THE BEST OF THE
HAIRY BIKERS

Si King & Dave Myers

THE BEST OF THE
HAIRY BIKERS

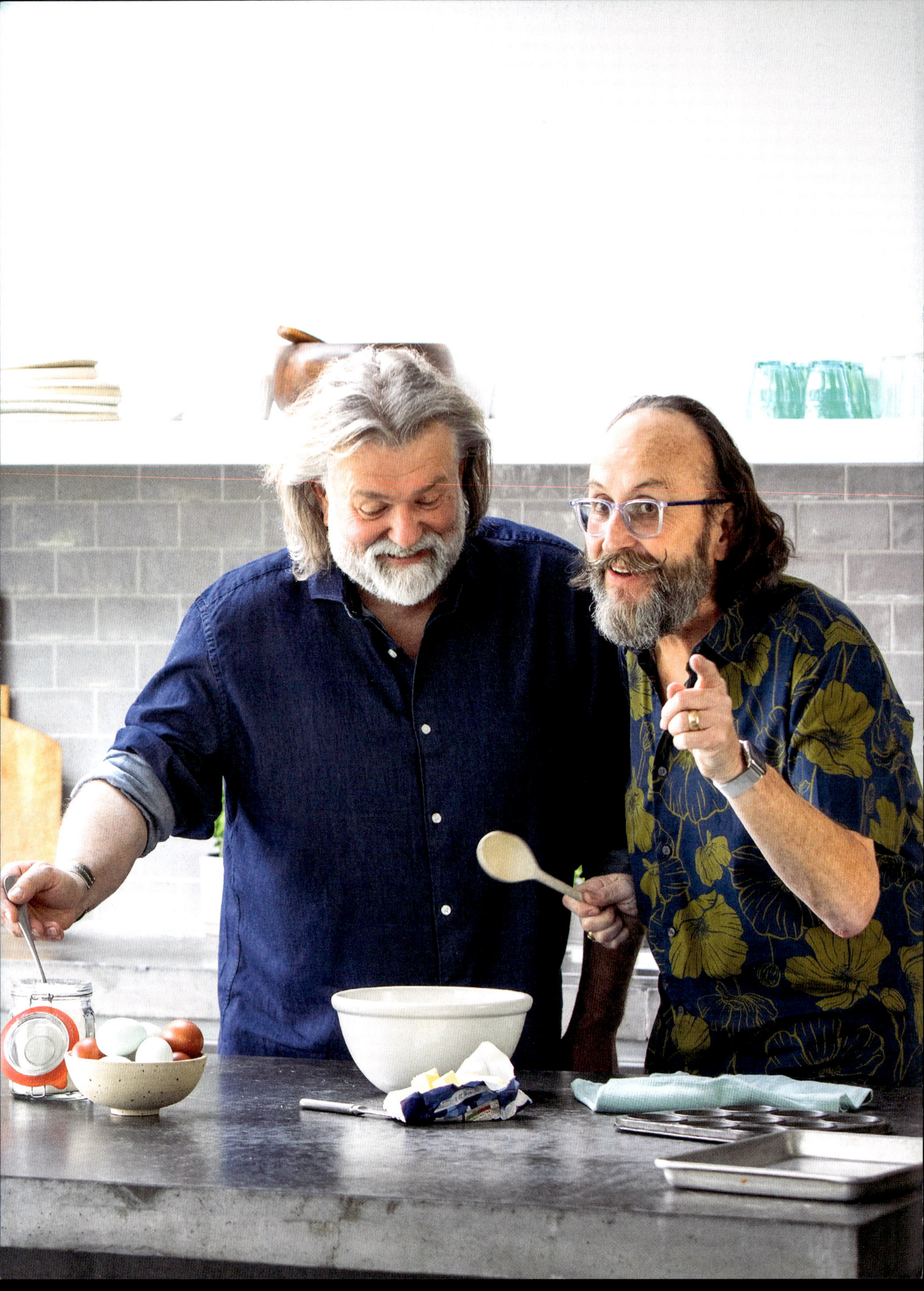

Introduction...6
1   Snacks...10
2   Soups...32
3   Salads...54
4   Pasta...76
5   Rice...98
6   Pies & traybakes...120
7   Curries...142
8   Veggie...164
9   Grills & roasts...186
10 Bakes...208
11 Puddings...230
12 Sides & basics...252
    Index...276
    The biggest thank you...287

It's been one hell of a ride! Working with Dave over the last twenty years or so on our television series, stage shows and, of course, our many cookbooks has been a complete blast. For the cookbooks, we travelled all over the world to find inspiration for our recipes, as well as explored the very best that our country has to offer. We've feasted on and written about curries, pies, meat, chicken and vegetarian dishes and much more besides and I hope we've given a great deal of pleasure to our amazing fans. We certainly had a shed-load of fun and we've been enriched as people by the journey.

Our Family Favourites, published in 2024, was the final book that Dave and I worked on together and I'd thought that was it. But, as a last hurrah to the Hairy Bikers, our publishers suggested doing a 'Best of' book, drawing on the hundreds of recipes we've written for our big cookbooks. The plan was for me to come up with what I thought were the ten best recipes in a number of categories, including salads, soups, curries, pies, and so on. Great idea, I said, and I started poring over the books.

Man – I have to say, it was so much more of a challenge than I'd ever thought. I'd pick ten great soups, job done, but then I'd say to myself, 'We have to include Scotch broth. And what about a seafood chowder?' And I'd start all over again. I knew we absolutely had to have meatballs in the book – Dave loved his meatballs – and there's no way I was going to leave out our vindaloo sausage rolls, and so it went on. Endless mind changing. I'd thought bakes and puddings might be easier than the savoury chapters, but I was struggling to choose my favourite crumble or the best trifle. Was that chocolate brownie really better than this one?

The painful thing was that for every extra recipe I decided I just had to include, something else had to go – otherwise I'd have ended up with doorstop of a book. But, on the other hand, I was so chuffed at looking back at all these great dishes we'd developed. And it was good remembering the excitement of endless discussions and reminiscing over times like when we were working on our *Ultimate Comfort Food* book and Dave came up with the idea of combining two of his all-time comfort favourites – risotto and spaghetti carbonara – in a risotto carbonara! He was as pleased as punch with that one and quite right too. It was a right laugh.

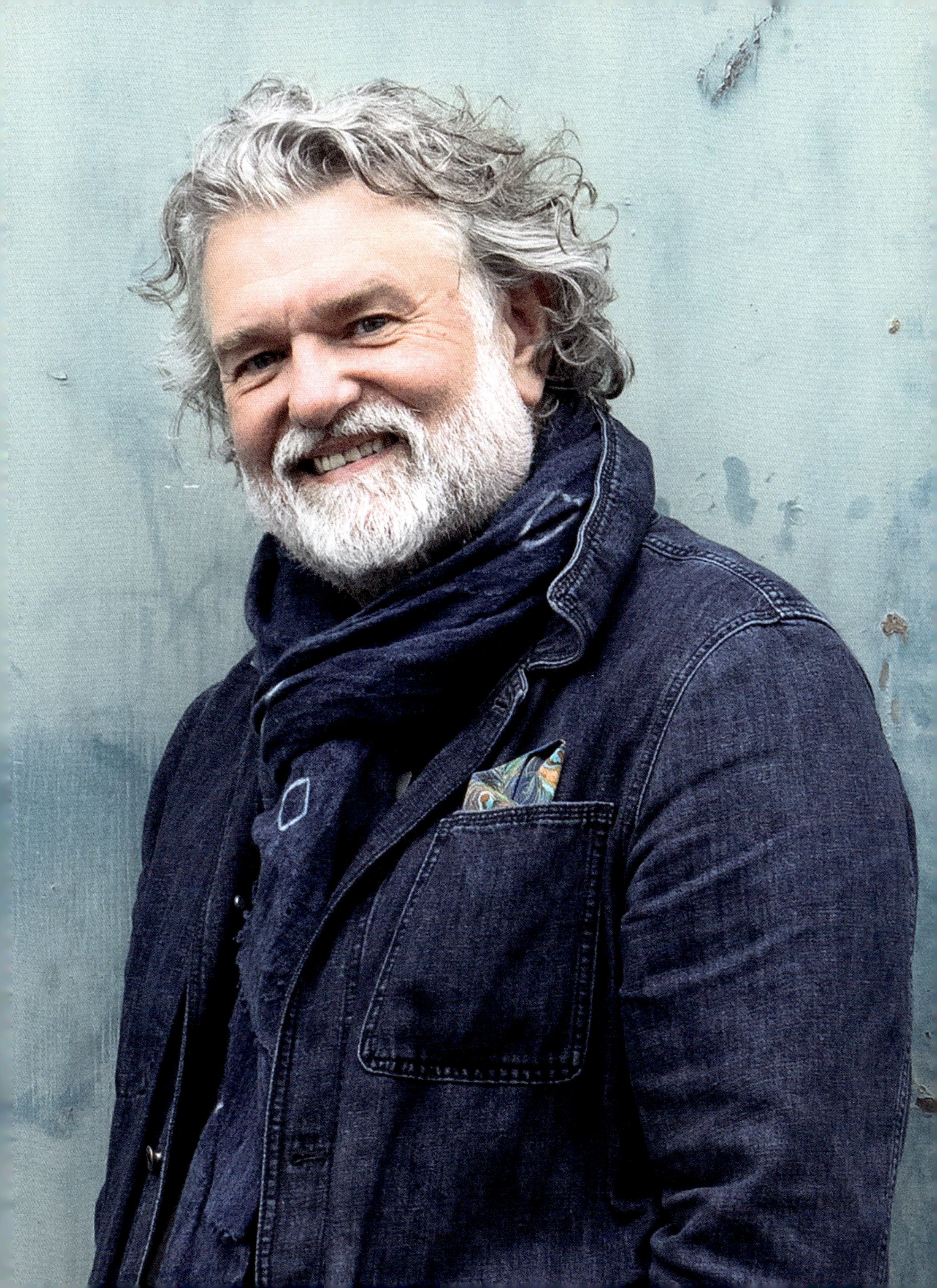

Of course, no two people are ever going to agree on a ten best selection of anything and I'm sure if Dave was here today we'd have been arguing endlessly – and probably doing lots of cooking and eating! But in the end the choices for this book were down to me and I hope you like what I've come up with. I've made some tweaks to the recipes to reflect changes over the years and I've had a fresh look at the introductions. I hope you will agree that there are a load of cracking dishes here.

As I've worked on this book, I've been very proud to look back at what we've achieved and, as always, I'll be forever grateful for all the love and support from you lovely people over the years. It's meant so much.

THANK YOU!

Love

Si xxx

A few top tips

1. Weigh all your ingredients and use proper measuring spoons and jugs. This is particularly important with baking recipes.

2. Every oven is different, so be prepared to cook dishes for a shorter or longer time, if necessary. I find a meat thermometer is a useful bit of kit to help you get perfectly cooked meat and chicken. They are readily available online and in kitchen shops.

3. Peel onions, garlic and other vegetables and fruit unless otherwise specified.

4. Use free-range eggs whenever possible. Dave and I have always believed that 95 per cent of good cooking is good shopping – great ingredients need less fussing with – so buy the best and freshest that your budget allows.

5. I've included a load of useful side dishes, spice mixes, sauces and a few stock recipes at the back of this book. Home-made stock is great to have in your freezer. But if you don't have time, you can find some good fresh stocks in supermarkets or you can use the little stock pots or cubes.

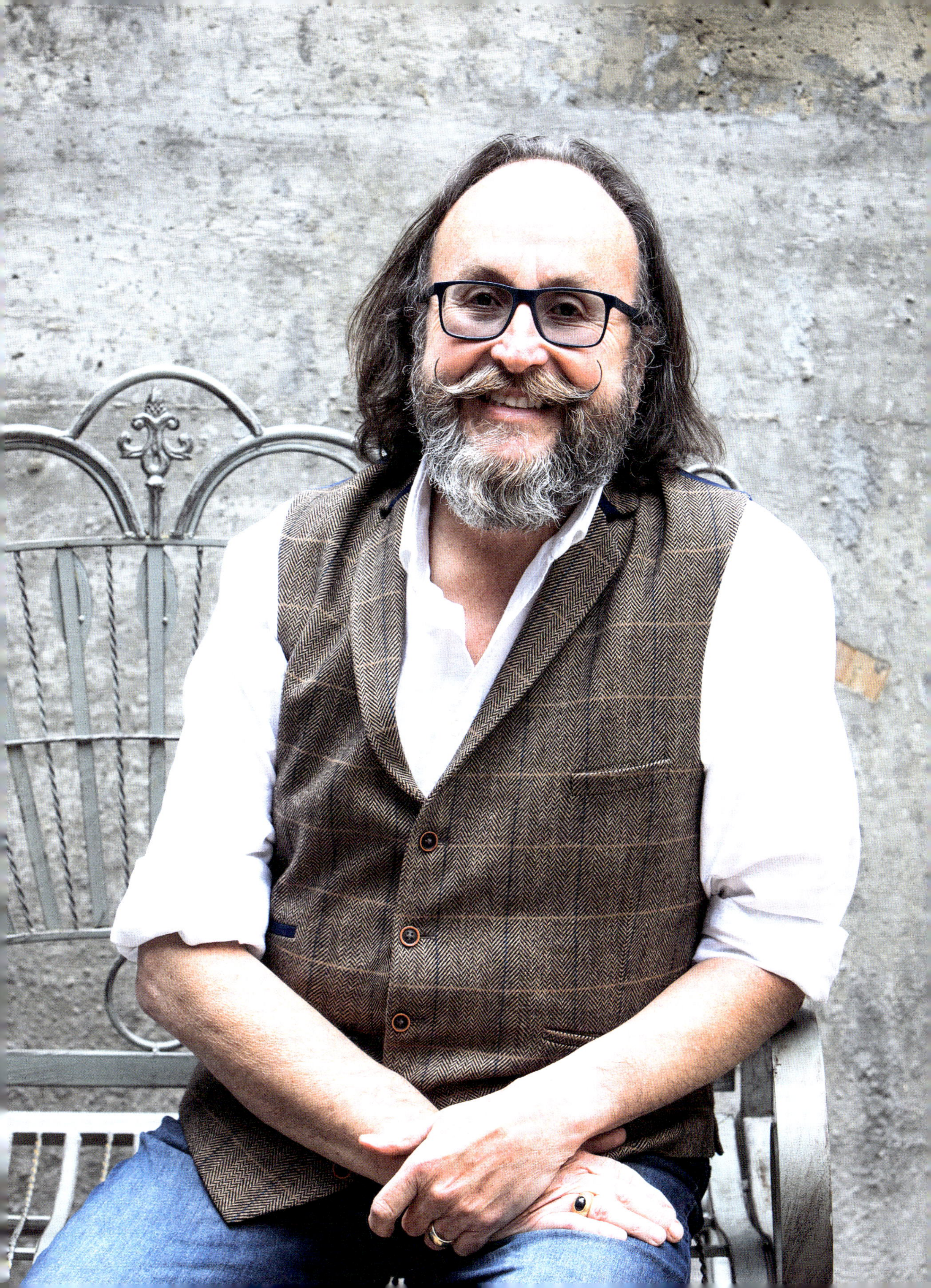

1. Vindaloo sausage rolls...12
2. Bruschetta...14
3. 'Nduja stromboli...16
4. Cheese & Marmite scones...18
5. Pickled onion bhajis...20
6. Garlic bread pizzas...22
7. Prawns on puri...24
8. Lamb chop pakoras...26
9. Scotch pickled eggs...28
10. Cornbread muffins with bacon jam...30

snacks

> *I'm sure you'll love these very tantalising temptations. They're great when you're peckish but are also fab as starters or as part of a buffet spread.*

Vindaloo sausage rolls

MAKES 24

500g sausage meat
a few coriander sprigs, finely chopped
1 x 320g sheet of ready-rolled puff pastry
pinch of ground turmeric
1 egg, beaten
1 tsp nigella seeds

VINDALOO PASTE
1 onion (see method)
15g root ginger, peeled and roughly chopped
3 garlic cloves, roughly chopped
3–4 red chillies, deseeded and roughly chopped
1 tbsp olive oil
1 tsp ground cumin
1 tsp ground turmeric
1 tsp ground coriander
1 tsp medium chilli powder
½ tsp ground fenugreek
½ tsp ground cinnamon
2 tbsp tomato purée
1 tbsp malt vinegar
2 tsp light brown soft sugar
salt

When we first thought of these little spicy delights we wondered what had taken us so long! We love sausage rolls and we love curry flavours so we combined the two and came up with a winner. Sausage rolls with attitude.

1. First make the vindaloo paste. Cut the onion in half. Roughly chop one half, put it in a food processor with the ginger, garlic and chillies, then purée to form a smooth paste, adding a little water if necessary.

2. Finely chop the remaining onion half. Heat the olive oil in a frying pan, add the chopped onion and fry until translucent. Add the spices and stir for another couple of minutes, then add the onion paste and the tomato purée. Stir for a few minutes – the aim is to cook the mixture a little, so it reduces until it's thick and starting to separate. Add the malt vinegar and sugar. Season with plenty of salt and cook for another couple of minutes or so to dissolve the sugar. Remove from the heat and leave to cool.

3. Break up the sausage meat and mix in the coriander. Preheat the oven to 180°C/Fan 160°C/Gas 4.

4. Unroll the pastry and cut it in half lengthways. Thickly spread the vindaloo paste down the centre of each piece of pastry. Leave a centimetre of border down each of the long sides, but make sure you go right to the edge of the short sides.

5. Divide the sausage meat into 2 pieces and shape them into logs the same length as the pastry. Place a log along one of the long edges on each piece of pastry.

6. Whisk the pinch of turmeric into the beaten egg. Brush the exposed edge of the pastry with egg, then roll up and make sure the edges are sealed. Cut each roll into 12 pieces.

7. Place the sausage rolls on a couple of baking sheets, then brush with the remaining egg and sprinkle with nigella seeds. Bake for about 25 minutes until the pastry is crisp and the filling is cooked through. Good hot or cold.

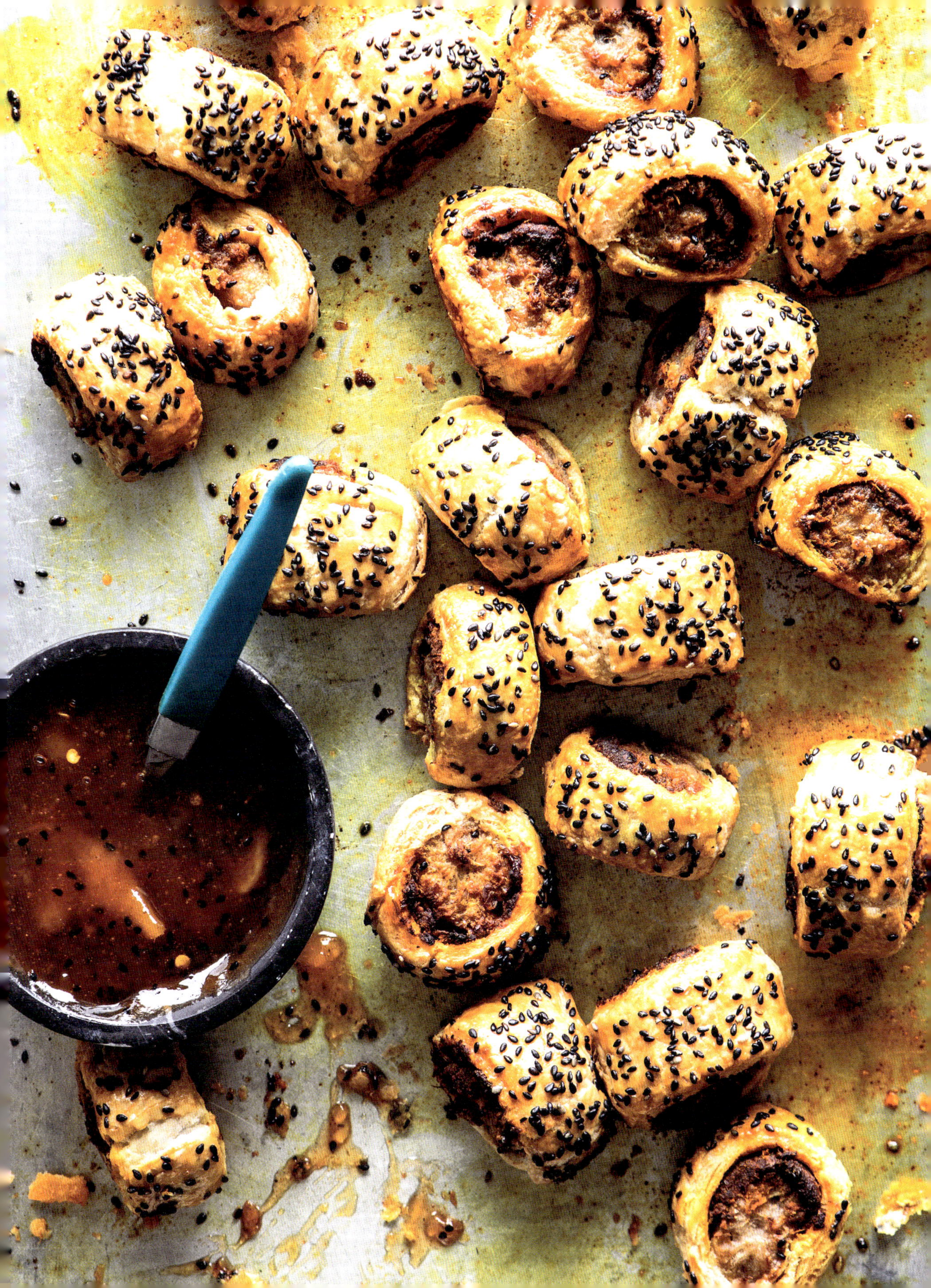

Bruschetta

BOTH FILLINGS MAKE ENOUGH FOR 4 SLICES OF BREAD

4 slices of rustic sourdough bread (about 1.5cm thick)
1 garlic clove, cut in half
salt and black pepper

TOMATO BRUSCHETTA
4–6 very ripe tomatoes, at room temperature
a few basil leaves, shredded
2 tbsp olive oil

RICOTTA & BROAD BEAN BRUSCHETTA
200g broad beans (podded weight)
250g ricotta
juice and zest of 1 lemon
2 tbsp olive oil
a few small mint leaves
a few basil leaves, shredded

As you know, the Hairy Bikers have always loved tasty things on toast and these little lovelies were inspired by our Mediterranean travels. They're great as a snack or as a starter with drinks - whatever you fancy. For the tomato version, make sure you get good tomatoes with great flavour and serve them at room temperature. Frozen broad beans are fine for that topping, but it really is worth taking the time to remove the tough greyish outer skins. The beans look better and taste better.

1. Toast the bread to a light golden brown. Rub the cut side of the garlic halves over the toast.

2. For the tomato bruschetta, roughly chop the tomatoes and put them in a bowl. Add most of the basil leaves, reserving a few for a garnish, and the olive oil. Season with a generous amount of salt and some black pepper. Stir and leave the tomatoes to stand for a few minutes to absorb the flavours.

3. Divide the tomato mixture between the slices of toast and garnish with a few more torn basil leaves. Serve at room temperature.

4. For the ricotta and broad bean bruschetta, bring a saucepan of water to the boil and cook the broad beans for about 2 minutes. Drain, run them under cold water, then remove their greyish outer skins to reveal the bright green beans beneath.

5. Break up the ricotta with a fork and add the lemon juice. Stir to combine, then spread this mixture over the toasted bread. Drizzle with a tablespoon of the olive oil. Toss the broad beans with the mint and basil leaves reserving a few for a garnish, then add the lemon zest and the remaining olive oil. Mix thoroughly and pile this on top of the ricotta. Season with salt and pepper and serve immediately.

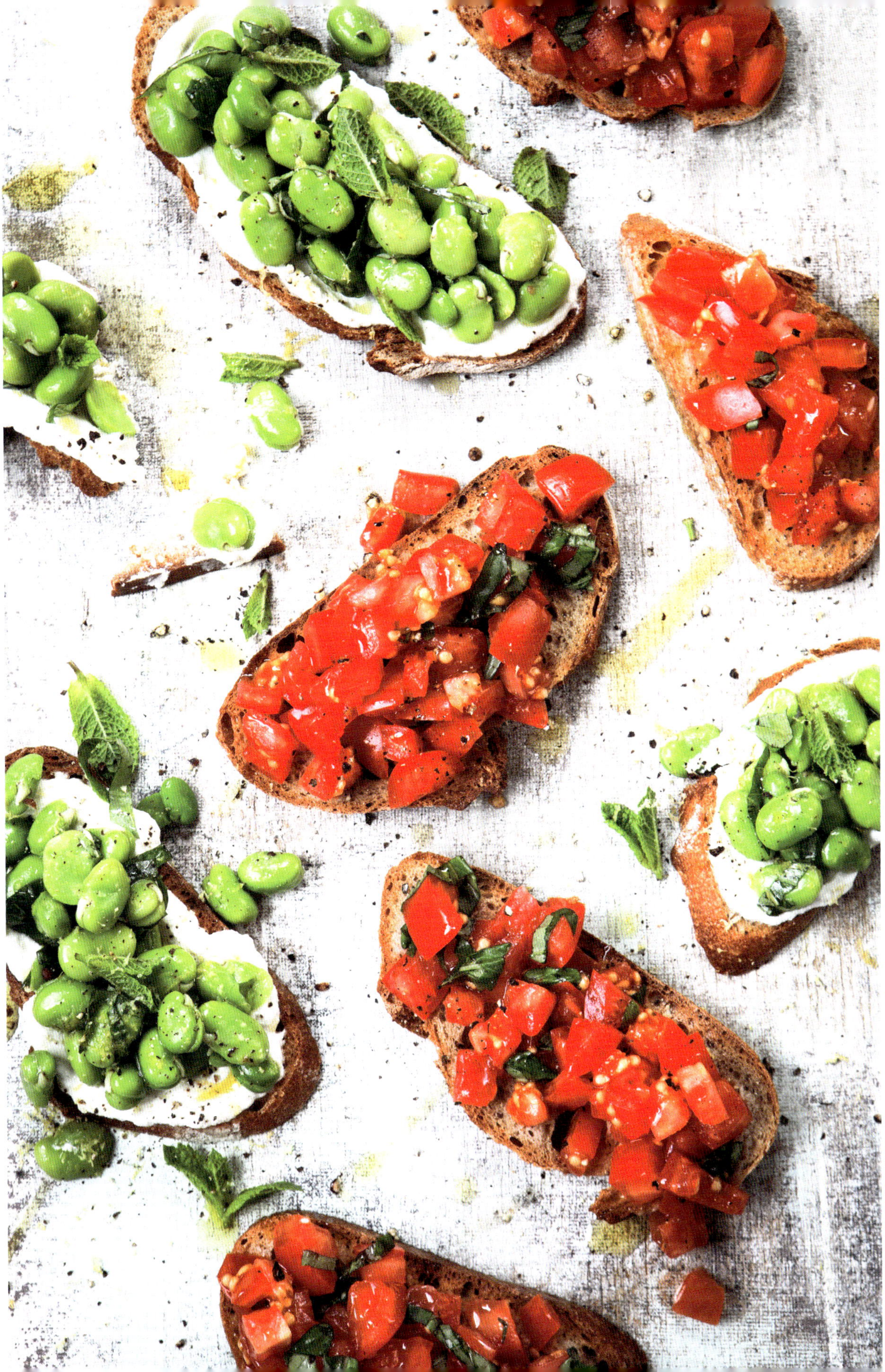

'Nduja stromboli

SERVES 4

DOUGH
450g strong white flour, plus extra for dusting
50g fine semolina
7g fast-action dried yeast
1 tsp salt
300ml tepid water
2 tbsp olive oil

FILLING
1 large or 2 small courgettes
2 tbsp olive oil
150–200g 'nduja
200g mozzarella, torn into pieces
1 tsp dried oregano (or 1 tbsp fresh oregano leaves)
small bunch of basil, leaves only
salt and black pepper

A stromboli is really a sort of rolled-up pizza and is just the thing for a snack or a TV dinner. You can use any filling you like, but I reckon this 'nduja and courgette version takes a lot of beating. 'Nduja is a totally epic paste that comes from southern Italy and is made of chillies, pork and salt, then smoked. It's hugely popular now and you can find it in most supermarkets. Some versions are spicier than others, so if you don't want to blow your socks off, be sure to taste it before you add the whole lot.

1. Mix the flour, semolina and yeast together in a large bowl, then add the salt. Make a well in the centre and gradually work in the water and the olive oil until the mixture comes together. Turn the dough out on to a floured work surface and knead until it's smooth and springy – this will take 10 minutes or so. Put the dough in a lightly oiled bowl and cover it with cling film or a damp tea towel. Leave the dough somewhere warm until it has doubled in size.

2. Prepare the filling. Very thinly slice the courgette on the diagonal. Toss the slices in a tablespoon of the olive oil and season with salt and pepper. Heat a griddle pan until it's very hot – too hot to hold your hand over. Turn the heat down slightly and then grill the courgette slices for 2–4 minutes on each side until soft and marked with char lines.

3. Preheat the oven to 200°C/Fan 180°C/Gas 6. Turn the dough out on to a lightly floured surface. Roll it out, stretching it constantly as it springs back, until you have a rectangle measuring about 45 x 30cm. Arrange the slices of courgette over the dough, leaving a 2cm border along the short and one of the long sides. Top with spoonfuls of 'nduja and pieces of mozzarella. Sprinkle over the herbs and season with salt and pepper.

4. Roll up the dough, starting with the borderless edge which will be the centre of the stromboli and pressing the short edges together as you go. Place it on a baking tray and brush it with the remaining olive oil. Cover with a damp tea towel and leave to stand for 30 minutes.

5. When the dough has risen again, put the stromboli in the oven and bake it for 25–30 minutes until golden brown. Leave it to cool for a few minutes, then cut into thick slices.

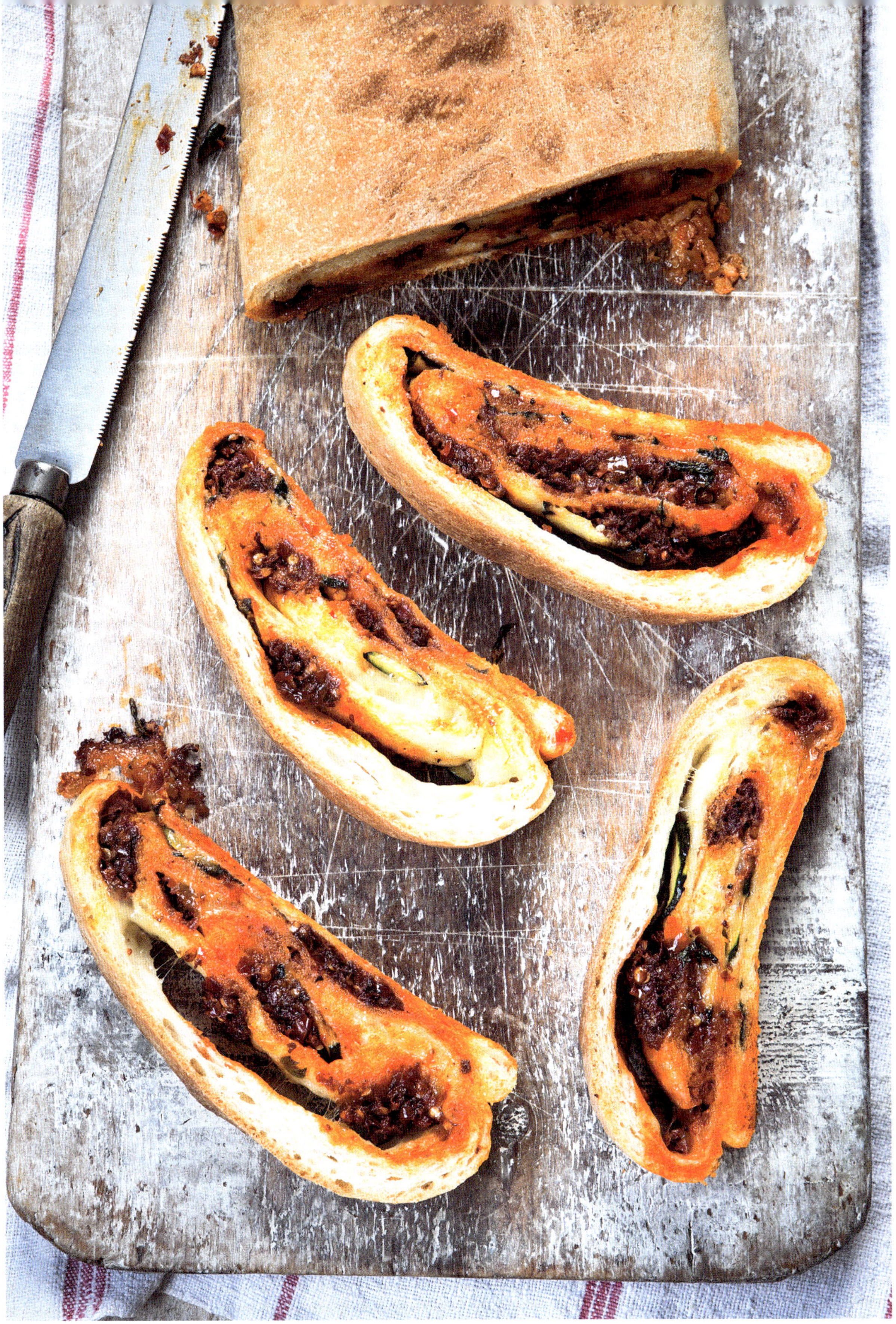

Cheese & Marmite scones

MAKES 8–9

150ml whole milk
1 tbsp Marmite
300g self-raising flour, plus extra for dusting
1 tsp baking powder
½ tsp salt
85g butter, chilled and cubed
150g Cheddar cheese, coarsely grated
1 tsp mustard powder
1 tbsp caster sugar

Everyone loves a scone and these, with the extra savoury hit of cheese and a touch of Marmite, are irresistible. They're easy to make, but if you want your scones to turn out as light as a feather, try not to mix the dough too much or they will be tough. Another top tip is to not twist the cutter as you press it down into the dough. This helps prevent the scones from turning out lopsided – but to be honest, once they're slathered with lashings of butter they'll still taste great, lopsided or not. Even if you're not a Marmite fan, I promise you'll love these.

1. Heat the milk in a pan until it's just starting to feel hot – blood temperature which is a bit hotter than tepid. Whisk in the Marmite until it has combined completely with the milk and the milk has turned a colour similar to milky coffee. Remove the pan from the heat and leave the milk to cool down. If you have time, chill it as well, but don't worry too much if you can't.

2. Mix the flour, baking powder and salt in a bowl. Add the butter and rub it in with your fingertips until the mixture is the texture of fine breadcrumbs. Add the grated cheese, mustard powder and sugar, then, if time allows, leave the mixture in the fridge to chill for half an hour.

3. Preheat the oven to 220°C/Fan 200°C/Gas 7. Line a large baking tray with baking paper.

4. Reserve a tablespoon of the milk and Marmite mixture to use as a glaze and pour the rest into the bowl of dry ingredients. Mix everything together as quickly as you can, using either a table knife or your fingers. Don't overwork the dough or the scones will be tough.

5. Turn the dough out on to a floured work surface and pat it down until it is about 3cm thick. Do this with your hands – no need for a rolling pin. Dip a 6cm cutter in flour and cut out rounds, pushing the cutter straight down. Squash the remaining dough together and cut out more scones. You should end up with 8 or 9.

6. Put the scones on the baking tray and brush them with the reserved milk and Marmite. Bake for 12–15 minutes until they are well risen and a deep golden brown in colour. Eat hot or cold, spread with butter.

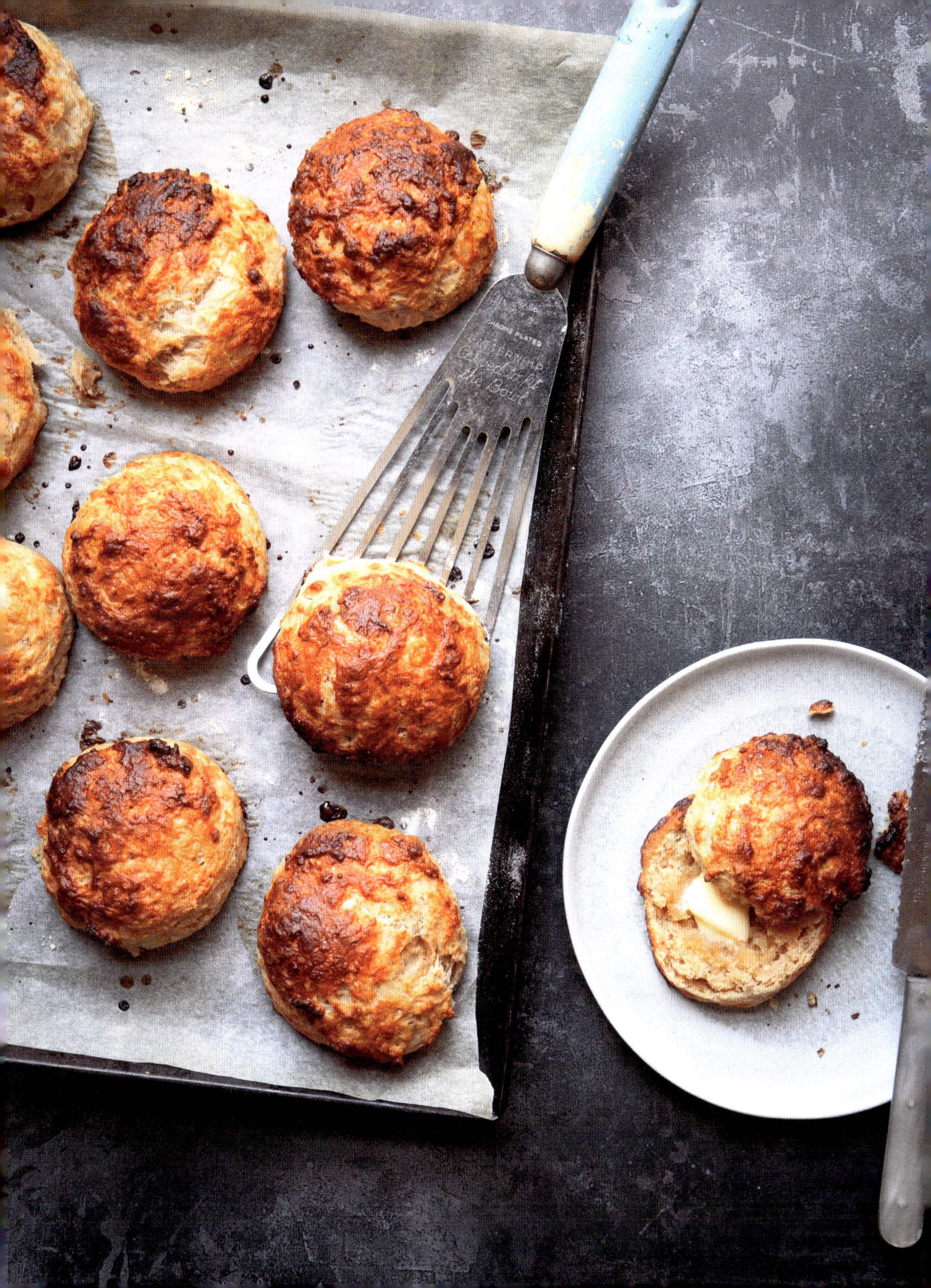

Pickled onion bhajis

SERVES 4

PICKLED ONIONS
1 tsp granulated sugar
2 tsp salt
1 tsp chilli flakes
50ml cider or red wine vinegar
2 medium onions, finely sliced

BATTER
70g gram (chickpea) flour
30g rice flour
1 tsp baking powder
1 tsp ground turmeric
1 tsp ground cumin
½ tsp ground cinnamon
15g root ginger, peeled and grated
3 garlic cloves, crushed or grated
2 green chillies, finely chopped
2 tbsp finely chopped coriander stems
1 tbsp coconut oil, melted, or 1 tbsp coconut yoghurt
1 tbsp lemon juice

TO FRY
vegetable or groundnut oil

TO SERVE
200ml natural yoghurt
50ml mango chutney
coriander leaves, finely chopped

Wow! Regular onion bhajis are fabulous enough but with the extra flavour that comes from lightly pickling the onion slices, these are something else. Make a plateful, pour yourself a cold beer and you'll feel mega content. Gram flour is available in supermarkets and if you can't find any rice flour, just blitz some rice to a powder in a spice grinder or a high-powered blender. The rice flour really helps to get the batter beautifully crisp. And there's a nice little mix of yoghurt and mango chutney on the side for dipping. This is a great vegetarian snack and if you want to make it vegan, use plant-based yoghurt.

1. First, pickle the onions. Mix the sugar, salt, chilli flakes and vinegar in a bowl. Stir until the sugar and salt have dissolved, then add the onions. Stir to coat and press them down into the vinegar, then top with just enough water to cover. Set aside for at least an hour, then drain them thoroughly and dry on kitchen paper.

2. Just before you are ready to fry the bhajis, make the batter mixture. Whisk all the ingredients together in a bowl, then add just enough water to make a batter that's roughly the consistency of double cream. Stir in the onions.

3. Half-fill a large saucepan or deep-fat fryer with oil and heat it to about 180°C. Do not leave the pan unattended.

4. Take heaped tablespoons of the mixture and drop them, a few at a time, into the oil. Fry the bhajis for 2–3 minutes on each side until they are a deep ochre brown, then drain on kitchen paper. Warning – don't try to fry more than a few at a time or the temperature of the oil will drop, and the bhajis may go soggy as opposed to crisp.

5. Mix the yoghurt, mango chutney and coriander together in a bowl, and serve with the hot bhajis.

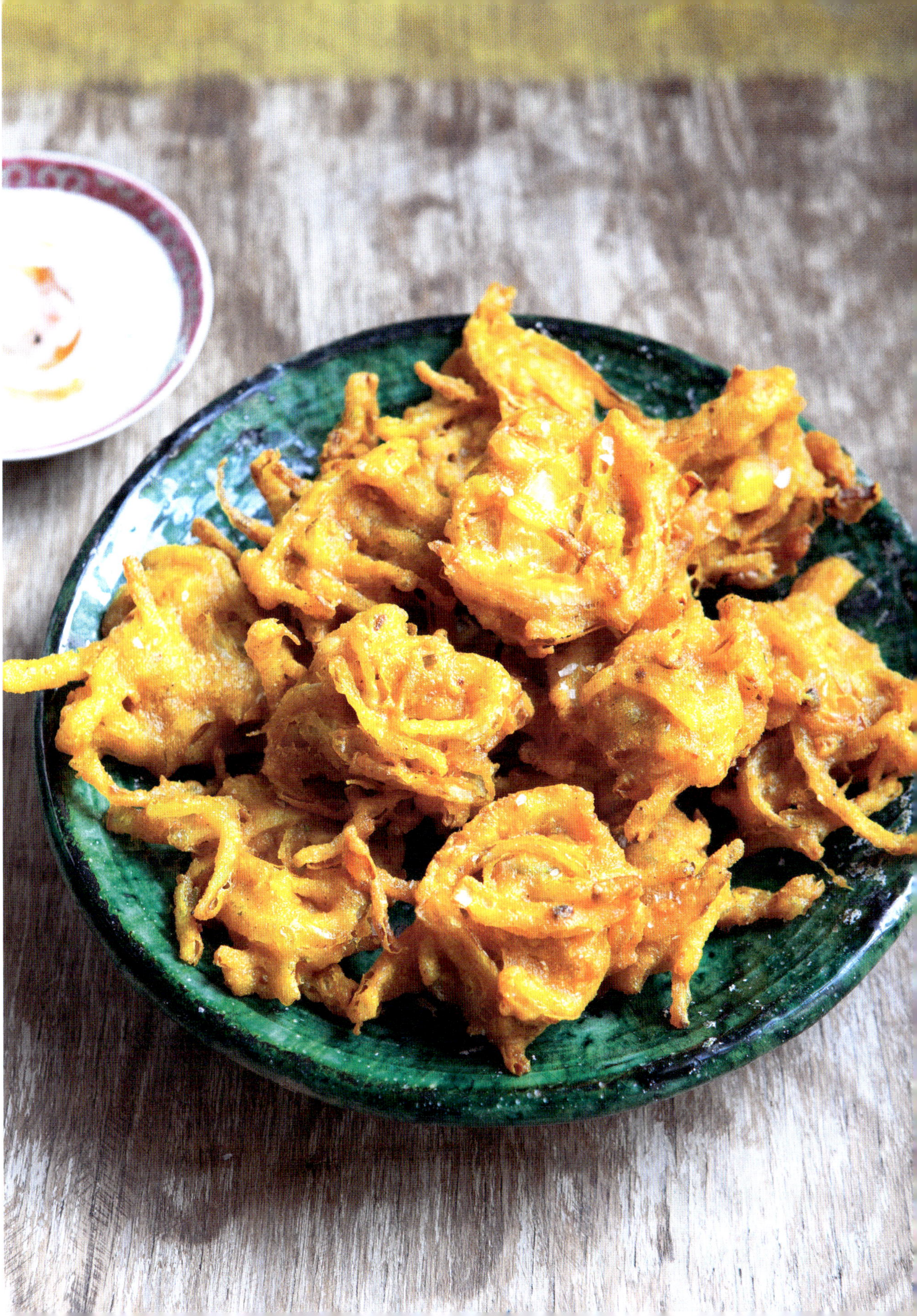

Garlic bread pizzas

SERVES 4

1 large baguette
100g butter, softened
4 garlic cloves, crushed
50g Parmesan cheese, grated
1 tsp garlic powder (optional)
salt and black pepper

TOPPING
1 tsp dried oregano
150g cherry tomatoes, chopped
200g mozzarella, sliced
1 tbsp olive oil
a few basil leaves

These have the great flavours of a classic pizza without all the faff of preparing the dough. They're super-quick to make and they taste amazing – the perfect comforting snack. You can buy garlic powder in the supermarket and it does add a nice smokiness to the flavour but feel free to leave it out if you don't happen to have any.

1. Preheat the oven to 200°C/Fan 180°C/Gas 6.

2. Trim off the ends of the baguette if you like, then cut it in half and split each half lengthways so you have 4 pieces of bread.

3. Put the butter in a bowl and add the garlic, Parmesan and garlic powder, if using. Season with salt and pepper and mix thoroughly. Spread the butter generously over the bread, then sprinkle over half the dried oregano.

4. Put the cherry tomatoes in a sieve and sprinkle them with salt. Toss gently and leave to stand for 10 minutes. Arrange the mozzarella over the bread slices, then top with the tomatoes. Drizzle with the olive oil, then add a few basil leaves and sprinkle with the remaining oregano.

5. Place on a baking tray and bake for about 15 minutes, until the bread is crisp and the cheese is well melted. Enjoy at once.

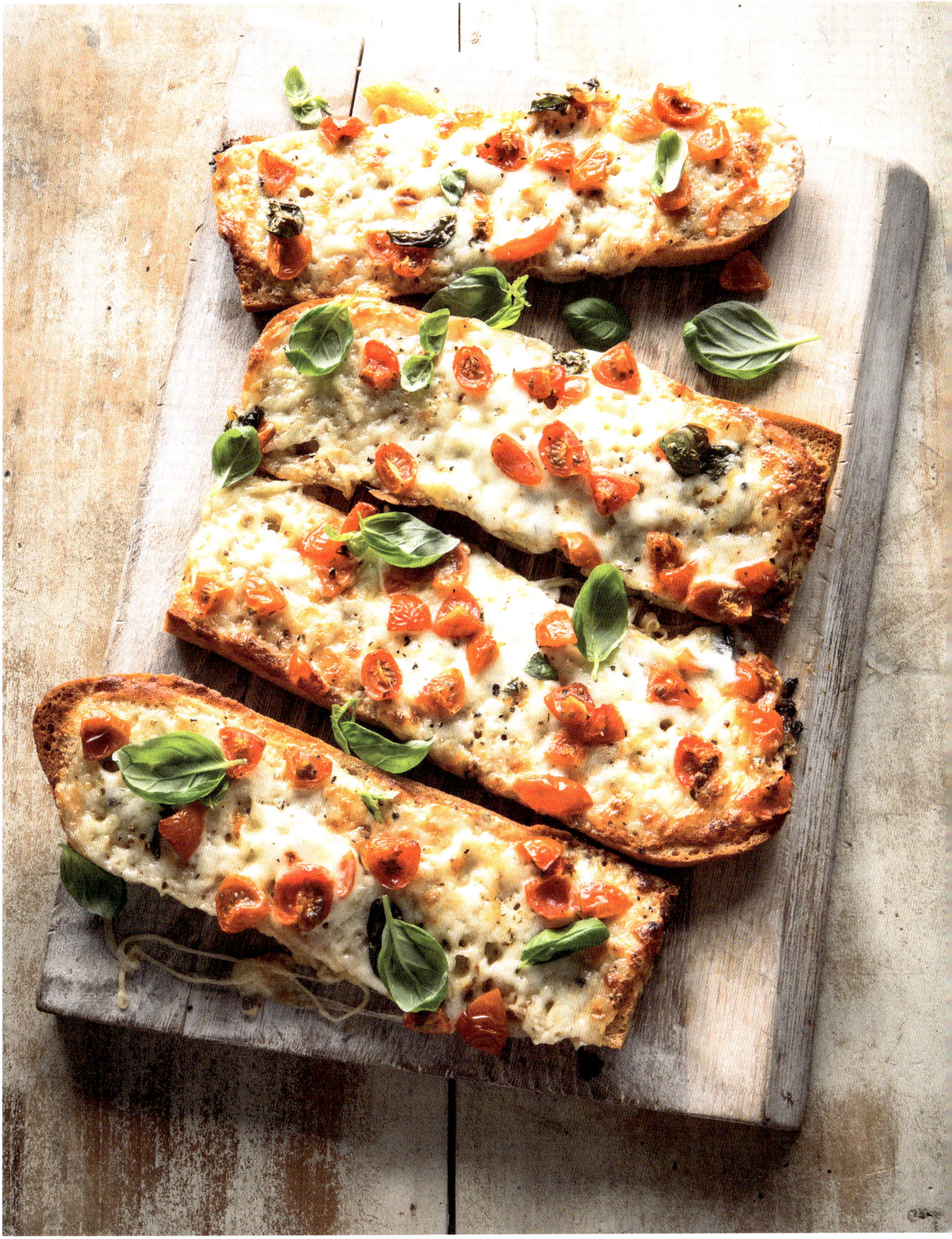

Prawns on puri

SERVES 6

4 tbsp vegetable oil
1 medium onion, finely sliced
1 long green chilli, deseeded and finely chopped
20g root ginger, peeled and finely grated
3 garlic cloves, crushed
1½ tsp garam masala (shop-bought or see p.269)
¼ tsp cayenne pepper
3 fresh ripe tomatoes, skinned and roughly chopped
3 tbsp lemon juice
1 tbsp caster sugar
400g cooked peeled prawns, defrosted
3 heaped tbsp finely chopped coriander, plus extra sprigs for garnishing
salt and black pepper

TO SERVE
Indian bread or 6 puris (see p.263)
lemon wedges, for squeezing

This quick, simple prawn curry is great served with any kind of Indian breads but is especially good served with puris, as in the photo opposite. If you fancy making puris, have a go at our recipe on page 263 and you'll be in for a real treat. Ordinary frozen prawns are fine for this recipe, but thaw them thoroughly and don't overcook them or they will go hard. And if you don't like prawns, try small cubes of chicken instead.

1. Place a large frying pan or wok over a medium-high heat. When it's hot, add the oil and stir-fry the onion and chilli for 3 minutes. Reduce the heat slightly, add the ginger and garlic and stir-fry for another 2 minutes. Sprinkle with the garam masala and cayenne pepper and continue to cook, stirring constantly, for 30 seconds.

2. Tip the tomatoes into the pan, then add the lemon juice, sugar and half a teaspoon of salt. Cook for 5 minutes, stirring constantly until the tomatoes have softened into a spicy sauce.

3. Add the prawns to the pan, season with some black pepper and cook for 1½–2 minutes until hot, while stirring. Remove the pan from the heat and stir in the coriander.

4. Serve the prawns on Indian bread or puris and garnish with sprigs of coriander. Add lemon wedges for squeezing over the prawns.

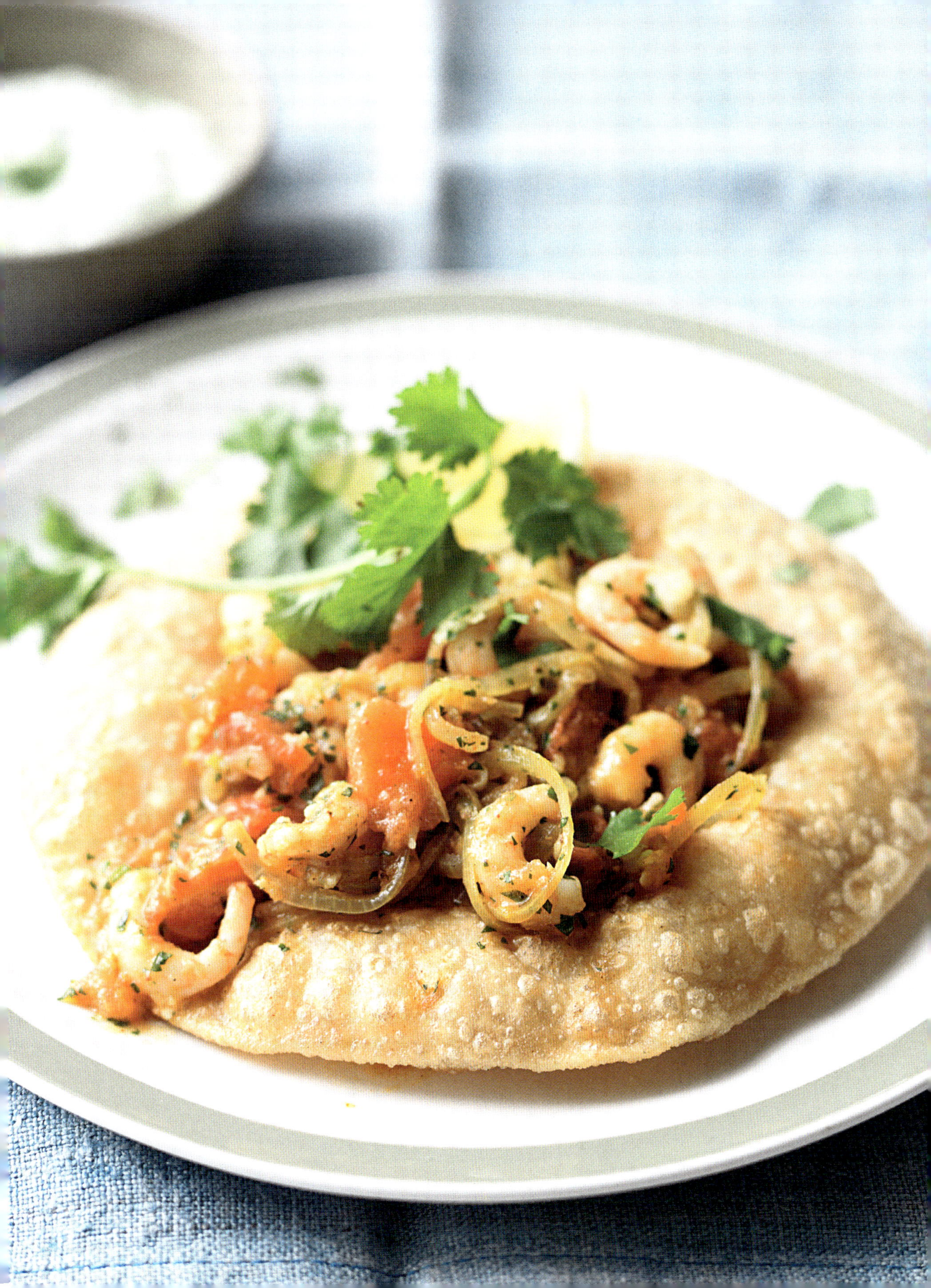

Lamb chop pakoras

SERVES 6 AS A STARTER

12–14 small lamb cutlets, French-trimmed
1 tsp cumin seeds
1 tsp coriander seeds
1 tsp black peppercorns
2–3 tbsp vegetable oil, plus extra for deep-frying

SPICE-INFUSED MILK
1 cinnamon stick
1 green chilli, thinly sliced
4 whole cloves
8 cardamom pods, crushed
15g root ginger, peeled and finely grated
½ onion, finely sliced
250ml whole milk

BATTER
125g gram (chickpea) flour
25g white self-raising flour
½ tsp cayenne pepper
½ tsp fine sea salt

TO SERVE
chutneys and relishes

Here we have the ultimate finger food – the scraped and cleaned bones of these cutlets make perfect handles as you enjoy the nuggets of spicy battered meat. These pakoras are not difficult to make and you can get everything ready ahead of time, then dip and fry at the last minute.

1. Start by making the spice-infused milk. Put the cinnamon stick, chilli, cloves, cardamom, ginger and onion in a saucepan and pour in the milk. Simmer for 5 minutes but don't let the milk boil over. Remove the pan from the heat and set aside for 20 minutes to allow the spices to infuse.

2. Check that the cutlets have been trimmed of any fat and the bones are scraped clean so you can use them as little handles. Heat a large frying pan and dry fry the cumin and coriander seeds until you can smell their aroma. Grind the seeds and peppercorns into a powder in a spice grinder or with a pestle and mortar. Coat the cutlets on both sides with the spices.

3. Heat 2 tablespoons of oil in the same pan. Working in batches so you don't overcrowd the pan, fry the cutlets for about 2 minutes on each side and then for a further minute to brown the edges. Once browned all over, transfer the cutlets to a plate to rest while you fry the next batch, adding a little extra oil if you need it.

4. To make the batter, put both flours, the cayenne and salt in a large bowl and make a well in the centre. Strain the infused milk through a fine sieve into a measuring jug. Slowly pour 200ml of the milk into the flour mixture, stirring it with a metal whisk to make a smooth batter.

5. Half fill a pan or deep fryer with oil and heat the oil to 170°C, checking it with a cooking thermometer. Dip a cutlet into the batter, gently shake off any excess, then carefully lower it into the hot oil. Repeat with a few more cutlets and fry them for 2–3 minutes, turning them regularly, until the batter is golden brown and crisp.

6. Put the fried cutlets on a baking tray lined with kitchen paper and keep them warm while you fry the rest. Be sure to bring the oil up to the right temperature between batches. Serve the cutlets with chutneys and relishes.

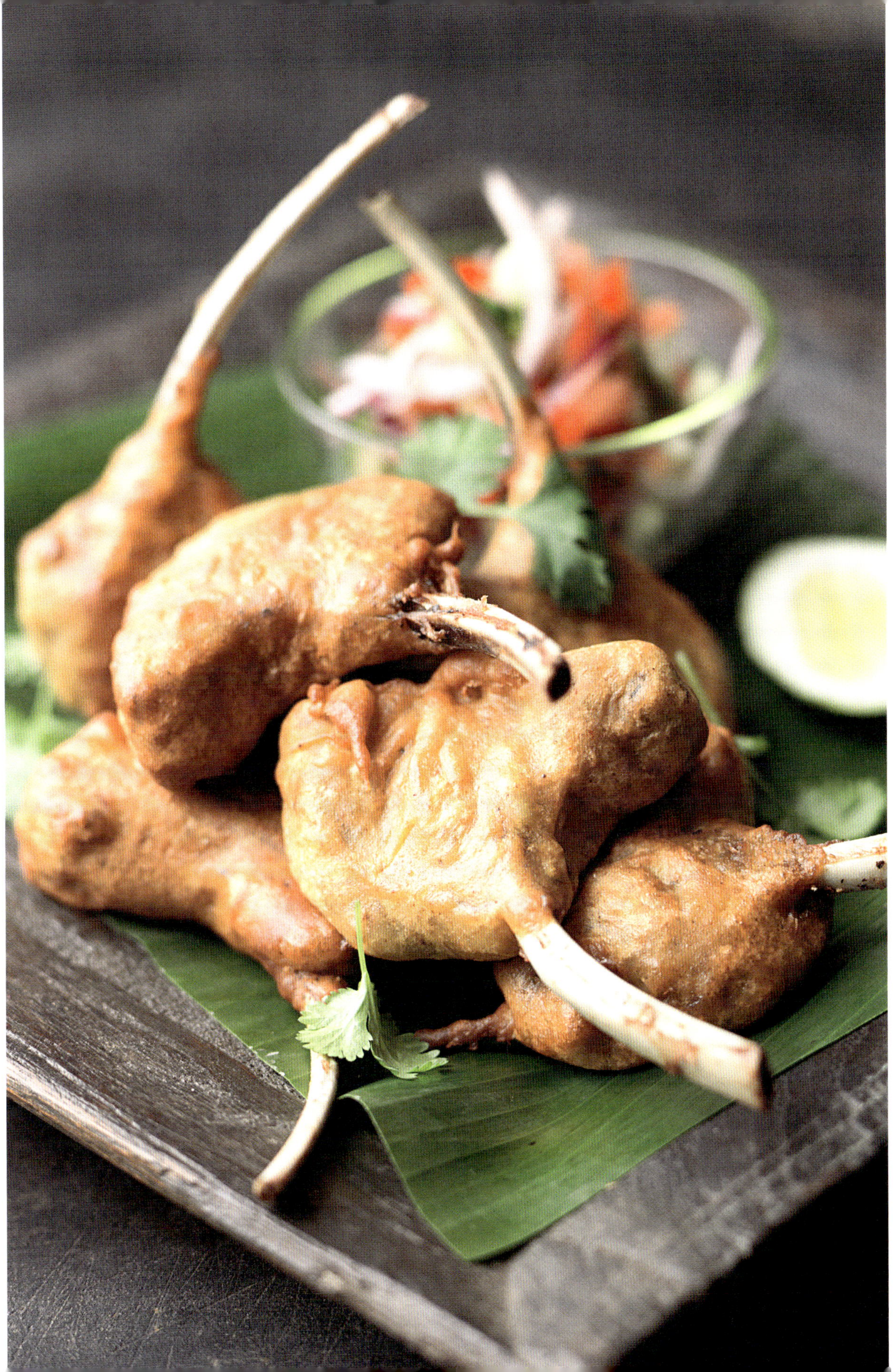

Scotch pickled eggs

MAKES 6

600g Cumberland sausages
2 tbsp celery salt
50g plain flour
100g panko breadcrumbs
1 packet of cheese and onion crisps, crushed
2 eggs
6 pickled eggs (shop-bought or see p.260)
oil, for frying
salt and black pepper

TO SERVE
mustard
cornichons and pickled onions

Dave and I have always been huge fans of a Scotch egg. Imagine our delight when in a pub in Scotland we saw people take a pickled egg from a big jar on the counter, mash it into a bag of cheese and onion crisps, then wash it down with a good swig of beer. So that got us thinking and we came up with this culinary keeper. Genius or what? You can buy jars of pickled eggs or if you make your own, you'll need to think ahead, as they need to be kept for at least a couple of weeks before eating.

1. Remove the sausage meat from the skins and put it all in a bowl. Cumberland sausages have a lovely peppery flavour, but you can use anything you fancy, from a herby Lincolnshire to a spicy chorizo.

2. Put the celery salt on one plate, then spread the flour on a separate plate and season it with salt and pepper. Mix the breadcrumbs with the crisps and put them on a third plate. Beat the eggs in a shallow bowl.

3. Take a pickled egg and roll it in celery salt, then the seasoned flour – the flour helps the sausage meat stick. Make a patty of sausage meat big enough to encase your egg, then wrap it round the egg and form it into a lovely round shape. It's easier to do this with wet hands. Repeat until you've made all your Scotch eggs.

4. Dip each sausage-coated egg into the seasoned flour, then the beaten egg and finally roll them in the crisp and crumb mixture.

5. If you want to deep-fry the eggs, half fill a pan or deep fryer with oil and heat the oil to 160°C. Add the eggs, a few at a time, and cook for about 6 minutes until golden. Make sure the oil comes back up to temperature after cooking the first batch.

6. Alternatively, you can shallow fry the eggs in oil, turning them occasionally until the sausage meat is cooked through and the outsides are golden. Serve up with some good mustard and a few cornichons and onions.

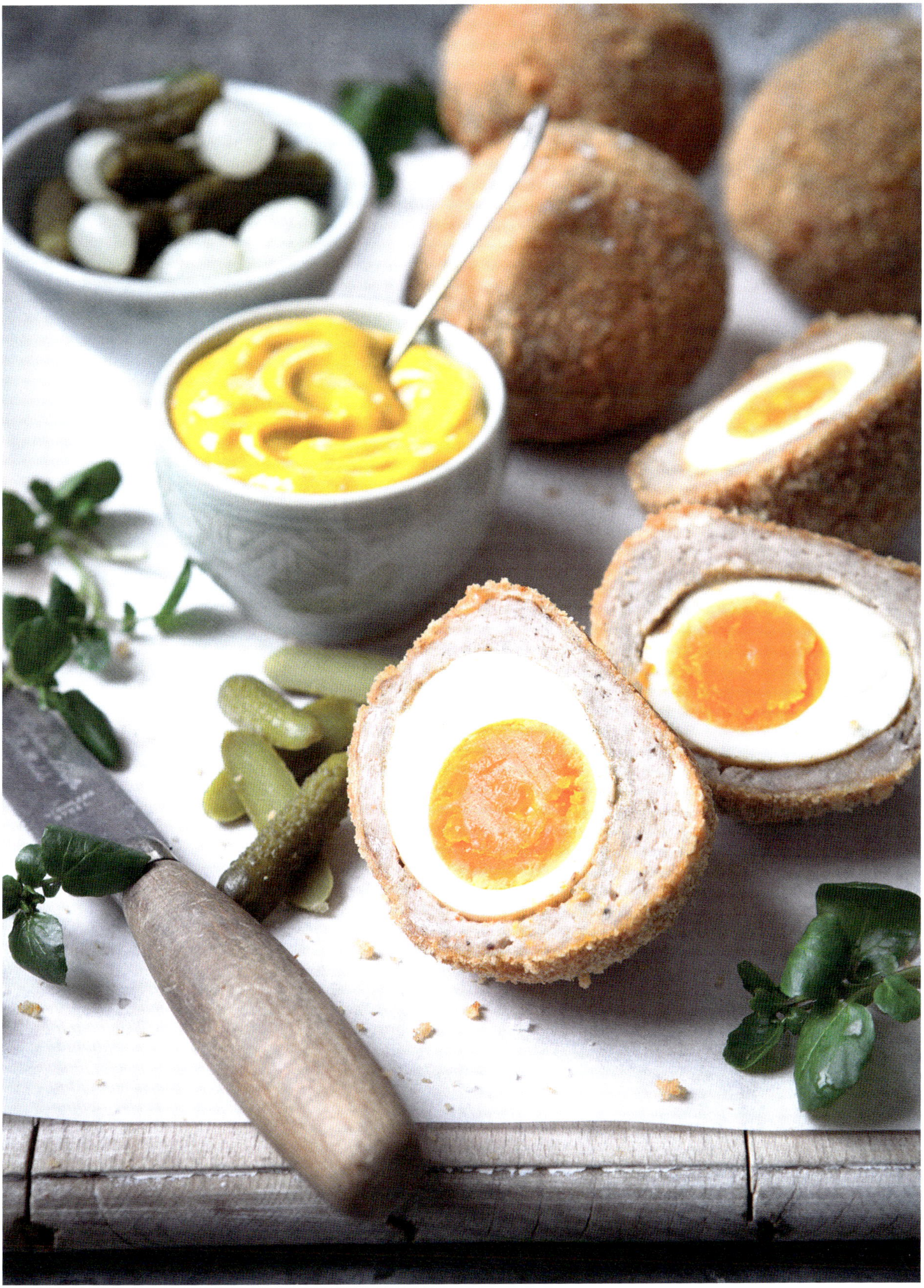

Cornbread muffins with bacon jam

MAKES 12

300g fine cornmeal or 150g cornmeal and 150g plain flour
1 tbsp baking powder
1 tbsp caster sugar
pinch of salt
300ml buttermilk
2 eggs
60ml olive oil or melted butter
125g canned sweetcorn, drained and patted dry
2 tbsp pickled jalapeños, chopped (optional)
4 tbsp bacon jam (shop-bought or see p.261)

Savoury muffins are always a treat but with the addition of some tasty bacon jam they reach another level. Doesn't bacon make everything just that bit better? Enjoy these warm from the oven if you can, or leave them to cool slightly and spread with butter or cream cheese. The muffins are naturally gluten-free if you go with all cornmeal, but you can also make them with half cornmeal, half flour if you want a softer crumb.

1. Preheat the oven to 200°C/Fan 180°C/Gas 6. Line a 12-hole muffin tin with paper cases.

2. Put the cornmeal or cornmeal and flour in a bowl with the baking powder, caster sugar and a generous pinch of salt. Stir to combine.

3. Put the buttermilk in a jug and beat in the eggs and the oil or melted butter. Pour this mixture into the bowl of dry ingredients and add the sweetcorn and the jalapeños, if using. Fold everything together, keeping the mixing to an absolute minimum. Don't worry if there's the odd streak of cornmeal – better that than risk overmixing the batter which makes for tough muffins.

4. Put a heaped tablespoon of the batter in each muffin case. Then top with a teaspoon of the bacon jam and give it a quick swirl to mix. Top with a further tablespoon of batter, followed by another half a teaspoon of bacon jam on top for a garnish. Push the bacon jam into the batter so it's flush with the batter rather than raised.

5. Bake the muffins in the oven for 15 minutes or until they are well risen and lightly browned. Enjoy warm or leave to cool.

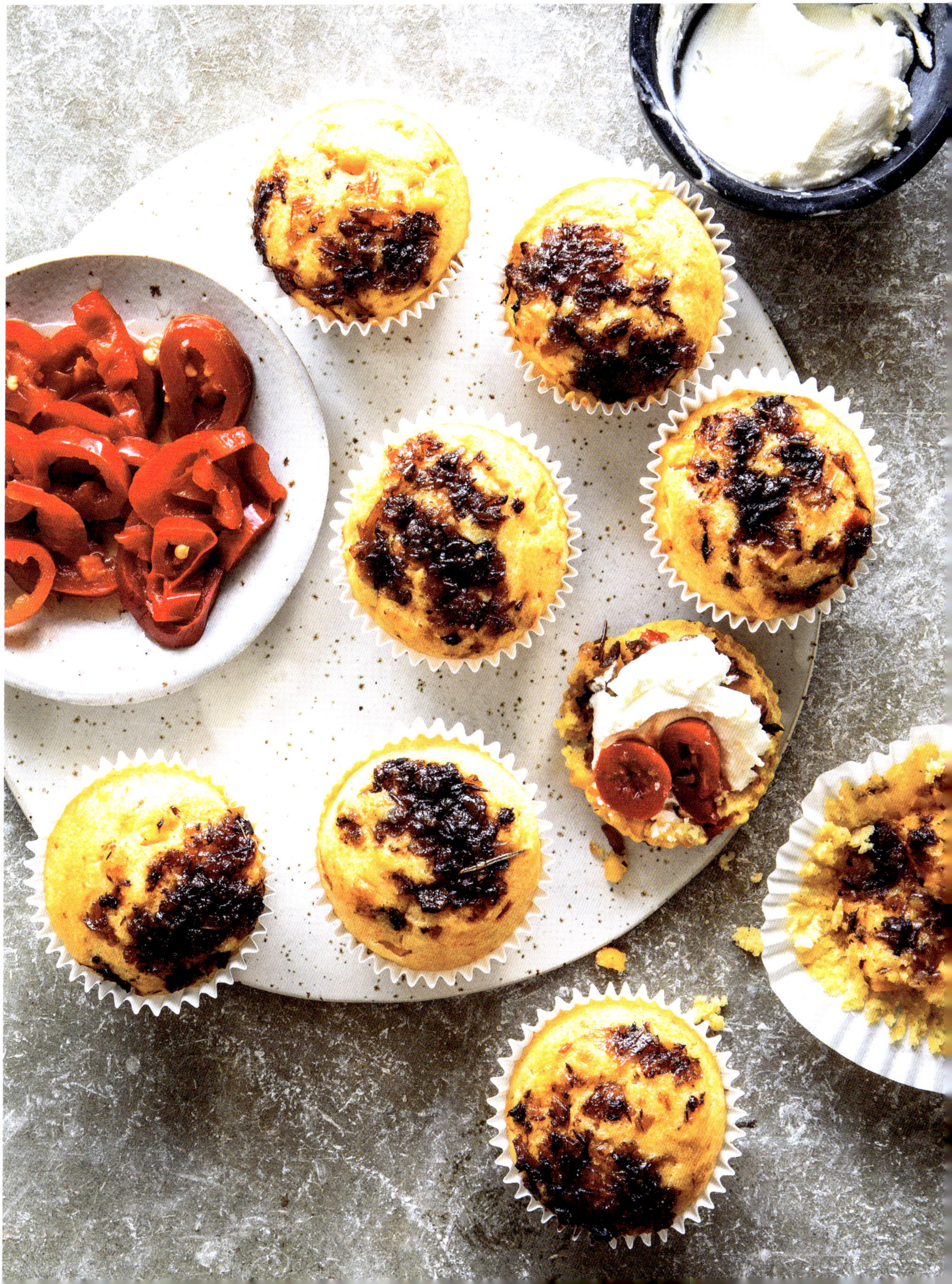

1. Moroccan tomato soup...34
2. Pea & watercress soup...36
3. Summery minestrone...38
4. French onion soup...40
5. Tom yum soup...42
6. Seafood chowder...44
7. Chicken soup...46
8. Oxtail soup with parsley dumplings...48
9. Pork ramen...50
10. Scotch broth...52

soups

> *A bowl of soup means comfort to me – a cuddle in a bowl. These are some of my favourites of the soups we've cooked over the years.*

Moroccan tomato soup

SERVES 4

2 tbsp olive oil
1 large onion, finely chopped
200g butternut squash, peeled and finely diced
2 large garlic cloves, finely chopped
2 tbsp harissa paste
50g red lentils, well rinsed
400g can of chopped tomatoes
800ml vegetable stock or water
salt and black pepper

GARNISH
1 tbsp olive oil
150g chickpeas (canned are fine)
1 tsp harissa paste
1 tbsp lemon juice
small bunch of parsley, finely chopped

Tomato soup is a classic and I reckon it's a favourite with everyone. The good old canned version always reminded Dave and I of childhood suppers and I love it still. but I also like to cook my own versions. This recipe has a North African vibe with a touch of harissa – a paste made of chilli and lots of spices and herbs that adds a great punch of flavour to any dish. Harissa is available in supermarkets.

1. Heat the oil in a large saucepan. Add the onion and cook over a low to medium heat until translucent. Add the squash and garlic and cook for several more minutes.

2. Stir in the harissa paste and the lentils. Mix thoroughly, then add the tomatoes and stock. Season with plenty of salt and pepper.

3. Bring to the boil, then reduce the heat to a steady simmer and partially cover the pan. Leave to simmer for about 20 minutes until the lentils and squash are tender. Purée the soup with a stick blender or in a jug blender, then taste and add more seasoning if necessary.

4. To make the garnish, heat the oil in a frying pan and add the chickpeas. Season with salt and pepper and stir in the harissa paste. Add the lemon juice, then cook, stirring constantly, until the pan looks dry.

5. Serve the soup garnished with the fried chickpeas and chopped parsley.

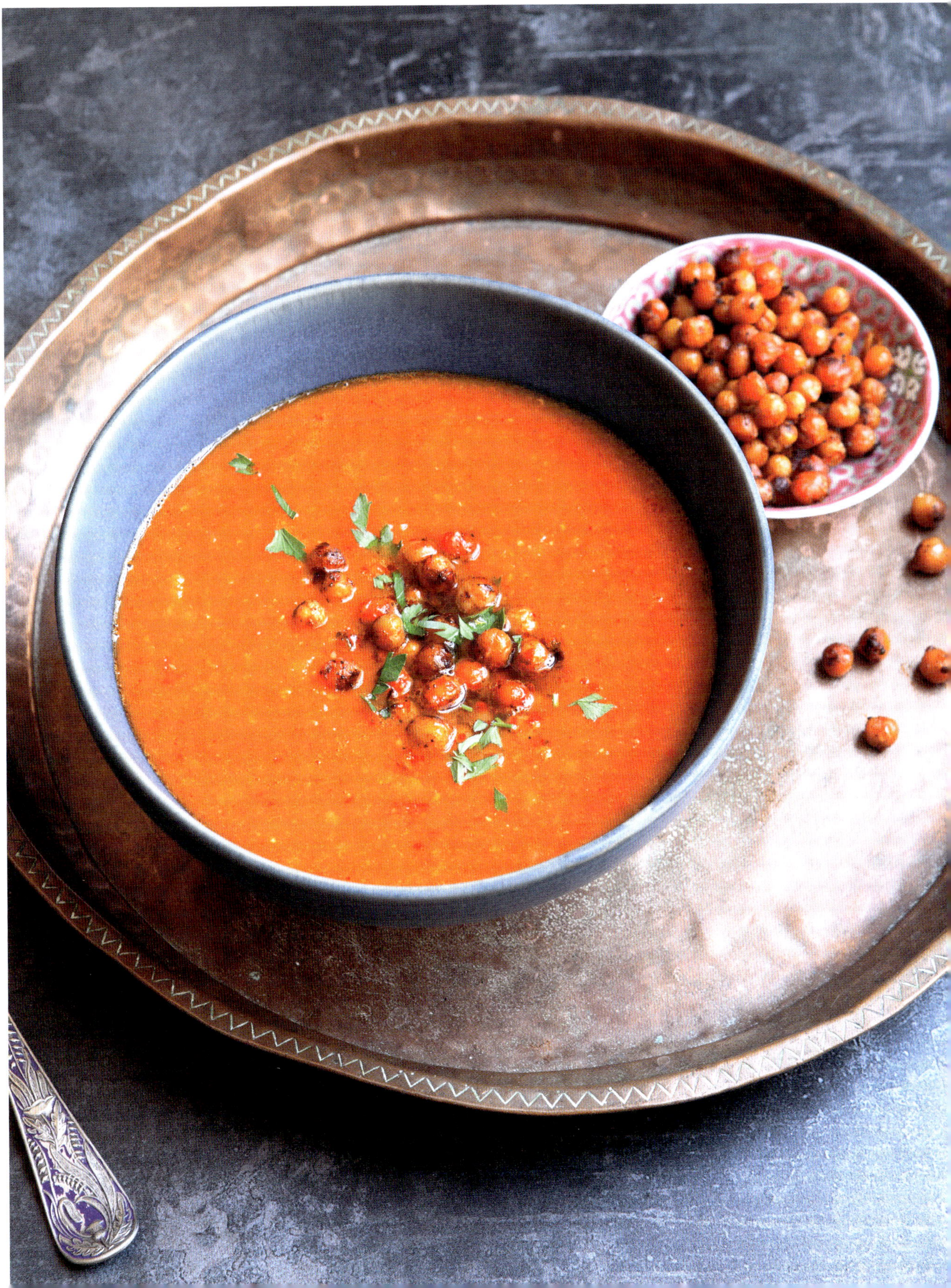

Pea & watercress soup

SERVES 4

1 tbsp olive oil
15g butter
2 leeks, finely diced
1 garlic clove, finely chopped
small bunch of fresh mint, leaves only, or 1 tsp dried mint
150g watercress, roughly chopped
800ml vegetable or chicken stock
500g frozen peas
salt and black pepper

TO SERVE
single cream
mint leaves

Sprightly, peppery watercress is a perfect partner to the sweetness of peas in this simple but tasty soup. The key to success here is the short cooking time which keeps the soup lovely and fresh and green. Stick to the timings below and you'll be on to a winner. Nourishing and delicious.

1. Heat the oil and butter in a large pan. When the butter has melted, add the leeks and cook them over a low heat for several minutes until soft and glossy. Add the garlic and cook for 2 more minutes.

2. Add the mint leaves or dried mint to the pan, together with the watercress. Stir until the watercress has wilted down, then pour in the stock. Add the peas and season with salt and pepper, then bring to the boil. Turn down the heat and simmer for 3–4 minutes.

3. Remove the soup from the heat and blitz with a stick blender or in a jug blender. You can make the soup completely smooth or, better still, leave it flecked with green. Reheat gently and serve immediately, topped with a swirl of cream and a few mint leaves.

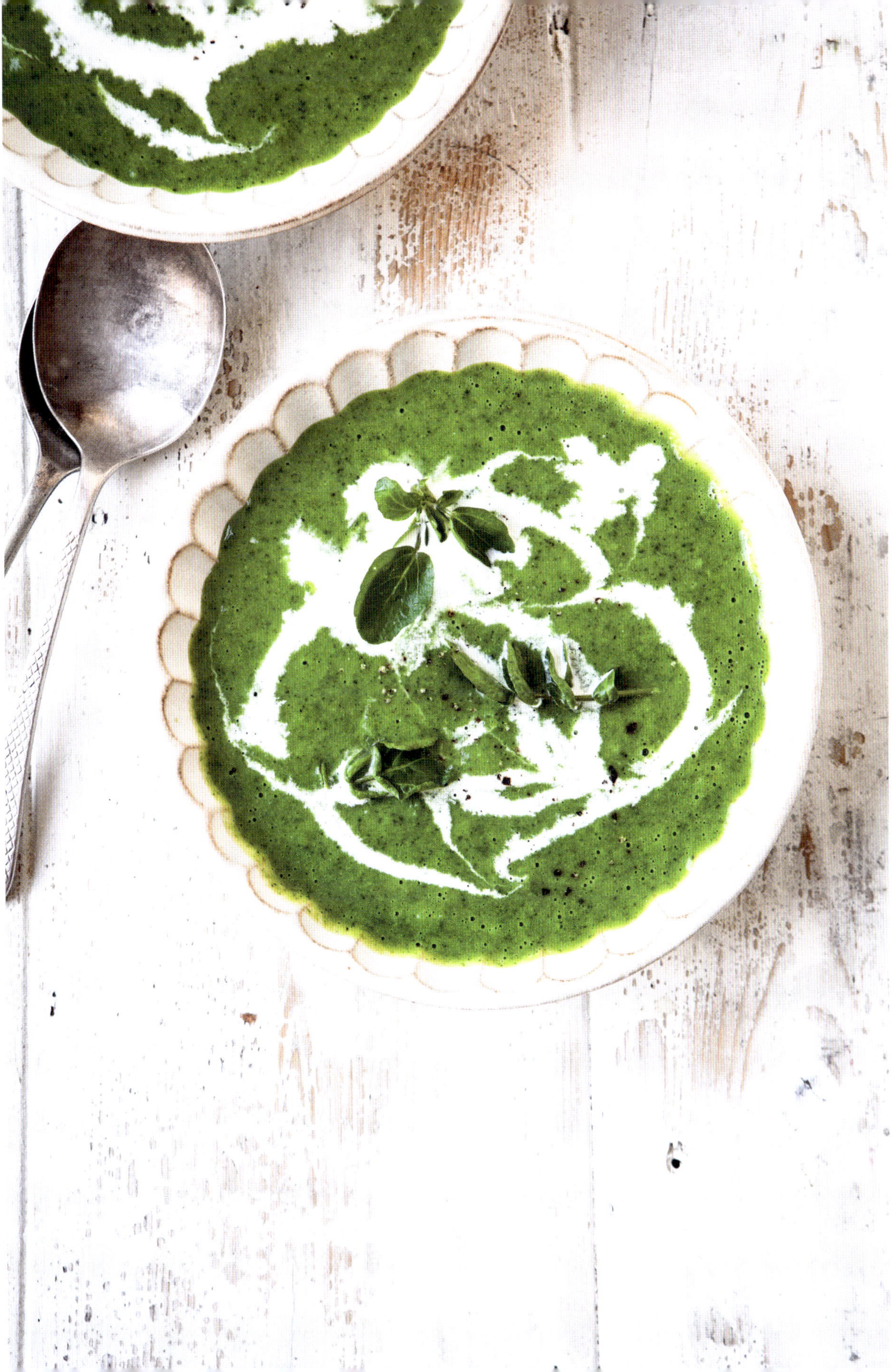

Summery minestrone

SERVES 4

2 tbsp olive oil
3 leeks, sliced on the diagonal
3 courgettes, sliced on the diagonal
200g runner beans, trimmed and cut into strips
2 garlic cloves, finely chopped
2 tarragon sprigs
1 parsley sprig
2 bay leaves
1 piece of pared lemon zest
1 litre vegetable or chicken stock
Parmesan rind (optional)
100g broad beans (fresh or frozen – remove the greyish outer skins if you have time)
3 little gem lettuces, quartered into wedges
400g can of cannellini beans, drained and rinsed
salt and black pepper

TO SERVE
basil leaves (optional)
mint leaves (optional)
basil pesto (shop-bought or see p.261)

The classic minestrone generally contains some broken-up spaghetti or other pasta, but when we came up with this recipe a few years ago, we decided to keep it light and just pack it with lots of lovely veg and beans. The special tip we picked up in Italy was to chuck in a Parmesan rind – that hard bit you can't grate any more without grating your fingers. It adds bags of flavour but remember to fish it out before you serve the soup.

1. Heat the oil in a large saucepan. Add the leeks and cook them over a medium to low heat until they are starting to soften. Add the courgettes, runner beans, garlic, herbs and lemon zest and cook for another 3–4 minutes.

2. Pour in the stock and season with salt and pepper. If you have a Parmesan rind, add it now – some of it will dissolve into the stock and provide extra flavour. Bring the soup to the boil, then turn the heat down and simmer, uncovered, until the vegetables are just tender. Add the broad beans and little gems and continue to cook until the little gems have wilted and their cores are tender.

3. Add the cannellini beans and heat them through. Fish out the remains of the Parmesan rind, the herb sprigs and the bay leaves. Serve the soup garnished with basil and mint leaves, if using, and spoonfuls of pesto.

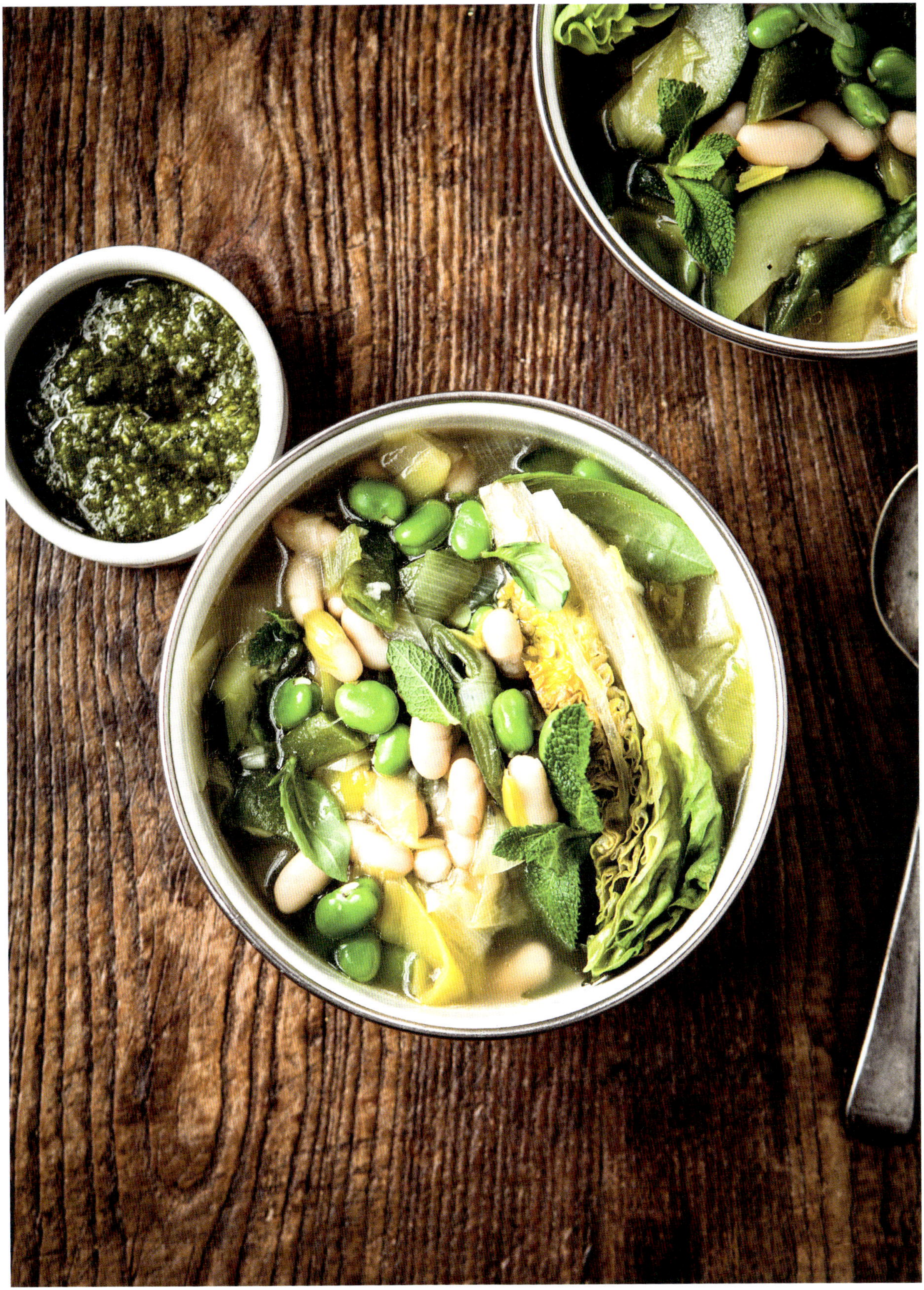

French onion soup

SERVES 4

75g butter
1kg onions, thinly sliced (about 3mm is good)
leaves from a large thyme sprig
large pinch of demerara sugar (optional)
1 tbsp plain flour
150ml dry sherry or white wine
1 tbsp sherry vinegar
1 bay leaf
850ml stock (beef, chicken or vegetable)
up to 1 tbsp brandy
salt and black pepper

CROUTONS

8 rounds of baguette
1 garlic clove, halved
butter, for spreading
100g Gruyère cheese, grated

You do need to be a bit patient when making this soup, as the onions need to cook for a long time to get that proper caramelised flavour, but man, is it worth it! On a cold winter day, a bowl of this onion soup is the best possible way of warming yourself up – it's central heating in a bowl. While some recipes suggest putting the bowls of soup topped with the cheesy croutons under the grill to brown, I prefer to grill the croutons first, then add them to the soup. Less likelihood of burning yourself and you get a nice mix of browned cheese and melting, stringy, soft cheese in the bowls.

1. Melt the butter in a large saucepan. Add the onions and thyme leaves and stir until everything is coated in buttery juices. Put a lid on the saucepan and leave the onions to cook for about 10 minutes over a low heat until they have softened.

2. Turn the heat up to medium and cook the onions until caramelised – this is not a fast process and will probably take at least an hour, perhaps longer. A fair amount of liquid will evaporate off first, as the onions release water and lose volume, then they will slowly brown. Stir them regularly, scraping up the brown layer which will coat the base of the pan. Add a splash of water from time to time if the onions are getting close to burning. Taste when you think they are caramelised enough and add a pinch of sugar if they need any additional sweetness.

3. Stir in the flour and cook it for a couple of minutes or so to get rid of the raw flavour. Add the sherry or white wine and bring it to the boil, stirring constantly to deglaze the base of the pan. Add the sherry vinegar, bay leaf and stock, then season with salt and pepper.

4. Bring the soup back to the boil, then turn down the heat, partially cover the pan and simmer for about 45 minutes. Add the brandy, a teaspoon at a time, stirring it in and tasting until you are happy with the flavour. Check the seasoning at the same time and adjust as necessary.

5. Heat a grill. Toast the baguette slices, rub them with the cut garlic and spread with butter. Divide half the cheese between the croutons and grill until the cheese has started to brown, then pile the rest of the cheese on top. Serve the soup with the croutons.

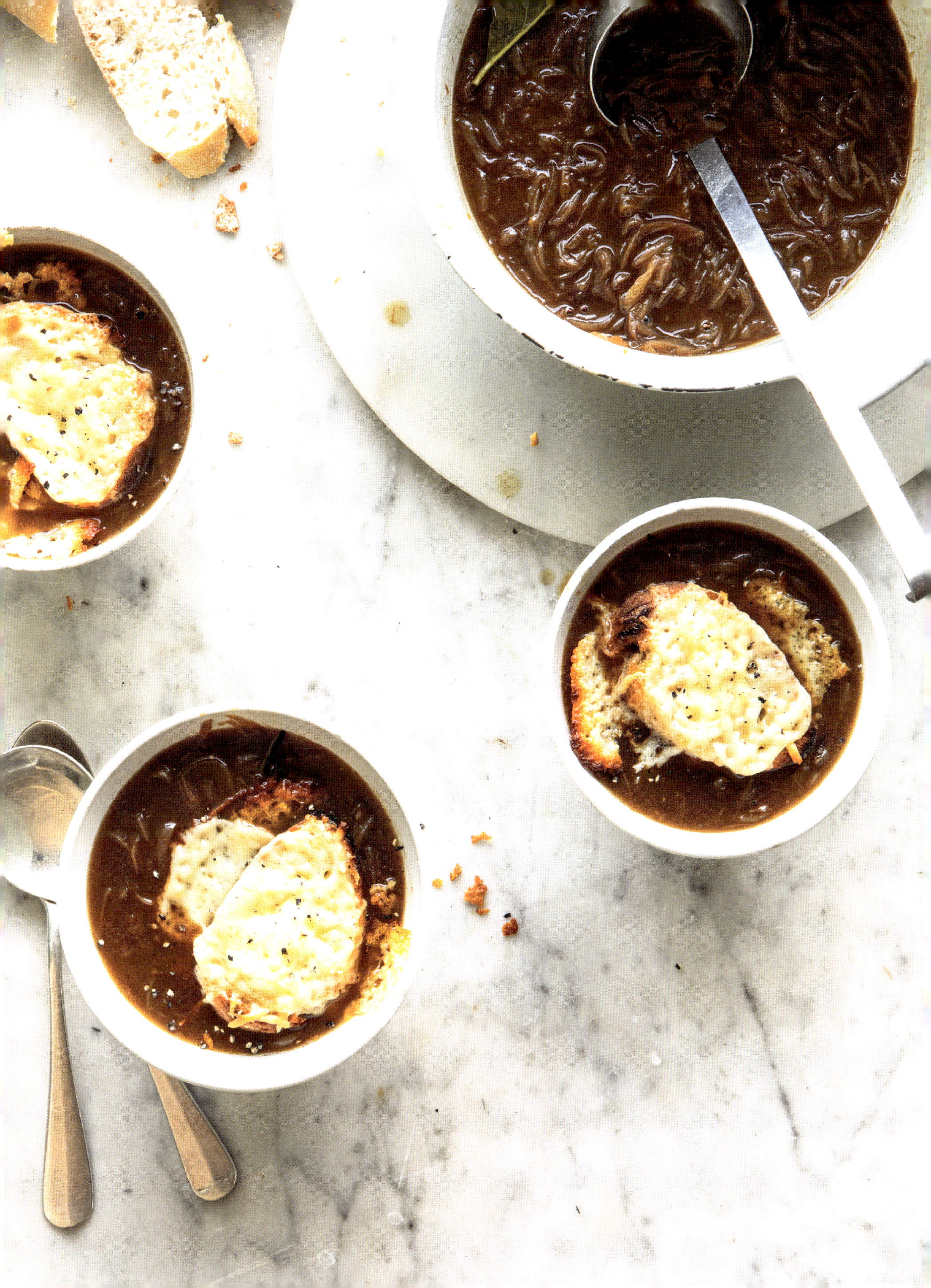

Tom yum soup

SERVES 4

TOM YUM PASTE
2 shallots, peeled
2 hot dried chillies
2–4 fresh red chillies, depending on the level of heat you like
4 garlic cloves, roughly chopped
25g galangal or root ginger, roughly chopped
2 lemongrass stalks, roughly chopped
zest of 1 lime
6 lime leaves

BROTH
1 carrot
4 heads of pak choi or similar
12 cherry tomatoes
4 lime leaves
1 bunch of coriander, stems and leaves separated
4 spring onions, to garnish
1 tbsp coconut oil
1 onion, finely sliced
1 litre vegetable stock
1 lemongrass stalk, left whole and bruised
200ml coconut milk
2 tbsp soy sauce
juice of 1 lime
1 tsp light brown soft sugar
1 block of silken tofu at room temperature, carefully cut into cubes
small bunch of Thai or regular basil
salt and black pepper

TO SERVE
lime wedges
chilli oil

This is our vegan version of the famous Thai hot and sour soup. Yes, there are a load of ingredients here, but you'll find them all in the supermarket and once they're chopped and ready the soup is quick to make and well worth it. In fact, while you're at it, make double the broth and pop some in the freezer so that's the bulk of the work done for another time. If you can't get Thai basil, it's fine to use the ordinary sort.

1. First make the paste. Put the shallots, dried chillies and fresh chillies into a frying pan and dry fry them for several minutes until they have started to blacken and smell very aromatic. Remove from the heat and set aside to cool.

2. Put the cooled shallots and chillies in a food processor with all the remaining paste ingredients and blitz to make a bright red paste. Keep pulsing and scraping down the sides of the bowl regularly. If you have trouble processing the mixture, add a couple of tablespoons of water.

3. For the broth, slice the carrot into ribbons with a potato peeler and cut the pak choi into thin pieces lengthways. Cut the tomatoes in half. Shred the lime leaves very, very finely and finely chop the coriander stems. Cut the spring onions in half lengthways, then shred them into pieces no larger than 1mm.

4. Heat the coconut oil in a large saucepan. Add the onion, fry it for a few minutes over a medium heat until it is a light golden brown, then add the paste. Fry for a few minutes, then add the stock and lemongrass. Bring to the boil and simmer for 5 minutes.

5. Add the coconut milk, soy sauce, lime juice and sugar. Stir to combine and to dissolve the sugar, then add the carrot ribbons, pak choi, cherry tomatoes, lime leaves and coriander stems. Check for seasoning and add salt and black pepper as necessary, then simmer until the vegetables are tender. Taste again and add more seasoning, lime juice and sugar to taste.

6. Divide the tofu between 4 large bowls. Ladle over the broth, then garnish with the spring onions, coriander and basil leaves. Serve with lime wedges and chilli oil to make it extra hot.

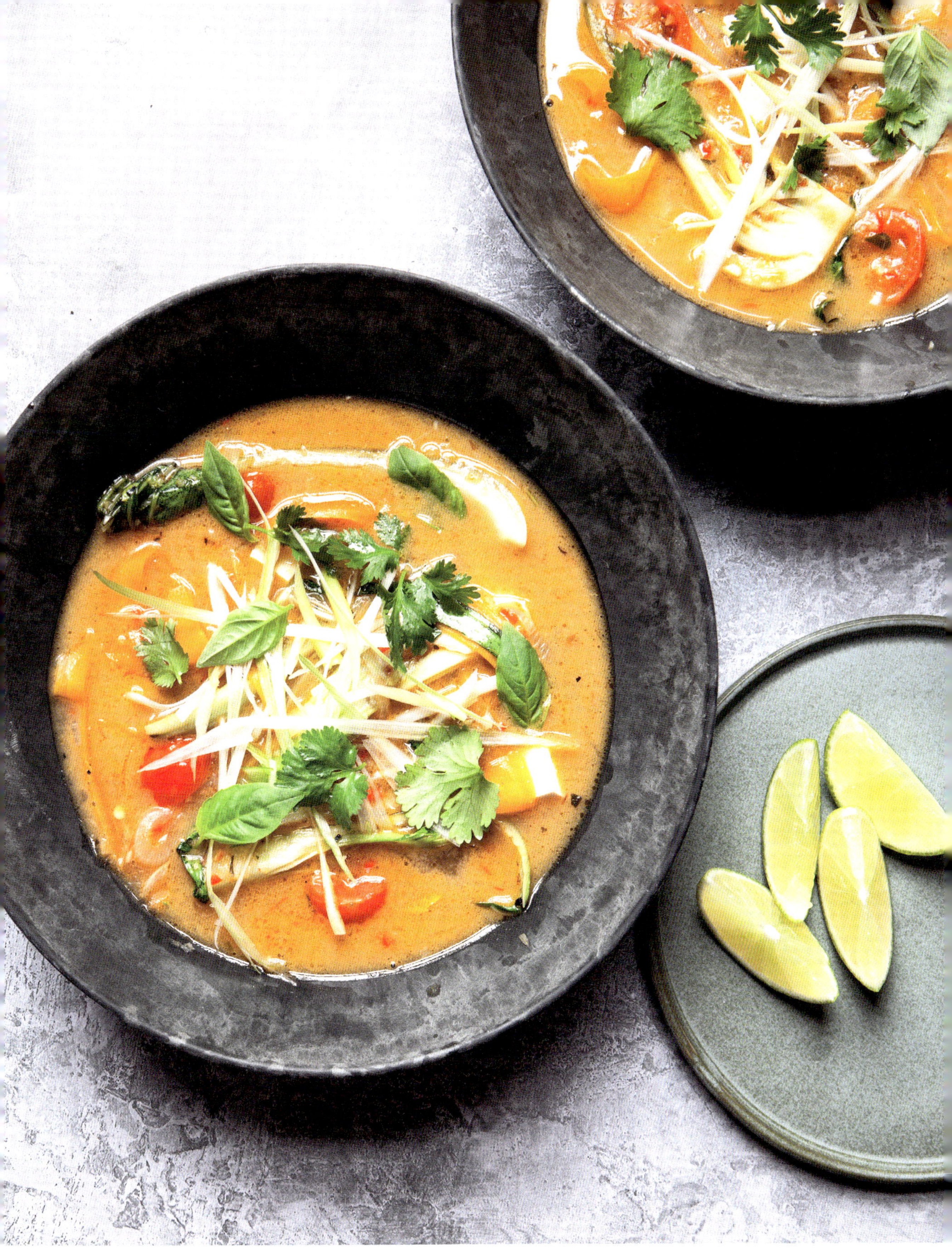

Seafood chowder

SERVES 4

25g butter
50g streaky bacon, cut into small strips
1 onion, diced
2 leeks, cut into rounds
2 celery sticks, sliced
1 tbsp plain flour (optional)
100ml white wine
300ml whole milk
300ml fish or chicken stock
300g floury potatoes, diced
2 bay leaves
2 thyme sprigs
1 mace blade
100ml double cream
500g frozen seafood mix, defrosted and well drained
salt and black pepper

TO SERVE
2 tbsp finely chopped parsley

Many moons ago, Dave and I cooked a cockle chowder on the beach in Southend for one of our first TV series. It was really good, but then we thought that instead of using cockles, which not everyone likes, a simpler idea would be to grab yourself one of those bags of frozen seafood in the supermarket. With one of those, this chunky chowder is a doddle to make and a real treat to eat. The mixes usually contain a selection of seafood, such as mussels, prawns, squid and white fish, but feel free to make your own selection if you prefer.

1. Heat the butter in a large pan. Add the bacon, onion, leeks and celery, then cook over a low heat for several minutes until the vegetables have started to soften and the bacon has rendered out some its fat and begun to crisp up.

2. This recipe includes potatoes which should thicken the chowder nicely, but you can also add flour to thicken it if you want. If using the flour, stir it into the buttery vegetables, then pour in the white wine. Allow the wine to bubble up, then stir until you have a thick paste. Add the milk and stock at the same time, along with the potatoes, herbs and mace, then season with salt and pepper. Bring the liquid almost to the boil, stirring constantly, then turn down the heat to a gentle simmer. Continue to cook, stirring regularly, until the vegetables are very tender and the soup has thickened.

3. Add the cream to the soup and cook for 2–3 minutes until piping hot. Add all the seafood and continue to cook for a further 3 minutes, then check the seasoning and add more salt and pepper if necessary. Serve the chowder garnished with chopped parsley.

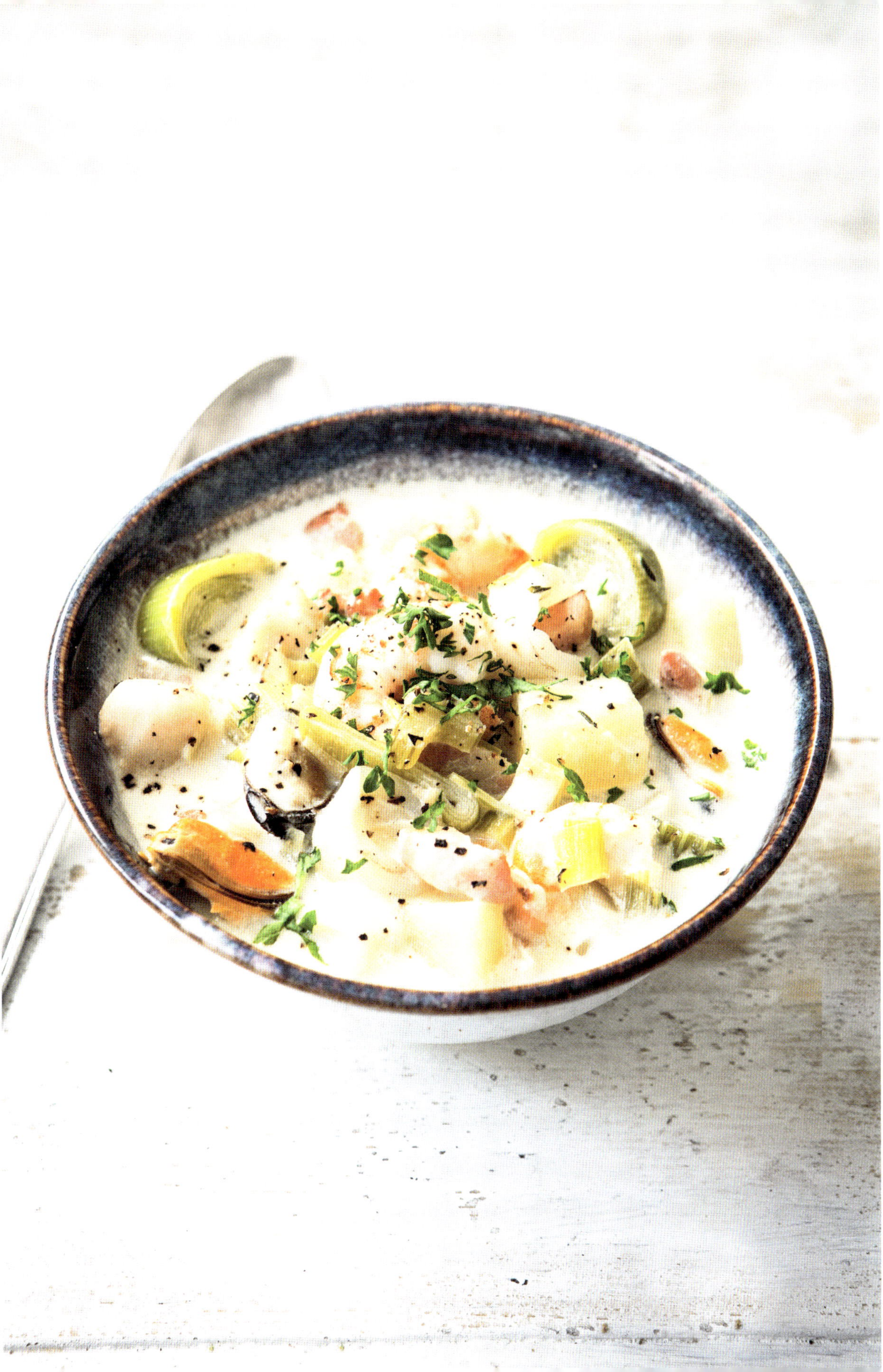

Chicken soup

SERVES 4

30g butter
1 onion, diced
2 large carrots, diced
2 celery sticks, diced
300g potatoes, diced
3 skinless chicken thigh fillets, diced
3 leeks, sliced into rounds
3 garlic cloves, finely chopped
leaves from 4 large tarragon sprigs, finely chopped, plus extra to garnish
100ml white wine
750ml chicken stock
50ml double cream
salt and black pepper

Here's a simple recipe for chicken soup that's packed with goodness and is also creamy and delicious. It's often said but I do believe that food like this is good for the soul. Warming and comforting, it's a meal in itself.

1. Heat the butter in a large saucepan and add the onion, carrots, celery and potatoes. Cook for 10 minutes over a gentle heat, stirring regularly.

2. Turn up the heat and add the diced chicken. Cook until the chicken is lightly coloured on all sides, then stir in the leeks, garlic and tarragon. Stir for another minute, then pour in the white wine and season with salt and pepper. Bring to the boil, cover the pan and leave to cook until the vegetables are tender – this will take about another 10–15 minutes.

3. Pour over the stock and bring to the boil. Lower the heat and simmer the soup gently for about 10 minutes, then check the vegetables – the potatoes should be breaking up and everything else should be cooked.

4. Stir in the cream and reheat until piping hot. Serve in bowls with a little more chopped tarragon sprinkled on top.

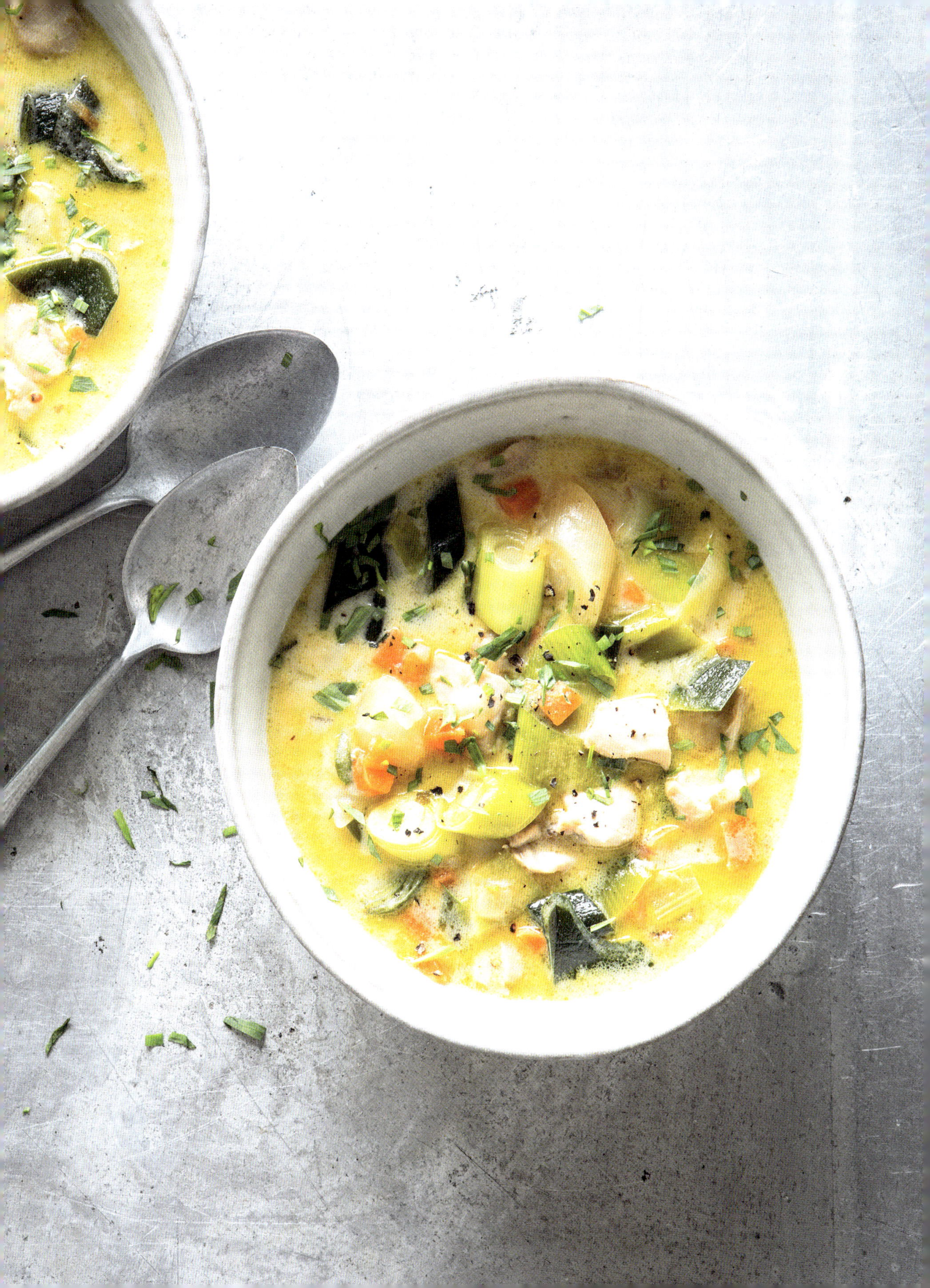

Oxtail soup with parsley dumplings

SERVES 6

1 whole oxtail (about 1.3kg), cut into chunky pieces
3 tbsp plain flour
3–4 tbsp olive oil
2 onions, halved and sliced
3 carrots, diced
2 celery sticks, trimmed and diced
2 garlic cloves, finely chopped
1 tsp dried thyme
2 bay leaves
300ml red wine
2 litres beef stock
2 tbsp tomato purée
2 tbsp cream sherry
salt and black pepper

PARSLEY DUMPLINGS
200g self-raising flour
100g shredded suet
3 tbsp finely chopped parsley
½ tsp salt

Oxtail soup was a fixture in our households when Dave and I were kids, but then it went out of fashion. Bring it back, I say, as it's dead tasty, and has great flavour and texture. Add a few delicious dumplings and you have a truly satisfying winter warmer.

1. Preheat the oven to 170°C/Fan 150°C/Gas 3½. Wash the oxtail pieces, pat them dry with kitchen paper and trim off any excess fat. Put the flour in a large bowl and season it well with salt and black pepper. Add the oxtail pieces and toss well until they are all coated with flour.

2. Heat 2 tablespoons of the oil in a frying pan. Brown the oxtail pieces over a medium heat for about 10 minutes, or until deeply coloured, turning them every now and then. It's probably best to do this in a few batches so you don't overcrowd the pan. Add extra oil if you need it. Put the browned oxtail pieces in a large, flameproof casserole dish.

3. Put the frying pan back on the hob and add the onions, carrots and celery, with a little extra oil if necessary. Cook them gently for about 10 minutes, or until softened and lightly browned, stirring occasionally. Add the garlic and cook for another couple of minutes. Tip the veg into the casserole dish with the oxtail and add the thyme and bay leaves, then stir in the wine, beef stock and tomato purée. Season and bring to a gentle simmer. Put the lid on the casserole dish, place in the centre of the oven and cook for 3 hours, stirring and turning the oxtail pieces halfway through the cooking time. The meat should be falling off the bones.

4. Remove the casserole dish from the oven, take out the oxtail pieces and set them aside to cool slightly. Skim off the fat from the surface of the soup and chuck it away. When the oxtail is cool enough to handle, pull the meat off the bones and discard any gristly bits. Cut the meat into small chunks and put it back in the casserole dish. Stir in the sherry.

5. To make the dumplings, mix the flour, suet, parsley and salt in a large bowl. Stir in enough water to mix to a soft, spongy dough – you'll probably need about 100–125ml. Roll the dough into 18 small balls.

6. Bring the soup to a gentle simmer on the hob, stirring occasionally. Season well, then drop the dumplings gently on top of the soup. Cover tightly with a lid and simmer for 15–18 minutes, or until the dumplings are well-risen and fluffy. Ladle the soup into deep bowls to serve.

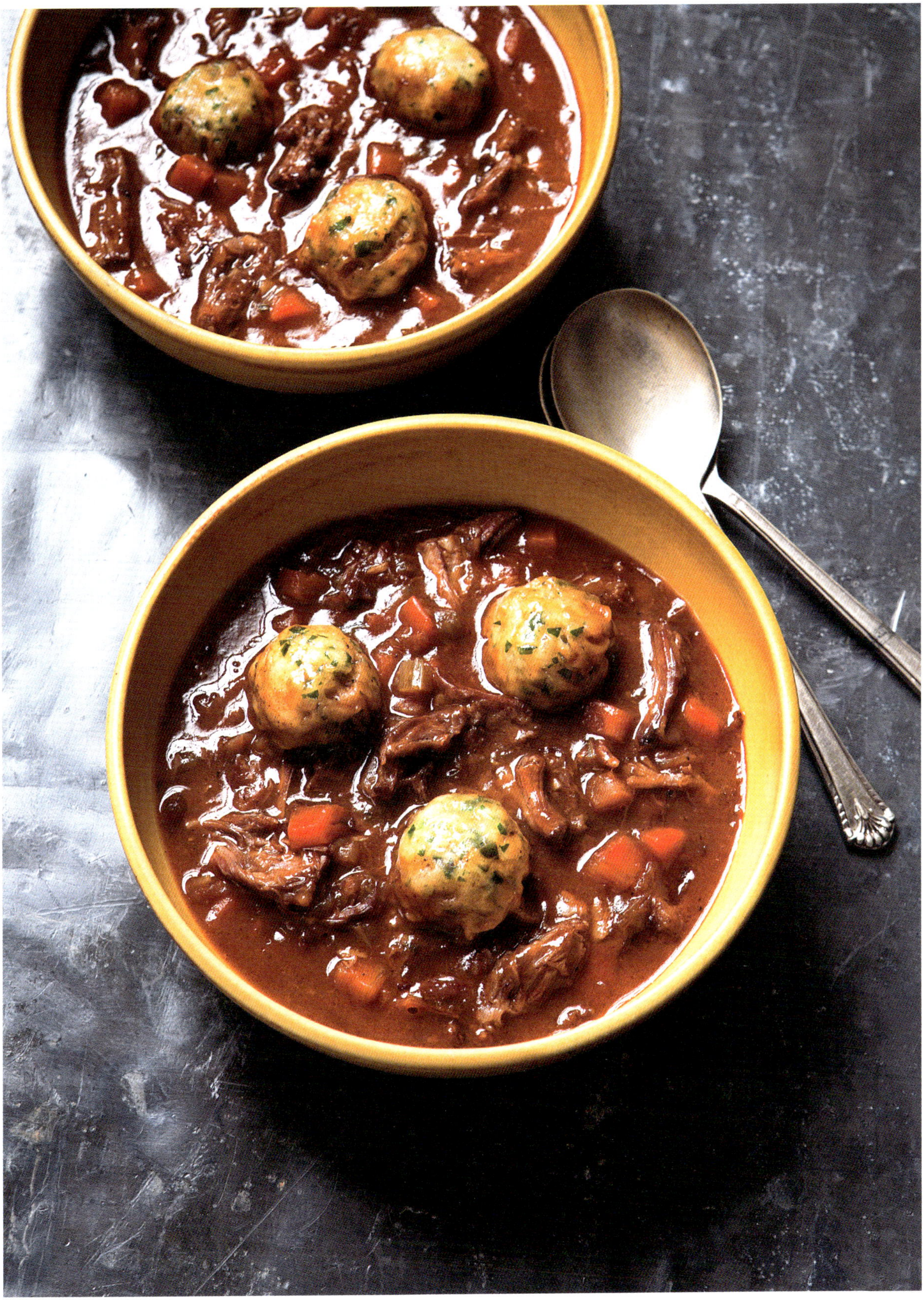

Pork ramen

SERVES 8–10

BROTH
1.5kg raw chicken carcasses
1.5kg pork bones, preferably spare ribs
1 pig's trotter
1 onion, skin included if clean enough, roughly chopped
2 carrots, roughly chopped
30g root ginger, roughly chopped
1 head of garlic, cloves separated but unpeeled
soy or tamari sauce

GARNISHES (ALL OPTIONAL)
cooked noodles
marinated eggs (tamago – see p.260)
slices of twice-cooked pork (char sui – see p.262)
bamboo shoots
Chinese greens, such as pak choi
Japanese mushrooms, such as enoki
bunch of spring onions, shredded
chilli oil
nori (seaweed strips)

First thing to say is that this isn't a quick midweek supper. Ramen needs love and attention and time and it's all about making a really rich and savoury stock. Feelings run high about the best way to make ramen and there are so many different recipes, but this is one that Dave and I came up with some years ago and we've always loved it. It does make a large quantity, so you can half the recipe if you like. Garnishes are optional, but if you want to try adding marinated eggs (page 260) and pork char siu (page 262) you will have something very special to enjoy.

1. Put the chicken carcasses, pork bones and the pig's trotter in a stock pot that holds 8–10 litres. Cover them with cold water and bring to the boil. When a mushroom-coloured foam starts to appear, start skimming it off. Continue skimming until the foam that appears is white.

2. Meanwhile, heat a griddle pan over a high heat. When it's too hot to hold your hand over – don't touch the pan – add the onion, carrots and ginger. Griddle them for several minutes, turning regularly, until fairly dark char lines appear on the vegetables.

3. Reduce the heat under the stock pot slightly so the stock is bubbling, not fiercely but harder than a simmer. Add the griddled onion, carrots and ginger and the garlic, then partially cover the pan and cook the broth for at least 3 hours – up to 5 if you can. Keep an eye on the liquid level – the stock shouldn't reduce too much, but don't let it boil away in the first hour or so, and top it up if necessary.

4. When your broth is a deep golden-brown and quite cloudy, strain it through a sieve. You can strain it again through muslin or a clean tea towel if you like, but that shouldn't be necessary. As this is such a rich broth, it's a good idea to skim off some of the fat. You can either do this when it settles on top, or to make the job easier, chill the broth until the fat has set and just scrape it off.

5. To serve, bring the broth back to the boil and season with soy sauce or tamari. Put cooked noodles in individual bowls, along with the marinated eggs, if using. Drop the cooked pork, if using, into the broth to heat through, then using chopsticks, divide it between the bowls and ladle over the broth. You can do the same with any of the other garnishes. Add a sprinkling of spring onions, and serve with more soy sauce, chilli oil or sauce and perhaps some pieces of nori seaweed. Fantastic!

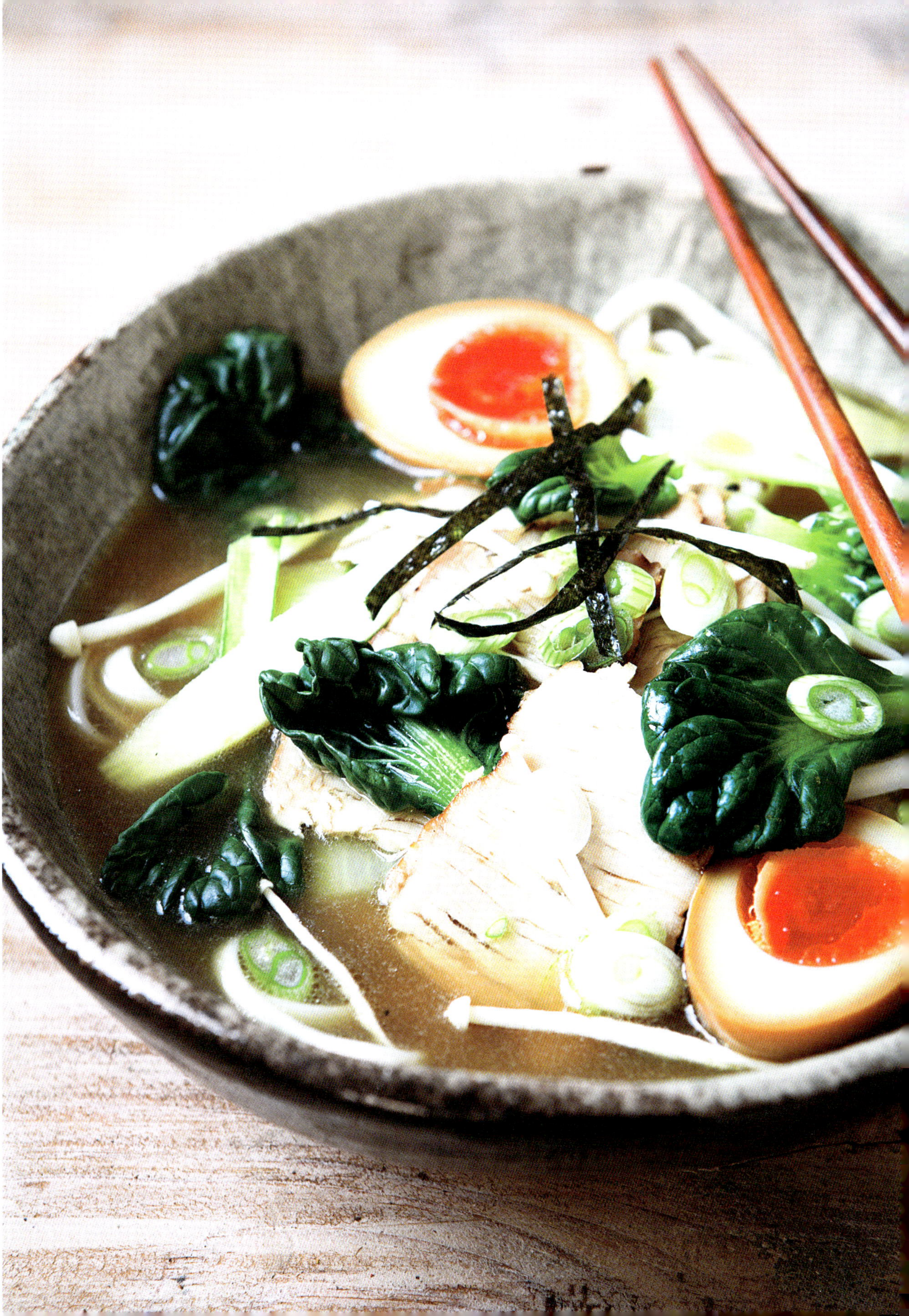

Scotch broth

SERVES 6

75g pearl barley
about 1kg lamb shoulder, on the bone
2 litres lamb stock or water
2 onions, chopped
1 bay leaf
a few fresh thyme sprigs
2 carrots, cut into 2.5cm pieces
2 turnips, cut into 2.5cm pieces (optional)
2 celery stalks, trimmed, cut into 2.5cm pieces
2 potatoes, cut into 2.5cm pieces
½ Savoy cabbage, cored and finely shredded
salt and black pepper

An old-school classic and none the worst for that. Scotch broth was something I loved as a child and it's a dish I make for my family now. Packed with veg, flavour and nourishment, this is a soup I never tire of.

1. Put the barley in a bowl, cover it with cold water and set it aside to soak.

2. Meanwhile, place the lamb in a large saucepan, cover it with the lamb stock or cold water and bring to a simmer. Skim off any scum, then add the onions, bay leaf and thyme to the pan. Bring back to a gentle simmer and cook for an hour, skimming occasionally.

3. Add the carrots, turnips and celery to the pan and season with a heaped teaspoon of salt and some black pepper. Bring back to a very gentle simmer, cover the pan with a lid and cook for 30 minutes.

4. When the 30 minutes is up, drain the barley and rinse it in a sieve under cold running water. Take the lid off the saucepan, turn the lamb over and add the pearl barley and potatoes. Cook gently for another 30 minutes, uncovered.

5. Stir in the cabbage and bring the broth back to a gentle simmer. Continue cooking, uncovered, for another 15 minutes or until the lamb is very tender and falling off the bone and the barley is softened. Remove from the heat.

6. Lift the lamb out of the pan with tongs or a large fork and put it on a board. Carve off all the meat, tearing it into largish chunks and discarding any skin and bone. Season the soup with more salt and pepper to taste and ladle it into large bowls. Divide the lamb between the bowls and serve at once.

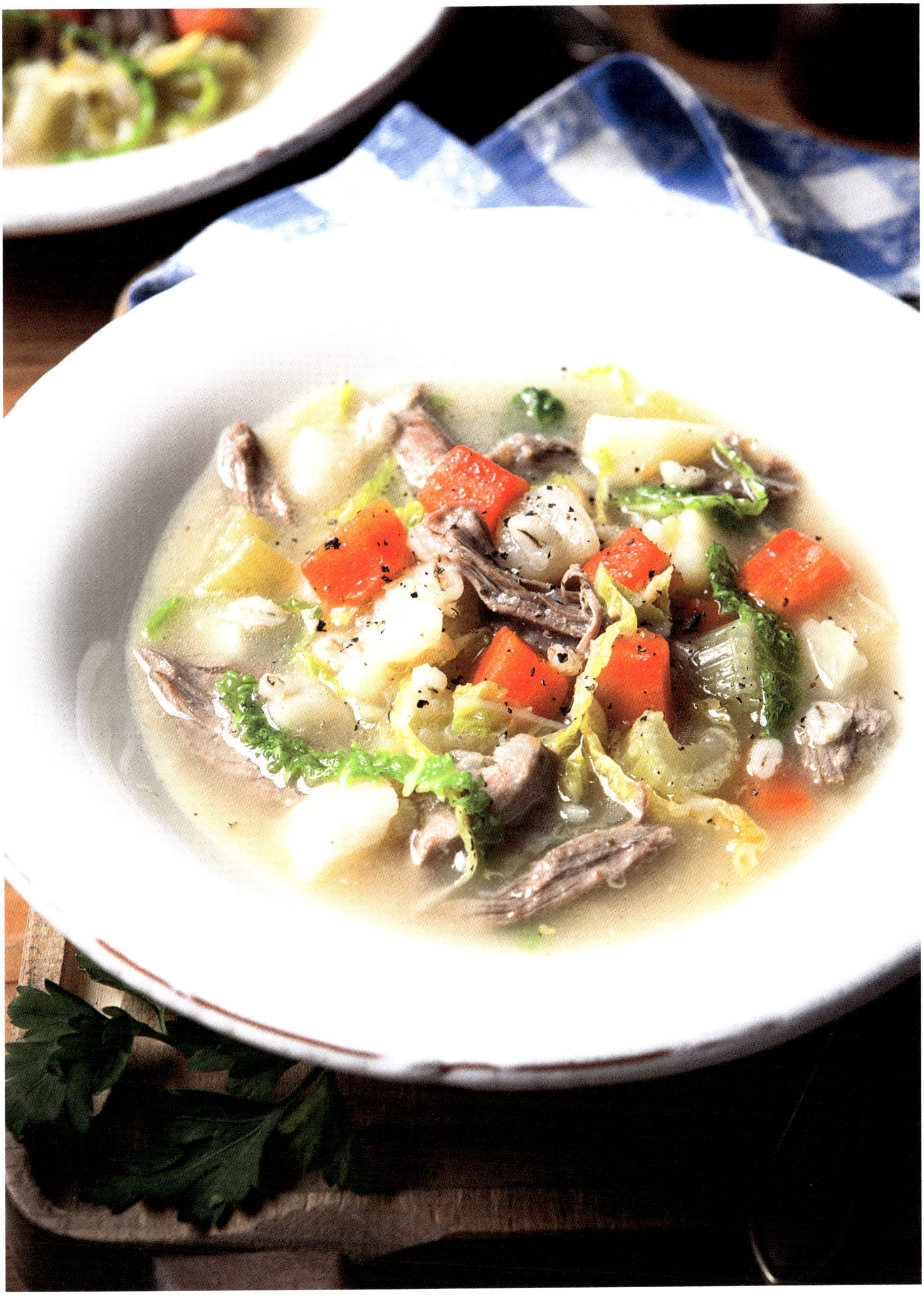

1 Burrata, Parma ham & grilled peach salad...56
2 Rainbow coleslaw...58
3 Roast beetroot, goat's cheese & apple salad...60
4 Grilled vegetable & freekeh salad...62
5 Waldorf salad...64
6 Caesar salad...66
7 Teriyaki chicken salad...68
8 Crispy noodles with prawns & crab...70
9 Thai prawn noodle salad...72
10 Steak & asparagus salad...74

salads

> *You'll find some real stars in this chapter, like the Waldorf and Caesar salads – what's not to love! – as well as some great Biker inventions. I'm particularly proud of the Thai prawn noodle salad and the steak and asparagus.*

Burrata, Parma ham & grilled peach salad

SERVES 4 AS A STARTER, 2 AS A MAIN MEAL

½ red onion, sliced into crescents
3 peaches, cut into wedges
1 tsp olive oil, plus 2 tbsp
100g rocket or other salad leaves
100g Parma ham, sliced
1 large burrata (or 2 balls of mozzarella)
2 tsp balsamic vinegar
handful of basil leaves, to garnish
salt and black pepper

Dave and I had a fantastic time travelling round parts of Italy, France and Spain while filming our **Mediterranean Adventure** *TV series a few years ago and enjoyed so much great food. This salad was one of our very favourite discoveries. We were already big fans of mozzarella but burrata is the luxury, gold-plated version – rich, creamy and extra delicious. You can, of course, make an excellent salad with mozzarella, but if you can lay your hands on some burrata, give it a try. You won't be disappointed.*

1. Add salt to a bowl of cold water, then add the slices of red onion. Leave them to soak for half an hour, then drain thoroughly.

2. Next grill the peaches. Heat a griddle pan until it's too hot to hold your hand over comfortably – don't touch it!. Toss the peach wedges in a teaspoon of olive oil, then griddle them on each cut side until charred with black grill marks – this should take about 2–3 minutes on each side. Set the wedges aside to cool slightly.

3. Arrange the leaves on a serving dish or in individual salad plates. Add the Parma ham, peach wedges and red onion slices, then break the burrata into pieces and add these too. Drizzle over 2 tablespoons of olive oil, followed by the balsamic vinegar and season lightly with salt and pepper. Garnish with basil leaves, then serve.

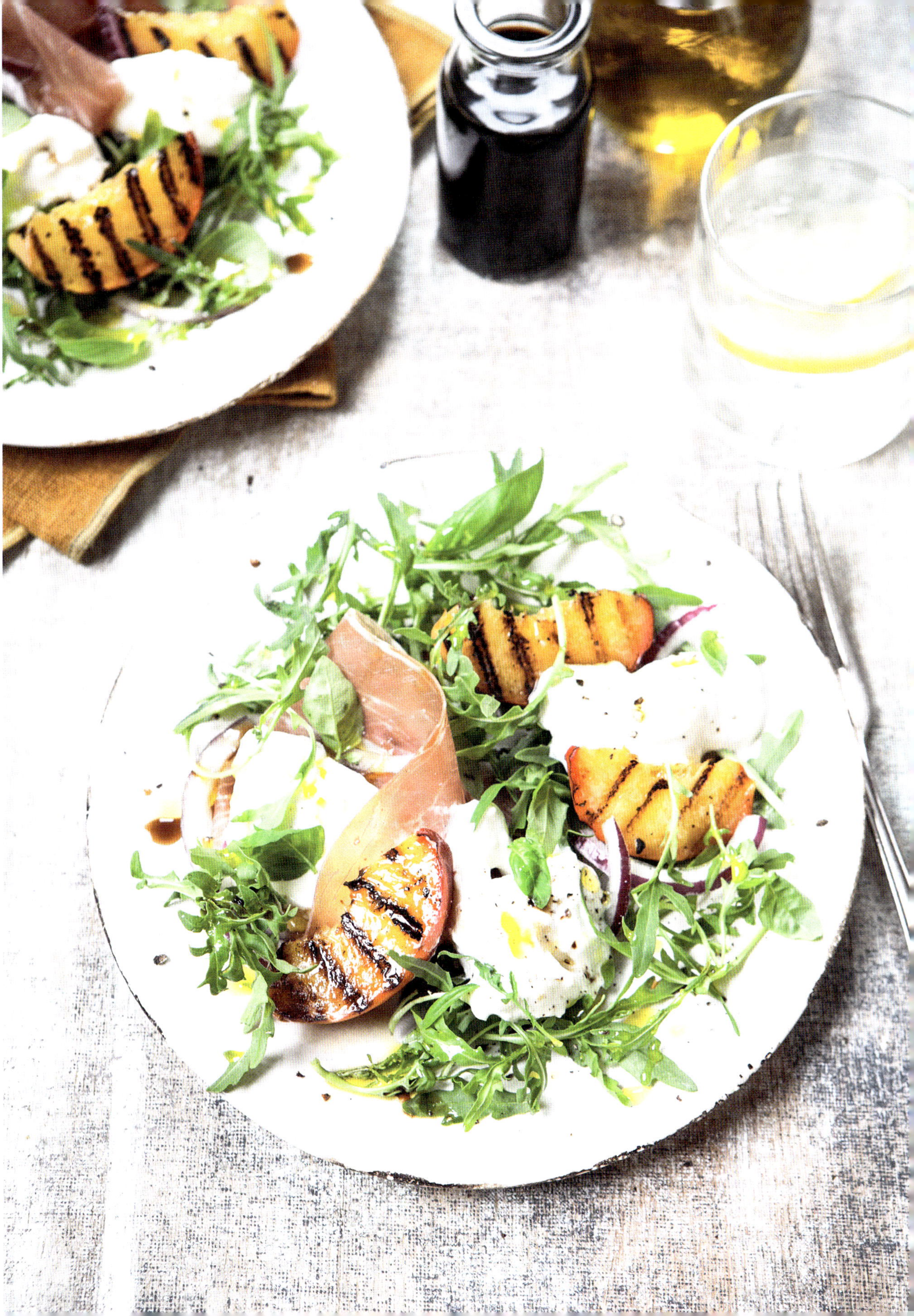

Rainbow coleslaw

SERVES 6

½ medium red cabbage
2 medium carrots, peeled
6 spring onions, trimmed and finely sliced
50g sultanas
1 apple, peeled, quartered, cored and cut into small chunks

DRESSING
150g mayonnaise
150ml natural yoghurt
1 small garlic clove, finely chopped
salt and black pepper

This is our version of a much-loved classic that has graced picnics, buffet tables and salad bars for many years. I like the red cabbage but you could use white cabbage if that's what you have. Fresh, crunchy and fabulous.

1. Remove any damaged outer leaves from the cabbage and cut out the tough central core. Shred the cabbage as finely as possible and put it in a large bowl. Coarsely grate the carrots lengthways into long, thin shreds.

2. Add the carrots, spring onions and sultanas to the bowl with the cabbage, then add the apple and toss lightly.

3. To make the dressing, mix the mayonnaise, yoghurt and garlic, then season with a little salt and plenty of pepper. Pour the dressing over the vegetables and toss gently.

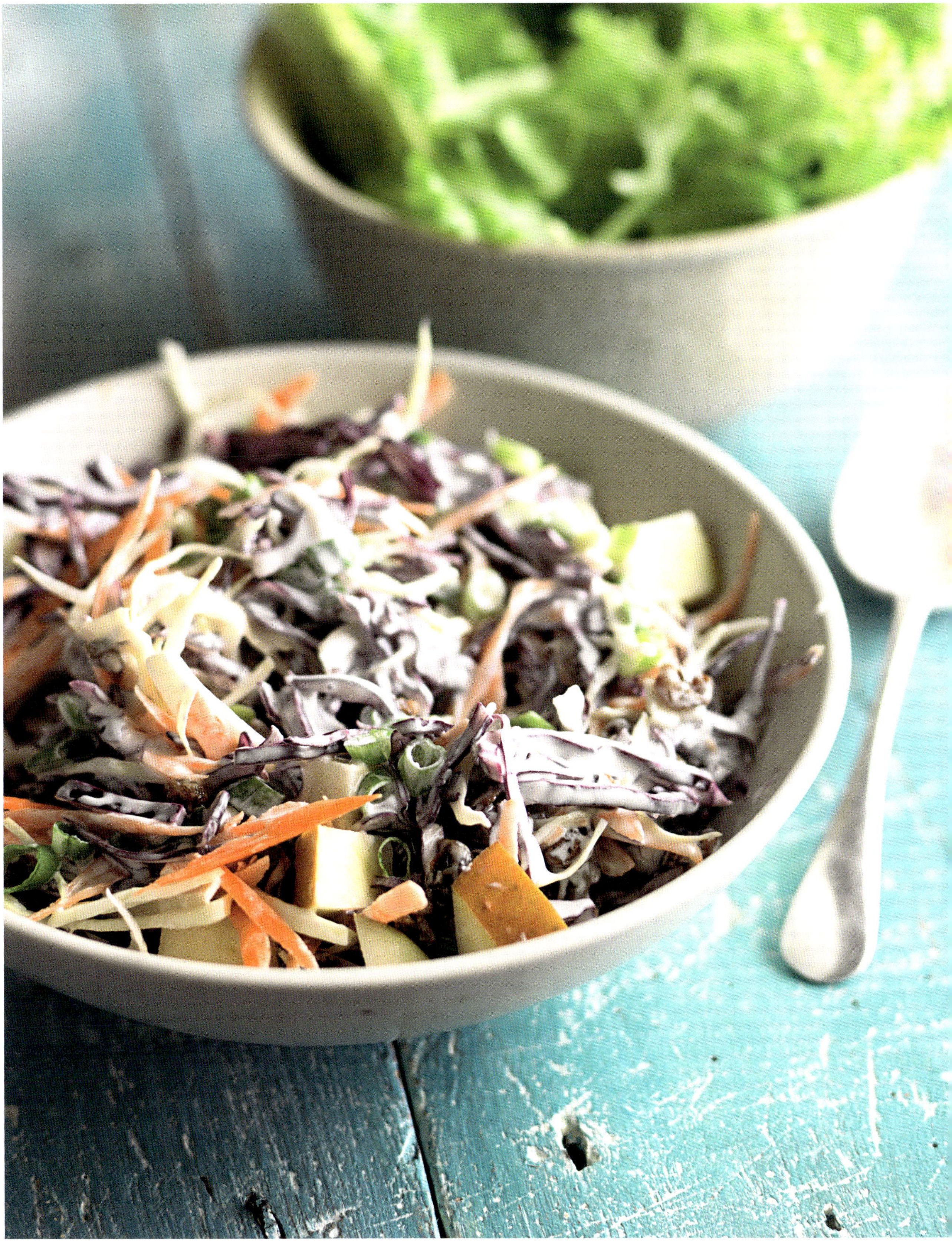

Roast beetroot, goat's cheese & apple salad

SERVES 4

6 fairly small beetroots
1 tbsp olive oil
a few thyme sprigs
100g watercress, broken into small sprigs
about 50g lamb's lettuce or other salad greens
1 or 2 crisp eating apples, cored and diced
about 150g goat's cheese log, thinly sliced
small bunch of parsley, torn into small sprigs
30g walnuts, roughly chopped
salt and black pepper

DRESSING
1 shallot, finely sliced
leaves from a thyme sprig
1 tbsp cider vinegar
3 tbsp walnut or olive oil

Beetroot and creamy goat's cheese go so well together and are just right for this robust, tasty salad. Fresh beetroots, if you have them, certainly work best in terms of texture and flavour and you can also use the leaves in the salad if they're fresh enough. If you don't have fresh beetroots or you don't have time to roast them, it's fine to use the vacuum-packed beetroots available in most supermarkets.

1. If you're using raw beetroots, preheat the oven to 200°C/Fan 180°C/Gas 6. Cut the stems off the beetroots about 1cm from the top – leaving this little bit of stem stops beetroots 'bleeding' as they cook. Wash and dry the beetroots thoroughly, put them in a roasting tin and drizzle over the oil. Add the thyme and season with salt and pepper. Cover the tin with foil and roast the beetroots for 40–50 minutes, depending on their size. They're ready once they're tender all the way through.

2. Leave the beetroots to cool for a few minutes until cool enough to handle, then rub off the skins. Set aside to cool, then dice. If using vacuum-packed beetroots, just dice them.

3. For the dressing, add the shallot and thyme leaves to the cider vinegar and leave to stand for 10 minutes. Season with salt and plenty of pepper, then whisk in the oil.

4. Assemble the salad on a large serving platter or in 4 individual bowls. Lightly toss the watercress and other salad leaves with the apple and beetroot. Top with the slices of goat's cheese and add the parsley sprigs and walnuts. Drizzle over the salad dressing and serve immediately.

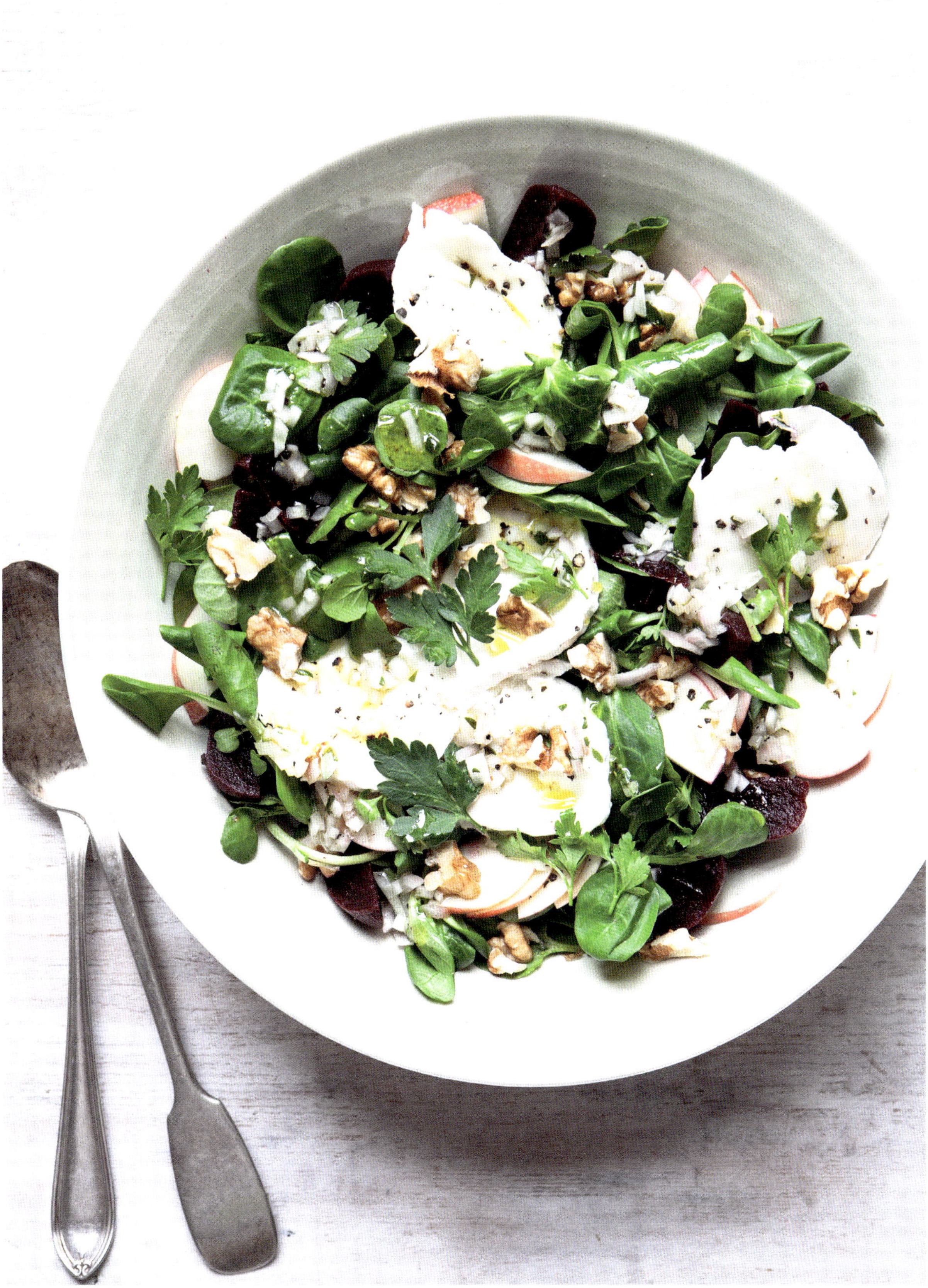

Grilled vegetable & freekeh salad

SERVES 4

FREEKEH
150g freekeh
1 tbsp olive oil
400ml vegetable stock or water
salt and black pepper

GRILLED VEGETABLES
2 courgettes, cut into thin strips on the diagonal
bunch of spring onions, trimmed
2 tbsp olive oil

DRESSING
1 tbsp tahini
2 tbsp olive oil
juice and zest of 1 lemon
½ tsp maple syrup or pomegranate molasses
1 garlic clove, crushed
¼ tsp ground cinnamon
¼ tsp ground allspice

SALAD
1 medium cucumber, finely diced
150g tomatoes, finely diced
large bunch of parsley, finely chopped
1 or more small bunches of mint, coriander or dill, finely chopped
20g pine nuts, lightly toasted

No need to freak out about freekeh! It's just a grain, like couscous and bulgur, and makes a good salad. It's easy to prepare and it's one of those things that's great to have in the store cupboard. Plenty of nice veg in this salad and you can vary them as you like, but do try the tasty dressing. It really lifts the salad into something special. Griddling the courgettes and spring onions does give extra flavour, but if you prefer you can just whack them all on a baking tray and cook them in the oven.

1. First cook the freekeh. Soak it for 5 minutes in plenty of cold water, then drain thoroughly. Heat the oil in a saucepan and add the freekeh. Toast until the freekeh is dry – it will give off steam to start with – then season with plenty of salt. Add 300ml of the stock or water and bring to the boil, then turn down the heat and cover. Simmer over a low heat for 15–20 minutes, until the freekeh is cooked and all the liquid has been absorbed. If it isn't quite done, add a splash more stock or water and continue cooking.

2. Grill the vegetables. Heat a griddle pan until it's too hot to hold your hand over – don't touch it, though! Toss the courgettes and the spring onions in the oil and season with salt and pepper. Grill the vegetables on each side until they have deep char lines and have softened. You may need to do this in more than one batch.

3. To make the dressing, whisk all the ingredients together with plenty of salt and pepper. Thin the dressing with a little water until it's about the consistency of single cream.

4. To assemble the salad, mix the freekeh with the cucumber, tomatoes and most of the herbs and pine nuts, reserving a few for a garnish. Toss with 2 tablespoons of the dressing.

5. Roughly chop the grilled spring onions, or leave them whole if you like, and arrange them over the freekeh along with the courgettes. Top with more of the dressing and the reserved herbs and pine nuts, then serve.

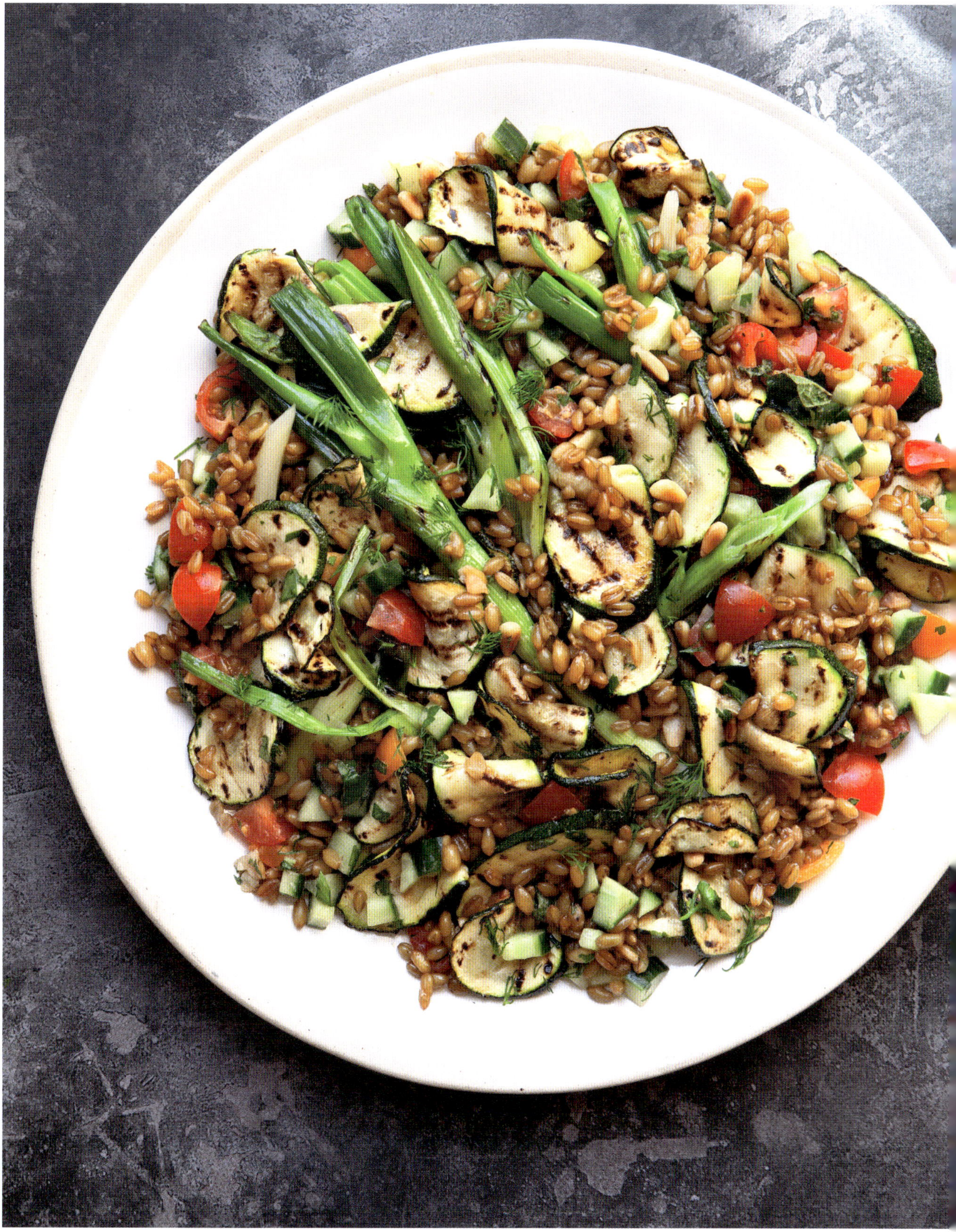

Waldorf salad

SERVES 4

MAYONNAISE
2 egg yolks
1 tbsp white wine vinegar
2 tsp Dijon mustard
½ tsp caster sugar
¼ tsp flaked sea salt
150ml sunflower oil
100ml crème fraiche
black pepper

WALDORF SALAD
65g shelled walnut halves
3 large celery sticks, finely sliced and leaves reserved
2 eating apples, quartered and finely sliced
250g seedless red grapes, halved
about 2 tsp fresh lemon juice

I can never think of Waldorf salad without remembering the **Fawlty Towers** *episode in which a tired and hungry American guest demands one from Basil's kitchen. Somewhat flummoxed, Basil replies: 'I think we're just out of waldorfs'. This salad is said, of course, to have been invented at a much fancier hotel, The Waldorf in New York, and when Dave and I were lucky enough to visit there we treated ourselves to big bowls of this creamy, crunchy deliciousness. It makes a great light lunch or an accompaniment to grilled chicken or meat.*

1. To make the mayonnaise put the egg yolks, vinegar, mustard and sugar into the small bowl of a food processor, or use a bowl and a stick blender. Season with salt and some black pepper.

2. Blend until smooth, then, with the motor running, very slowly and gradually add the oil and blend until smooth and thick. Add the crème fraiche and 1–2 tablespoons of cold water. Blend for a few seconds more until the sauce has a soft dropping consistency. Spoon into a bowl, cover and chill in the fridge until needed.

3. For the salad, place the walnut halves in a small frying pan over a medium-high heat for a few minutes until nicely toasted, tossing them regularly. Remove the pan from the heat and leave the nuts to cool.

4. Add the sliced celery to a large bowl with the apples and grapes. Pour over the lemon juice and toss well. This will keep the apples from going brown. Mix in the mayonnaise, toasted walnut halves and celery leaves, then serve.

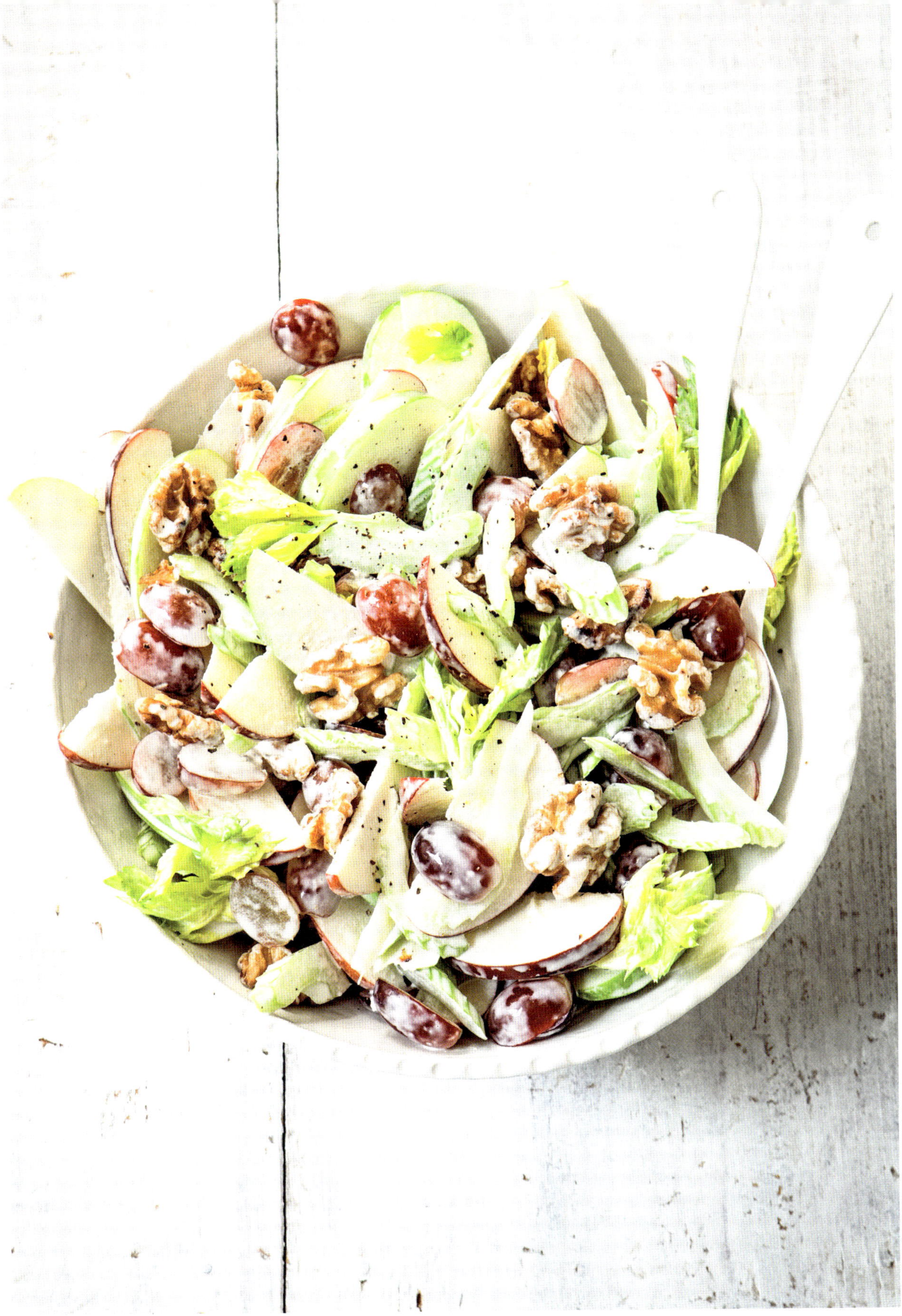

Caesar salad

SERVES 4

CHICKEN (OPTIONAL)
2 boneless, skinless chicken breasts
2 tbsp olive oil
juice of ½ lemon
1 tsp dried oregano or thyme
salt and black pepper

CROUTONS
½ ciabatta loaf, cut into cubes
4 tbsp olive oil
1 garlic clove, crushed

DRESSING
6 anchovy fillets, finely chopped
juice of ½ lemon
1 tsp white wine vinegar
1 tsp Dijon mustard
4 tbsp olive oil

SALAD
1 garlic clove, cut in half
2 romaine/cos lettuce hearts, torn up
25g Parmesan cheese, grated
1 egg yolk

Caesar salad is one of the all-time greats – a magical taste combo of crunchy lettuce, anchovy, Parmesan, croutons and egg yolk. It's fabulous kept simple, but if you want a more substantial salad, add some grilled chicken as here, or some cooked prawns. Whichever way, this is a truly wonderful salad and it also makes a good filling for a wrap. Note that this recipe does contain raw egg.

1. First prepare the chicken breasts, if using. Place a chicken breast on your work surface. Take a sharp knife and insert it along the long side of the breast. Slice into the breast, stopping just short of the other side, then open it out like a book. Repeat with the other chicken breast.

2. Put the olive oil, lemon juice and oregano or thyme into a bowl and season with salt and pepper. Add the chicken breasts and leave them to marinate for 30 minutes. Heat a griddle pan over a high heat until it's too hot to hold your hand over comfortably, then add the chicken. Griddle the breasts on each side for 3–4 minutes until they are completely cooked through and have deep char lines. Remove the chicken from the griddle, then when it's cool enough to handle, cut or tear it into strips.

3. To make the croutons, put the cubes of bread in a bowl and toss them with the olive oil until coated. Season with salt and pepper. Put the bread in a frying pan and sauté over a medium-high heat, stirring regularly until it's all crisp and brown. When the bread is crisp enough, add the garlic and cook for another couple of minutes.

4. For the dressing, mash the anchovies into the lemon juice, vinegar and mustard. Drizzle in the olive oil, whisking constantly until the mixture thickens. Season with salt and pepper to taste.

5. To assemble the salad, take the garlic halves and rub them around the inside of a salad bowl. Add the lettuce, the chicken, if using, and the croutons. Sprinkle the Parmesan into the bowl and pour over the dressing. Drop the egg yolk on to the salad and toss thoroughly until the dressing, egg yolk and Parmesan have clung to the rest of the ingredients. Serve immediately.

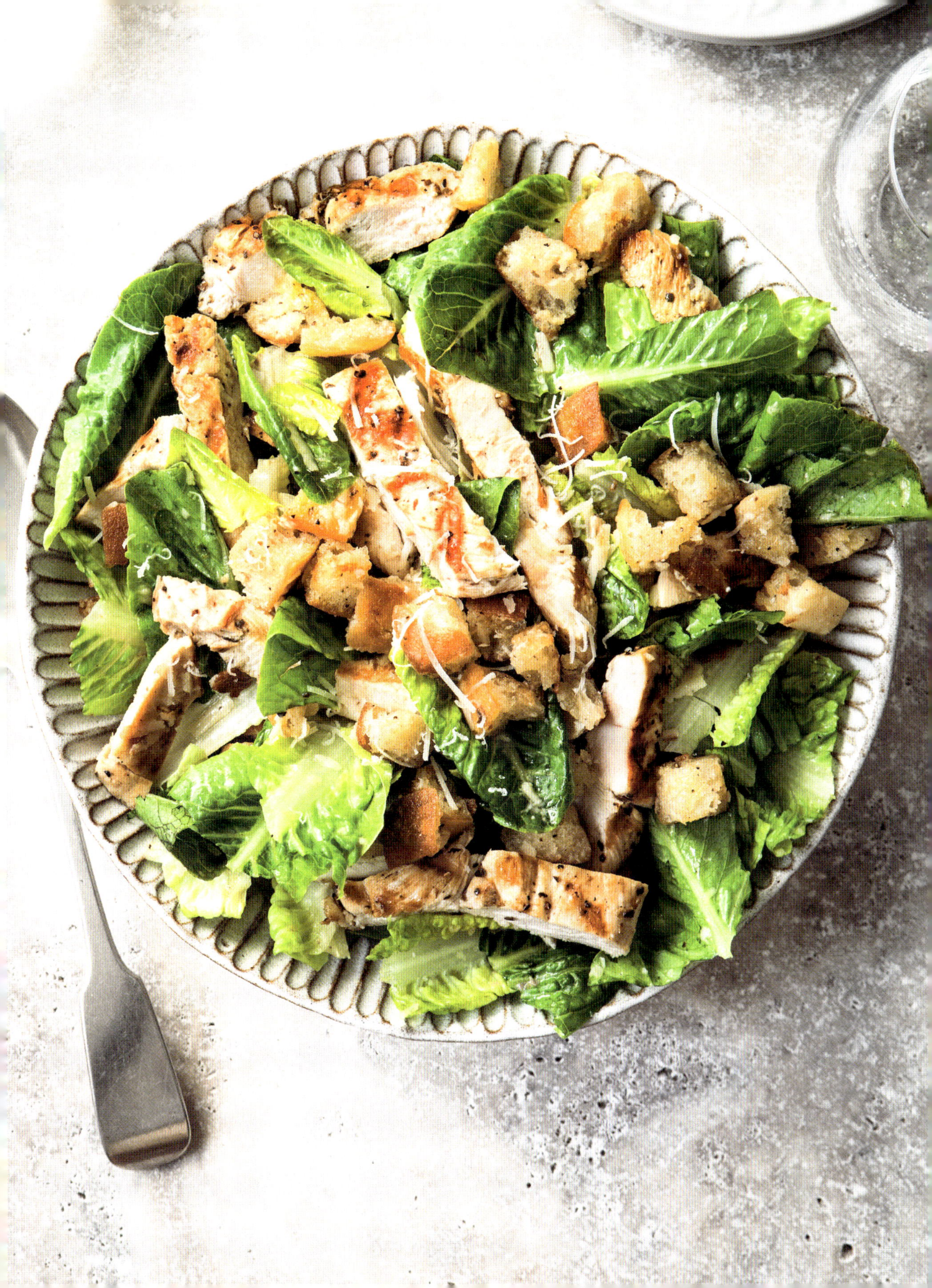

Teriyaki chicken salad

SERVES 4

6 chicken drumsticks
2 tbsp sunflower or groundnut oil
2 tsp sesame oil

TERIYAKI SAUCE
50ml dark soy sauce
100ml mirin
1 tbsp rice wine vinegar or cider vinegar
1 tbsp light brown soft sugar
15g root ginger, sliced
3 fat garlic cloves, sliced
black pepper (optional)

RANCH DRESSING
50g soured cream
50g buttermilk
30g mayonnaise
1 tbsp rice wine or cider vinegar
pinch of sugar
1 tsp garlic powder
dash of Worcestershire sauce
dash of hot sauce (such as Tabasco)
salt and black pepper

SALAD
1 large iceberg lettuce, shredded
200g radishes, sliced
200g cherry tomatoes, halved
6 spring onions, sliced (whites and greens separated)
a few coriander sprigs, chopped, to garnish
2 tsp sesame seeds, to garnish

This is a really special salad – rich, comforting and packed with flavour. It's easy to make but it is important to steam the drumsticks before stir-frying them, as the chicken skin will then have a much better texture. Save the steaming liquid to use as a light stock in another recipe.

1. First cook the drumsticks. Put them in a steamer basket and steam over simmering water until cooked through, which should take about 20 minutes. The skin will shrink and become much less flabby during this process.

2. To make the teriyaki sauce, whisk everything together. Do not add salt – the soy sauce will reduce when cooked and become saltier as it does so. Add some black pepper if you like.

3. To make the ranch dressing, whisk everything together and season with salt and pepper. Taste and adjust the amount of vinegar, sugar and hot sauce to your liking.

4. As soon as the chicken is cool enough to handle, cut or pull the meat away from the bones, discarding any tendons or cartilage as you go.

5. Heat the oil in a wok. When you can see the air above the oil shimmer, add the chicken and stir-fry until well browned. Pour in the teriyaki sauce and continue to stir regularly until it has reduced into a sticky coating around the chicken. Drizzle over the sesame oil.

6. Put the lettuce, radishes, tomatoes and the whites of the spring onions into a salad bowl and pour over the ranch dressing. Toss to coat everything, then add the chicken. Garnish with the coriander, spring onion greens and sesame seeds before serving.

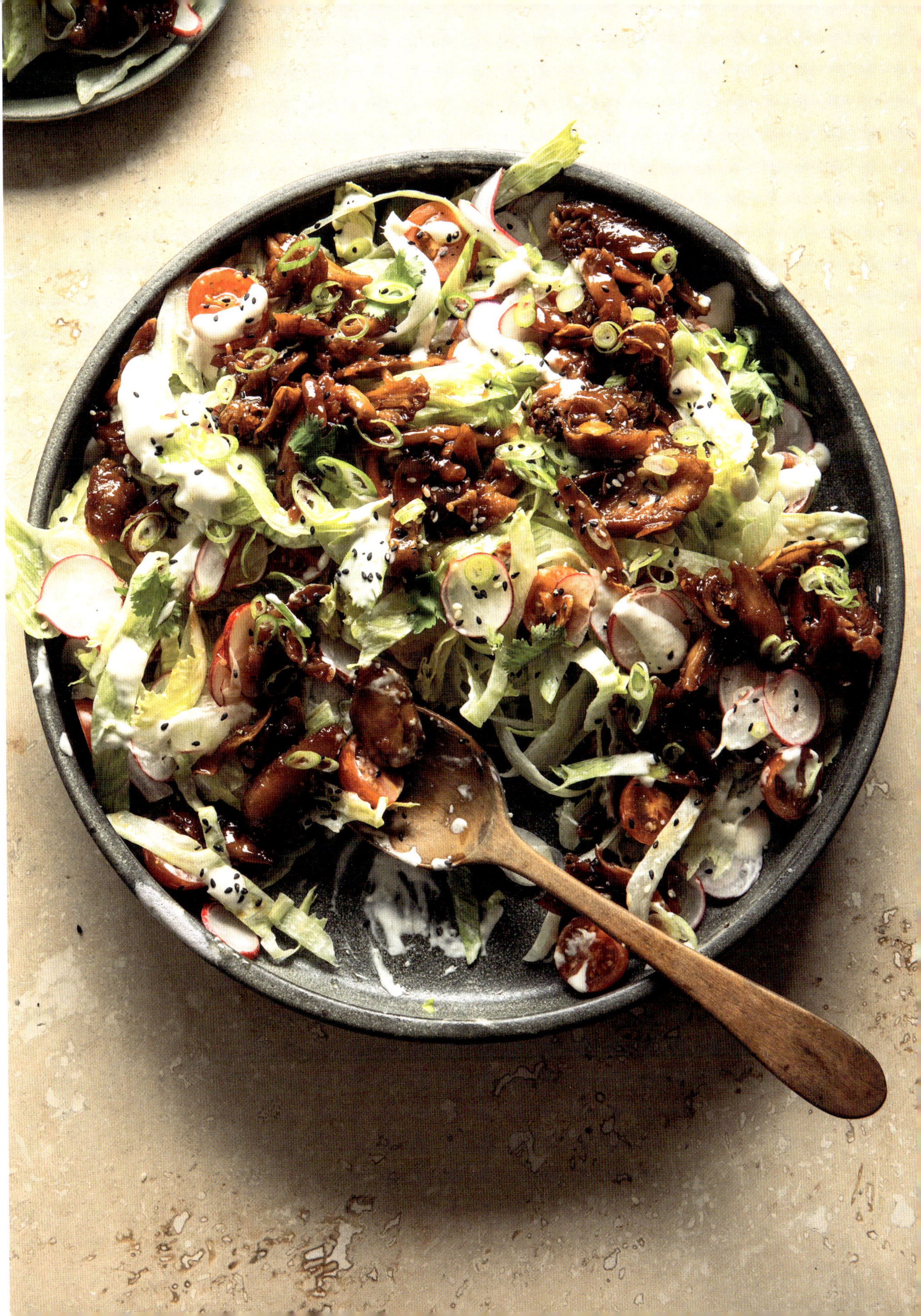

Crispy noodles with prawns & crab

SERVES 4

vegetable or groundnut oil
125g thin rice noodles
5 Thai shallots (or 1 banana shallot), thinly sliced
400g raw, peeled tiger prawns, deveined
20g root ginger, peeled and finely grated
3 garlic cloves, grated or crushed
20g galangal, finely grated
3 spring onions, cut lengthways and thinly sliced
150g fresh bean sprouts
3 kaffir lime leaves, sliced and cut into matchstick strips
200g fresh picked white crabmeat
big handful of fresh coriander, roughly chopped
big handful of mint, leaves picked from the stems (do not chop or the leaves will go brown)
big handful of holy basil

DRESSING

2 heaped tbsp grated palm sugar
5 tbsp Thai fish sauce
3 tbsp fresh lime juice

GARNISH

1 large red chilli, sliced at an angle
2 limes, cut into wedges

I remember this amazing salad so well. Dave and I cooked it alongside the ruins of Ayutthaya, once the capital of old Siam as Thailand used to be called, when filming our **Asian Adventure** *series. Yes, there are quite a few ingredients but most can be prepared in advance and the dish really is worth the effort. Just keep the noodles, herbs, prawn and crab mix separate and put them all together at the last minute. The noodles don't need blanching – you can just drop them straight into hot oil. They do expand though, so be sure to cook them in batches.*

1. First make the dressing. Stir the palm sugar into the fish sauce until the sugar dissolves. Add the lime juice and stir, then set aside.

2. Pour enough oil for deep-frying into a wok or a large deep saucepan and heat to 180–190°C. Check the temperature with a cooking thermometer or if you don't have one, add a small cube of bread. If the oil is hot enough, the bread will turn crisp and golden and float to the top in a few seconds. Fry the noodles in batches – each batch will cook in seconds. Add a batch to the pan and cook until the noodles are puffed up and turning a pale golden colour. Remove the noodles with a slotted spoon and set aside to drain on kitchen paper.

3. Wipe the wok or pan with kitchen paper and add 3 tablespoons of fresh oil, then fry the shallots until crispy. Remove them from the wok, drain on kitchen paper and set aside.

4. Put the wok or pan back on the heat and add another tablespoon of oil. When the oil is hot, add the prawns and stir until they are slightly opaque. Add the root ginger, garlic and galangal and sauté for a couple of minutes. Continue to cook and stir until the prawns are cooked. Tip the contents of the pan into a large bowl and add the crispy shallots.

5. Add the spring onions, bean sprouts, lime leaves and crabmeat to the bowl, then the dressing and herbs. Mix everything together, but be gentle so you don't crush the herbs. You'll find your hands are best for this task. Mix the salad with the crispy noodles, then garnish with slices of chilli and lime wedges, then serve straight away.

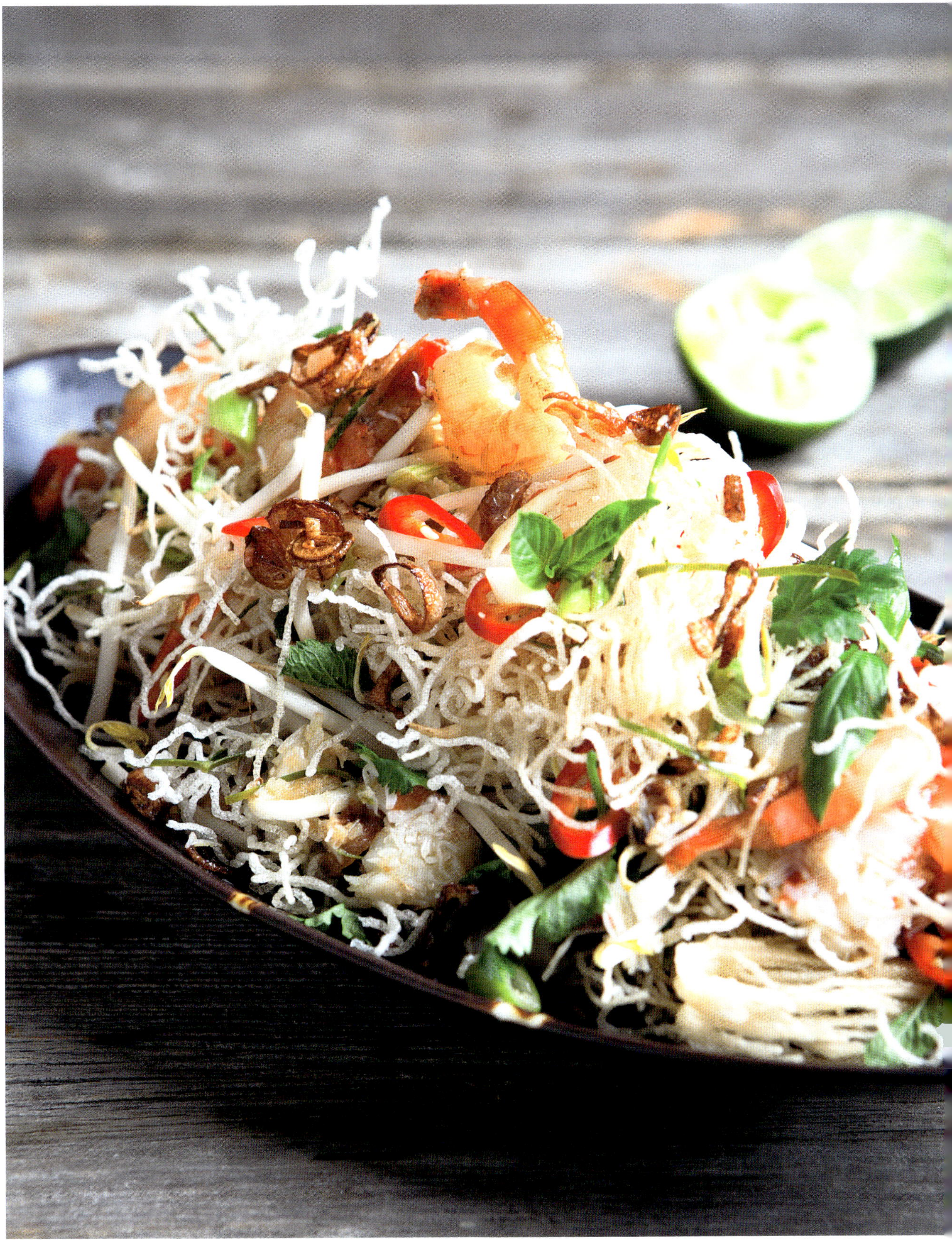

Thai prawn noodle salad

SERVES 4

250g glass noodles
40g peanuts
groundnut oil or vegetable oil, for frying
20 Thai shallots (or about 8 banana shallots), finely sliced
3 red bird's-eye chillies, deseeded and finely sliced
12 cherry tomatoes, cut in half
3 sticks of Chinese celery or 1 celery stick, trimmed and cut into 2.5cm pieces
juice of 2 limes
4 tbsp Thai fish sauce
40g dried shrimp
4 large garlic cloves, thinly sliced
500g raw, peeled tiger prawns (tails left on), deveined
large handful each of fresh coriander, Thai basil and mint leaves, roughly chopped

This is a great favourite of mine – a tantalising combination of salty dried shrimp, crunchy peanuts, succulent tiger prawns and glass noodles. These very thin noodles, also known as cellophane noodles, become transparent when cooked. Interestingly, most glass noodles are made from mung bean or sweet potato starch so are gluten-free.

1. Put the noodles in a large bowl, cover them with freshly boiled water and leave to soak for 15 minutes. Drain the noodles, then cut them into pieces with scissors to make them easier to eat. Toast the peanuts in a dry pan, then chop them roughly and set aside.

2. Place a wok over the heat, add 2 tablespoons of oil and gently fry half the shallots until they're golden brown and slightly crispy. Tip them into a large mixing bowl, then add the remaining raw shallots, the chillies, tomatoes, celery, lime juice and fish sauce to the bowl. No need to wash the wok, as you'll need it again.

3. Add another tablespoon of oil to the wok and fry the dried shrimp for 4–5 minutes, until slightly crispy. Add them to the bowl with the shallots and other ingredients.

4. Heat 2 tablespoons of oil in the wok and add the sliced garlic. Cook gently until the garlic is just turning light gold, then add the raw tiger prawns. Fry, stirring or tossing them regularly to coat the prawns in the garlicky oil, until they have all turned pink and are cooked through.

5. Add the prawns to the bowl with the salad, then add the roughly chopped herbs. Toss in the noodles and give the salad a really good mix with your hands. Transfer to a serving dish and garnish with the toasted peanuts.

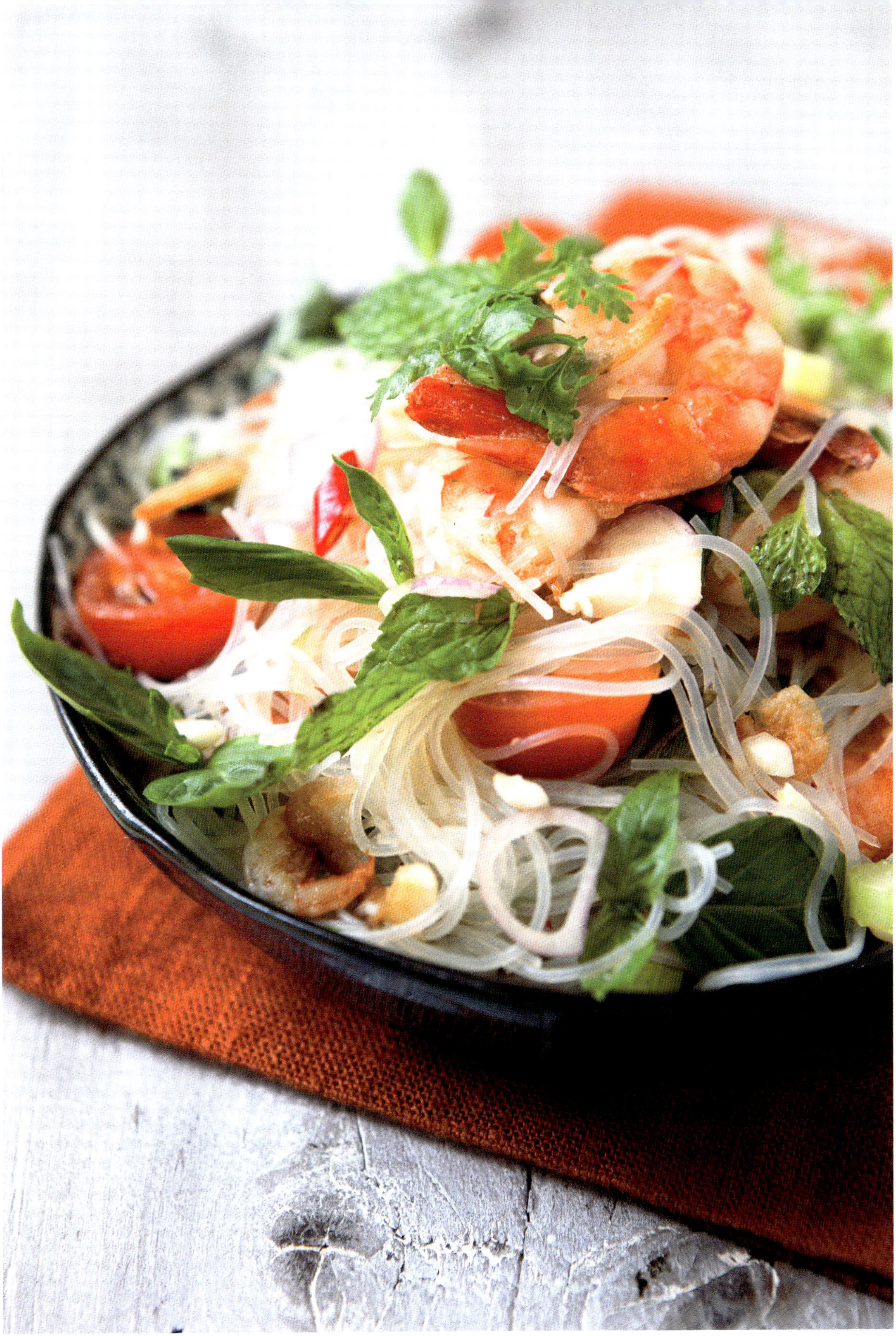

Steak & asparagus salad

SERVES 4

400g salad or baby new potatoes
a few mint sprigs
2 sirloin steaks (about 2cm thick)
bunch of asparagus, trimmed
150g salad leaves
small bunch of chives, to garnish
sea salt

DRESSING
1 tbsp olive oil
2 tbsp crème fraiche
1 tsp mustard
1 tsp sherry vinegar
1 tsp honey
2 tsp black peppercorns, crushed

A proper hearty salad. this is a real treat when asparagus is in season. At other times of year you could substitute something such as long-stemmed broccoli. Serve some crusty bread on the side and maybe a little tomato and red onion salad as well and you have a lunch fit for – well. me!

1. First make the salad dressing. Whisk everything together, season with salt and set aside.

2. Bring a pan of water to the boil, add the potatoes and mint sprigs, then season with salt. Boil until the potatoes are just tender, then drain them thoroughly and set aside.

3. Meanwhile, heat a large griddle pan. Season the steaks with plenty of salt, then grill them to your liking. For rare meat, cook for 1½ minutes on the first side, then 1 minute on the second; for medium-rare, cook for 2 minutes on the first side, then 1½ on the second. For medium, cook for 2 minutes on each side.

4. Remove the steaks and set them aside to rest for 5–10 minutes. Add the asparagus to the griddle and cook, turning regularly until the stems have char lines and are knife tender.

5. Slice the rested steak into strips and add any juices to the salad dressing. Arrange the salad leaves, potatoes, steak and asparagus on a large platter and drizzle over the dressing. Snip the chives over the top and serve.

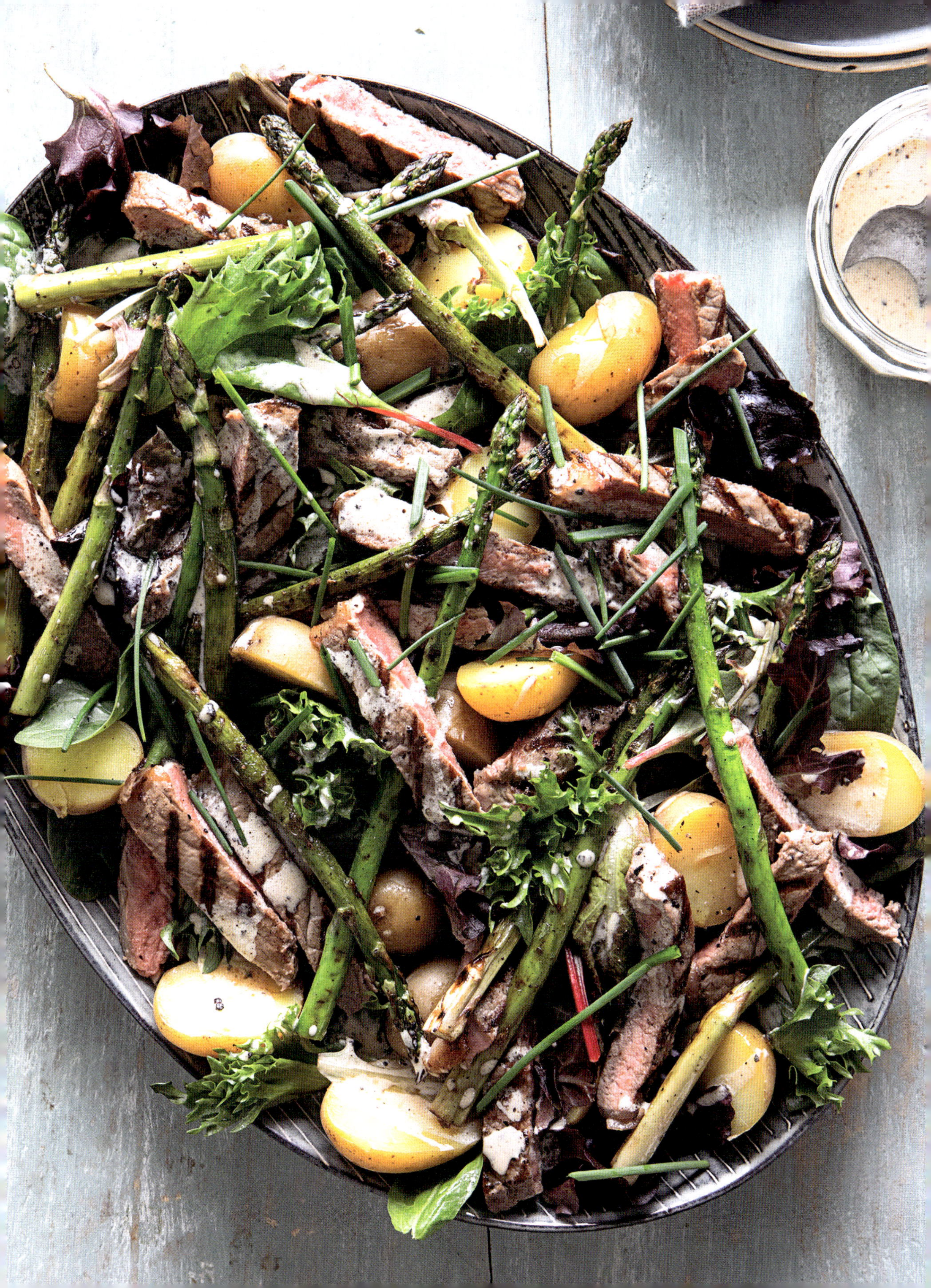

1. Spaghetti & meatballs...78
2. Our 'proper' Bolognese...80
3. Chicken Kiev pasta bake...82
4. Lobster mac 'n' cheese...84
5. Seafood with saffron fregola...86
6. Celebratory lasagne...88
7. Spaghetti carbonara...90
8. 'Nduja linguine...92
9. Spaghetti alla greens...94
10. Roasted aubergine pasta...96

pasta

❝ *A good bowl of pasta is a go-to meal for most people. Here are some winners, from the fasta-pasta carbonara to a lasagne that's fit for any Italian family celebration.* ❞

Spaghetti & meatballs

SERVES 4

TOMATO SAUCE
1kg ripe tomatoes or 2 x 400g cans of chopped tomatoes
2 tbsp olive oil
1 onion, finely chopped
2 garlic cloves, finely chopped
1 tsp dried oregano
100ml white wine
pinch of sugar (optional)
handful of basil, chopped
salt and black pepper

MEATBALLS
1 tbsp olive oil
1 onion, finely chopped
2 garlic cloves, finely chopped
1 tsp dried oregano
zest of 1 lemon
½ tsp chilli flakes (optional)
500g pork mince
25g pine nuts, roughly chopped
handful of basil, finely chopped
75g breadcrumbs
1 egg

TO SERVE
400g spaghetti
basil leaves, to garnish
Parmesan cheese, grated

Dave always did love a meatball so I wanted to include this recipe – one of his great favourites. These meatballs are really packed with flavour and, partnered with a gutsy tomato sauce, a good helping of pasta and plenty of Parmesan, they make a meal to put a smile on everyone's face. I think it's well worth making this with good fresh tomatoes if you can.

1. First get the tomato sauce started. If using fresh tomatoes, peel them. To do this, core each tomato and score a cross on the base, then plunge it into boiling water for a count of 10 (less ripe tomatoes may need a little longer). Roughly chop the tomatoes or put them in a food processor and pulse. Do not strain – there's a lot of flavour in the liquid/jelly around the seeds.

2. Heat the oil in a large saucepan. Add the onion and sauté, stirring regularly, until it's very soft and translucent. Add the garlic and cook for another couple of minutes, then add the oregano and white wine. Allow the wine to reduce by half, then add the tomatoes (fresh or canned) and season with plenty of salt and pepper. Bring to the boil, then turn down the heat, cover the pan and simmer for half an hour. Uncover and taste. If the sauce is too acidic, add a generous pinch of sugar. Continue to simmer gently until the sauce is well reduced. Add the basil towards the end of this simmering time.

3. While the sauce is simmering, make the meatballs. Preheat the oven to 200°C/Fan 180°C/Gas 6 and line a baking tray with baking parchment. Heat the oil in a frying pan and add the onion. Sauté over a low heat until soft and translucent, add the garlic and cook for another minute or so. Take the pan off the heat and then add the oregano, lemon zest and chilli flakes, if using. Season well.

4. Put the pork mince into a bowl and add the contents of the frying pan along with the remaining ingredients. Add more seasoning and mix thoroughly until quite stiff. Divide into 20 balls and place them on the baking tray. Bake in the oven for about 15 minutes until browned and just cooked through. Add the meatballs to the sauce and let them simmer for a few minutes.

5. Cook the spaghetti in a large pan of salted water, according to the packet instructions. Spoon the meatballs and sauce over the spaghetti and garnish with basil. Serve with plenty of grated Parmesan.

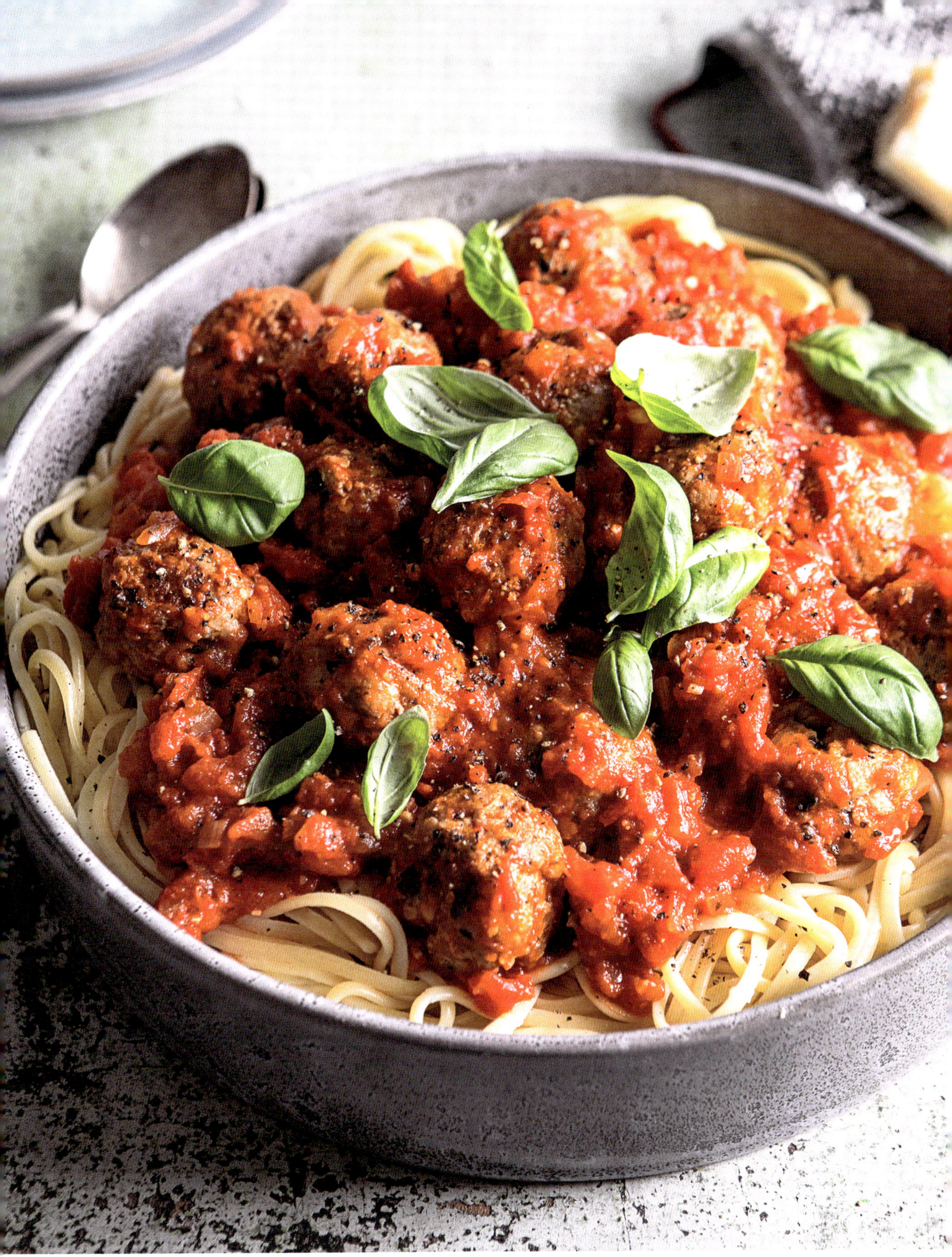

Our 'proper' Bolognese

SERVES ABOUT 8 WITH PASTA

750g stewing beef, in large chunks
2 tbsp plain flour
3 tbsp olive oil
2 onions, finely chopped
1 large carrot, finely chopped
2 celery sticks, finely chopped
250g pork mince
4 garlic cloves, finely chopped
2 tbsp tomato purée
pinch of cloves
pinch of ground cinnamon
2 bay leaves
1 thyme sprig
2 tsp dried oregano
leaves from 1 rosemary sprig, finely chopped
700ml red wine
200g puréed tomatoes (preferably fresh)
salt and black pepper

TO SERVE
pasta, such as tagliatelle
Parmesan cheese, grated

We called this recipe 'proper' when we first published it because sadly, what's served up as Bolognese sauce is all too often a mere shadow of the real thing. A good Bolognese needs to contain chunks of beef as well as pork mince and should be simmered gently for a few hours to get the authentic rich flavour. This recipe serves eight, but even if you're only feeding a few of you it's well worth cooking up a whole batch of the sauce while you're at it and stashing some in the freezer for another time. Use good stewing beef, such as shin, featherblade or even ox cheek, and make sure it has a nice marbling of fat – fat provides flavour. The pork mince should also contain some fat – lean mince just isn't right here.

1. Put the beef into a bowl and season it with salt and pepper. Sprinkle over the flour and toss to coat the meat well, then pat off any excess.

2. Heat a tablespoon of the oil in a frying pan. Sear the beef on all sides, making sure you allow the meat to develop a good crust. It's best to do this in batches so you don't overcrowd the pan, setting each batch aside as it is browned.

3. Heat the remaining oil in a large saucepan or a flameproof casserole dish. Add the onions, carrot and celery and sauté over a gentle heat until soft and translucent. You can cover the pan with a lid in between stirs to help it along if you like.

4. Turn up the heat and add the pork mince and garlic. Cook until the pork has browned, then stir in the tablespoons of tomato purée, the spices and herbs.

5. Pour in the wine and bring to the boil. Allow it to bubble vigorously for about 5 minutes, then turn the heat down to a simmer. Add the seared beef and pour in the puréed tomatoes. Season with salt and pepper.

6. Cover the pan and leave to simmer for 2–3 hours, until the beef is tender. Remove the chunks of beef from the pan and gently tear them apart into much smaller pieces, then put these back in the pan. Leave the sauce to simmer, uncovered, until it is well reduced. Serve the sauce with pasta and Parmesan or freeze in portions for another time.

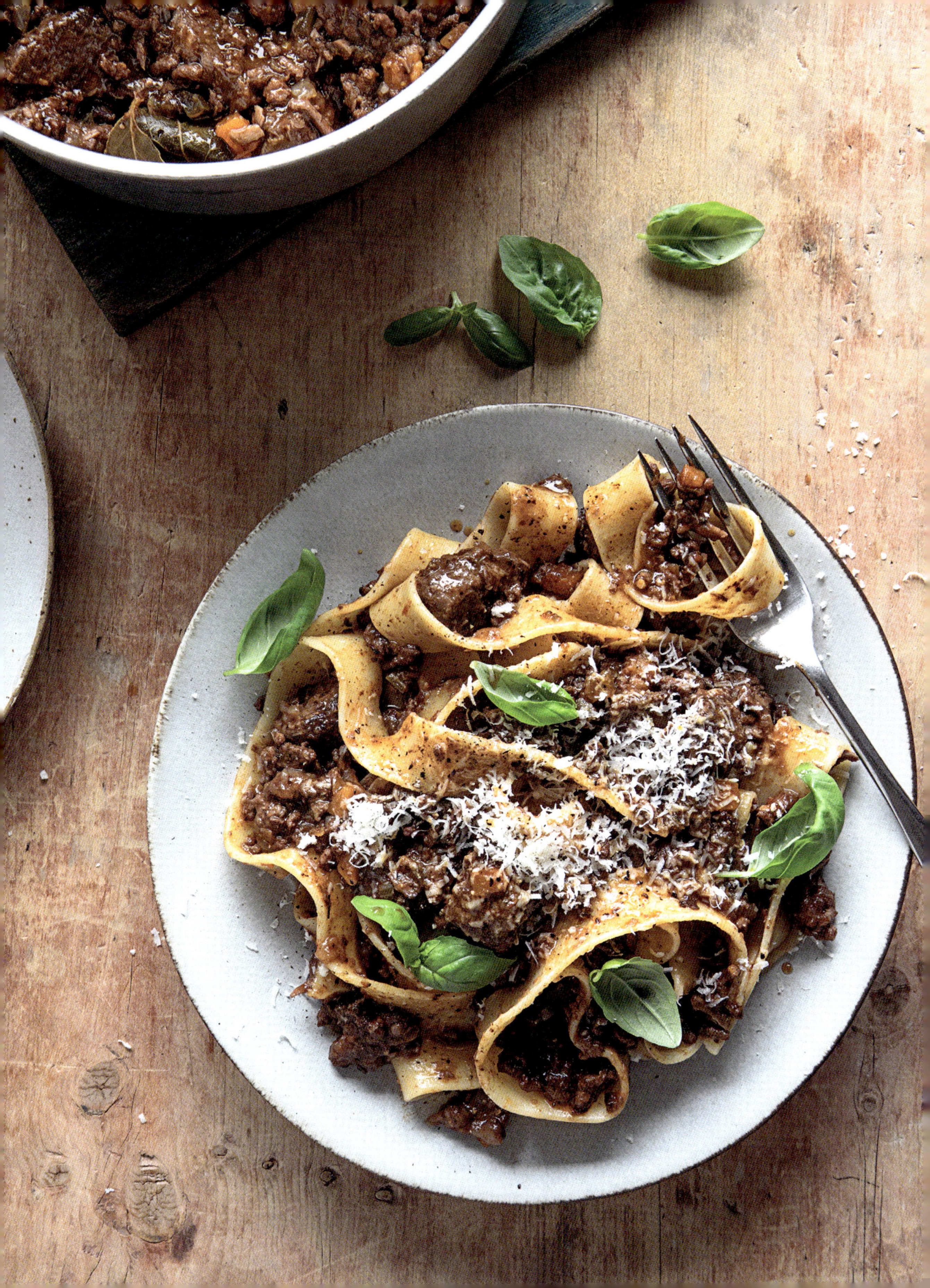

Chicken Kiev pasta bake

SERVES 4

2 large onions, cut into slim wedges
500g boneless chicken thighs (skinned if you like)
zest and juice of ½ lemon
1 tsp herbes de Provence or Italian mixed dried herbs
2–3 tbsp olive oil
300g short pasta
100g parsley, coarsely chopped
a few basil leaves
100g Parmesan cheese, coarsely grated
3 large garlic cloves, roughly chopped
30g butter
50g panko breadcrumbs
salt and black pepper

A great family supper. this has all the comfort of a pasta bake with the herby, garlicky flavours of a chicken Kiev. Two favourites rolled into one – what a feast! It's simple to make and you can prepare it in advance, ready to pop in the oven for the final stage of cooking. All you need alongside is a green salad or some green veg. Epic.

1. Preheat the oven to 200°C/Fan 180°C/Gas 6. Put the onion wedges and chicken thighs into a large roasting tin. Sprinkle over the lemon zest and juice and the herbs. Season with salt and lots of black pepper and drizzle with the olive oil. Roast in the oven for 30 minutes, stirring every so often to keep the onions from catching. Remove from the oven and roughly slice or tear the chicken thighs into pieces, then put them back in the tin.

2. Meanwhile, cook the pasta in a large pan of salted water according to the packet instructions. When the pasta is al dente, drain it, reserving a couple of ladlefuls (about 200ml) of the cooking water.

3. Put the parsley, basil, Parmesan and garlic in a food processor with some salt and black pepper. Blitz to a coarse paste, add a little of the pasta water, then continue to process until you have a green-flecked sauce.

4. Mix the sauce with the rest of the reserved pasta water. Add this and the pasta to the chicken and onion in the tin, along with 20g of the butter and mix thoroughly. Sprinkle with the breadcrumbs and dot with the remaining butter. Bake in the oven (200°C/Fan 180°C/Gas 6) for 20 minutes until the panko breadcrumbs are lightly golden and everything is piping hot.

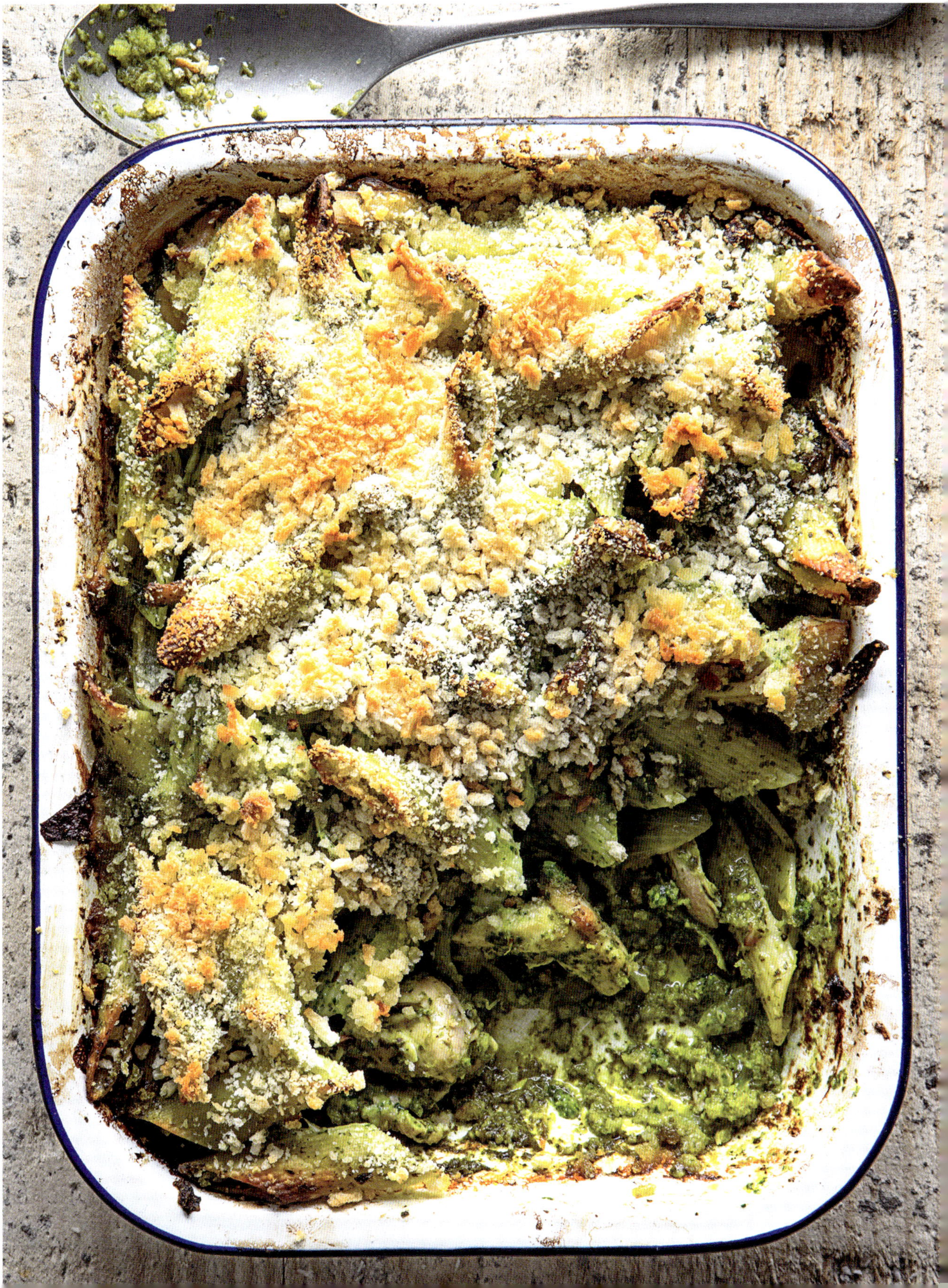

Lobster mac 'n' cheese

SERVES 4–6

salt
500g macaroni

INFUSED MILK
4 lobster tails, shell on, or 400g large prawns, shell on
1 tbsp olive oil
100ml white wine
750ml milk
2 bay leaves
slice of onion
1 mace blade

SAUCE
50g butter
1 onion, finely diced
50g bacon lardons
2 garlic cloves, finely chopped
1 thyme sprig
50g plain flour
1 tsp mustard powder
¼ tsp cayenne
100g Cheddar cheese, grated
100g Gruyère cheese, grated

TO SERVE
50g fresh breadcrumbs
a few basil leaves, shredded

This is not just any mac 'n' cheese, it's our very special mac 'n' cheese – a recipe that Dave used to call 'the footballer's Saturday night special'. The addition of shellfish elevates this to a luxury dish and although lobster can be expensive, you can sometimes pick up some amazing bargains at supermarket fish counters. If not, large prawns give a great result too. Try this, I beg you. It really does taste the business.

1. Preheat the oven to 200°C/Fan 180°C/Gas 6. Bring a large saucepan of water to the boil and salt it generously. Add the macaroni and cook it according to the packet instructions until just shy of al dente. Drain and set aside.

2. Separate the lobster flesh from the tails – or peel the prawns – and reserve the shells. Heat the oil in a saucepan and add the lobster flesh or peeled prawns. Cook them quickly on each side, then remove and set aside.

3. Put the shells in the same pan and heat over a high heat, shaking the pan until they have taken on some colour. With the heat on high, pour in the white wine and allow it to bubble fiercely. Pour in the milk, then add the bay leaves, onion and mace. Heat slowly until the milk is just below boiling point, then remove the pan from the heat. Leave the milk to infuse until it's at room temperature, then strain it into a jug and set aside.

4. For the sauce, heat the butter in a large pan. Add the onion and bacon and fry until the onion is lightly caramelised and the bacon is crisp and brown. Add the garlic cloves and thyme, then stir in the flour, mustard powder and cayenne. Stir until you have a roux (it will be lumpy because of the onion and bacon), then gradually add the infused milk, stirring in between each addition, until it is all incorporated. Add 75g of each of the cheeses and stir over a low heat until the cheese has melted.

5. Mix the sauce with the macaroni and stir in the lobster meat or prawns. Pour into a large, shallow ovenproof dish. Mix the breadcrumbs with the remaining cheese and the basil. Sprinkle this over the macaroni. Bake in the oven for 30–35 minutes until it is piping hot, browned on top and bubbling.

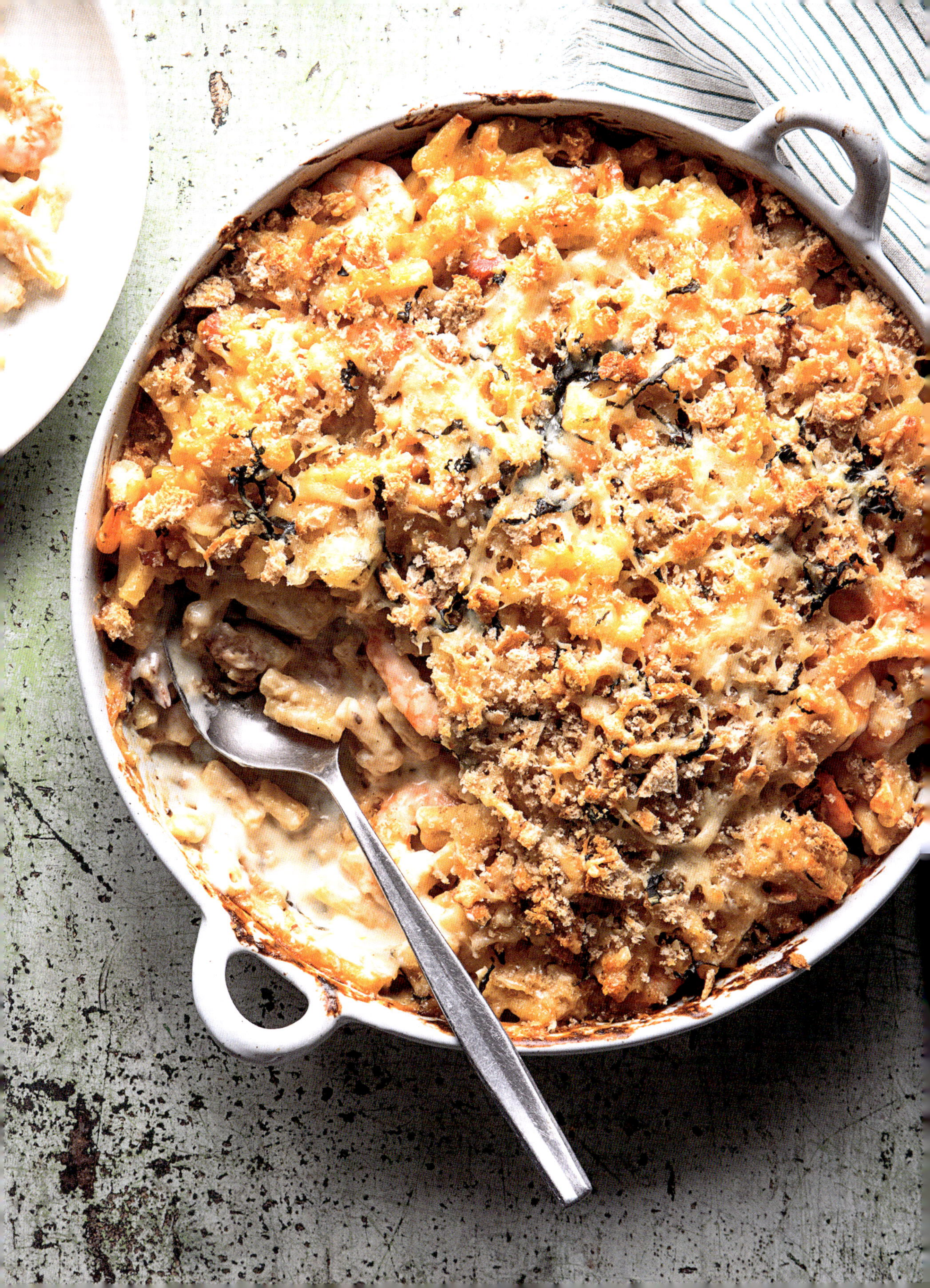

Seafood with saffron fregola

SERVES 4

200g mussels
200g clams
600g shell-on prawns
4 tbsp olive oil
300ml fish stock
500g fregola
1 onion, finely chopped
2 garlic cloves, finely chopped
1 red chilli, finely chopped, or ½ tsp chilli flakes
1 thyme sprig
1 tsp dried oregano
pinch of saffron, ground
100ml white wine or vermouth
4 medium tomatoes, peeled and roughly chopped
12 small scallops, shelled and cleaned
salt

TO SERVE
small handful of chopped basil and parsley
lemon wedges

Dave and I first ate this in Sardinia and immediately wanted to cook it ourselves. Fregola is actually little balls of pasta made from semolina and marries well with this lovely selection of seafood. A touch of saffron and a gentle hit of chilli are the perfect finishing touches. Give it a go – I think you'll love it. If you can't get fregola you could use jumbo couscous.

1. Wash the mussels and clams well and discard any with broken shells or any that are open and don't close when given a sharp tap. Take the heads and shells off the prawns and devein them – remove the little black line along the back of each one. Set the prawns and the shells and heads aside.

2. Heat a tablespoon of the oil in a large, lidded frying pan and add the prawn shells and heads. Fry them for a minute or so until they've turned pink, then pour in the stock. Allow it to bubble up, while stirring vigorously, then leave it to simmer for 5 minutes. Remove the pan from the heat, then strain the stock into a jug and set it aside. Discard the prawn shells and heads.

3. Bring a large pan of water to the boil and add plenty of salt and the fregola. Simmer the fregola for about 10 minutes until it is just al dente, then drain it and set it aside.

4. While you are cooking the fregola, heat 2 tablespoons of the oil in the frying pan. Add the onion and fry it until softened, then add the garlic, chilli, herbs and saffron. Pour in the wine or vermouth and allow the liquid to reduce for a couple of minutes, then add the reserved stock and the tomatoes. Simmer for 5 minutes, then stir in the cooked fregola. Put the clams and mussels on top, cover the pan and cook for another 2–3 minutes or until the shellfish have opened. Discard any clams and mussels that don't open.

5. In a separate frying pan, heat the remaining olive oil. Sear the prawns on both sides very quickly, then add them to the fregola. Repeat with the scallops. Stir in the basil and parsley and serve immediately with lemon wedges on the side.

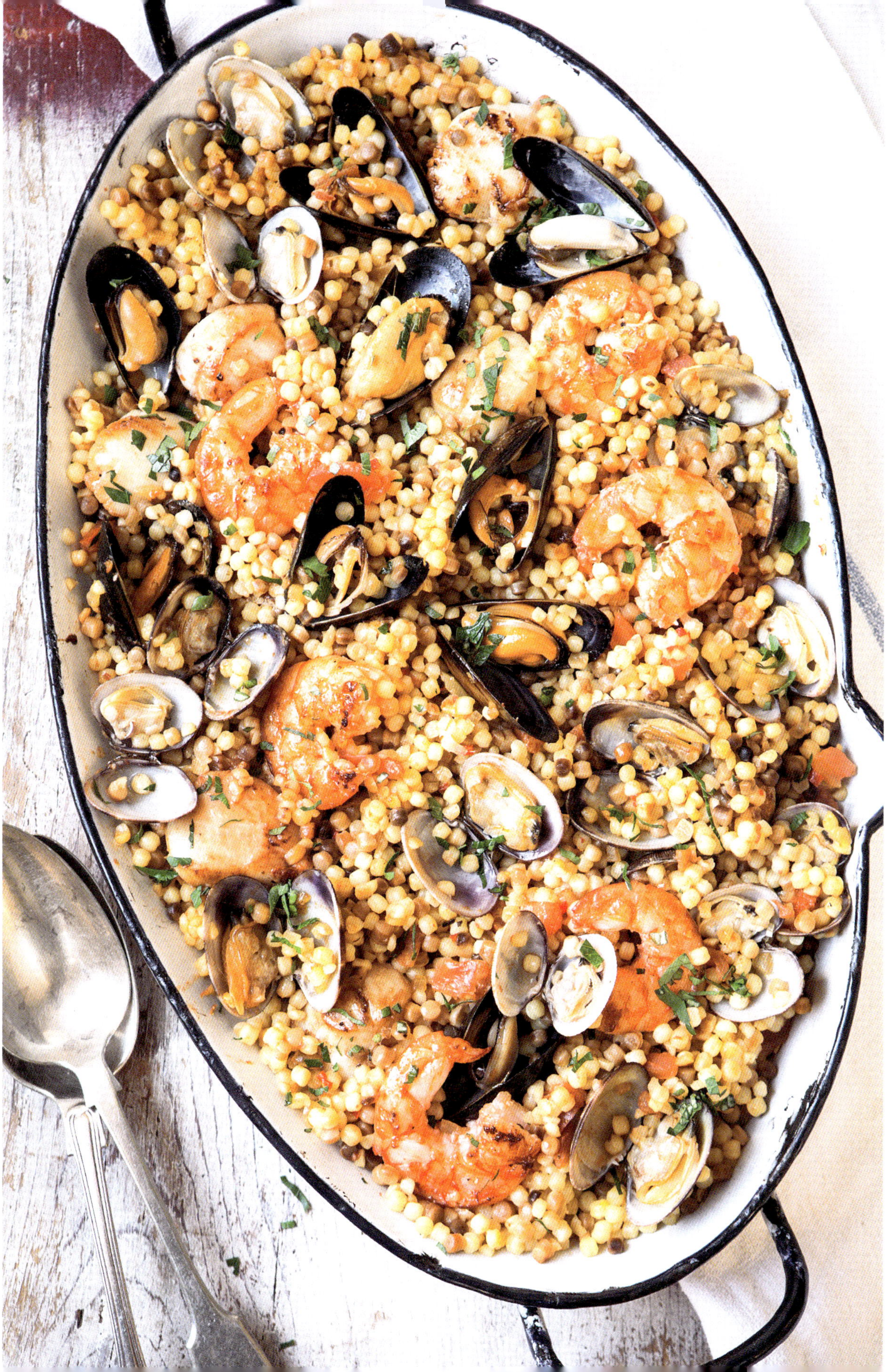

Celebratory lasagne

SERVES 8

MEATBALLS
150g minced beef
150g minced pork
50g breadcrumbs
2 garlic cloves, crushed
1 tsp dried sage
1 tsp dried oregano
1 egg
2 tbsp milk
grating of nutmeg
2 tbsp olive oil
salt and black pepper

TO ASSEMBLE
4 large sausages (preferably Italian style with fennel seed)
1 quantity of tomato sauce (see p.267)
½ quantity of fresh pasta (see p.264), or 18 dried lasagne sheets
300g ricotta cheese
600g mozzarella
200g Parmesan, grated
bunch of basil, shredded (reserve a few whole leaves)

This really is something for a special occasion – big, bold and packed with great flavour. A proper feast. It's been a hugely popular dish and I've heard there are people out there who can barely read the recipe in **Mediterranean Adventure,** *where it was first published, because the page is so spattered with sauce! You'll find a recipe for fresh pasta on page 264 or you can use bought fresh pasta or dried lasagne sheets.*

1. To make the meatballs, put all the ingredients, except the olive oil, in a bowl and season generously with salt and pepper. Mix thoroughly, then form the mixture into small balls of about 20g each – you should get 18–20. Chill the meatballs for 30 minutes. Heat the olive oil in a large saucepan or frying pan (it needs to be big enough to hold the tomato sauce later) and brown the meatballs briefly on all sides. Remove the meatballs from the pan.

2. Skin the sausages and shape them into small rounds about the same size as the meatballs. Fry these on all sides too. Put the meatballs back in the pan and pour over the tomato sauce. Bring to the boil, and leave to simmer for 10 minutes. This helps keep the meatballs and sausage moist during the oven cooking time and also adds flavour to the sauce.

3. Preheat the oven to 200°C/Fan 180°C/Gas 6. You'll need an oven dish or roasting tin for assembling the lasagne – one about 25 x 35cm is ideal. If using fresh lasagne, roll it out and cut it into 6 sheets – each should be the length of your dish or tin.

4. Remove the meatballs and sausages from the tomato sauce with a slotted spoon and set them aside. Ladle about a quarter of the tomato sauce into the bottom of your dish, then cover with either 2 sheets of fresh pasta or 6 dried sheets. Top with the next quarter of tomato sauce, then cover with half the meatballs and sausage. Take 100g of the ricotta and spoon teaspoons of it over the sauce, in between the meatballs and sausage meat. Sprinkle over 100g of the mozzarella and 50g of the grated Parmesan, followed by some of the basil leaves.

5. Top with another layer of pasta and repeat, using up another quarter of the tomato sauce, the rest of the meatballs and sausage meat, another 100g each of the ricotta and mozzarella, 50g of the Parmesan and more basil.

6. Finish with a layer of pasta and cover with the remaining tomato sauce. Top with the rest of the ricotta, mozzarella and Parmesan and add a few basil leaves, tucking them in so they are not too exposed while in the oven.

7. Bake in the oven for 45–50 minutes, by which time the pasta will be cooked and the top should be brown and bubbling. Remove the lasagne from the oven and leave it to stand for about 10 minutes before cutting. Each serving should stand up well without being sloppy.

Spaghetti carbonara

SERVES 4

400g spaghetti
2 tbsp olive oil
200g pancetta, thickly sliced, then diced
2 garlic cloves, crushed
50ml vermouth, such as Noilly Prat, or white wine
2 eggs
50g Pecorino cheese, finely grated
50g Parmesan cheese, finely grated
salt and black pepper

TO ASSEMBLE
2 tbsp finely chopped parsley

This is one of those recipes that is so simple, yet so perfect. Made with everyday ingredients – eggs, bacon, pasta and cheese – it is the very definition of comfort and it takes no time to make. Pecorino, by the way, is an Italian cheese made from sheep's milk. The flavour is just right for this dish, but if you can't find any, use extra Parmesan instead. You may sometimes see carbonara recipes that include cream but don't go there – cream is definitely not needed.

1. First get the spaghetti going. Bring a large saucepan of water to the boil and add salt. Once the water is boiling, add the spaghetti and cook for 10–12 minutes until al dente.

2. Meanwhile, heat the olive oil in a large frying pan. Add the pancetta and cook it over a medium heat until it's nicely crisped. Add the garlic and fry gently for a couple more minutes.

3. Pour in the vermouth or white wine and let it bubble for a couple of minutes until well reduced. Remove the pan from the heat.

4. Crack the eggs into a bowl large enough to hold the pasta and beat them well, then stir in the cheeses. Season with a small amount of salt and lots of black pepper.

5. Strain the pasta in a colander. Don't do this too thoroughly as you don't want the pasta to be completely dry. Add the pasta to the egg and cheese mixture and mix thoroughly, making sure all the pasta is well coated. Then add the pancetta and garlic to the spaghetti and mix thoroughly again. Serve at once sprinkled with parsley.

BIKER TIP

Italian cooks often suggest not draining the pasta too thoroughly, as it's good to have a little of the cooking water to lubricate the sauce.

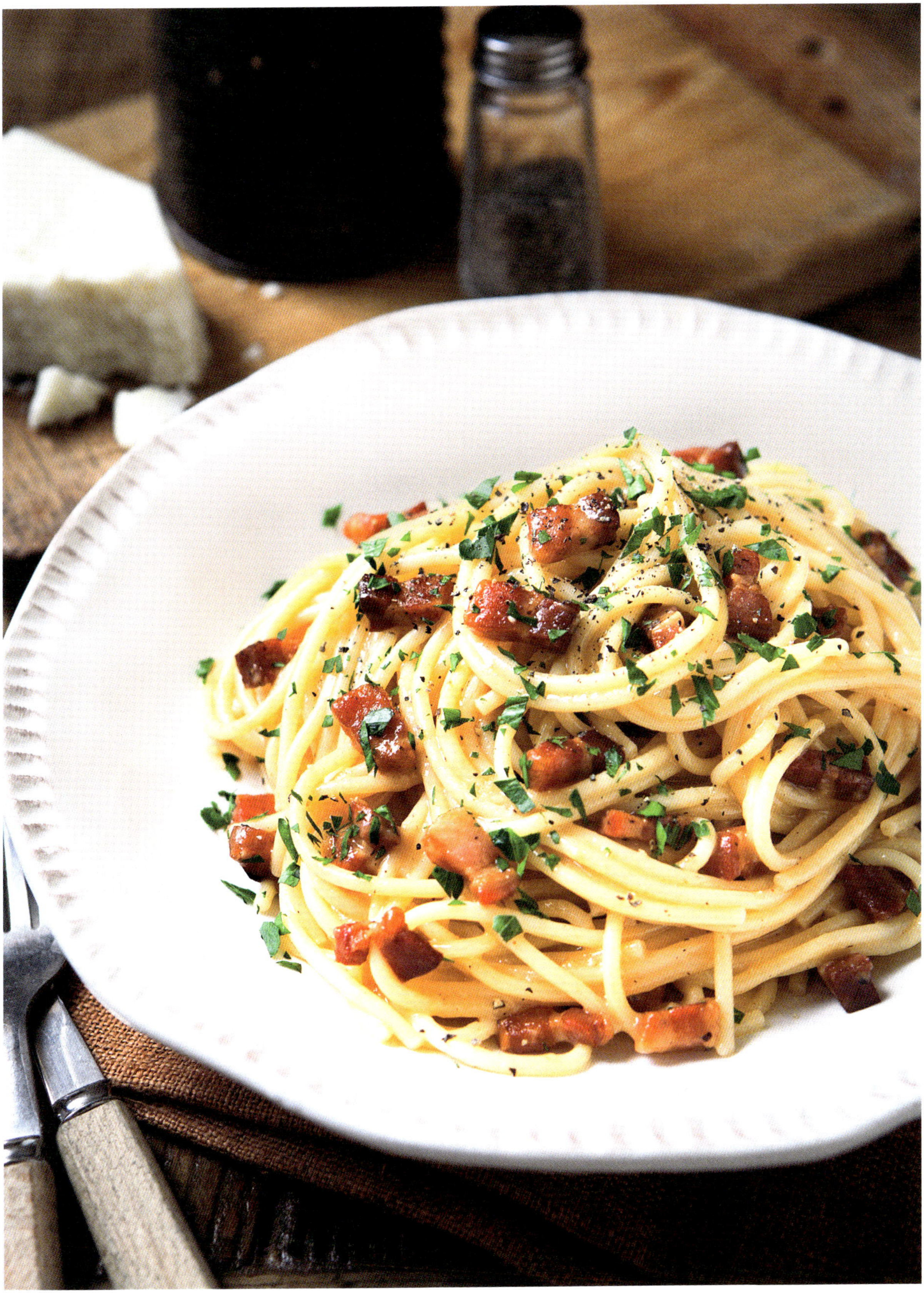

'Nduja linguine

SERVES 4

400g linguine

SAUCE
2 tbsp olive oil
1 small onion, very finely chopped
3 garlic cloves, very finely chopped
250g cherry tomatoes, puréed
1 tsp dried oregano
150g 'nduja
50ml vodka
50ml double cream
salt and black pepper

TO SERVE
basil leaves
grated Parmesan
chilli flakes (optional)

The Italian spicy pork and pepper paste known as 'nduja adds a great blast of flavour to this quick pasta recipe. There's a shot of vodka in here too which blends beautifully with the other ingredients and enhances the dish still further. Be sure to let the vodka cook for long enough though, so your supper doesn't taste of alcohol.

1. First make the sauce. Heat the oil in a saucepan, add the onion and cook over a low-medium heat until soft and translucent. Add the garlic and continue to cook for another 2–3 minutes.

2. Pour in the tomatoes and add the oregano and 'nduja. Break up the 'nduja as much as possible, so it crumbles and starts to dissolve into the tomatoes. Season with plenty of salt and pepper. Bring the sauce to the boil, then turn down the heat and leave to simmer while you cook the pasta.

3. Cook the linguine in plenty of salted, boiling water until al dente. Drain the pasta, reserving a ladleful of the cooking water, then tip the pasta back into the saucepan.

4. Add the vodka to the sauce and let it simmer for a couple of minutes before adding the double cream and about 100ml of the cooking water. Simmer for a few more minutes – the cooking liquid will help thicken the sauce.

5. Pour the sauce over the linguine and mix thoroughly. Serve in shallow pasta bowls and garnish with basil leaves and some grated Parmesan. Offer a bowl of chilli flakes for anyone who wants some extra heat.

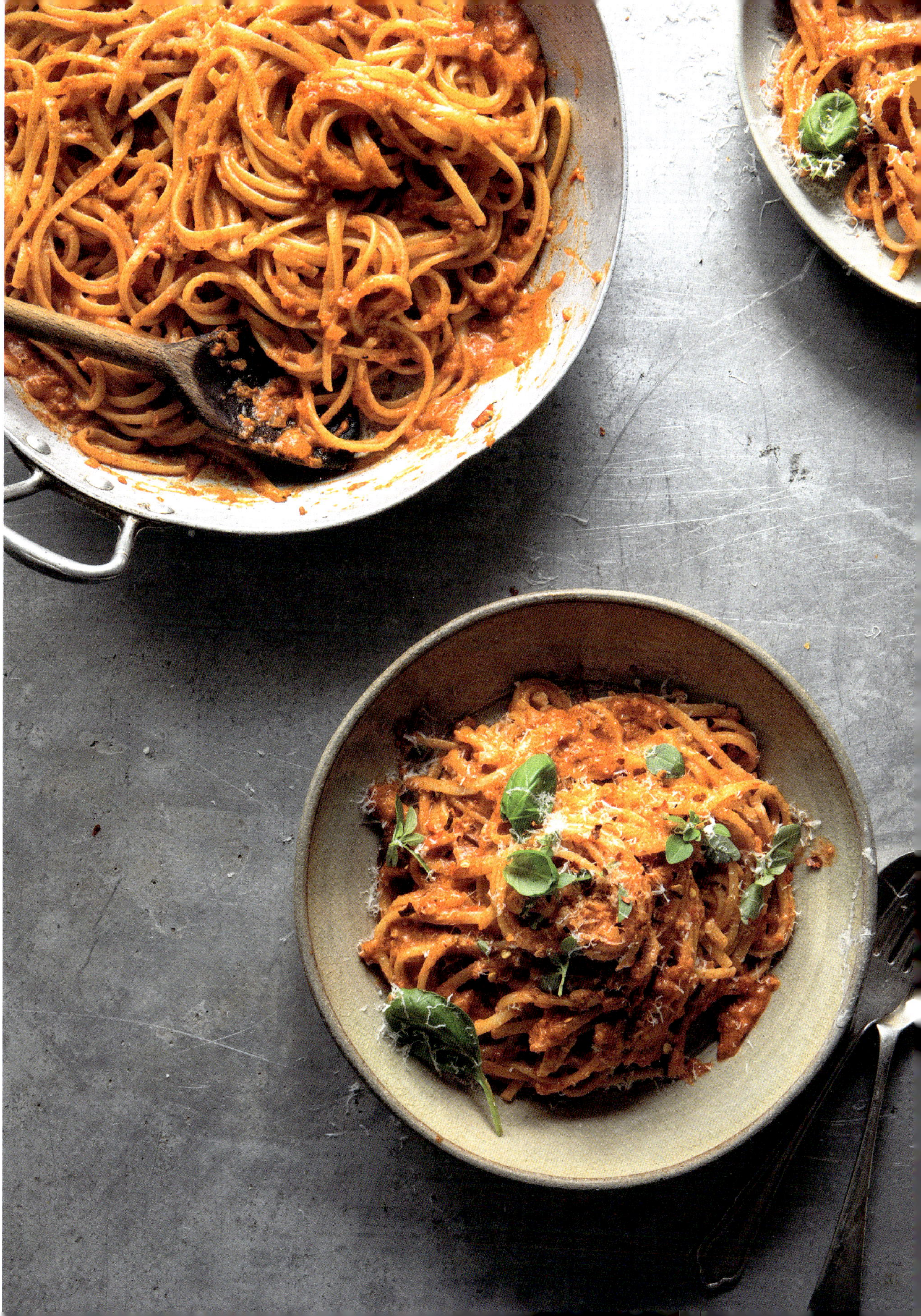

Spaghetti alla greens

SERVES 4

400g spaghetti or linguine
150g broad beans (frozen are fine)
150g spinach or rocket
1 tbsp olive oil
1 large courgette, coarsely grated and excess liquid squeezed out
1 garlic clove, crushed
zest of 1 lemon
75g Parmesan cheese, grated
handful of basil leaves, shredded
salt and black pepper

We came up with this great pasta dish when working on our **One Pot Wonders** *book. Keeping a careful eye on your timer, you cook everything – pasta and veg – in one pan, then finish with a little of the cooking liquid, some oil, seasonings and lemon. Super-fresh and zesty, this meal is on the table before you know it. It makes a good veggie or vegan option too if you use vegetarian cheese or a vegan alternative.*

1. Heat a large pan of water. When it is at a rolling boil, add plenty of salt and the pasta. Check the cooking instructions on the pasta packet and make a note of the cooking time.

2. When the pasta is 3 minutes away from being ready, add the broad beans – no need to remove the skins unless you feel like it. After a further 2 minutes, add the spinach or rocket. When the greens have wilted down and the pasta is al dente, reserve a couple of ladlefuls of the cooking liquid and drain the pasta thoroughly.

3. Tip the pasta back into the pan and add the olive oil. Toss lightly, add the courgette, garlic, lemon zest and Parmesan, then season with more salt and plenty of black pepper. Stir in some of the reserved cooking liquid – you don't want the sauce to be too runny, so add just enough to stop the pasta looking claggy or dry. Stir in the basil and serve immediately.

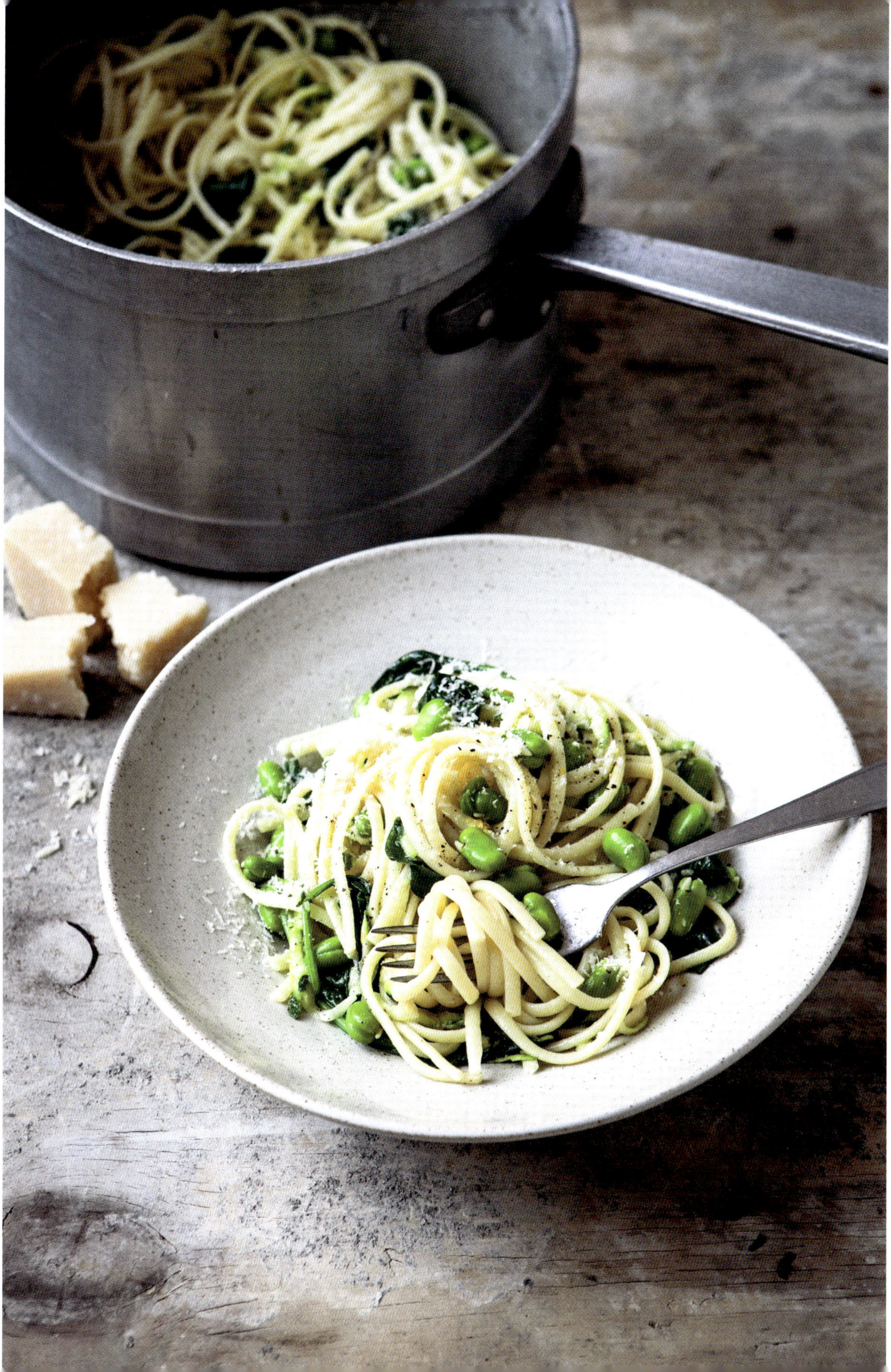

Roasted aubergine pasta

SERVES 4

2 aubergines, cut into 2–3cm cubes
4 tbsp olive oil
1 onion, finely chopped
3 garlic cloves, finely chopped
100ml red wine
400g can of tomatoes
½ tsp chilli flakes
¼ tsp ground cinnamon
400g tube-shaped pasta
50g black olives, pitted and sliced
25g capers, rinsed
salt and black pepper

TO SERVE
a few basil leaves, torn
a few shavings of hard sheep's cheese, such as Pecorino (optional)

We based this on a classic Sicilian pasta dish called pasta alla norma. In the traditional version, the aubergines are fried but as you know they can soak up loads of oil, so Dave and I decided to roast them which makes for a lighter result. A few chilli flakes, a hint of spice and some capers and black olives all contribute to what is a truly flavourful feast.

1. Preheat the oven to 200°C/Fan 180°C/Gas 6. Put the aubergine cubes on a couple of baking trays and drizzle up to 2 tablespoons of the oil over them. Sprinkle with salt and pepper, then roast for about 30 minutes, until tender and golden brown.

2. Meanwhile, heat the remaining oil in a large pan. Add the onion and cook gently until soft and translucent. Add the garlic and continue to cook for another 2 or 3 minutes. Turn up the heat, pour in the red wine and allow it to bubble up, then continue to cook until it has reduced down by half. Add the tomatoes and spices, season with salt and pepper, then cook for about half an hour until the sauce has thickened and reduced.

3. While the sauce is simmering, bring a large saucepan of water to the boil and add salt. Add the pasta and cook until tender but still with a little bite to it – al dente.

4. Add the olives and capers to the sauce, then stir in the aubergines. Simmer for a few more minutes just to make sure everything is piping hot. Serve with the pasta and garnish with basil leaves and shavings of cheese, if using.

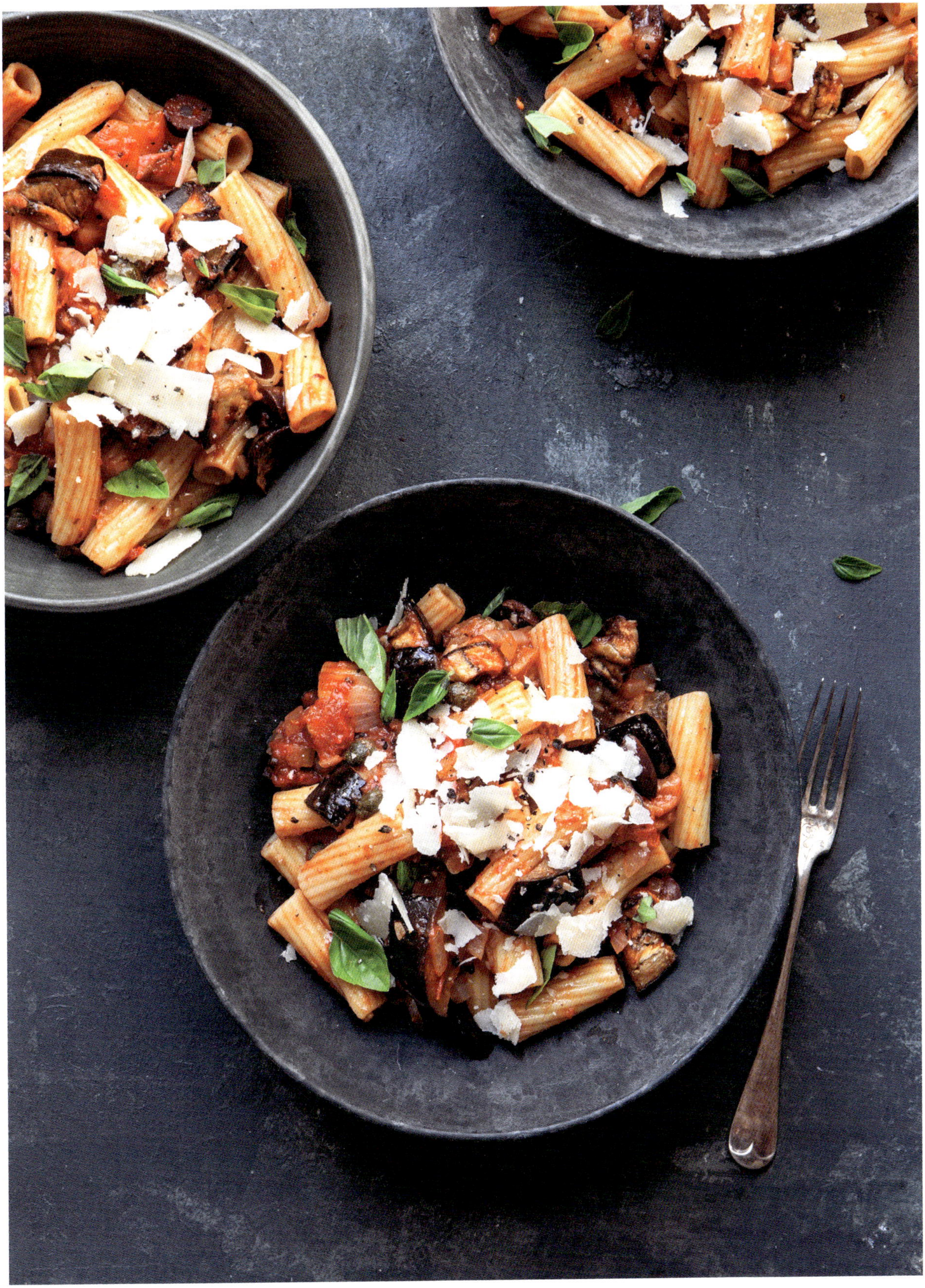

1 **Vegetable biryani...100**
2 **Egg fried rice...102**
3 **Special fried rice...104**
4 **Mushroom risotto...106**
5 **Hairy Biker paella...108**
6 **Really good kedgeree...110**
7 **Turkish lamb pilaf...112**
8 **Arroz al horno...114**
9 **Risotto carbonara...116**
10 **Spring vegetable pilaf...118**

rice

"Rice is one of the world's most popular foods and can be cooked in the most extraordinary variety of ways. Dishes like egg fried rice can make the quickest of suppers, while a beautiful biryani makes any occasion special."

Vegetable biryani

SERVES 6

FRIED ONIONS
vegetable oil
2 large onions (about 300g), thinly sliced into crescents
1 tsp cumin seeds
salt and black pepper

RICE
300g basmati rice
juice of ½ lemon

VEGETABLES & SAUCE
250g carrots
300g runner beans
300g cauliflower
1 tbsp vegetable oil
5 cardamom pods
1 x 5cm cinnamon stick
1 star anise
3 cloves
2 bay leaves
4 fat garlic cloves, crushed
15g root ginger, grated
½ tsp mild chilli powder
1 tsp ground cumin
½ tsp ground turmeric
1 tsp garam masala
3 tbsp coriander stems, finely chopped
1 large tomato, diced
150ml natural yoghurt
juice of 1 lime

TOPPINGS
large pinch of saffron
30g butter
50ml single cream

TO SERVE
sliced green chillies
sprigs of coriander
lime wedges
raita (see p.188)

A biryani is a proper showstopper of a dish, but actually our vegetarian version is easier than it looks to make and so worth it. Just take your time, don't overcook the cauliflower and be sure to rinse and soak the rice well and you'll be fine.

1. Start by cooking the onions. Cover the base of a large frying pan with a thick layer of vegetable oil and fry the onions over a medium to high heat until they are crisp and dark brown. Keep stirring regularly to make sure they don't burn. Add the cumin seeds for the last few minutes, then season with salt and pepper. Drain the onions on kitchen paper, then set aside.

2. Put the rice in a large bowl and cover with water. Swill it around a couple of times until the water is cloudy, then drain. Repeat until the water is fairly clear. Leave the rice to soak for 30–45 minutes.

3. While the rice is soaking, slice the carrots and runner beans on the diagonal and cut the cauliflower into small florets. Bring a large pan of water to the boil and add plenty of salt. Add the carrots and simmer for 5 minutes, then add the cauliflower and beans. Continue to cook for another 3–4 minutes until the carrots are just tender but still firm and the cauliflower is al dente. It's important that the cauliflower shouldn't be cooked through, so check it after 3 minutes.

4. Heat the oil in a large flameproof casserole dish. Add the whole spices and bay leaves and fry for a minute, then add the garlic, ginger and remaining spices. Stir for a couple of minutes, then stir in the rest of the ingredients. Season and add the vegetables. Remove the dish from the heat and set aside.

5. For the topping, toast the saffron in a dry frying pan, then leave it to cool. Put it in a mortar with a pinch of salt and grind it to a fine powder with the pestle. Add 2 tablespoons of just-boiled water and leave to stand.

6. When the rice has finished soaking, bring a large pan of water to the boil and add 2 teaspoons of salt and the lemon juice. Add the rice and cook for 4–5 minutes until it's almost but not quite cooked through. When you squeeze a grain of rice it should break up into several pieces and still be firm, not mushy. Drain the rice, but don't shake it dry – it needs some residual moisture. Taste the rice and add more salt if you like. Preheat the oven to 200°C/Fan 180°C/Gas 6.

7. Add a third of the fried onions to the vegetables and sauce in the casserole dish and stir. Add another third to the rice, then spoon the rice over the vegetables. Melt the butter and add the cream, then pour this over the rice. Finally, drizzle over the saffron water.

8. Cover the dish with 2 layers of foil. Put it over a high heat, then as soon as you can hear the contents bubble and the foil starts to puff up a little from the steam, put the dish in the oven for about 20 minutes.

9. Remove the dish from the oven and leave to stand for 15 minutes before removing the foil. The rice should be beautifully dry and fluffy. Add the remaining fried onions, then serve with the green chillies, coriander, lime wedges and some raita.

Egg fried rice

SERVES 4

2 tbsp vegetable oil
1 skinless, boneless chicken breast, cut into small dice
200g mushrooms, quartered
2 garlic cloves, finely chopped
1 red chilli, finely chopped (optional)
500g cooked and chilled long-grain rice
2 eggs, beaten
200g frozen peas, defrosted
bunch of spring onions, sliced into rounds
2 tbsp soy sauce
1 tsp sesame oil

Dave and I were really happy with our one-wok version of egg fried rice which is the quickest, tastiest supper you could hope to make. Protein, veg and carbs all in one pot, full of flavour and hardly any washing up. What more could you want?

1. Heat the oil in a large wok. When the air above the oil is shimmering, add the diced chicken breast and the mushrooms. Stir-fry the chicken and mushrooms until cooked, then add the garlic and the chilli, if using. Stir-fry for another minute, then add the rice and continue to stir-fry for a minute.

2. Push everything to one side of the wok, then add the beaten eggs. Stir constantly until they are lightly scrambled, then stir them into the rice, together with the peas and the spring onions. Cook for a couple of minutes more, then add the soy sauce and the sesame oil. Serve at once.

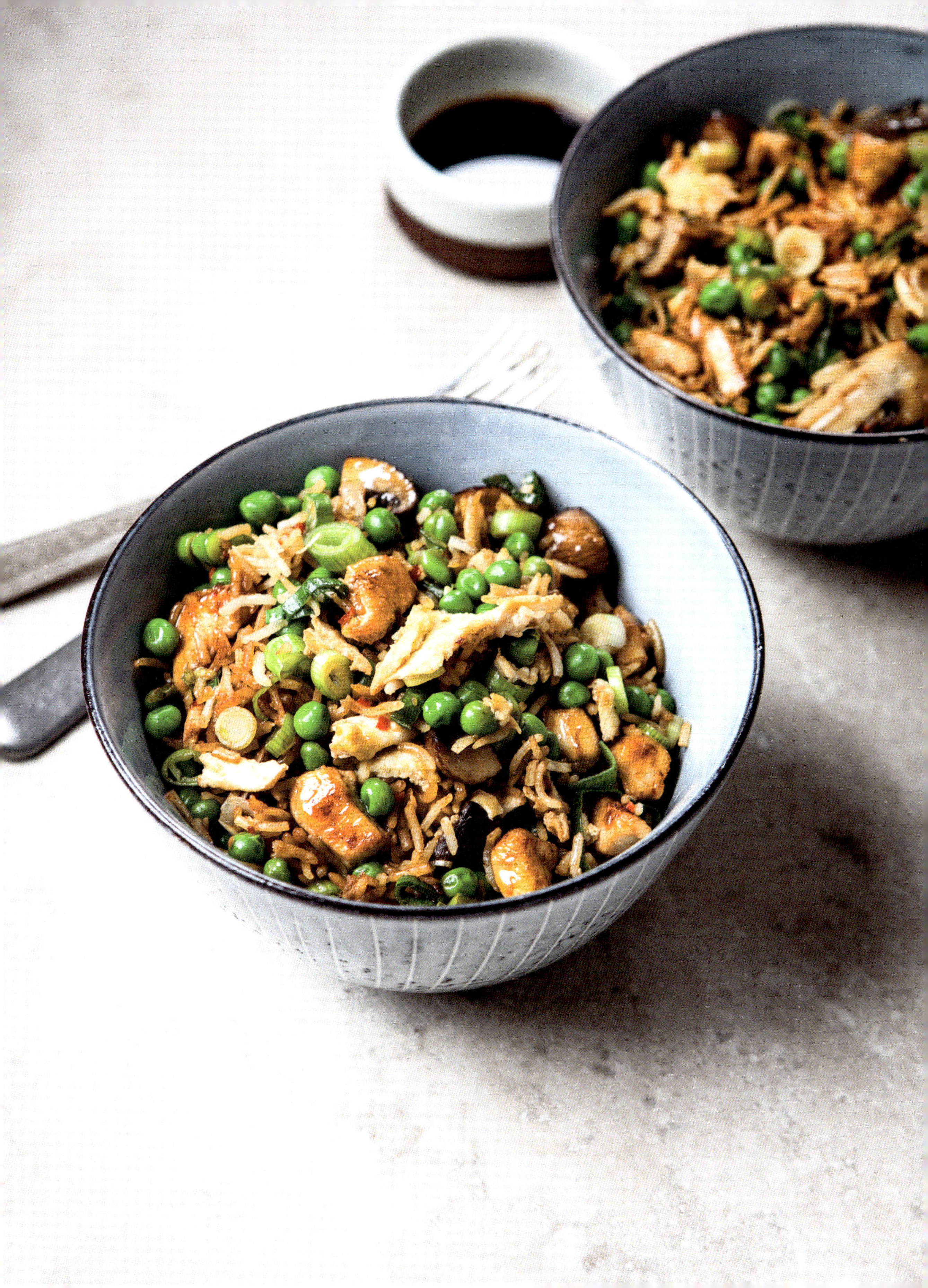

Special fried rice

SERVES 4

2 tbsp vegetable oil
2 eggs, beaten
200g shelled raw prawns (optional)
2 bacon rashers, finely diced
1 onion, diced
1 red pepper, diced
1 carrot, finely sliced on the diagonal
100g baby corn, sliced into rounds
10g root ginger, cut into matchsticks
2 garlic cloves, finely chopped
½ tsp Chinese 5-spice powder
150g cooked chicken, shredded
150g peas, defrosted if frozen
400g cooked and chilled basmati rice
4 spring onions, finely sliced (include the greens)
1 tsp sesame oil
salt

SAUCE
2 tbsp soy sauce
1 tbsp rice vinegar
1 tbsp rice wine
1 tsp hot sauce (optional)

TO SERVE
soy sauce
chilli oil

This is our poshed-up, extra-tasty version of fried rice – and a great way of using up odds and ends in the fridge. We've suggested adding prawns, bacon and chicken but it's up to you – just use whatever you have available. The addition of raw prawns does add extra flavour, but you could add cooked ones at the end instead if you prefer.

1. Mix together the sauce ingredients in a small bowl.

2. Heat 2 teaspoons of the oil in a wok. Season the eggs with a pinch of salt and add them to the wok. Scramble the eggs very quickly, then as soon as they are set, turn them out on to a plate and set aside.

3. Wipe out the wok and add the remaining oil. Add the prawns, if using, and stir-fry them until pink and cooked through. Remove them from the wok and set aside. Add the bacon and fry until crisp, then add the onion, red pepper, carrot and baby corn. Stir-fry over a high heat until just al dente, then add the ginger and garlic. Sprinkle in the Chinese 5-spice powder and continue to stir-fry for 2 minutes.

4. Add the chicken and peas to the wok and fry for one minute, then add the rice. Continue to stir-fry until the rice is heated through, then pour the sauce over the contents of the wok. Stir-fry for another minute, then stir through the prawns, if using, the spring onions and the scrambled eggs. Leave to stand over the heat for a couple of minutes.

5. Drizzle over the sesame oil and serve immediately, with soy sauce and chilli oil at the table for everyone to add for themselves.

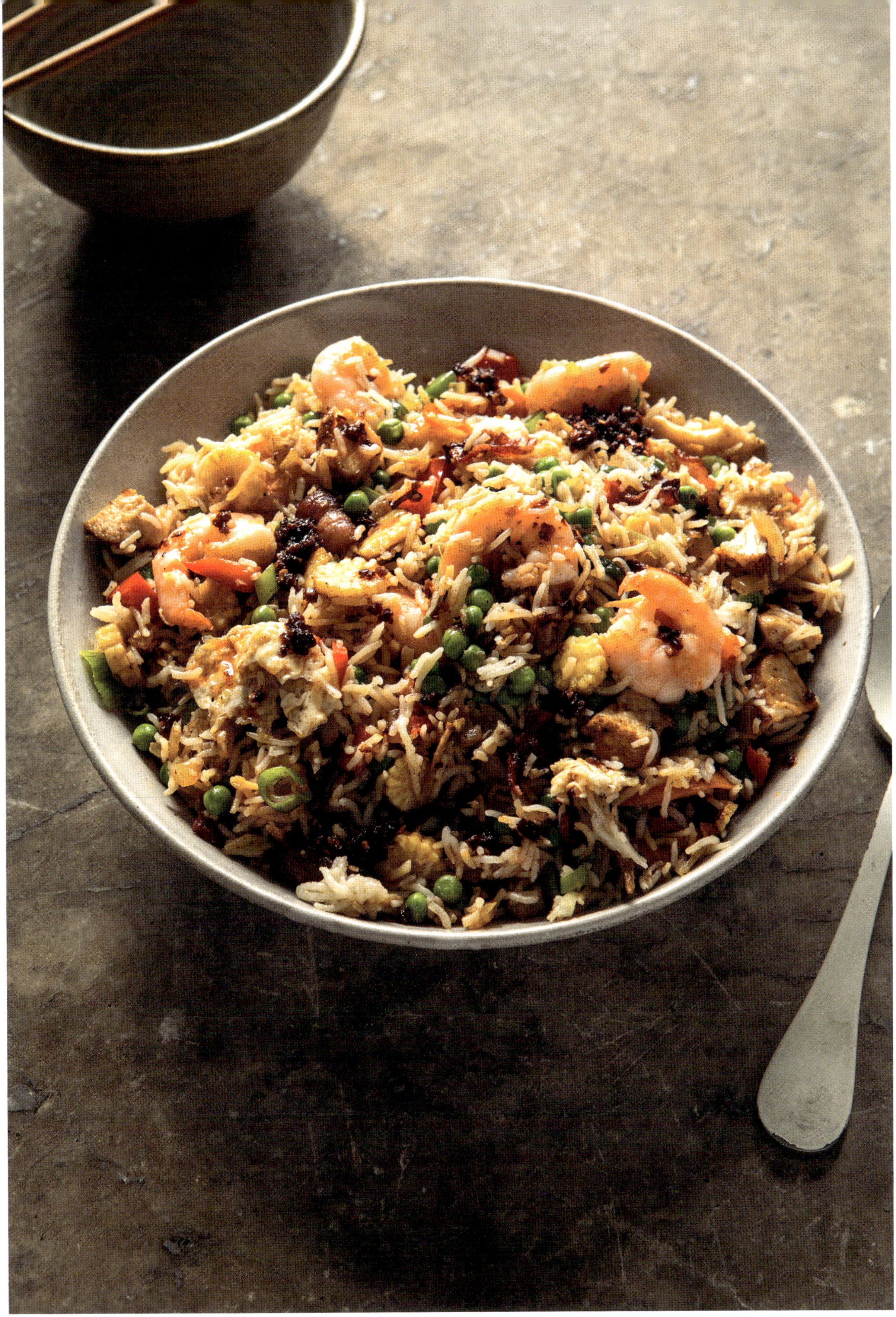

Mushroom risotto

SERVES 4

25g dried wild mushrooms
2 tbsp olive oil
50g butter
1 large onion, finely chopped
500g mixed fresh mushrooms, 200g finely chopped, 300g sliced
3 garlic cloves, finely chopped
300g risotto rice
100ml white wine
a few thyme sprigs
about 1.25 litres hot mushroom or vegetable stock
squeeze of lemon juice
50g Parmesan cheese, grated
handful of parsley, very finely chopped
salt and black pepper

TO SERVE
a few drops of truffle oil (optional)
extra Parmesan, grated or shaved

This is a proper tasty risotto, given extra flavour by including a few dried wild mushrooms and their soaking liquid. For the fresh mushrooms, use a mixture of button, field and chestnut mushrooms or whatever you have handy. And for a really luxurious dish, add a touch of truffle oil if you happen to have some.

1. Soak the dried mushrooms in a small bowl of warm water for half an hour or so. Heat a tablespoon of the olive oil with 25g of the butter in a large sauté pan. Add the onion and cook gently until soft and translucent.

2. Strain the dried mushrooms, then rinse them to get rid of any grit. Reserve the soaking liquid after straining off any sediment. Finely chop the soaked mushrooms and put them in the pan with the onion, then add the 200g of finely chopped fresh mushrooms. Cook over a medium-high heat until the mushrooms have given off their liquid and it has evaporated. Add the garlic and cook for another couple of minutes.

3. Pour in the risotto rice and stir until it is glossy. Pour in the wine and leave to bubble until most of it has evaporated. Add the soaking liquid and thyme to the stock. Season the rice, then turn down the heat and start adding the hot stock a ladleful at a time, stirring constantly in between each addition. Make sure most of the liquid has been absorbed before you add more. When the rice is al dente and creamy, stop adding stock – you may not need it all. Add a squeeze of lemon juice and stir.

4. Add the remaining butter and the cheese and beat them into the risotto for extra creaminess. Remove the pan from the heat and cover it with a lid while you prepare the mushroom garnish.

5. Heat the remaining oil in a frying pan and add the 300g of sliced fresh mushrooms. Fry them over a high heat until golden brown, then season with salt and pepper. Serve the risotto in bowls, garnished with the fried mushrooms and chopped parsley. Add a drizzle of truffle oil, if using, and grate or shave some extra cheese over the top.

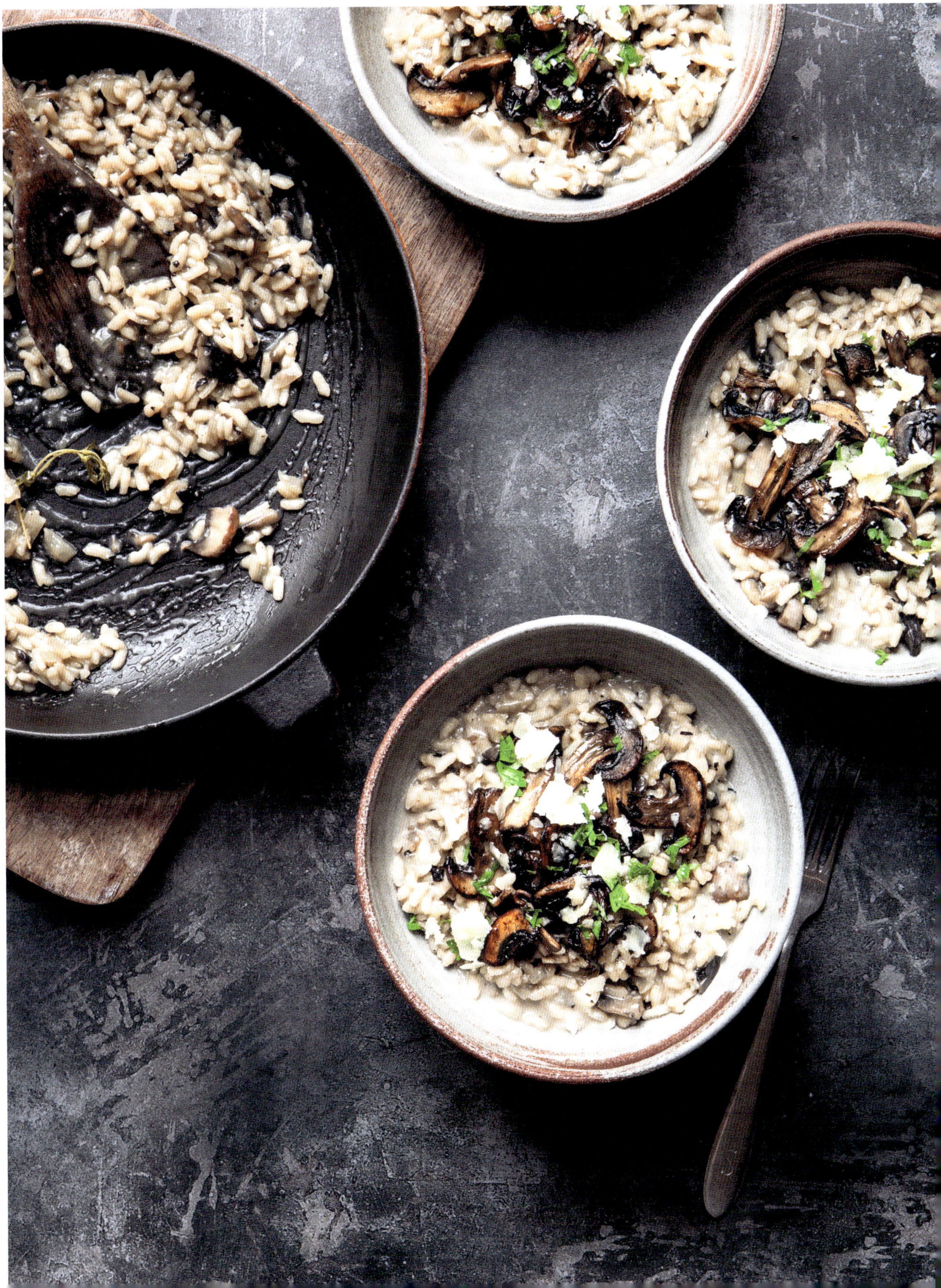

Hairy Biker paella

SERVES 8

1 tbsp olive oil
600g chicken thigh fillets, skinned and diced
150g cooking chorizo, diced or sliced
4 garlic cloves, finely chopped
300g large tomatoes, skinned and roughly chopped
1 tsp smoked paprika
zest of 1 lemon
1.5 litres hot chicken stock
3 bay leaves
2 thyme sprigs
200g green beans, cut into short lengths
500g paella rice
1 tsp saffron threads, soaked in a little warm water
a couple of handfuls of mussels
12 raw king prawns
salt and black pepper

TO SERVE
lemon wedges

I'm not claiming this is a totally authentic paella recipe but it's one that Dave and I have cooked at home and on TV for many years and everyone loves it. I'm a big fan of these dishes that are cooked all in one pan so you can put it on the table and let everyone dig in and help themselves. As you'll see, this serves eight – at least – so is great for a party or a family gathering. All you need on the side is some crusty bread and a green salad.

1. Heat the oil in a large sauté pan over a medium heat. Season the chicken with salt and pepper, then fry for 5 minutes, turning the pieces regularly until lightly coloured. Add the chorizo and cook for a further minute.

2. Add the garlic and cook for another couple of minutes, then push everything to one side of the pan. Add the tomatoes and fry them for a few minutes, then mix everything together and sprinkle in the paprika and lemon zest. Pour in all but a large ladleful of the chicken stock and bring back to the boil. Add the bay leaves, thyme and green beans and season with salt.

3. When the chicken stock has come back to the boil, turn the heat down to a simmer and sprinkle in the rice, trying to get it into as even a layer as possible. Pour in the saffron with its soaking water and stir – this is the only time you should stir your paella once the rice has been added! Bring to the boil again, then cook for 5 minutes.

4. Turn the heat down and leave the rice to simmer slowly for 12–15 minutes. If the pan is getting dry, taste the rice – if it's still too firm, add some of the reserved stock and cook for a few more minutes.

5. Meanwhile, prepare the mussels. Wash them thoroughly, scraping off any barnacles and pulling out the beards. Discard any mussels with broken shells or any that do not close tightly when you tap them sharply.

6. When the rice is ready, arrange the mussels and prawns over the paella. Cover the pan with a damp tea towel or a lid if you have one and wait for the mussels to steam open and the prawns to turn nicely pink. I prefer to leave the prawns unshelled so everyone can peel their own, but shell them if you prefer. Discard any mussels that don't open. Serve the paella with some lemon wedges.

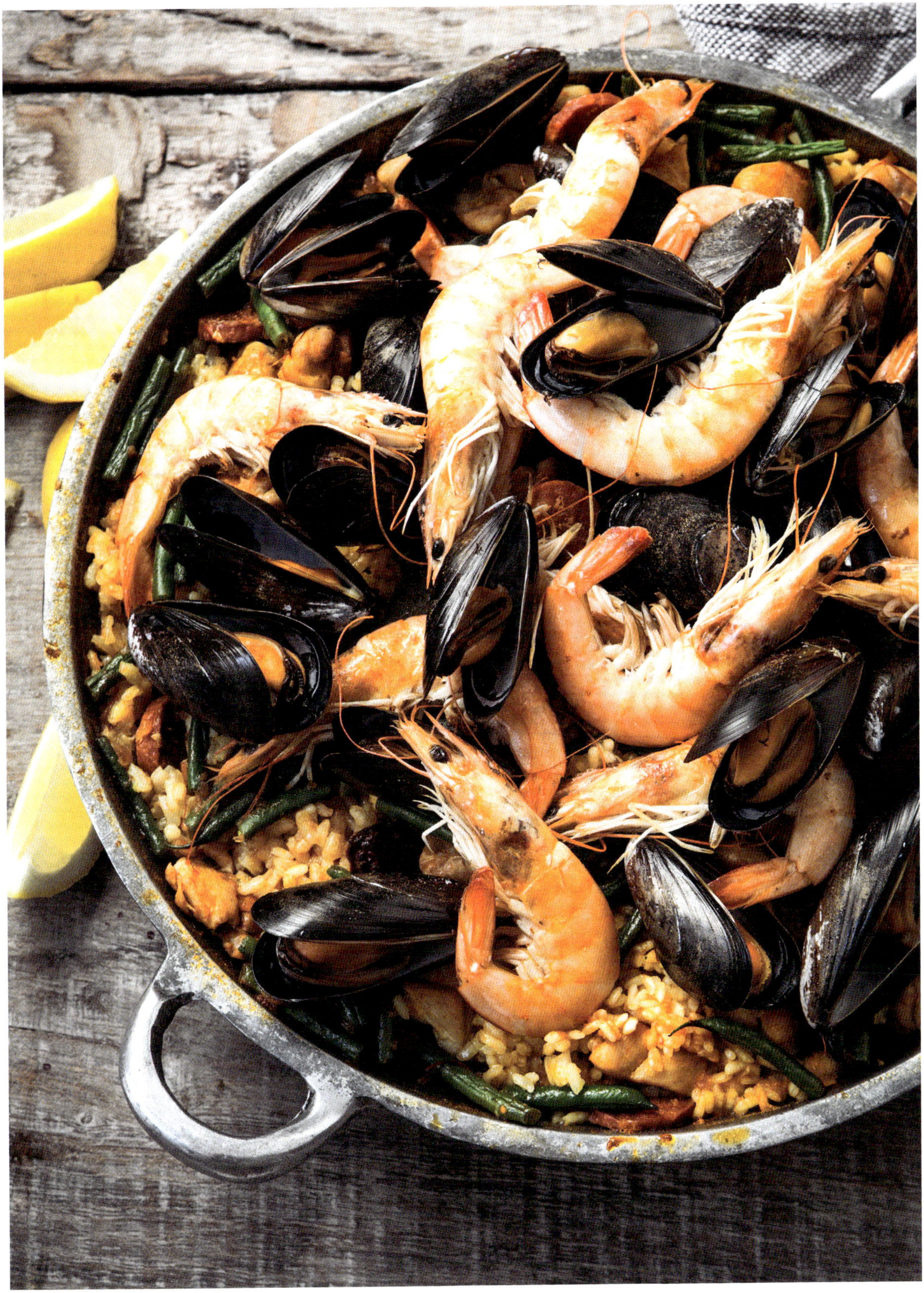

Really good kedgeree

SERVES 6

475g undyed smoked haddock fillet, halved
2 bay leaves
200g basmati rice, rinsed in cold water, then drained
4 eggs
100g frozen peas (optional)
40g butter
1 tbsp vegetable oil
1 onion, finely chopped
1 heaped tbsp medium curry powder
3 tbsp double cream
3 tbsp chopped parsley
juice of ½ lemon
black pepper

Kedgeree originated in India and is thought to have been brought to Britain by returning colonials. In the nineteenth century, it became popular as a breakfast dish in grand country houses, but regular people like me tend to enjoy it later in the day. There are loads of versions but I reckon we got it right with this one. If not serving immediately, tip the kedgeree into a warm dish and dot with a few cubes of butter. Cover the dish with foil and keep the kedgeree warm in a low oven for up to twenty minutes before serving.

1. Place the haddock in a large frying pan, skin-side up. Pour over 500ml of water, add the bay leaves and bring the water to a gentle simmer. Cook the fish for 8–10 minutes until it is just done and flakes easily. Drain it in a colander set over a bowl and discard the bay leaves. Pour the cooking liquor into a saucepan.

2. Stir the rice into the cooking liquor. Cover the pan with a lid and bring the liquor to the boil, then reduce the heat and leave to simmer very gently for 10 minutes. Turn off the heat and leave the rice covered for 3–5 minutes longer. By this time it should have absorbed all the liquid.

3. While the rice is cooking, bring some water to the boil in another pan, add the eggs and cook them for 8 minutes. Drain them in a sieve and cool under cold running water, then peel and set aside. Defrost the peas, if using, in boiling water and drain.

4. Melt the butter with the oil in a large pan and cook the onion over a low heat for 5 minutes until softened, stirring occasionally. Add the curry powder and cook for another 3 minutes, stirring constantly. Add the cooked rice to the pan and stir in the onion. Then add the peas, cream, parsley and a few twists of black pepper.

5. Flake the fish into chunky pieces, discarding the skin, and add them to the pan. Gently stir in the lemon juice and cook for a couple of minutes. Cut the eggs into quarters and place them on the rice. Cover the pan with a lid and leave it over the heat for 2–3 minutes or until the eggs are warm, then serve.

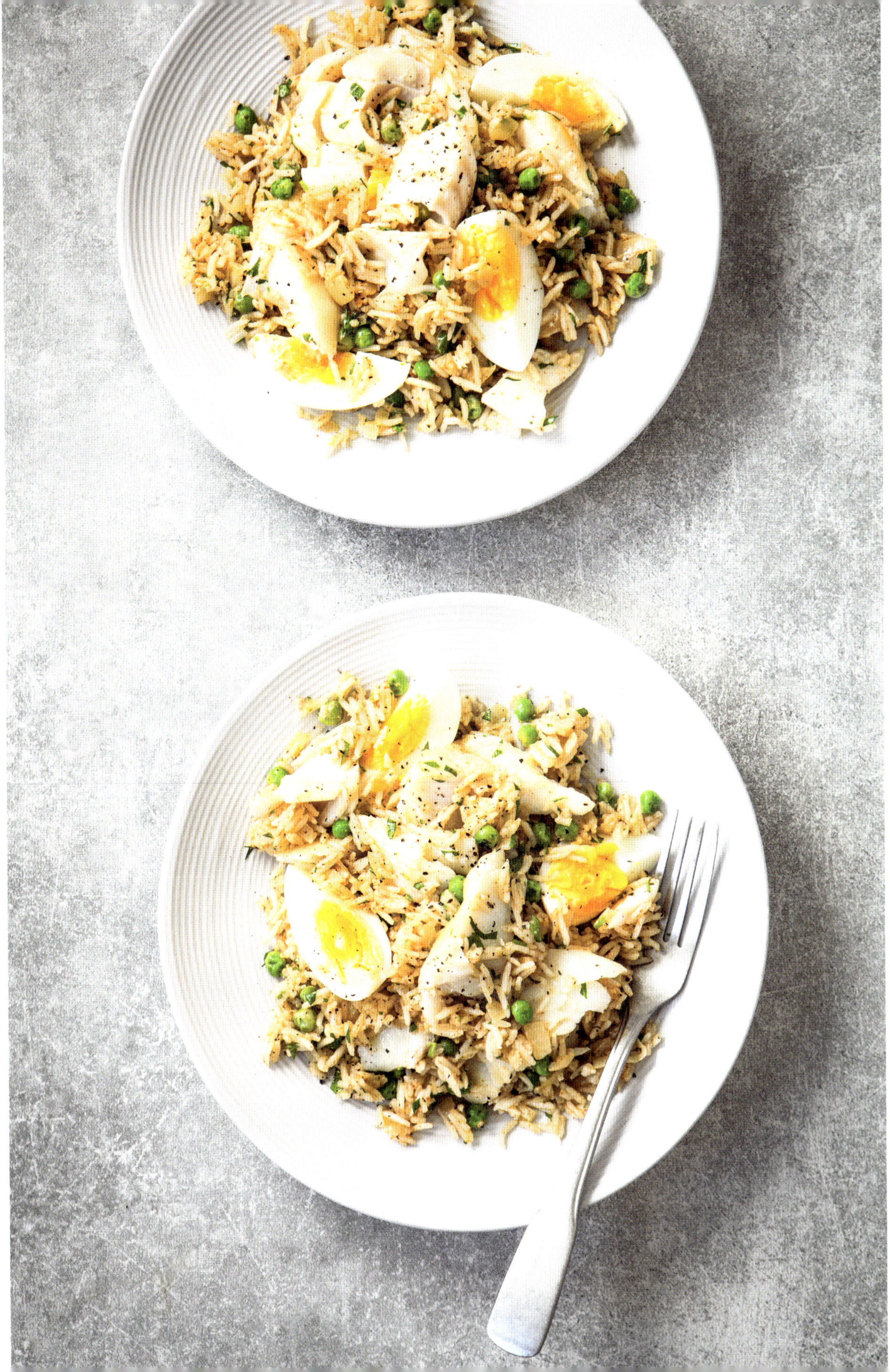

Turkish lamb pilaf

SERVES 6–8

1 tbsp olive oil
600g lean lamb (leg is good), diced into 2cm pieces
½ tsp black peppercorns
½ tsp allspice berries
4 cloves
5cm cinnamon stick
large pinch of saffron, soaked in a little warm water
500ml chicken stock or water
15g butter
1 large onion, sliced vertically into thin strips
500g long-grain rice, rinsed and soaked for 30 minutes in warm water
100g sultanas, soaked with the rice
50g pine nuts
a small bunch of fresh mint or dill leaves
salt

YOGHURT DIP
300ml Greek yoghurt
½ cucumber, peeled and deseeded
1 tsp dried mint
pinch of sumac

This is a beautiful dish for a special occasion. It does take a while to cook but there's nothing difficult about it and the result is superb. Sumac is a lemony-flavoured spice popular in Middle Eastern cooking and it's available in supermarkets. Use golden sultanas if you can find them.

1. Heat the olive oil in a large flameproof casserole dish. Add the pieces of lamb and sear them on all sides.

2. Lightly crush the peppercorns, allspice berries and cloves with a pestle and mortar, then sprinkle them over the lamb. Stir for a minute or so, then add the cinnamon and the saffron with its soaking water. Pour over the stock or water and season with salt. Bring to the boil, then turn the heat down to a simmer. Put a lid on the casserole dish and cook for about an hour, until the lamb is tender.

3. Remove the lamb from the casserole dish with a slotted spoon and set it aside, then drain off the cooking liquid into a measuring jug. Top this liquid up to 1 litre with water (or more chicken stock if you prefer) and set it aside. Wipe out the casserole dish, then add the butter and melt it over a medium heat. Add the onion and cook it for about 10 minutes until golden-brown. Stir regularly so the strips of onion colour evenly.

4. Put the lamb back in the dish, shredding it into pieces if you like. Drain the rice and sultanas and add them too. Stir to coat the rice in the juices from the onion and pour in the topped-up cooking liquid.

5. Bring to the boil, then turn down the heat and put the lid on the dish. Simmer for 20 minutes, until the rice is cooked and has absorbed all the liquid, then remove the casserole dish from the heat. Take off the lid, put a folded tea towel over the casserole dish, then replace the lid. Leave the pilaf to stand for 15 minutes, during which time the rice will become fluffier.

6. Meanwhile, toast the pine nuts in a dry frying pan for a couple of minutes, until light golden-brown.

7. To serve, pile the pilaf on to a warm platter. If a crust has formed on the bottom of the casserole, try to peel this off in one piece and serve it on the side – this is the 'tahdig', considered a special treat and usually served to honoured guests. Sprinkle the pilaf with the pine nuts and freshly chopped mint or dill and serve with a bowl of refreshing yoghurt dip.

YOGHURT DIP

Put the yoghurt in a bowl. Coarsely grate the cucumber and strain it through a sieve, or wring it out in a clean tea towel to remove as much water as possible. Stir the cucumber and dried mint into the yoghurt, then season with salt and pepper and a pinch of sumac.

Arroz al horno

SERVES 4

2 tbsp olive oil
150g black pudding, sliced
100g spicy cooking chorizo, sliced
2 red onions, sliced into slim wedges
2 red peppers, diced
3 garlic cloves, finely chopped
100g tomatoes, fresh or canned, finely chopped or puréed
1 tbsp smoked paprika
pinch of saffron, soaked in 2 tbsp warm water (optional)
2 bay leaves
leaves from a few rosemary sprigs, finely chopped
zest and juice of 1 lemon
1 litre chicken stock
400g can of chickpeas, drained
300g paella rice
1 head of garlic
chopped parsley, to garnish
salt and black pepper

The idea for this recipe came from one of the many wonderful people who cared for Dave while he was in hospital. A Spanish nurse, called Monica, told Dave about one of her favourite dishes from her homeland– arroz al horno, which means 'rice in the oven'. He loved the sound of it and this is the version we came up with, made with British black pudding instead of Spanish morcilla. It's warming, filling and totally delicious.

1. Preheat the oven to 200°C/Fan 180°C/Gas 6.

2. Heat a tablespoon of the olive oil in a wide, shallow, flameproof casserole dish. Quickly fry the black pudding, then remove it with a slotted spoon and set it aside. Add the chorizo and fry until lightly browned, then remove it from the pan and set it aside with the black pudding.

3. Heat the remaining oil in the casserole dish and add the onions and peppers. Sauté until they have softened and the onion is translucent, then stir in the garlic. Cook for another minute, then add the tomatoes, paprika, the saffron and its soaking water, if using, the herbs and the lemon zest. Stir for a minute, then pour in the stock and add the chickpeas. Season with plenty of salt and pepper. Bring to the boil and cook for a couple of minutes.

4. Put the black pudding and chorizo back in the casserole dish. Sprinkle in the rice as evenly as you can, pushing it under the liquid where necessary but without stirring. Season again.

5. Pierce the head of garlic all over with the tip of a sharp knife, making sure you go right through each clove. Push the garlic head into the centre of the casserole dish so only the top is left exposed.

6. Put the dish in the oven and bake, uncovered, for 20–25 minutes until the rice has absorbed the liquid and is swollen and tender. Remove the dish from the oven, cover with a tea towel and a lid, and leave to stand for 10 minutes. This step isn't essential, but it does improve the texture of the rice.

7. Pour over the lemon juice and serve sprinkled with parsley. Break open the head of garlic and divide the cloves between each serving – the garlic flesh can be squeezed out and eaten with the rice.

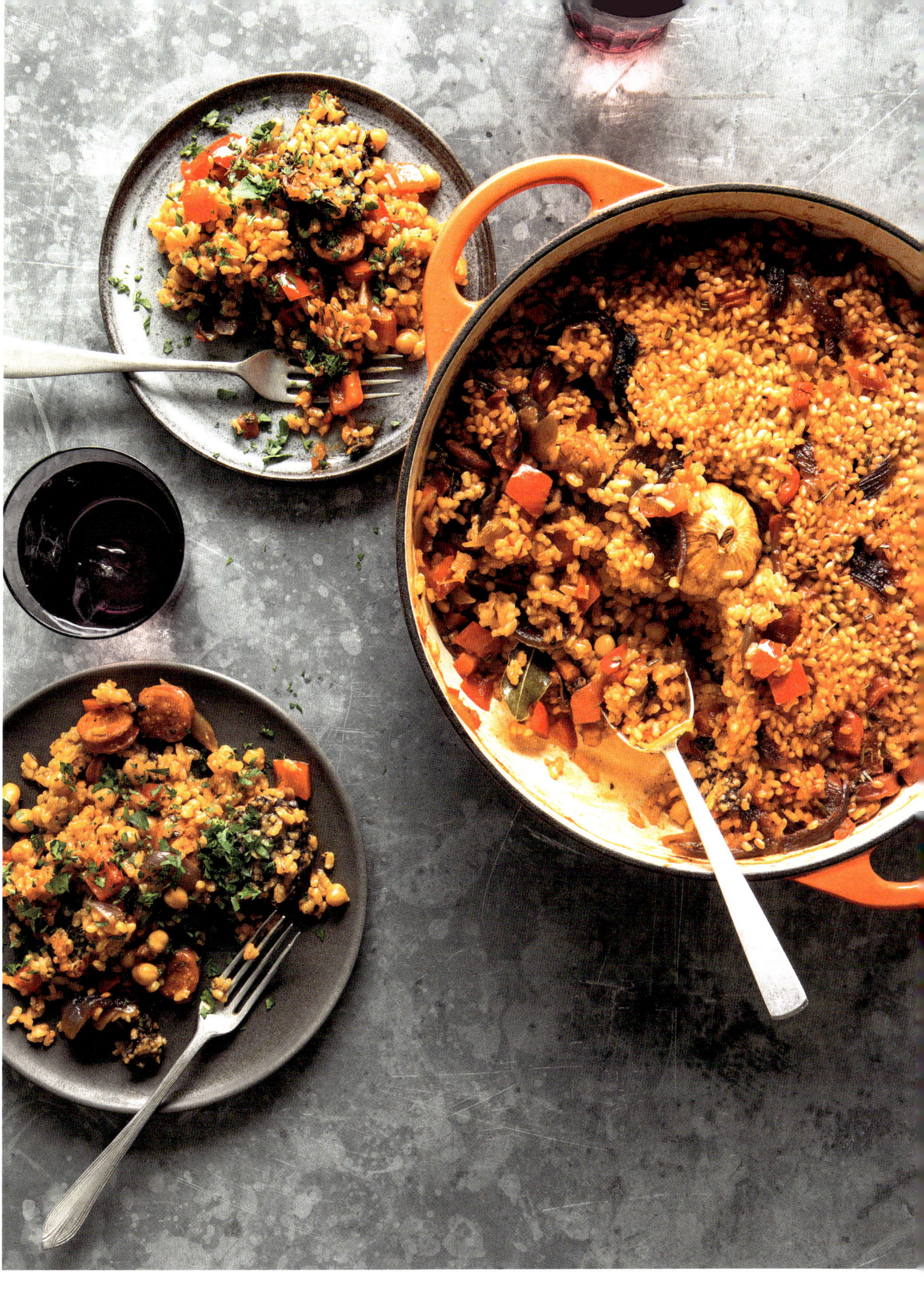

Risotto carbonara

SERVES 4

1 tbsp olive oil
150g pancetta, diced
30g butter
1 onion, finely chopped
3 garlic cloves, finely chopped
leaves from a large thyme sprig
300g risotto rice
100ml white wine
1 litre hot chicken stock
2 egg yolks
50g Parmesan, grated
salt and black pepper

I don't know what my Italian friends make of this, but Dave and I were chuffed to bits when he came up with the idea of combining two of our very favourite dishes – risotto and spaghetti carbonara. I don't want to boast too much but I have to say, it's genius. You'll love it.

1. Heat the oil in a large sauté pan and add the pancetta. Fry over a high heat until crisp and browned, then remove it with a slotted spoon and set aside.

2. Add half the butter to the pan. When it has melted, add the onion and sauté it over a low-medium heat until soft and translucent. Add the garlic, thyme leaves and rice, then stir until the rice is glossy with oil and butter. Season with salt and black pepper.

3. Pour in the wine and bring to the boil. When the wine has almost completely boiled off, add a ladleful of stock. Stir the stock into the rice over a medium heat and keep stirring until most of it has been absorbed by the rice. Repeat until you have used all the stock – this process will take at least 20 minutes. By this time the rice should be slightly al dente and surrounded by a creamy sauce. Have a taste – the rice should still have a very little bite to it.

4. Beat in the egg yolks, followed by the rest of the butter and half the grated Parmesan. Stir in two-thirds of the pancetta, and leave the risotto to stand for a couple of minutes to heat through.

5. Serve garnished with the rest of the pancetta and Parmesan.

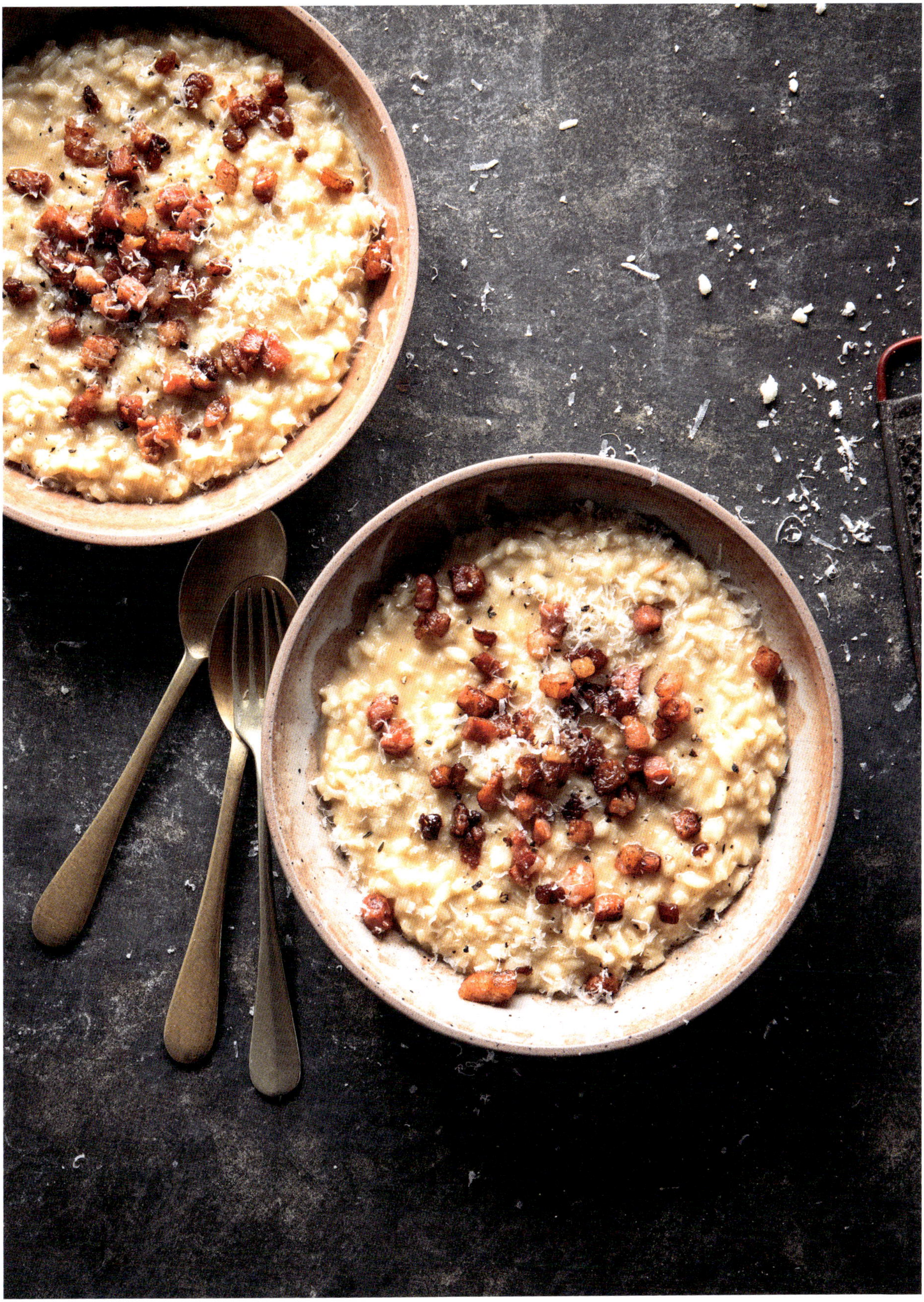

Spring vegetable pilaf

SERVES 4

2 tbsp olive oil
15g butter
1 onion, finely chopped
small bunch of chard, stems and leaves separated and shredded
1 large courgette, finely chopped
300–400g frozen broad beans
300g basmati rice
½ tsp ground allspice
¼ tsp ground cinnamon
pinch of saffron
bunch of asparagus tips, thinly sliced on the diagonal
100g frozen peas
large bunch of dill, finely chopped
small bunch of mint, leaves only, chopped
zest of 1 lime
salt

TO SERVE
lime wedges
Greek yoghurt

A truly fabulous vegetarian meal, this recipes was inspired by a Turkish broad bean and dill side dish we cooked way back. We've added loads more veg to make it into a main meal and you can vary them if you like – use spinach or kale instead of chard, for instance. I do think it's a good idea to peel the skins off the broad beans as they look and taste miles better, but if you don't have time I won't tell anyone. This can be a good vegan dish if you leave out the butter and use an extra tablespoon of oil instead and serve with plant-based yoghurt.

1. Heat the oil and butter in a large flameproof casserole dish. When the butter has melted, add the onion, chard stems and courgette. Cook over a gentle heat until the onion is soft and translucent.

2. While the onion is cooking, prepare the broad beans. Pour a kettle of boiling water over them, then drain and slip off the grey outer skins. You should end up with about 300g of beans, so if you don't want to peel your broad beans, just use this amount instead.

3. Cover the rice in cold water and swill it around until the water turns cloudy. Strain and repeat until the water runs clear.

4. When the onion is cooked, add the spices to the pan, then pour in 500ml of water and add plenty of salt. Bring to the boil, then add the rice, followed by the chard greens. Give everything a quick stir, then add the asparagus, broad beans and peas. Cover and leave to cook for 15 minutes. Check – if the rice is still very firm, leave for another 3–4 minutes, then remove the pan from the heat and leave to stand for at least another 10 minutes to steam.

5. Stir through the dill and mint leaves. Serve immediately with wedges of lime and plenty of yoghurt.

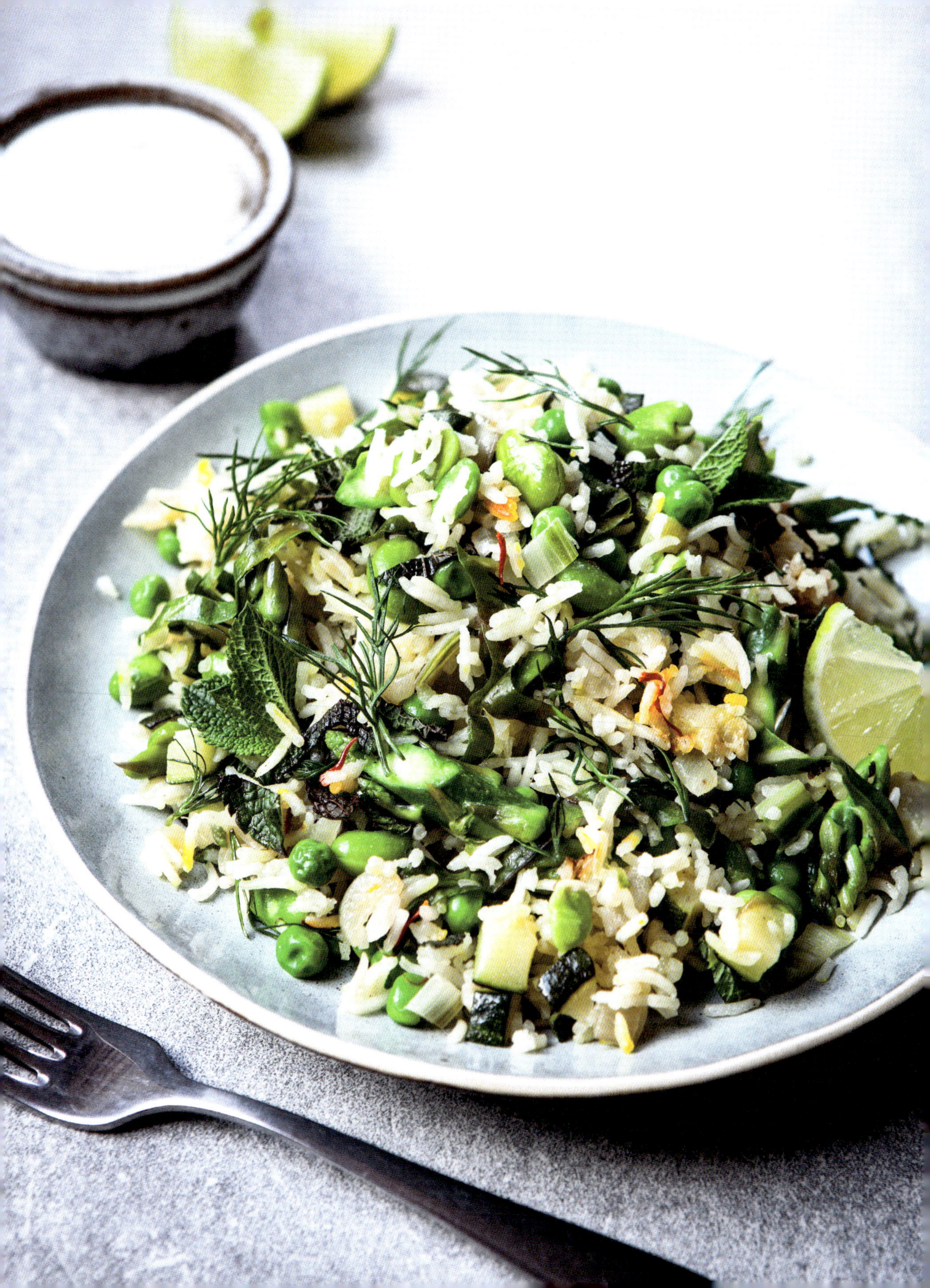

1. Classic cheese & onion pie...122
2. Salmon pie with spinach...124
3. Chicken, ham & leek pie...126
4. Curried chicken pie...128
5. Steak & mushroom pie...130
6. Cumberland sausage pie...132
7. Shepherd's or cottage pie...134
8. Fish & chorizo traybake...136
9. Chicken & sausage traybake...138
10. Traybake Christmas dinner...140

pies & traybakes

“ *Dave and I shared a passion for pies – which is why we maintained our pie-like shape! We grew up eating them and we both loved making 'em. Traybakes have always been a favourite too – quick to prepare and proper tasty.* ”

Classic cheese & onion pie

SERVES 4–6

400g waxy potatoes, cut into 1cm dice
1 medium onion, finely chopped
125g Lancashire cheese, coarsely grated
125g mature Cheddar cheese, coarsely grated
1 egg, beaten
salt and black pepper

PASTRY

350g plain flour, plus extra for dusting
½ tsp baking powder
100g butter
100g lard (or just 200g butter)
1 egg yolk
1 egg, beaten, for brushing

Cheese and onion is one of the all-time great flavour combinations and this is a pie that everyone will love. Dave used to tell me how when he was a teenager at college he would eat a couple of cheese and onion pies for breakfast every day! Made with two tasty British cheeses, this is a treat for any occasion, or you can pack a chunky slice in a lunchbox to take to work. You could, of course, use shop-bought pastry, but this one is nice.

1. For the pastry, put the flour and baking powder in a bowl with a pinch of salt. Add the butter or butter and lard, if using, then rub in the fat until the mixture resembles breadcrumbs. Stir in the egg yolk with a knife, then add ice-cold water a little at a time, cutting it in as you go, until the pastry starts to come together. You can do this in a food processor if you prefer. Shape the pastry into 2 discs, one a little larger than the other, wrap them in cling film and leave them in the fridge until you are ready to roll them.

2. Bring a pan of salted water to the boil and add the potatoes. Bring back to the boil, then cook for 2 minutes. Add the onion and cook for a further minute, then drain thoroughly and set aside to cool. Put the grated cheese into a large bowl and add the cooled potato and onion and the beaten egg. Mix thoroughly and season with salt and pepper.

3. Preheat the oven to 200°C/Fan 180°C/Gas 6.

4. Take the smaller of the pastry balls and roll it out on a well-floured surface, then use a large dinner plate to cut out a round of about 25cm in diameter. Carefully transfer the disc to a baking tray.

5. Pile all the filling on to the disc, making sure you leave a border of at least 2cm. Flatten the filling down so it is even – it should be around 2cm high.

6. Roll out the other disc of pastry with any trimmings from the first disc, making sure it is large enough to cover the filling. Brush the edges of the bottom layer of pastry with beaten egg and place the larger one on top, moulding it around the filling. Make sure the edges are well sealed then trim and press a fork around it. Brush the whole pie with beaten egg and cut 2 slits in the centre.

7. Bake the pie in the preheated oven for 30–35 minutes. Serve hot, straight from the oven, at room temperature, or cold.

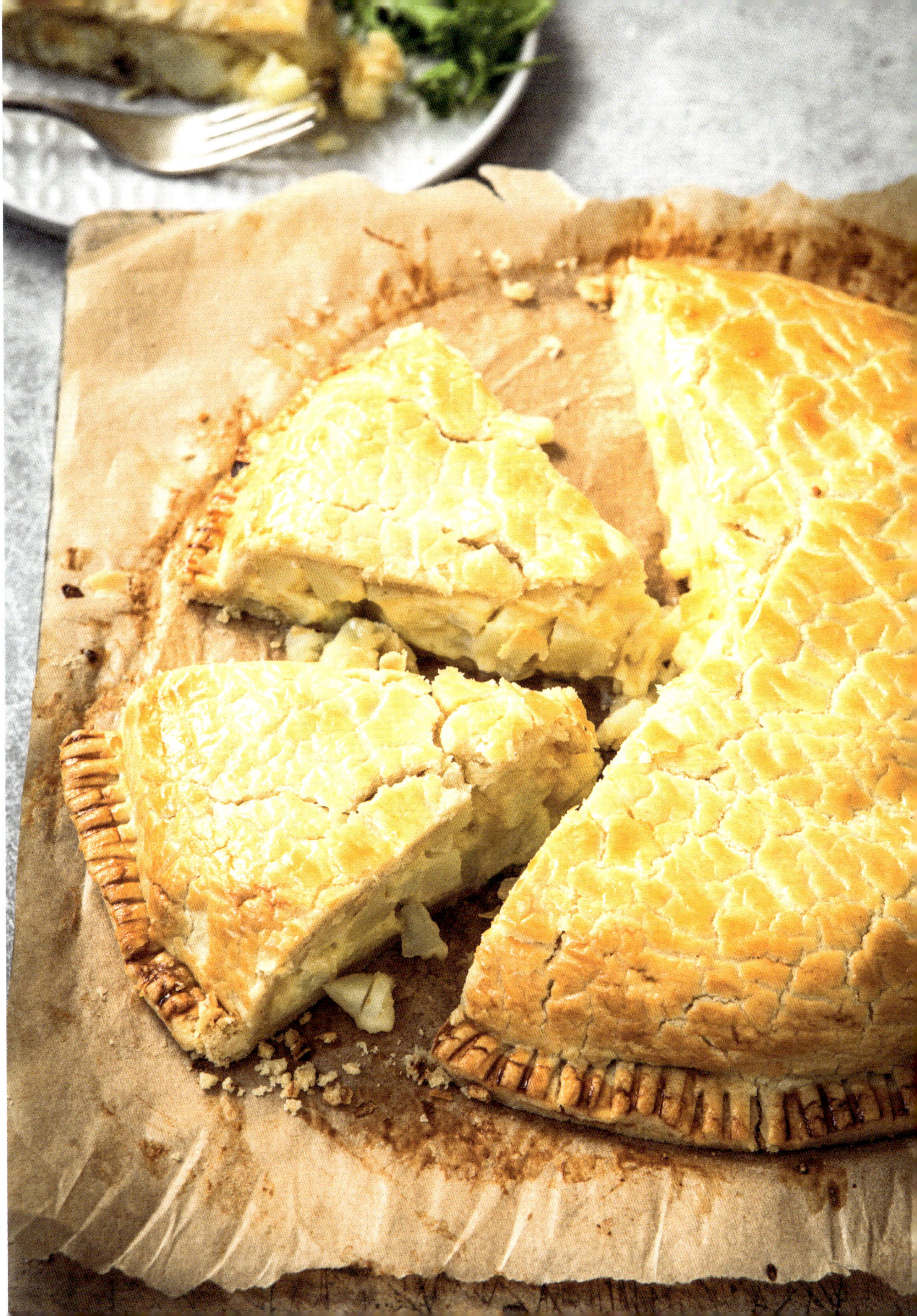

Salmon pie with spinach

SERVES 4

4–5 tbsp hollandaise sauce (see p.266)
500g salmon fillet
450–500g baby leaf spinach
400–500g ready-made puff pastry
grated zest of 1 lemon
1 tbsp finely chopped tarragon (optional)
1 egg, lightly beaten
salt and black pepper

This is quite a fancy pie but it's not difficult to prepare and you can use ready-made puff pastry. Don't be daunted about the hollandaise sauce – just follow our instructions and you'll be fine. Dave and I first cooked this with some trout we'd caught when fishing in Scotland, but since then we've used salmon which is easier to find in the shops. Creamy and luxurious, this is a really impressive dish.

1. First make the hollandaise sauce. Leave it to cool by putting the bowl of sauce into a larger bowl filled with iced water.

2. Put the salmon in a large pan and add cold water just to cover. Bring to the boil, then cover the pan and simmer the fish for 2 minutes. Remove the pan from the heat and leave for another 5 minutes. Strain off the liquid and leave the salmon to cool. Flake the flesh, keeping the pieces as large as possible. Discard the skin.

3. Wash the spinach, then, without draining it too thoroughly, put it in a pan. Place the pan over a medium heat and push the spinach down with a wooden spoon – it will wilt down quite quickly. When it has completely collapsed leave it to cool, then squeeze out as much liquid as you can.

4. Preheat the oven to 200°C/Fan 180°C/Gas 6. Roll out the puff pastry. Arrange half of the salmon over the bottom half of the pastry, leaving a 2cm border along the bottom edge. Season with salt and pepper, and top with half the spinach. Stir the lemon zest and the tarragon, if using, into the hollandaise, then spread half of the hollandaise over the spinach. Repeat these layers with the remaining salmon, spinach and hollandaise.

5. Brush the border and exposed pastry with beaten egg. Fold the pastry over and roll the edges to seal. Trim off any excess. Brush the pie with beaten egg and cut a few slits along the top of the pastry.

6. Bake the pie in the oven for 35–45 minutes, or until the pastry has puffed up and is a rich golden-brown, and the filling is piping hot.

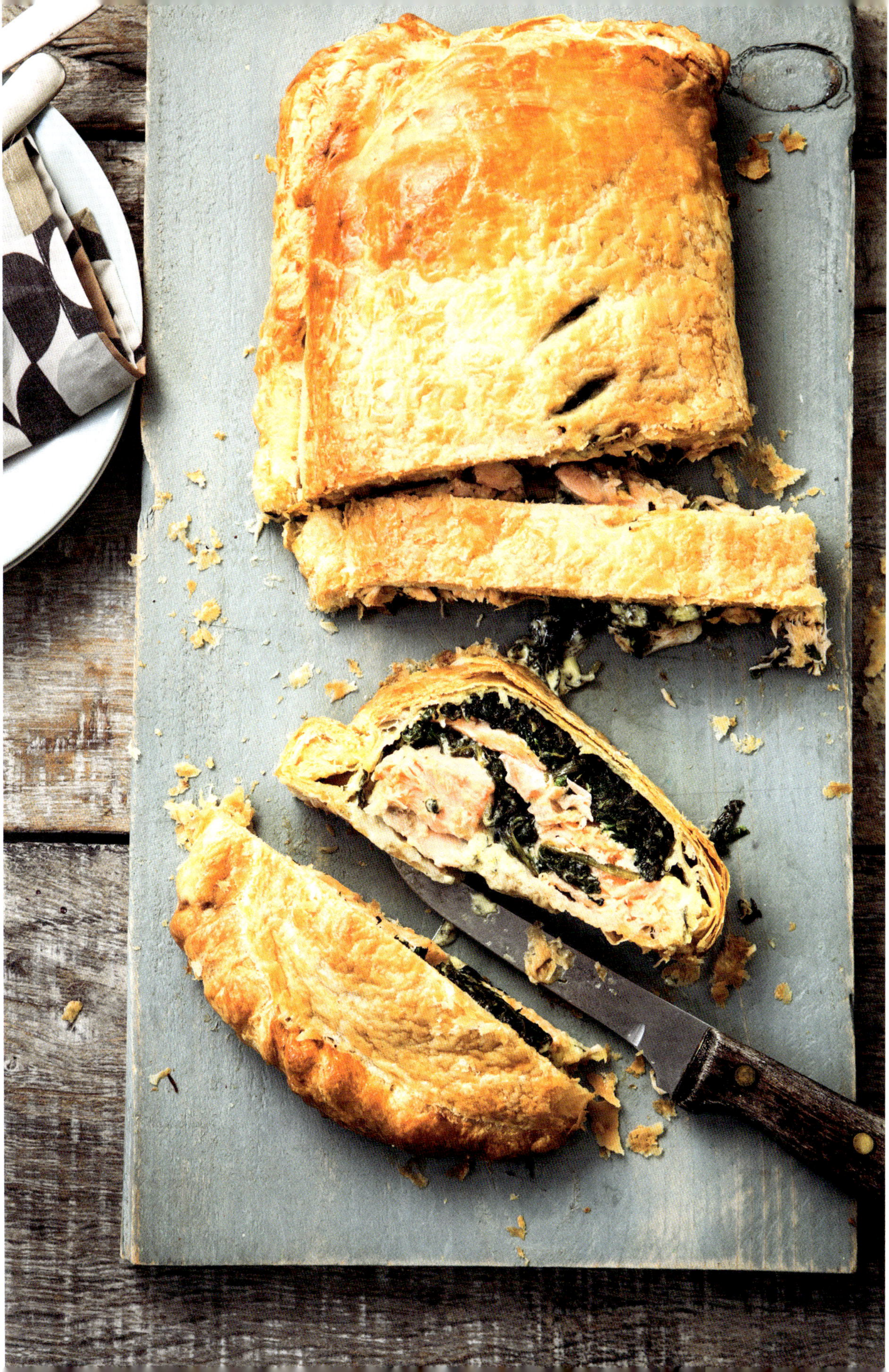

Chicken, ham & leek pie

SERVES 6

450ml chicken stock
3 skinless, boneless chicken breasts
75g butter
2 leeks, trimmed and cut into 1cm slices
2 garlic cloves, finely chopped
50g plain flour
200ml whole milk
2–3 tbsp white wine (optional)
150ml double cream
150g thickly sliced ham, cut into 2cm chunks
salt and black pepper

PASTRY
500g shortcrust pastry (shop-bought or make your own – see p.265)
flour, for dusting
1 egg, beaten, to glaze

A great favourite from our **Chicken & Egg** *book. this is one of the best of all pies I reckon. And if you like, you could make it with leftover turkey for a fabulous post-Christmas treat. Just miss out the first step and add chunks of cooked turkey with the ham.*

1. Heat the stock in a saucepan. Add the chicken and bring the stock to a low simmer, then cover the pan and cook for 10 minutes. Remove the breasts and set them aside, then pour the stock into a jug for later.

2. Melt 25g of the butter in a large saucepan. Stir in the leeks and fry them gently for 2 minutes, stirring occasionally, until just softened. Add the garlic and cook for a further minute. Add the remaining butter, then once it has melted, stir in the flour. Cook for 30 seconds, stirring constantly.

3. Slowly pour the milk into the saucepan, a little at a time, stirring well. Gradually add 250ml of the stock, then the wine, if using, and stir until the sauce is smooth and slightly thickened. Bring to a gentle simmer and cook for 3 minutes. Season the sauce to taste, then remove the pan from the heat and stir in the cream. Pour the sauce into a large bowl and cover the surface with cling film to prevent a skin forming. Set aside to cool.

4. Preheat the oven to 200°C/Fan 180°C/Gas 6. Put a baking tray in the oven to heat up.

5. Cut off about a third of the pastry to use for the lid of the pie. Roll out the remaining pastry on a lightly floured surface until it's about 5mm thick and 4cm larger than the pie dish and use it to line the pie dish. Cut the chicken breasts into bite-sized pieces and stir them and the ham and leeks into the sauce. Pour all the filling into the pie dish.

6. Roll out the rest of the pastry and lay it over the filling. Trim the edges and crimp them together, then cut a small steam hole in the top. Brush the pastry with the rest of the beaten egg. Put the dish on the preheated tray in the oven and bake for 35–40 minutes until piping hot and golden brown on top.

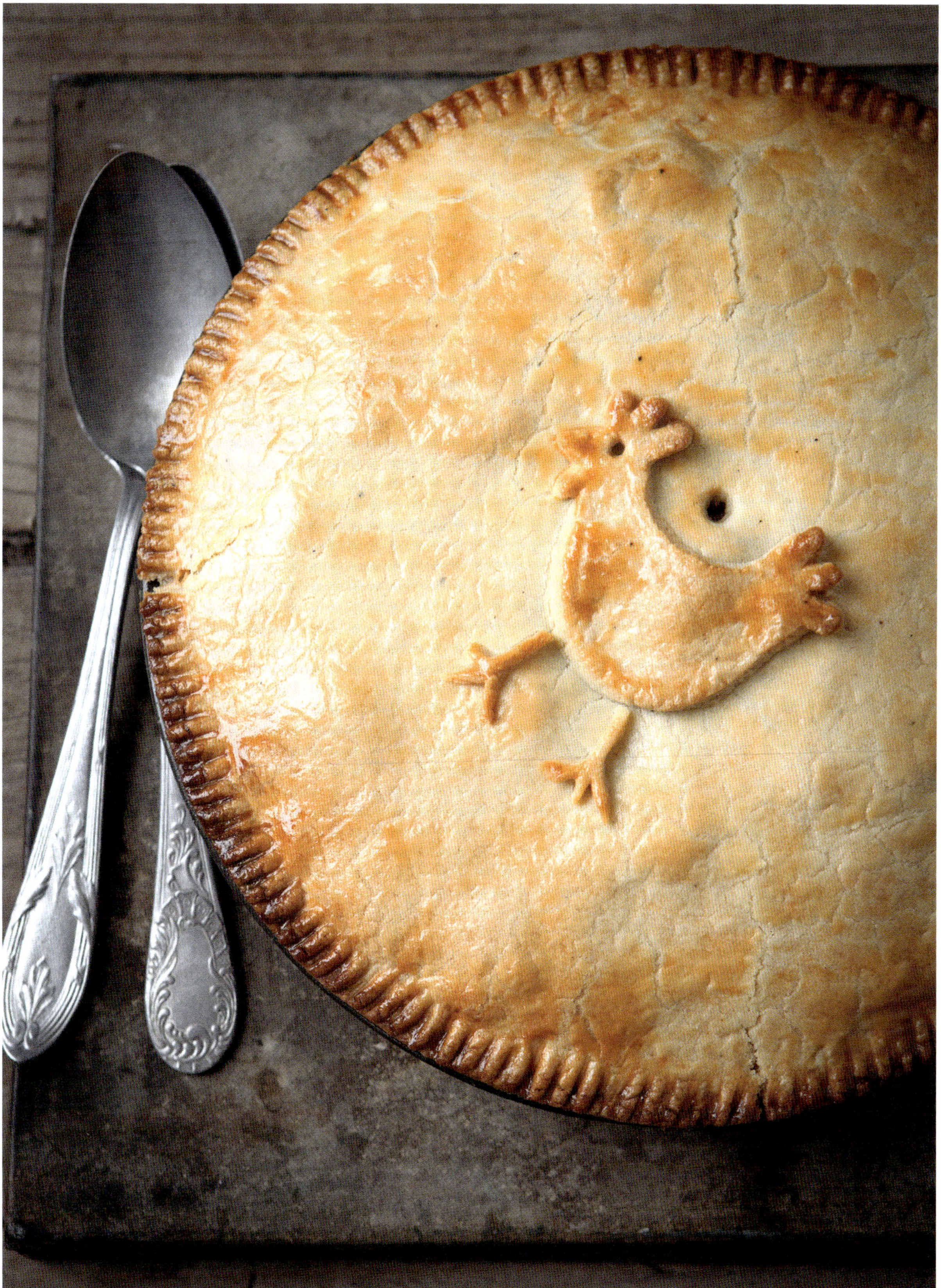

Curried chicken pie

SERVES 6

1 tbsp vegetable or coconut oil
1 large onion, diced
1 red pepper, diced
250g butternut squash or pumpkin, diced
500g skinless, boneless chicken thighs, diced
1 scotch bonnet, finely chopped
3 garlic cloves, finely chopped
15g root ginger, peeled and finely chopped
1 tsp dried thyme
1 tbsp mild Caribbean curry powder (shop-bought or see p.269)
1 tbsp plain flour
100ml chicken stock or water
200ml coconut milk
salt and black pepper

PASTRY

300g plain flour, plus extra for dusting
½ tsp ground turmeric
¼ tsp curry powder
150g lard
2–3 tbsp iced water
milk, for brushing

SALSA

2 mangos, peeled and diced
1 red onion
juice and zest of 1 lime
½ scotch bonnet, finely diced
parsley leaves
a few mint sprigs

Curry and pie – two of my very favourite things and here they are, all in one lush plateful. The curry has a Caribbean flavour and it's all encased in a special turmeric-spiced pastry. And to complete the Caribbean vibe, serve the zesty mango salsa on the side.

1. To make the filling, heat the oil in a large flameproof casserole dish and add the onion, pepper and squash. Cook for several minutes until the onion is starting to look translucent, then add the chicken, scotch bonnet, garlic and ginger. Season with salt and pepper. Stir until the chicken is browned, then add the thyme, curry powder and flour. Stir until a paste forms around the chicken and vegetables.

2. Stir in the stock or water, followed by the coconut milk. Bring to the boil, then turn down the heat and cook, stirring regularly, until the vegetables and chicken are cooked through and the sauce has reduced down – this will take about 15 minutes. Leave to cool completely.

3. To make the pastry, mix the flour, turmeric and curry powder with half a teaspoon of salt. Rub in the lard, then add just enough iced water to make a smooth dough. Wrap the pastry and chill it until you are ready to roll it out.

4. Preheat the oven to 200°C/Fan 180°C/Gas 6. Take two-thirds of the pastry and roll it out on a floured work surface. Use it to line a pie dish, then add the cooled filling. Brush the edges of the pastry with water.

5. Roll out the remaining pastry and place it over the filling. Press all around the edges to seal and crimp them together. Brush the pastry with milk. Bake for about 30 minutes until the pie is golden brown around the edges and piping hot.

6. For the salsa, mix everything together and season with salt and pepper. Serve the pie with the salsa on the side.

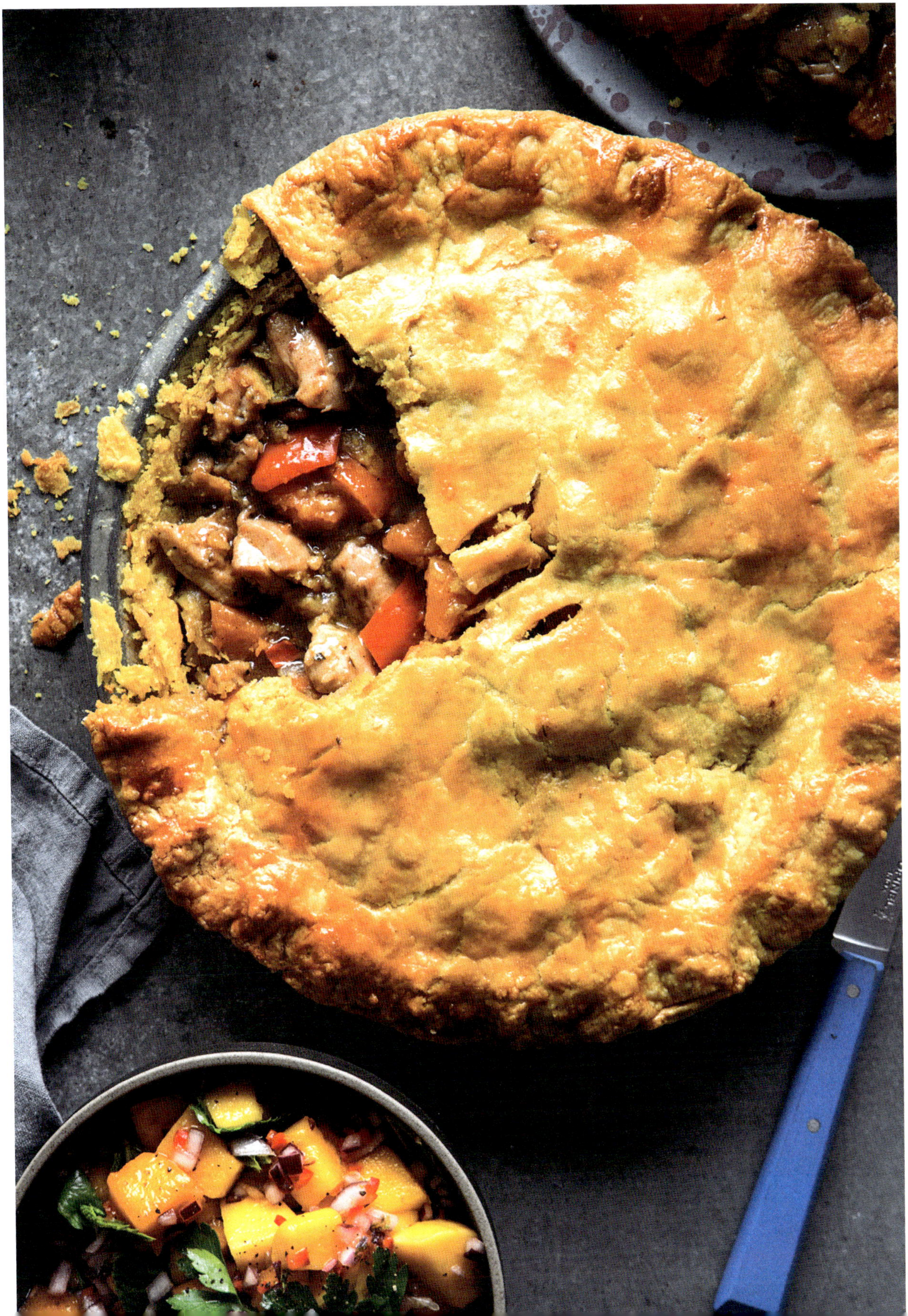

Steak & mushroom pie

SERVES 6

320g ready-rolled puff pastry
750g braising steak, diced
50g plain flour
3 tbsp olive oil
300g chestnut mushrooms, halved
1 large onion, finely chopped
3 garlic cloves, chopped
1 large thyme sprig
2 bay leaves
300ml red wine
300ml beef stock
1 tsp Worcestershire sauce
½ tsp Dijon mustard
1 can of smoked mussels or oysters (optional)
1 egg, beaten with 1 tbsp water
salt and black pepper

We wrote this recipe for a top-crust pie to fill the brief for our **One Pot Wonders** *book, cooking the filling in a casserole dish or ovenproof pan, then covering it with ready-rolled puff. Of course, if you're not bothered about this being one pot, feel free to cook the filling in whatever pan you like, then bake the pie in a pie dish. More washing up though! You might be surprised at the idea of oysters and mussels, but they are a traditional addition to steak pies and add a nice smoky flavour. Go on – give them a try.*

1. Unroll the pastry and cut a round or rectangle that will fit snugly into your flameproof casserole dish or pan. Lay it on a piece of greaseproof paper and put it in the fridge to chill until needed. If you're feeling artistic, use the scraps to cut out decorations for the top of the pie.

2. Season the steak with salt and pepper and dust it with flour. Pat off any excess. Heat a tablespoon of the oil in your casserole dish or pan and fry the steak until nicely browned. It's best to do this in a couple of batches so you don't overcrowd the dish. Remove the browned meat and set it aside, then add the remaining oil and briskly fry the mushrooms. When they're brown, remove them and set aside, then add the onion. Turn down the heat and cook the onion until soft, then stir in the chopped garlic and cook for another couple of minutes.

3. Put the beef back in the dish or pan and add the thyme and bay leaves. Turn up the heat and pour in the red wine. Leave it to bubble for a few minutes, then add the beef stock, Worcestershire sauce and mustard – the steak should be just about covered with liquid. Season with salt and pepper.

4. Bring to the boil, then turn down the heat to a simmer and put the lid on the dish or cover tightly with foil. Leave to simmer for an hour and a half, checking regularly to make sure the mixture isn't sticking. Add the cooked mushrooms and continue to simmer for another 30 minutes or until the beef is tender. Remove the lid and simmer to reduce the liquid – it needs to be the consistency of gravy. Set the dish aside so the beef can cool down.

5. When you want to finish cooking the pie, preheat the oven to 200°C/Fan 180°C/Gas 6. Roughly chop the mussels or oysters, if using, and scatter them on top of the beef. Lay the pastry over the top and add any decoration, then brush with beaten egg. Cut a couple of slits in the centre of the pastry.

6. Bake in the oven for 35–40 minutes until the pastry is a rich golden brown and well risen and the filling is piping hot and bubbling.

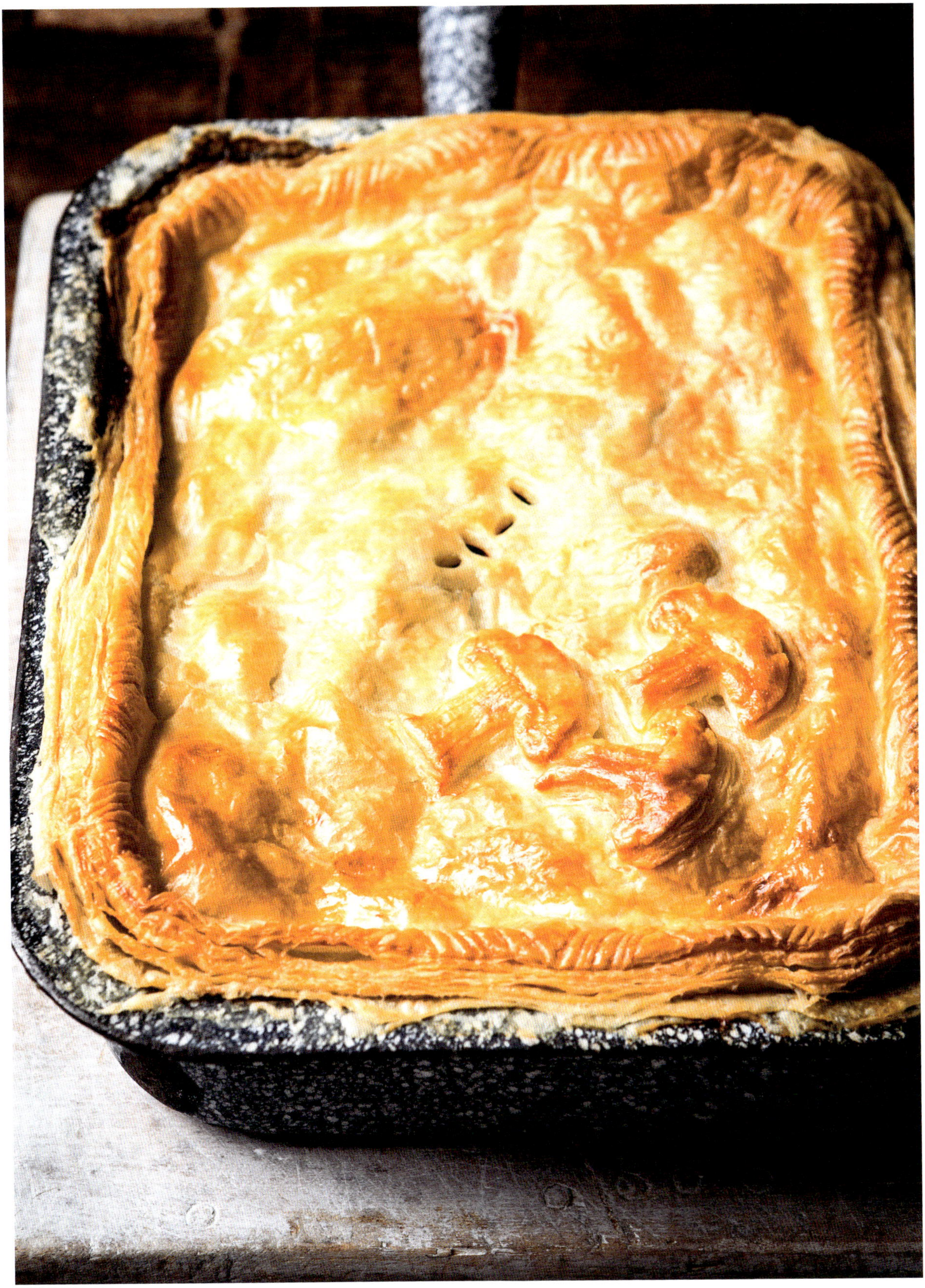

Cumberland sausage pie

SERVES 4–6

8 Cumberland sausages (about 500g)
3 tbsp olive oil
15g butter
1 large onion, diced
2 large carrots, diced
2 celery sticks, diced
1 tbsp plain flour
2 tbsp tomato purée
100ml red wine
400ml beef stock
1 tsp Worcestershire sauce
2 bay leaves
1 large thyme sprig
1–2 tbsp Cumberland sauce
1 tsp orange zest (optional)
salt and black pepper

TOPPING

1kg floury potatoes, cut into chunks
30g butter
1 bunch of spring onions, cut into rounds
1 tbsp Dijon mustard (optional)
50ml single cream
100g Cheddar cheese, grated

A really tasty, family-friendly meal, this is basically a shepherd's pie with a filling of sausage balls and plenty of juicy veg. Add a topping of cheesy mash and you have proper comfort food.

1. Skin the sausages. Divide each sausage into 4 and roll the pieces into balls. Heat a tablespoon of the oil in a pan and lightly fry the sausage balls until browned on all sides, then set them aside.

2. Heat the remaining olive oil with the butter in a large pan or a flameproof casserole dish. Add the vegetables and sauté them for a few minutes, until well coated with the oil and butter. Cover and then leave to cook, stirring regularly, until tender – this will take at least 10 minutes.

3. Stir in the flour, then when it has disappeared into the oil, stir in the tomato purée. Turn up the heat and cook for a couple of minutes, stirring constantly, then pour in the red wine. Bring to the boil and continue to stir, then add the stock, Worcestershire sauce and herbs. Stir in the Cumberland sauce and the orange zest, if using, then add the sausage balls. Season with plenty of salt and pepper.

4. Bring to the boil, then turn the heat down to a simmer. Cook the mixture for 20 minutes until it has reduced down a bit and thickened. Stir every so often to make sure it doesn't catch on the bottom.

5. Meanwhile, make the topping. Bring a large saucepan of water to the boil. Add the potatoes, season with plenty of salt and cook until tender. Preheat the oven to 200°C/Fan 180°C/Gas 6.

6. Drain the potatoes and mash them until nice and smooth. Melt the butter in a saucepan and add the spring onions. Fry until they start to soften, then add the potatoes to the pan with the mustard, if using, and the cream. Beat together until well combined.

7. Spoon the filling into a pie dish or casserole dish. Spread the mashed potato over the top, then rough it up with a fork. Sprinkle with the grated cheese. Bake in the oven for 25–30 minutes until well browned and piping hot.

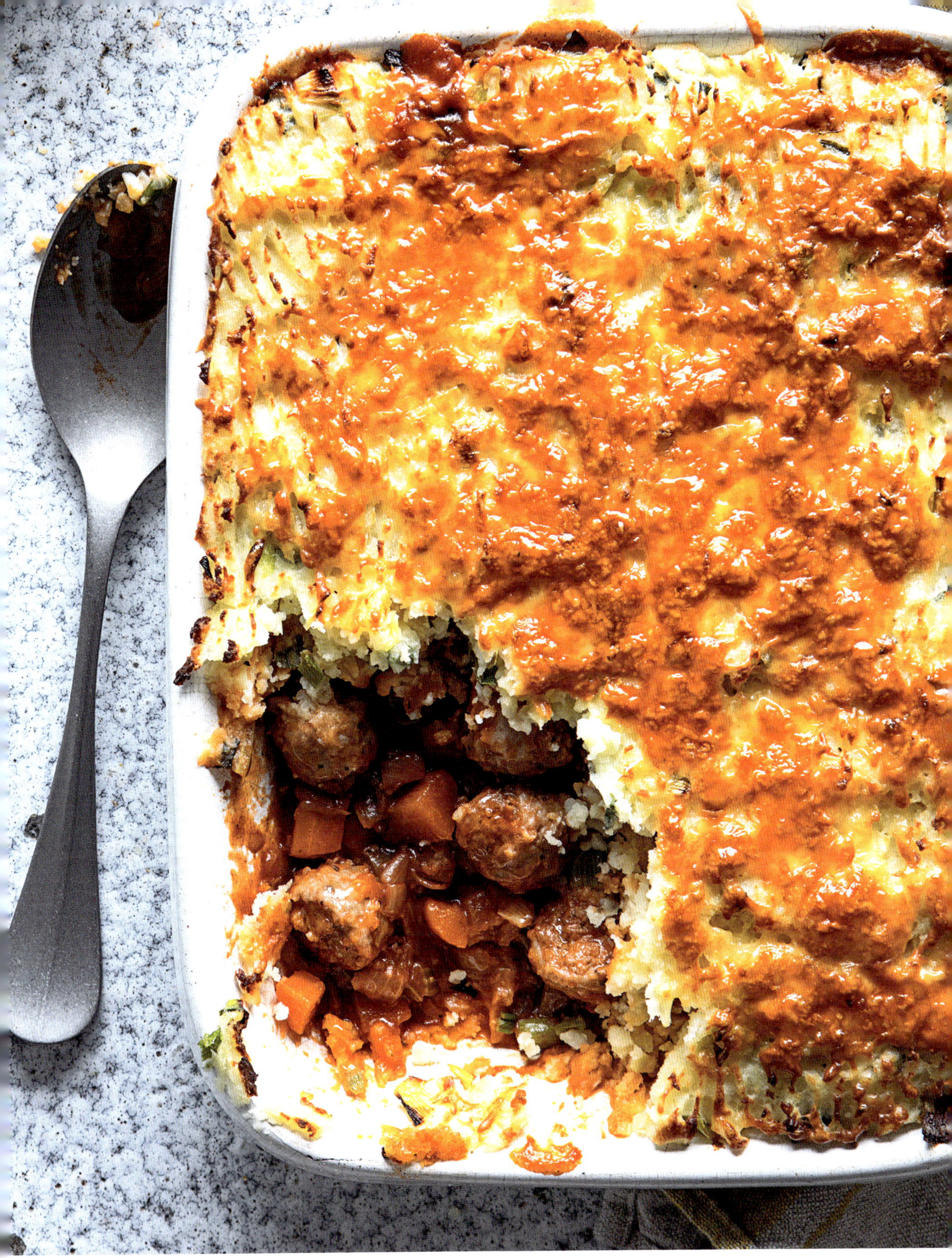

Shepherd's or cottage pie

SERVES 4–6

about 600g leftover roast meat
1 tbsp olive oil
1 large onion, finely diced
2 carrots, finely diced
1 celery stick, finely diced
2 garlic cloves, finely chopped
1 large rosemary sprig, leaves finely chopped
1 thyme sprig, leaves finely chopped
300ml red wine
1 tbsp tomato purée or ketchup
300ml leftover gravy or stock
dash of Worcestershire sauce
salt and black pepper

TOPPING

1kg floury potatoes, cut into chunks
large knob of butter, plus extra for dotting on top of the pie

I've always believed that shepherd's and cottage pies were invented as a thrifty way of eking out any leftover Sunday roast into a satisfying meal for Monday. I do know that leftover roast meat makes a much better pie than mince, but if you don't have any leftovers, use finely diced fresh meat. This pie is topped with regular mash, but you could try a topping of mashed sweet potato or other root veg for a change if you like.

1. Chop all the meat into small dice. This is best done by hand, but if you want to use a food processor, cut the meat into slices first, then process it very carefully, as you don't want it chopped too fine.

2. Heat the oil in a large saucepan or a flameproof casserole dish. Add the onion, carrots and celery, then fry them gently over a medium heat for up to 10 minutes, until they are softening and just starting to take on some colour.

3. Turn up the heat, add the meat and cook it over a medium heat for a few minutes. Keep the stirring to a minimum at first until the underside is well browned, then stir until it's well coloured. Add the garlic and herbs and season with salt and pepper.

4. Pour in the wine and let it bubble until it has reduced almost completely, then add the purée or ketchup, gravy or stock and the Worcestershire sauce. Bring the mixture to the boil, then turn down the heat and simmer for about 20 minutes. Keep an eye on it and if the mixture looks as if it is drying out, add a little more stock or water. Preheat the oven to 200°C/Fan 180°C/Gas 6.

5. Meanwhile, make the topping. Bring a large saucepan of water to the boil. Add the potatoes, season with plenty of salt and cook until tender. Drain and tip them back into the pan, then add the butter. Mash until smooth, adding a tiny bit of milk if they appear dry – they shouldn't be.

6. Pour the filling into an ovenproof dish (about 30 x 20 x 5cm). Using a spatula, spread the potatoes over the top in as even a layer as possible, then rough up the surface with a fork. Dot with butter.

7. Put the dish on a baking tray and bake the pie in the oven for 25–30 minutes until it's piping hot inside and well browned on top.

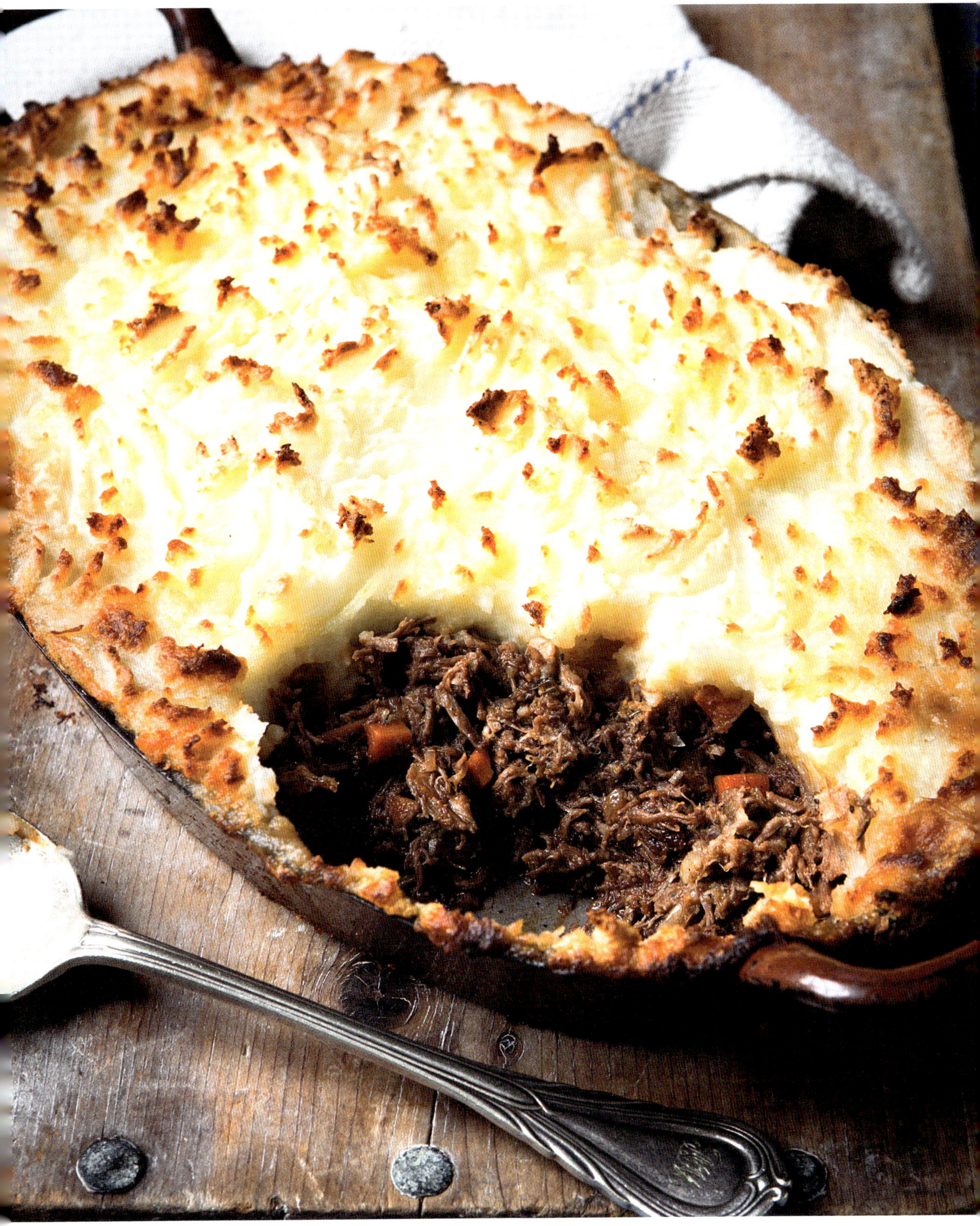

Fish & chorizo traybake

SERVES 4

2 red onions, cut into wedges
2 red peppers, cut into thick strips
2 large courgettes, cut into chunks
2 tbsp olive oil
zest of 1 lemon
3 thyme sprigs
100ml red wine
2 x 400g cans of butter beans, drained
250g cherry tomatoes
salt and black pepper

FISH & CRUST

100g chorizo, skinned and sliced
100g breadcrumbs
1 garlic clove, finely chopped
a few basil leaves
4 fairly thick fillets of white fish, such as cod, haddock or hake, skinned

Dave and I first cooked fish with a chorizo crust many years ago on one of our early filming trips. It's such an easy way of cooking fish and it's been really popular, so it seemed like a good idea to take the basic idea and make it into a tasty traybake with lots of lovely veg. It's a winner.

1. Preheat the oven to 200°C/Fan 180°C/Gas 6. Arrange the onions, peppers and courgettes in a roasting tin and drizzle over the oil. Sprinkle the lemon zest over the veg and mix thoroughly. Add the thyme sprigs to the tin and season with salt and pepper, then roast in the oven for 20 minutes.

2. Pour in the red wine and add the butter beans to the tin, then put it back in the oven for a further 10 minutes.

3. Meanwhile, make the crust. Put the chorizo in a dry frying pan and fry until it's crisp and much of the fat has rendered out. Drain on kitchen paper.

4. When the chorizo is cool, put it in a food processor with the breadcrumbs, garlic and basil leaves. Blitz until the mixture is finely textured and has a paste-like quality. Season the fish fillets, then press some chorizo mixture on top of each one.

5. Add the fish fillets to the roasting tin and dot the cherry tomatoes around them. Put the tin back in the oven for a further 15 minutes until the fish is cooked through and the topping is nicely browned.

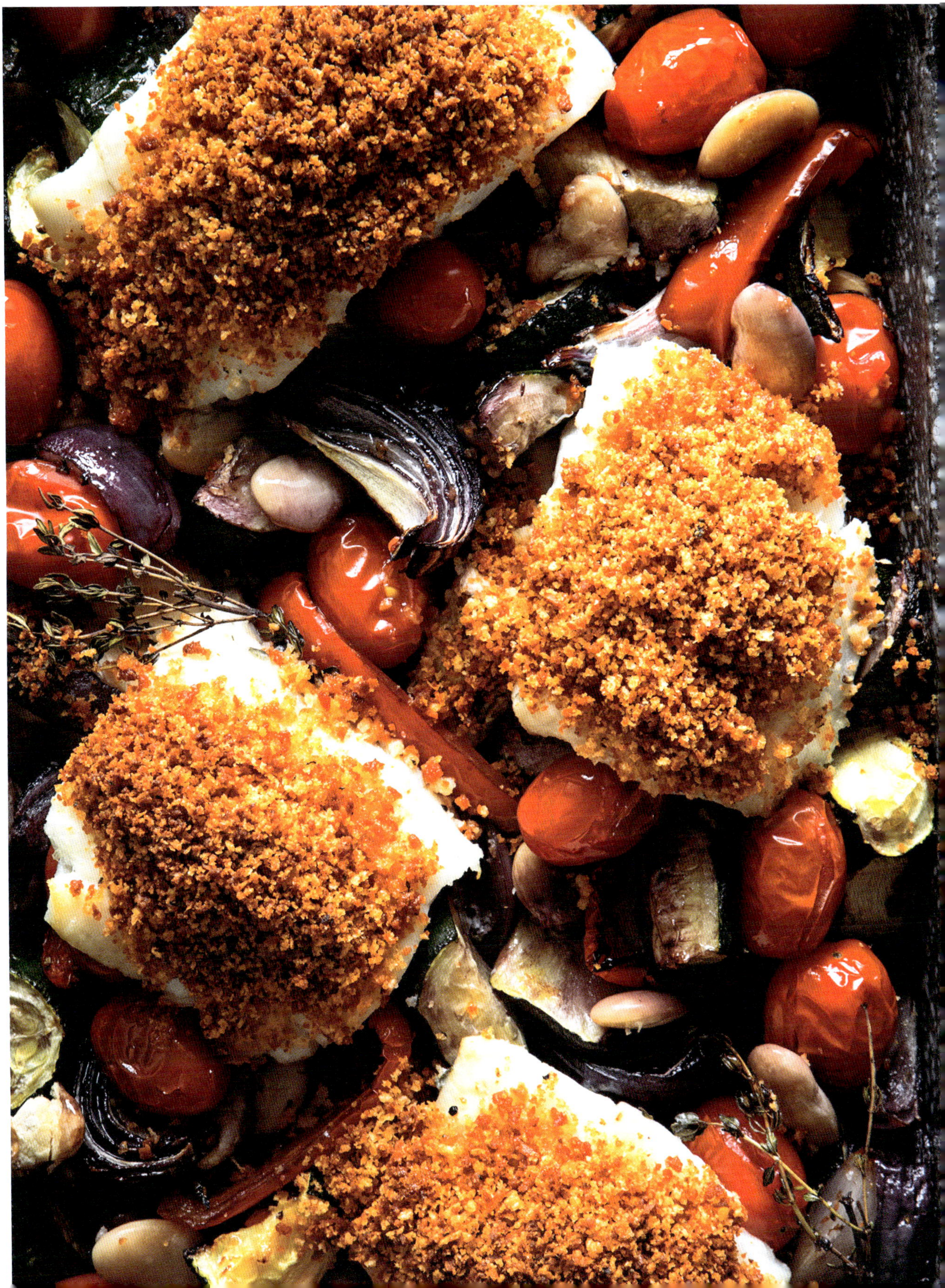

Chicken & sausage traybake

SERVES 4

4 chicken thighs, bone in and skin on
4–6 meaty pork sausages
500g piece of pumpkin or squash, cut into wedges
2 onions, cut into wedges
a few thyme sprigs or 1 tsp dried thyme
1 tbsp olive oil, plus extra to drizzle
50ml red wine
1 tbsp maple syrup
1 tsp red wine vinegar
½ tsp chilli flakes (optional)
200g chestnut mushrooms, halved
salt and black pepper

This one-pot wonder takes moments to put together, then you can just whack it in the oven and wait for the magic to happen. Full of flavour, it's a deeply satisfying dish that you'll make again and again.

1. Preheat the oven to 220°C/Fan 200°C/Gas 7.

2. Place the chicken thighs skin-side up in a roasting tin with the sausages, pumpkin or squash and the onions and season them all with salt and pepper. Sprinkle the thyme over everything and drizzle over the tablespoon of olive oil. Mix the red wine with 100ml of water and pour it into the tin, then place the tin in the oven and roast for 30 minutes.

3. Remove and turn the sausages so they can brown all over. Mix the maple syrup with the vinegar and spoon it over the contents of the roasting tin. Sprinkle over the chilli flakes, if using, then add the mushrooms and drizzle with a little more olive oil.

4. Roast for a further 25–30 minutes until everything is cooked through and well browned.

5. Serve the chicken, sausages and veg with any pan juices spooned over them and a good pile of greens.

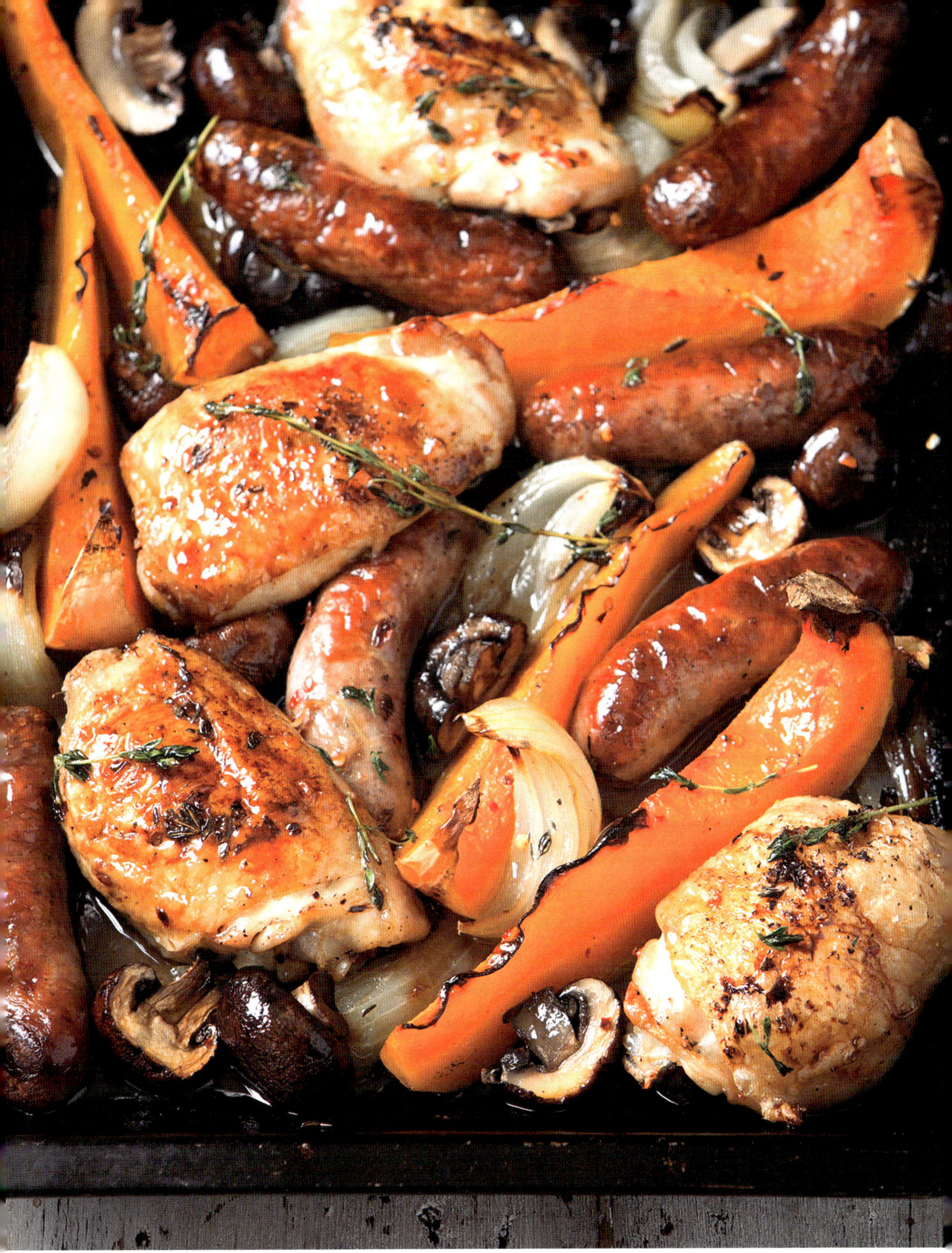

Traybake Christmas dinner

SERVES 4

4 chicken thighs, bone in and skin on
olive oil
1 large onion, sliced into wedges
salt and black pepper

STUFFING BALLS
15g butter
1 onion, finely chopped
35g dried cranberries
50ml just-boiled water
50g cooked chestnuts (vacuum-packed are fine), crumbled
75g breadcrumbs
1 tsp dried thyme
1 egg

PIGS IN BLANKETS
4 slices of streaky bacon
8 chipolatas

VEGETABLES
3 floury potatoes, cut into chunks
2 parsnips, cut into chunks
3 carrots, cut into batons
25g lard, dripping or duck fat

TO SERVE
chicken gravy (see p.272)
cranberry relish (see p.265)

Here's a Christmas dinner all cooked in a couple of roasting tins – chicken, pigs in blankets, stuffing balls and a selection of veggies. Great for a stress-free feast on the day or for a winter Sunday lunch. If Christmas dinner is incomplete for you without Brussels sprouts, add some to the veg. Cut them in half, toss them in oil and add them half way through the cooking time.

1. Preheat the oven to 200°C/Fan 180°C/Gas 6.

2. First make the stuffing balls. Melt the butter in a frying pan and add the finely chopped onion. Sauté until very soft and translucent, then remove the pan from the heat. Put the cranberries in a small bowl, cover with the just-boiled water, then leave to soften and swell. The cranberries should absorb all the water but if not, drain them. Put the onion and cranberries in a bowl with the remaining ingredients, then season and mix thoroughly. Shape the mixture into 8 balls.

3. For the pigs in blankets, cut each piece of bacon in half and stretch each half out with the flat side of a knife. Wrap each stretched half around a chipolata.

4. Season the chicken thighs and rub the skins with olive oil. Place the onion wedges in the base of a roasting tin and drizzle with oil. Arrange the chicken thighs, pigs in blankets and stuffing balls on top of the onion.

5. Now prepare the vegetables. Bring a large saucepan of salted water to the boil. Add the potatoes, followed by the parsnips, then the carrots and simmer for 5 minutes. Drain thoroughly. Shake the pan around a bit to fluff up the edges of the potatoes and parsnips.

6. Put the lard, dripping or duck fat in another roasting tin and place it in the oven. When the fat is smoking hot, remove the tin from the oven and add all the vegetables. Shake the tin to distribute the veg evenly and season with salt and black pepper.

7. Put both roasting tins in the oven, with the chicken on the top shelf and the vegetables below. Roast for 40–45 minutes, checking regularly and turning the tins round to make sure everything cooks evenly and is well browned, Serve with plenty of gravy and some cranberry relish.

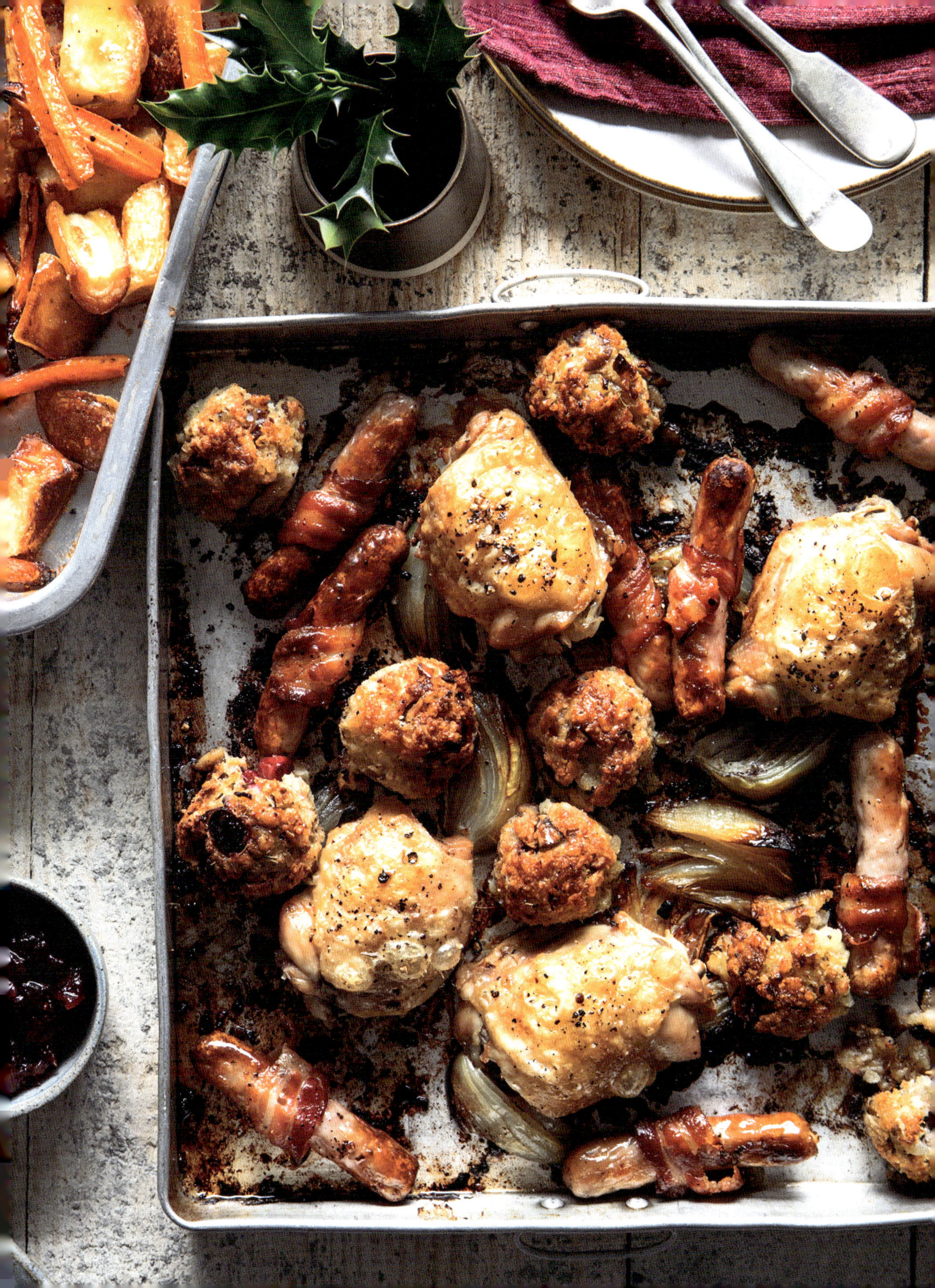

1 **Crunchy palak paneer**...144
2 **Cauliflower tikka masala**...146
3 **Auntie Daeng's green curry**...148
4 **Keralan king prawn curry**...150
5 **Chicken tikka masala**...152
6 **Lamb kofte vindaloo**...154
7 **Extra-special lamb biryani**...156
8 **Lamb pasanda**...158
9 **Traditional lamb saag**...160
10 **Dry Keralan beef curry**...162

curries

❝ *Who doesn't love a curry! Dave and I first became mates over a curry in a pub and these fragrant, spicy dishes were always among our favourite things to cook and share.* ❞

Crunchy palak paneer

SERVES 4

3 tbsp coconut oil or ghee
2 medium onions, finely chopped
20g root ginger, finely grated
3 garlic cloves, finely chopped
1 tsp ground cumin
1 tsp ground coriander
1 tsp ground turmeric
1 whole green chilli, split lengthways
400g can of chopped tomatoes
1 tsp caster sugar
400g young spinach leaves
salt and black pepper

PANEER

1 tsp garam masala (shop-bought or see p.269)
3 tbsp semolina
220g paneer
3–4 tbsp coconut or olive oil
squeeze of fresh lemon juice, about 1 tsp

Paneer is a fresh soft cheese that's used in many Indian vegetarian dishes. It's much more readily available than it was when we first published this recipe more than a decade ago, and you'll find it in many supermarkets. It absorbs flavours well and with a crunchy coating of spiced semolina it combines beautifully with the juicy mix of spinach, tomatoes and spices.

1. Heat the oil or ghee in a large saucepan. Gently fry the onions with the ginger and garlic for 6–8 minutes until they are soft and very lightly coloured, stirring regularly.

2. Add all the dry spices, the whole chilli and a teaspoon of salt and fry for another minute, stirring. Tip the chopped tomatoes into the pan and add the sugar. Bring to a gentle simmer, then cook for 20 minutes, stirring regularly, until the sauce is well reduced. Taste and add some extra salt and pepper if necessary.

3. While the sauce is cooking, mix the garam masala with the semolina in a large bowl. Cut the paneer into pieces roughly the size of a stock cube and add them to the bowl. Toss well to coat all the cubes.

4. Add enough of the oil to cover the base of a large frying pan and place it over a medium heat. Fry the cubes of paneer for 4–5 minutes, turning occasionally, until they are browned and crisp on all sides.

5. Stir the spinach into the pan with the spiced tomato sauce and cook for about 2–3 minutes, stirring until the leaves are well wilted. Tip the sauce and spinach into a warmed serving dish and gently toss with the paneer. Add a squeeze of lemon juice to sharpen the flavour and serve at once.

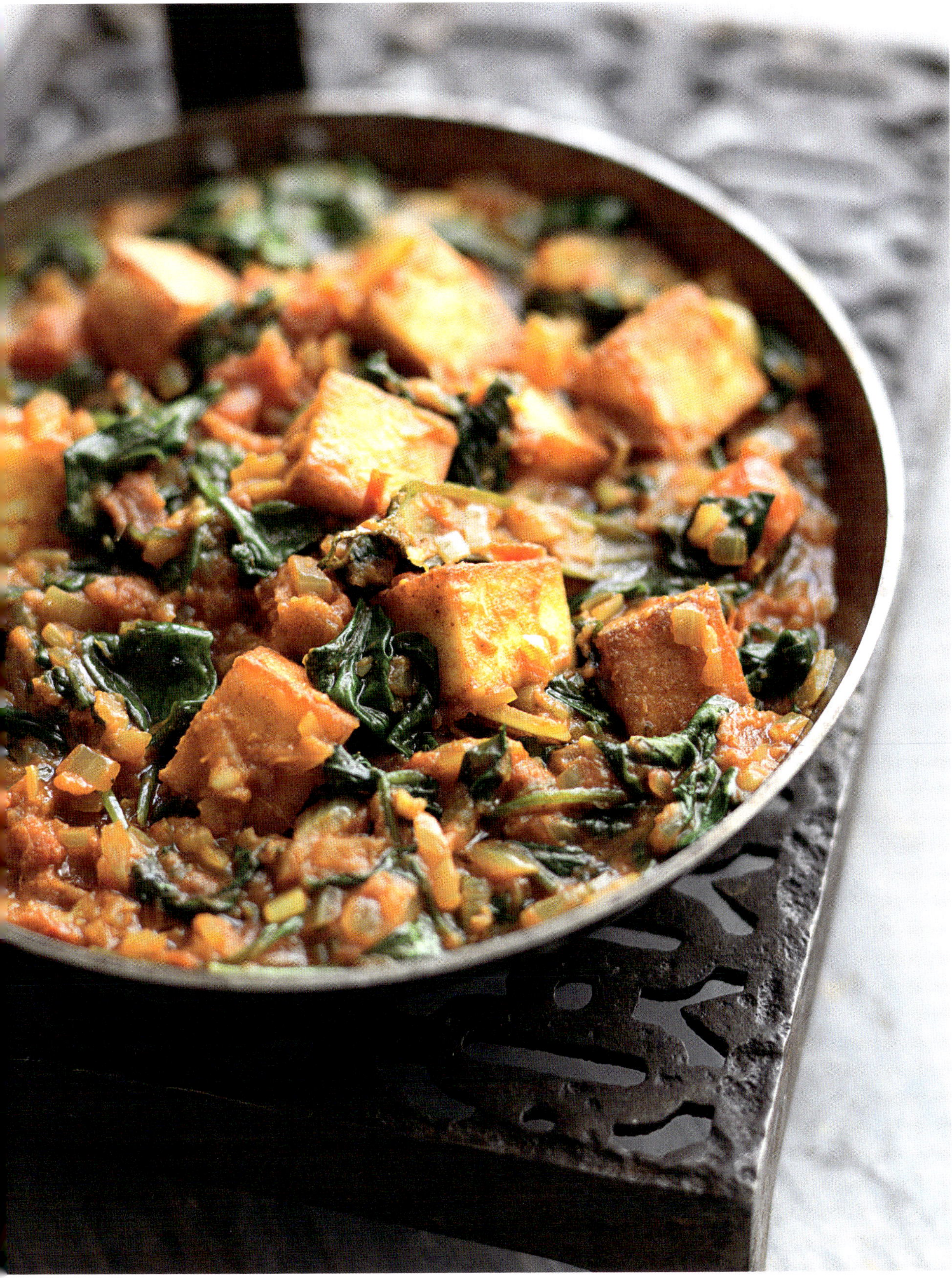

Cauliflower tikka masala

SERVES 4

1 large cauliflower, broken into florets
400g can of chickpeas, drained (optional)

MARINADE
150ml Greek yoghurt
1 tbsp olive oil
juice of 1 lemon
1 tsp Kashmiri chilli powder
1 tsp garam masala
½ tsp nigella seeds
salt and black pepper

SAUCE
1 onion, finely chopped
3 garlic cloves, finely chopped
15g root ginger, chopped
1 tbsp coconut or olive oil
1 tsp Kashmiri chilli powder
1 tsp ground cumin
1 tsp ground coriander
1 tsp garam masala
½ tsp ground cinnamon
¼ tsp ground cloves
800ml passata or 2 x 400g cans of tomatoes puréed until smooth
50g butter (optional)
50ml double cream
pinch of sugar (optional)

TO SERVE
coriander leaves
lemon wedges
naan bread or basmati rice

Chicken tikka masala is one of the most popular curries, so it made sense to us to come up with a vegetarian version for our **Veggie Feasts** *book. The cauli florets are marinated, then bathed in a spicy sauce and you can add some chickpeas too, if you like, for a bit of extra protein. Totally epic and great served with naan bread or rice.*

1. Preheat the oven to 200°C/Fan 180°C/Gas 6. Mix all the ingredients for the marinade together in a bowl and season with salt and pepper. Add the cauliflower florets and turn them over in the marinade until completely coated. Place them, well spaced out, on a baking tray and roast for 20–25 minutes, turning them over halfway through, until lightly browned and tender to the point of a knife.

2. To make the sauce, purée the onion, garlic and ginger together in a food processor until smooth. Heat the oil in a large saucepan and add the purée. Fry for a few minutes, stirring regularly, until it thickens, then sprinkle in all the spices and fry for another couple of minutes.

3. Pour in the passata or puréed tomatoes and season with salt and pepper. Bring to the boil, then turn the heat down and simmer for a few minutes until the sauce has reduced by about a third.

4. Add the butter, if using, and whisk to make sure it combines with the sauce. Stir in the cream, then taste. If the sauce tastes acidic, add a pinch of sugar. Add the cauliflower and the chickpeas, if using, and cook for a few minutes to make sure everything is piping hot but don't let it boil. Garnish with plenty of coriander and lemon wedges and serve with naan bread or basmati rice.

BIKER TIP

You can adapt this to make a good vegan dish. Use plant-based yoghurt in the marinade, leave out the butter and use plant-based yoghurt in the sauce instead of cream.

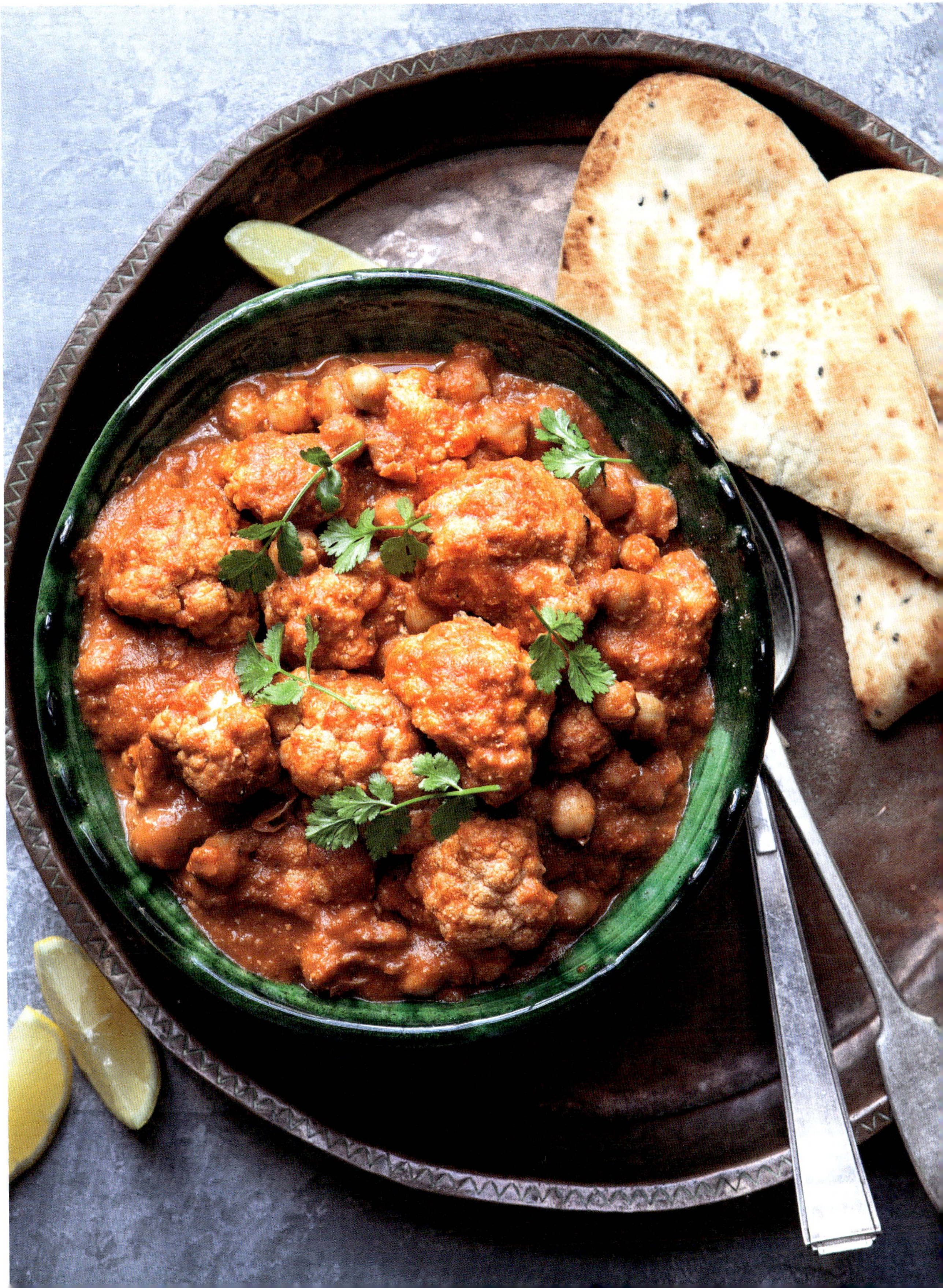

Auntie Daeng's green curry

SERVES 4

vegetable oil
50g green curry paste (see below)
600ml coconut milk
50g coconut cream, grated
3 tbsp Thai fish sauce
2 tbsp grated palm sugar
2 long green Thai chillies, deseeded and chopped
6 kaffir lime leaves, cut into very thin strips
5 apple aubergines
400g shelled raw prawns

GREEN CURRY PASTE

1 tbsp coriander seeds
1 tsp cumin seeds
1 tsp dry white peppercorns
15 green chillies (add a small amount first and taste, as they vary in heat)
1 tsp salt
1 tsp finely chopped galangal
1 tbsp crushed lemongrass
½ tsp grated kaffir lime zest or ordinary lime zest
1 tsp grated coriander root
9 garlic cloves, crushed
3 Thai shallots (or 1 banana shallot), finely chopped
1 tsp shrimp paste

TO SERVE

handful of Thai basil, torn (optional)
Thai rice

When Dave and I were filming our **Asian Adventure** *series we went to a little restaurant in Bangkok run by the amazing Chef Chanchavee Skulkant, affectionately known as Auntie Daeng. We were told she used to cook for the Thai royal family, then opened her own place serving amazing traditional food at very reasonable prices. I don't know if the restaurant is still there but she was kind enough to share her green curry recipe with us and it is so good. I like to make it with prawns, but you could also use some fish or diced chicken, pork or beef. The apple aubergines are smaller than the ones we're used to and you can find them in Asian stores. You could also use pea aubergines which are even smaller. I suggest making the green curry paste before you start the rest of the recipe.*

1. To make the green curry paste, put the coriander and cumin seeds in a mortar with the peppercorns and crush them. Tip them out and set aside, then add the chopped green chillies and salt to the mortar and pound with the pestle to make a paste.

2. Add the galangal, lemongrass, lime zest and coriander root and continue to pound. Mix in the crushed seeds, then the garlic, shallots and shrimp paste and pound everything to a paste. If you don't have the energy of the amazing Auntie Daeng, you could do all this in a food processor.

3. For the curry, place a wok on the heat and add a tablespoon of oil. Add 50g of the curry paste and stir-fry, then add 200ml of the coconut milk. Continue to stir fry until the pan is almost dry, then add another 200ml of coconut milk. Repeat until all the milk has been used.

4. Now add the coconut cream and stir, then cover the pan until the mixture comes to the boil. Add the fish sauce, palm sugar, green chillies and kaffir lime leaves. Cut the apple aubergines into quarters and add them to the pan. Cook until the aubergines are nearly soft, then add the prawns and cook until they have turned pink.

5. Add the Thai basil, if using, and serve with rice.

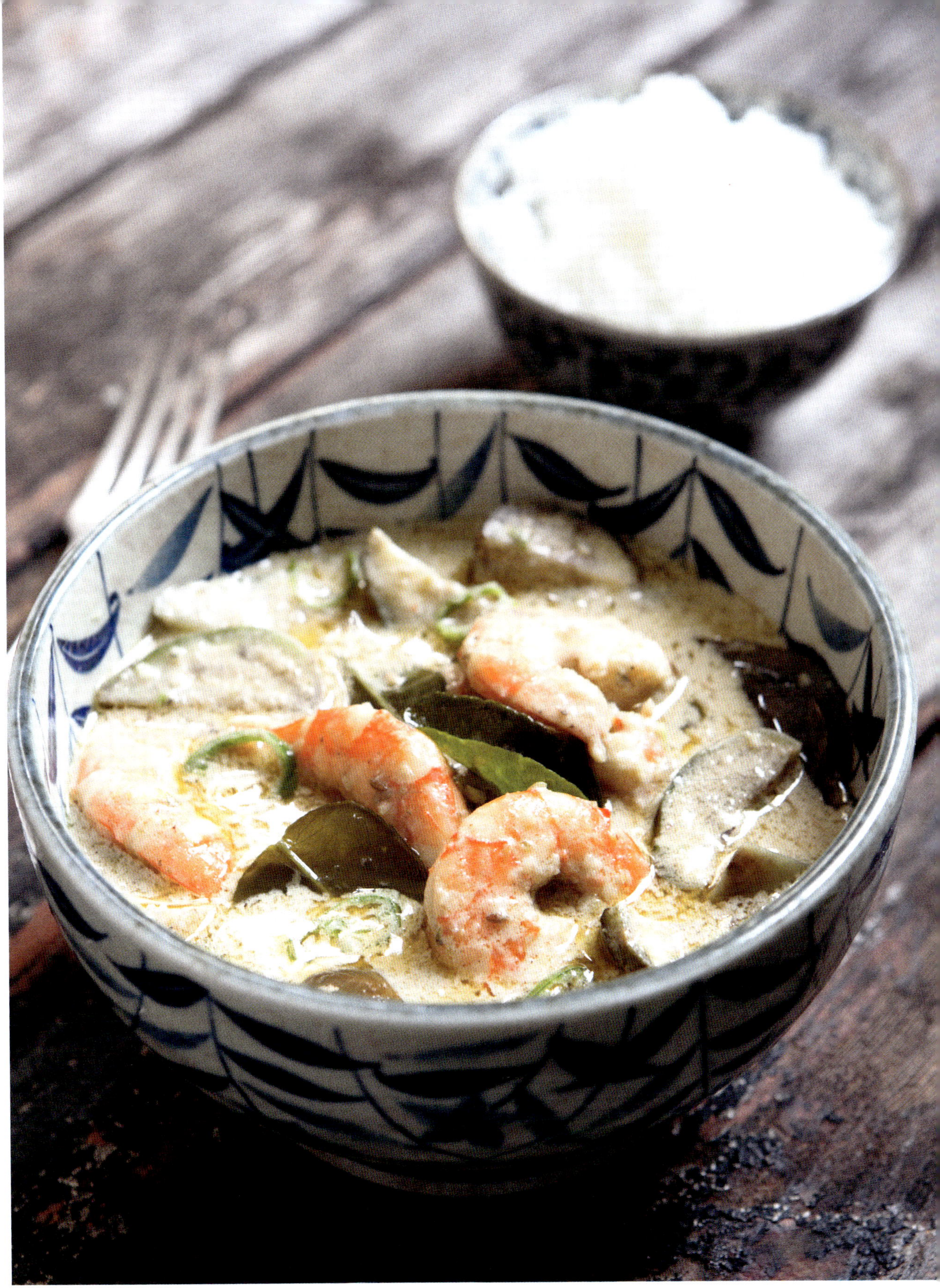

Keralan king prawn curry

SERVES 3–4

500g jumbo king prawns, defrosted
1 onion, peeled and roughly chopped
1 long red chilli, deseeded
2 garlic cloves
25g root ginger, peeled and roughly chopped
2 tbsp coconut or olive oil
12 fresh curry leaves
1 tsp black mustard seeds
½ tsp ground fenugreek
pinch of asafoetida
½ tsp ground turmeric
200ml coconut milk
juice of 1 lime
salt and black pepper

TO SERVE

4 tbsp chopped coriander leaves
1 lime, cut into wedges
basmati rice or Indian bread

Dave and I did a number of theatre tours during our career together, in which we larked about on stage and did a bit of cooking. This dish, based on the amazing curries we'd enjoyed in South India, was dead quick to make and smelled amazing so went down really well. I reckon we must have cooked it in eighty theatres around the country!

1. First peel the prawns, removing their heads but leaving the tails on to look decorative. Slit the prawns down the back and remove the black stuff – it's not good to eat.

2. Put the onion, chilli, garlic and ginger in a food processor and blitz them to a paste. You might need to remove the lid of the food processor and push the mixture down with a rubber spatula a few times.

3. Heat the oil in a frying pan over a medium heat. Add the curry leaves, mustard seeds, fenugreek and asafoetida, then fry for 20–30 seconds, or until you smell the delicious aroma. Add the onion, chilli, garlic and ginger paste and fry for another 1–2 minutes.

4. Add the turmeric, king prawns and a tablespoon of cold water and cook for 1–2 minutes or until the prawns are pink and the water has evaporated. Stir well to cover the prawns in the spice mixture.

5. Pour in the coconut milk and season to taste with salt and pepper. Bring the mixture to a simmer and cook for 1–2 minutes until the coconut milk is warmed through and the prawns are done. Squeeze over the lime juice.

6. Garnish with the chopped coriander and lime wedges and serve with rice or Indian bread.

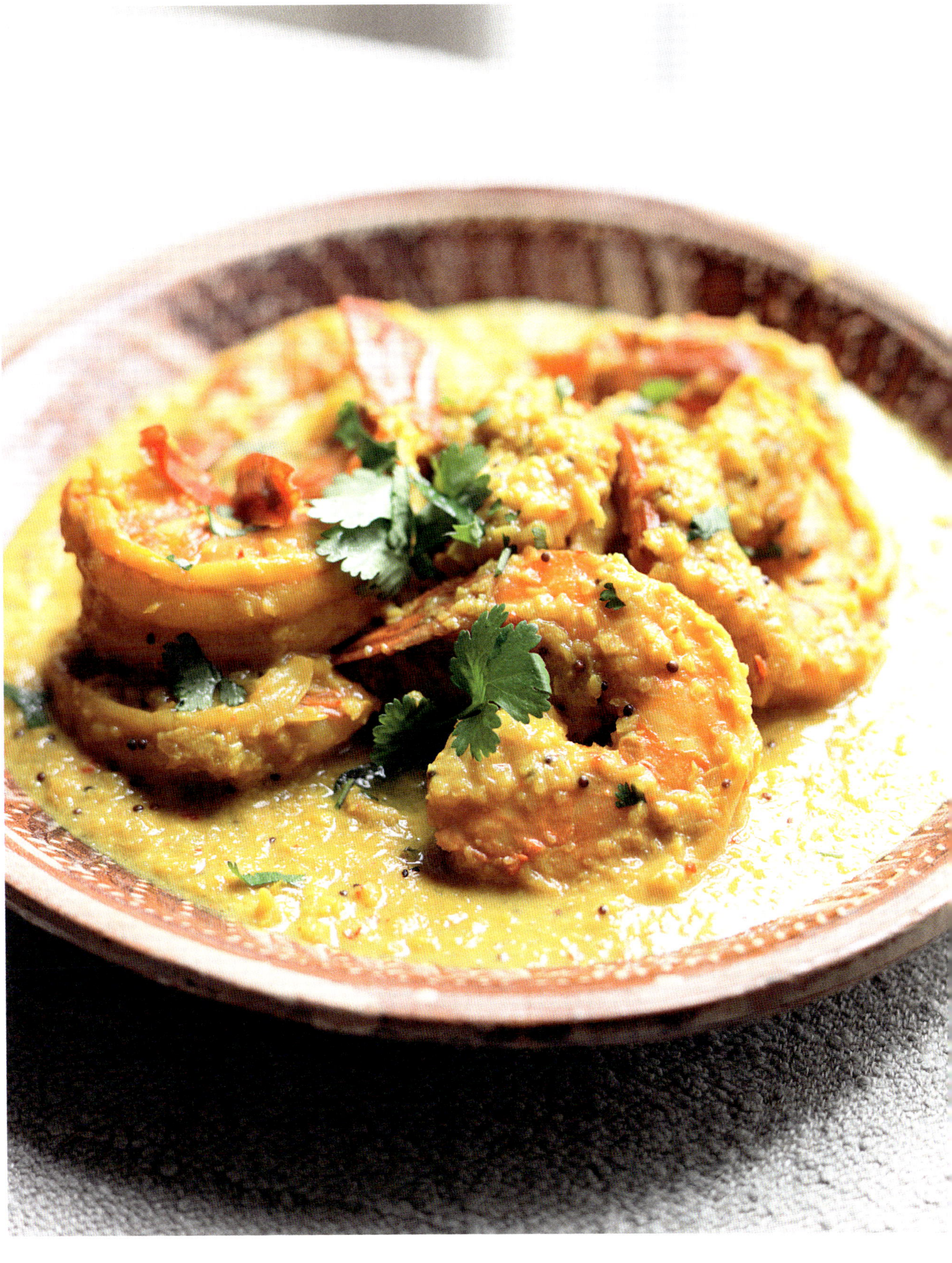

Chicken tikka masala

SERVES 4

2 tbsp cumin seeds
2 tbsp coriander seeds
2 whole cloves
1 tsp black peppercorns
small piece of cinnamon stick
½ tsp ground fenugreek
1½ tsp ground turmeric
2 tsp ground paprika
½–1 tsp hot chilli powder
2 garlic cloves, crushed
20g root ginger, peeled and finely grated
4 tbsp natural yoghurt
4 boneless, skinless chicken breasts, each cut into 7 or 8 pieces
oil, for greasing skewers
salt

MASALA SAUCE
4 tbsp ghee, or
   2 tbsp softened butter and 2 tbsp sunflower oil
3 medium onions, chopped
4 garlic cloves, crushed
25g root ginger, peeled and finely grated
½ tsp ground turmeric
3 tbsp tomato purée
2 tsp caster sugar
2 tbsp double cream

TO SERVE
rice

Yes, there is a long list of ingredients here, but it really is worth making your own masala paste instead of using a jar. It doesn't take long and it you will be rewarded with a truly tasty, fragrant gem of a dish. You'll need some metal skewers for the chicken.

1. Put the cumin and coriander seeds, cloves, peppercorns and cinnamon stick in a dry frying pan over a medium heat. Cook for 1–2 minutes, stirring regularly until lightly toasted. Tip everything into a mortar or an electric spice grinder, then add the fenugreek, turmeric, paprika, chilli powder and a teaspoon of salt. Grind everything to a fine powder.

2. Spoon 3 tablespoons of this spice mixture into a mixing bowl and stir in the garlic, ginger and yoghurt. Mix thoroughly and set aside. Stir the chicken pieces into the spiced yoghurt, cover and leave in the fridge to marinate for at least 4 hours or ideally overnight.

3. To make the masala sauce, heat the ghee (or butter and oil) in a large non-stick saucepan and add the onions, garlic and ginger. Cover and cook over a low heat for 10 minutes, stirring occasionally. Remove the lid, increase the heat slightly and stir in the rest of the powdered spices, plus the half teaspoon of turmeric. Fry for 3 minutes, stirring regularly.

4. Stir in the tomato purée, caster sugar and a teaspoon of salt and fry for 2–3 minutes, stirring constantly. Add 400ml of water, bring to a gentle simmer and cook for 5 minutes more, adding the cream for the last 30 seconds of the cooking time. Remove from the heat and blitz with a stick blender or in a food processor to form a sauce that's as smooth as possible. Pour it into a bowl, cover and chill until you're ready to cook the chicken.

5. Thread the chicken pieces on to lightly greased, long metal skewers. You should be able to fit about 6 chunks of chicken on to each skewer, leaving 1–2cm between each piece. Preheat the grill to its hottest setting and place the skewers on a rack over a grill pan lined with foil. Slide the pan on to a shelf, putting it as close as possible to the heat, and cook the chicken for 5 minutes. Turn each skewer, holding it with an oven cloth, and cook on the other side for another 4–5 minutes or until the chicken is cooked through and lightly charred.

6. While the chicken is grilling, tip the masala sauce into a large frying pan. Bring to a gentle simmer and cook for 2–3 minutes, stirring regularly. Take the chicken skewers from under the grill and slide a fork down the length of each skewer to plop the pieces into the hot sauce. Stir well and leave to bubble for a few seconds more. Serve hot with rice.

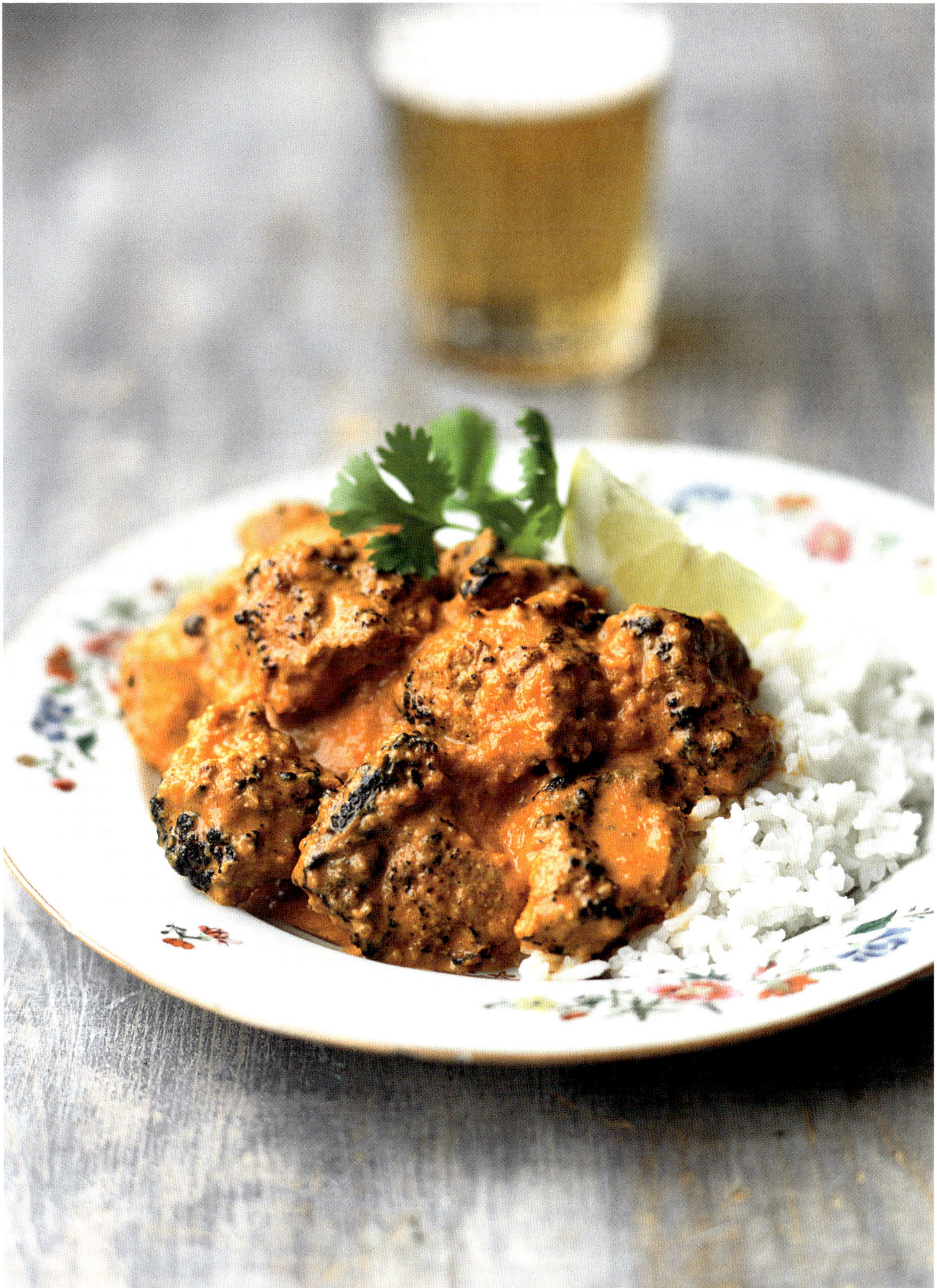

Lamb kofte vindaloo

SERVES 4

MEATBALLS
1 tbsp olive oil
1 onion, finely chopped
2 garlic cloves, finely chopped
500g minced lamb
1 tsp dried oregano
zest of 1 lemon
½ tsp chilli flakes (optional)
25g pine nuts, roughly chopped
small bunch of basil, finely chopped
75g breadcrumbs
1 egg
salt and black pepper

CURRY
3 tbsp vegetable or coconut oil
3 onions, finely sliced
2–3 tbsp vindaloo spice paste (see p.268 or shop-bought)
up to 1 tsp light brown soft sugar or jaggery

TO SERVE
green chillies, sliced
coriander leaves

As I'm sure you all know, my mate Dave was a huge fan of meatballs and we have both always loved a curry, so this fab fusion was just meant to be. It is totally epic and great served with Indian bread or rice. You can, of course, buy some vindaloo paste in the supermarket but it is well worth making your own if you have time. There's a recipe on page 268. Jaggery, by the way, is a type of sugar that's popular in India and is made of palm tree sap, but it's fine to use ordinary brown soft sugar.

1. Preheat the oven to 200°C/Fan 180°C/Gas 6. Line a baking tray with baking parchment.

2. Put all the meatball ingredients in a bowl and season them generously with salt and pepper. Mix everything together very thoroughly, then shape into 20 balls or torpedo shapes. Place the balls on the baking tray and bake them in the oven for 10 minutes. Remove and set aside.

3. For the curry, heat the oil in a large saucepan or a flameproof casserole dish. Fry the onions over a medium heat until they've turned a deep golden brown, then add the vindaloo paste and stir for a few more minutes. Add 600ml of water, plenty of seasoning and half the sugar. Bring to the boil then turn down the heat and simmer for 20 minutes or so until the sauce is reduced, but not too thick – it will continue reducing when you add the meatballs. Taste for seasoning and add the rest of the sugar and more salt if necessary.

4. Add the meatballs to the sauce and continue to simmer gently for another 5–10 minutes until the meatballs are piping hot and the sauce has reduced to a thick gravy. Serve with sliced chillies and coriander.

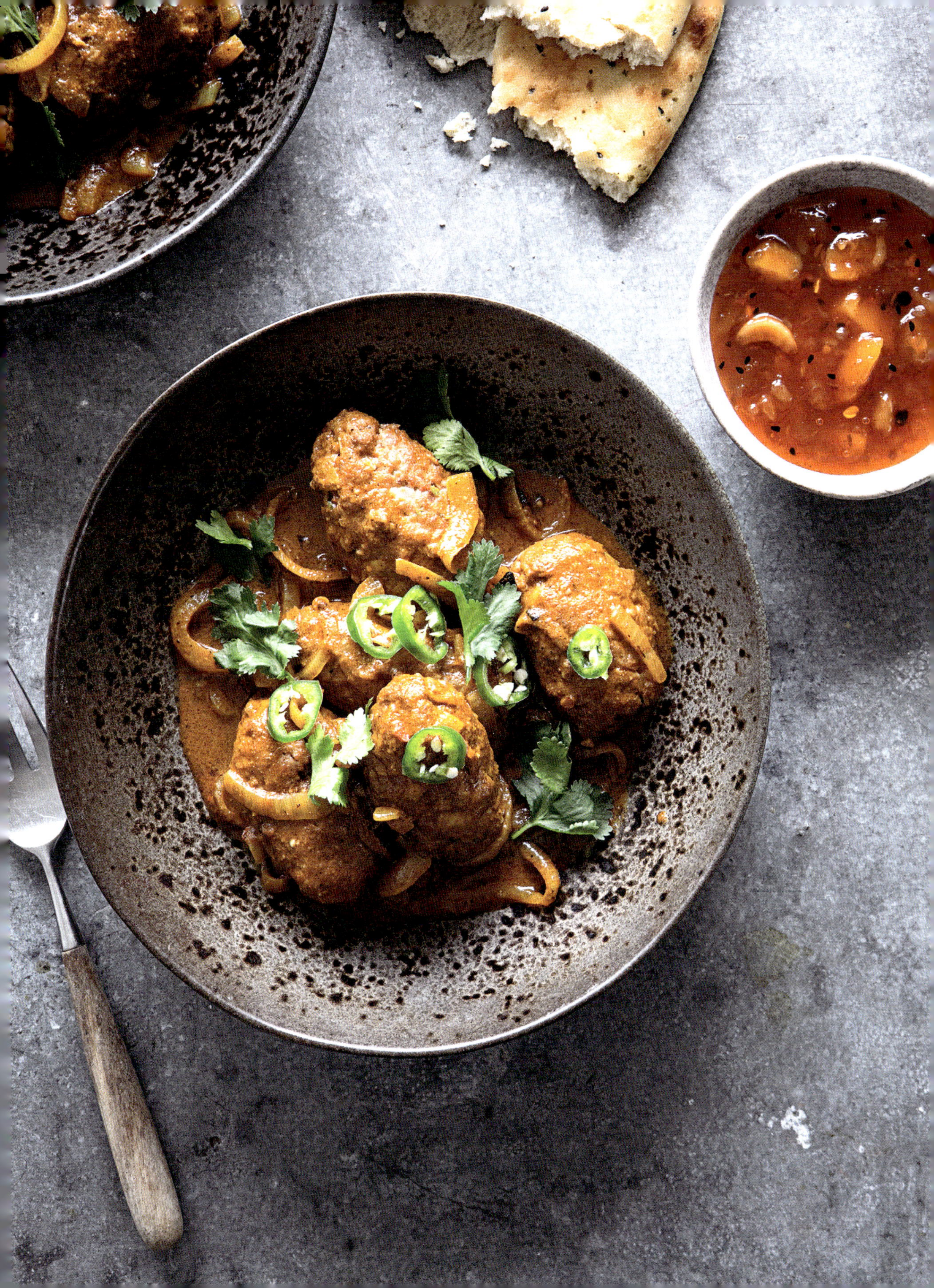

Extra-special lamb biryani

SERVES 6 GENEROUSLY OR 8–10 AS PART OF A LARGER MEAL/BUFFET

100ml whole milk
1 small sachet of saffron (0.4g) or 1 heaped tsp
4 medium onions
4 garlic cloves
25g root ginger, peeled and roughly chopped
1 plump fresh red chilli, deseeded and roughly chopped
50g flaked almonds
6 cloves
2 tsp cumin seeds
2 tsp coriander seeds
¼ cinnamon stick
10 cardamom pods
½ nutmeg, finely grated
900g–1kg lamb shoulder meat
sunflower oil
200ml natural yoghurt
2 bay leaves
50g sultanas
350g basmati rice
40g butter
3 large free-range eggs
4–5 tbsp roughly chopped fresh coriander, plus extra to garnish
salt and black pepper

This is a spectacular dish for a party and can be eked out to serve loads by adding perhaps a veg curry and plenty of rice and breads. It does take a while, but you can spread the work over a couple of days by cooking the lamb well ahead of time. You then put the lamb in the dish it's going to be baked in, cover and chill it for up to 24 hours. Roughly one and a half hours before serving, bring the lamb up to room temperature, half cook the rice as below and scatter it over the lamb. Bake for a bit longer than mentioned below, 45–50 minutes, until the lamb is piping hot and the rice is tender.

1. Pour the milk into a small pan, add the saffron and heat gently for a few minutes without boiling. Remove from the heat and set aside for 2–3 hours or overnight.

2. Roughly chop 2 of the onions and then put them in a food processor with the garlic, ginger, chilli and half the flaked almonds. Add 50ml of cold water and blend to a paste. Put the cloves, cumin and coriander seeds in a mortar or an electric spice grinder with the cinnamon, the seeds from the cardamom pods and a teaspoon of salt. Pound or grind until as powdery as possible. Add the grated nutmeg, sprinkle with black pepper and tip into the onion paste. Blitz briefly until all the ingredients are combined.

3. Trim the lamb of any hard fat and cut into bite-sized pieces. Heat a couple of tablespoons of oil in a frying pan, season the lamb with salt and black pepper, then fry, a few pieces at a time, until browned on all sides. Tip each batch into a large heavy-based saucepan as it is browned. Add more oil as needed.

4. Pour another 3 tablespoons of oil into the same frying pan and cook the onion paste until lightly browned, stirring often. Add a little water if the paste begins to stick. Tip into the pan with the lamb. Stir in the yoghurt and bay leaves. Place the pan over a low heat and stir in 300ml of water. Bring to a gentle simmer, cover and cook over a low heat for 45–60 minutes or until the lamb is tender, stirring occasionally.

5. Cut the remaining 2 onions in half and slice thinly. Heat 2 tablespoons of oil in a large frying pan and cook the onions for 6–8 minutes until softened and golden brown, stirring often. Drain on kitchen paper. Put the rest of the almonds in the pan and cook for 2–3 minutes, turning often, until lightly toasted. Stir the sultanas into the pan, then tip into a bowl and leave to cool.

6. When the lamb is tender, remove the lid and increase the heat. Boil the sauce until reduced and thick, stirring often. This will probably take around 10 minutes, depending on how long the lamb has been cooking. Add a little more seasoning if necessary.

BIKER TIP
This makes a fairly mild curry. If you would prefer something a bit hotter, add an extra chilli or two.

7. Meanwhile, put the rice in a large bowl and cover with water. Swill a couple of times until the water is cloudy, then drain. Repeat until the water is fairly clear. Leave the rice to soak for 30–45 minutes. Bring a large pan of water to the boil and add 2 teaspoons of salt. Add the rice and cook for 4–5 minutes, then drain.

8. Pile the meat and sauce into a large, fairly deep ovenproof dish. Spoon over the part-cooked rice and drizzle with the soaked saffron threads and milk. Dot with the butter, scatter with half the fried onions, then cover the dish with 2 layers of tightly fitting foil. Bake for 30 minutes.

9. While the meat and rice are baking, hard-boil the eggs for 10 minutes. Peel the eggs and cut into quarters. Put the reserved fried onions in a small frying pan and heat through over a low heat. Take the dish of lamb and rice out of the oven and remove the foil. Gently mix in the chopped coriander, then garnish with the eggs, hot onions, toasted almonds and sultanas. Add a few fresh coriander leaves and serve.

Lamb pasanda

SERVES 6

1kg boneless lamb leg meat
2 tbsp ghee or vegetable oil
2 medium onions, sliced
7 cardamom pods, crushed
1½ tsp fenugreek seeds
1 tbsp garam masala
   (shop-bought or see p.269)
2 tbsp ground almonds
1 tsp caster sugar
1 cinnamon stick
2 bay leaves or 2 tsp dried
   fenugreek leaves
5–6 tbsp double cream

MARINADE
200g natural yoghurt
2 tsp ground coriander
2 tsp ground cumin
1 tsp ground turmeric
¼ tsp hot chilli powder
3 garlic cloves, peeled
25g root ginger, peeled
   and roughly chopped

TO SERVE
rice or bread

A pasanda is a rich creamy curry, with a beautiful flavour of mild spices and ground almonds. It's often made with chicken but I've always liked our lamb version. The meat is flattened and then marinated in yoghurt, spices, garlic and ginger.

1. Trim the lamb, removing any visible fat or sinew and cut it into rough 3cm chunks. Place a few between 2 sheets of cling film and bash with a rolling pin or the flat side of a meat mallet until they are about 5mm thick. Continue until all the pieces are flattened.

2. Put the marinade ingredients in a food processor or blender and blitz until as smooth as possible. Scrape the mixture into a bowl. Stir the meat into the marinade and turn the pieces to coat them all. Cover the bowl and leave the lamb to marinate in the fridge for at least an hour before cooking. You can prepare the meat in the morning, then leave it in the fridge all day before cooking it in the evening if you like.

3. To make the sauce, heat the ghee or oil in a large flameproof casserole dish or a saucepan. Add the onions and fry for about 10 minutes or until softened and lightly browned, stirring regularly, so they brown without burning. Remove the onions from the heat and blitz them with a stick blender until they are as smooth as possible. Alternatively, let the onions cool for a few minutes and blend them in a food processor.

4. Return the pan to the heat and add the cardamom pods, fenugreek seeds and garam masala. Cook for 2 minutes more, stirring constantly. Tip the lamb and marinade into the pan and cook over a medium heat for 2–3 minutes, stirring constantly. Add the ground almonds, sugar, cinnamon, a teaspoon of salt and 500ml of water. Drop the bay leaves or fenugreek leaves on top, stir well and bring to a gentle simmer.

5. Cover the pan loosely with a lid and leave to simmer for 1 hour, or until the lamb is tender. Remove the lid and stir the curry occasionally as it cooks. When the lamb is tender, stir in the double cream and increase the heat. Simmer the curry for about 10 minutes or until the sauce is thick, stirring very regularly. Serve with rice or bread.

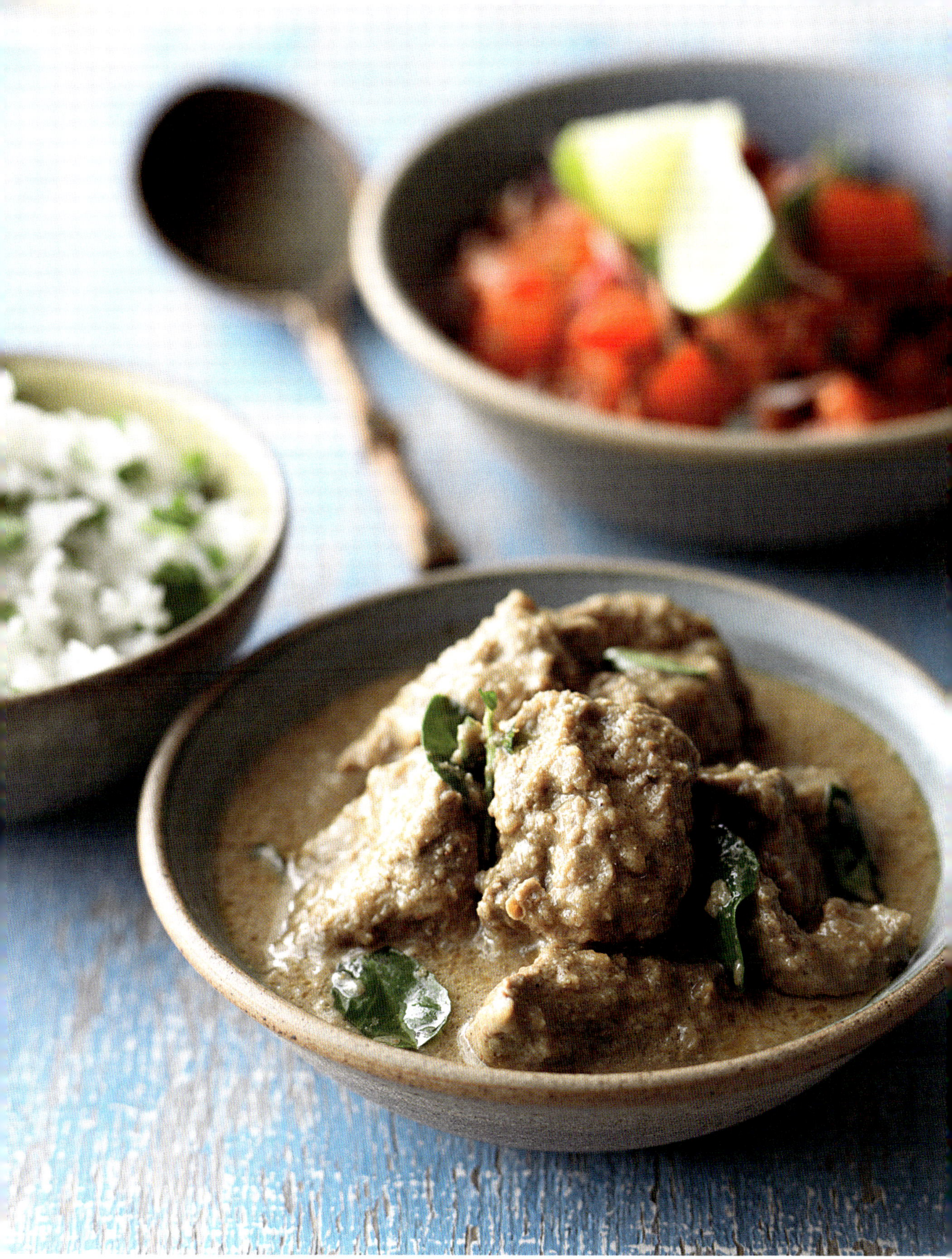

Traditional lamb saag

SERVES 6

5 tbsp vegetable oil
4 large onions, sliced
10 cardamom pods
1 tbsp cumin seeds
2 tsp mustard seeds
½ cinnamon stick
2 long red chillies, sliced
6 large garlic cloves, roughly sliced
1 tbsp ground coriander
2 tsp ground turmeric
500g mature spinach leaves (not baby spinach), tough stalks removed
900g boneless lamb leg meat, cut into chunks of about 4cm
1 bay leaf
2 tbsp tomato purée
salt and black pepper

TO SERVE
rice or bread

In Indian cookery, saag can mean any kind of bitter greens but I usually like to go with spinach. This is a magical dish and I know it has long been a favourite with many of our readers. It's medium-hot but if you prefer a milder curry, remove the seeds from the chillies.

1. Heat 3 tablespoons of the oil in a large frying pan. Cook the onions gently for 20 minutes until softened and golden brown, stirring regularly.

2. Lightly crush the cardamom pods to split them, then open each pod and scrape out the seeds into a bowl. Add the cumin and mustard seeds and the cinnamon stick, then grind to form a fairly fine, dry powder using a pestle and mortar or a spice grinder.

3. When the onions are ready, remove about half of them and set aside on a plate. Put the pan back over the heat, stir in chillies and garlic and cook for 3 minutes, stirring. Add the ground spices and the coriander and turmeric, then cook for 2 minutes more, stirring constantly.

4. Drop about 300g of the spinach into the pan and cook for 2–3 minutes, turning it with the onions until well wilted. Remove the pan from the heat, scrape everything into a bowl and leave to cool. Tear the remaining spinach leaves in half, then set aside.

5. Put the pan back on the hob and add another tablespoon of oil. Season the lamb with salt and black pepper. Working in batches, fry the lamb over a medium-high heat until browned on all sides, adding more oil if necessary. Transfer each batch to a flameproof casserole dish. Preheat the oven to 170°C/Fan 150°C/Gas 3½.

6. Transfer the cooled onions and spinach mixture to a food processor and blitz to form a thick green paste. Stir this into the casserole dish with the lamb and add the bay leaf, tomato purée and 800ml of water. Season with salt, stir well and bring to a simmer.

7. Remove the casserole dish from the hob and cover the surface of the curry with some crumpled baking parchment. Cover with a lid and cook the curry in the oven for 2½–3 hours or until the meat is very tender and the sauce is thick. Stir halfway though cooking if possible.

8. Take the curry out of the oven, remove the paper and stir in the reserved onions and the rest of the spinach. Cover with just the lid – no paper – and put the dish back in the oven for a further 15–20 minutes or until the onions are hot and the spinach has wilted. Serve with rice or warm bread.

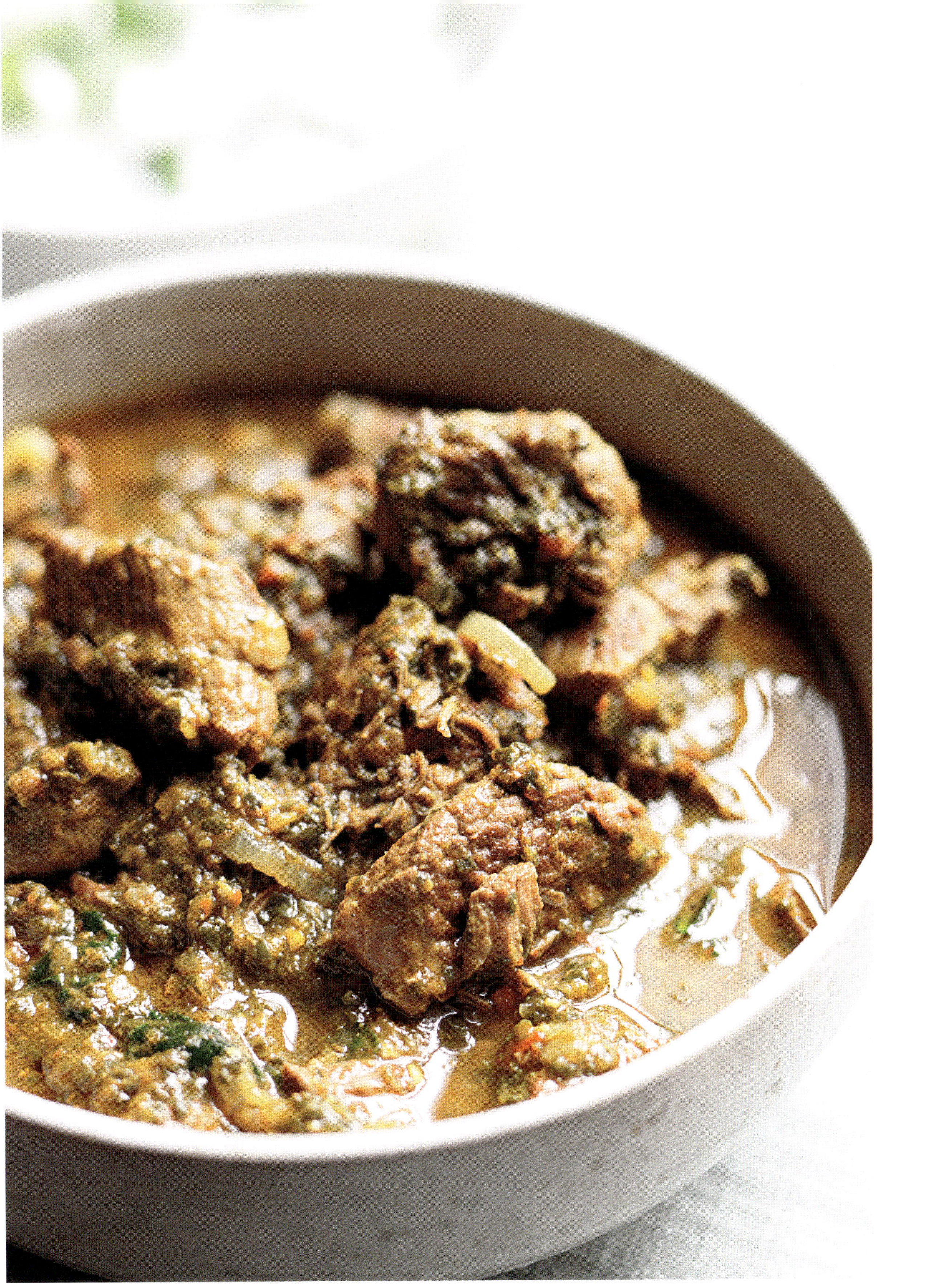

Dry Keralan beef curry

SERVES 4-5

2cm cinnamon stick
4 cloves
2 tsp fennel seeds
4 extra-hot dried chillies (bird's-eye)
1 tbsp coriander seeds
1 tsp ground turmeric
800g chuck steak (braising beef), trimmed and cut into 2.5cm chunks
25g root ginger, peeled and finely grated
4 garlic cloves, finely sliced
1 long green chilli, deseeded and finely chopped
1 tbsp red or white wine vinegar
2 medium onions, halved and thinly sliced
10 fresh or 15 dried curry leaves
25g fresh or 15g dry shredded coconut strips (optional)
4 tbsp coconut oil or vegetable oil
salt and black pepper

TO SERVE

bread or rice
chutneys
lime halves, for squeezing

This is a drier than usual curry with a wonderful, slightly aniseedy flavour and it makes a nice change from the usual saucy dishes. Dave and I first tasted this at a roadside stall in Kerala when on one of our filming trips and fell in love with it. If you don't want to prepare your own ground spices you could use two heaped teaspoons of garam masala and two teaspoons of fennel seeds instead. It won't taste quite the same but will still be good.

1. Put the cinnamon, cloves, fennel seeds, chillies and coriander seeds in a spice grinder or a mortar and grind them to a fine powder. Tip the spices into a large bowl and add the turmeric and 2 teaspoons of fine salt. Stir well to mix. Add the beef, ginger, garlic, chilli, vinegar, half the onion slices and half the curry leaves, then season with lots of pepper and toss well. Cover the bowl and leave to marinate in the fridge for 1 hour.

2. Preheat the oven to 180°C/Fan 160°C/Gas 4. Transfer the beef mixture to a flameproof casserole dish and stir in 350ml of water. Bring to the boil over a high heat then cover the dish with a lid and transfer it to the oven. Cook for 1½–2 hours or until the beef is very tender.

3. Remove the lid and place the casserole dish back on the hob. Bring to the boil and cook for about 5 minutes or until all the liquid has evaporated. This will take about 5 minutes. You'll need to stir it regularly as the drier the curry becomes, the more likely it is to stick. Remove from the heat. At this point, the beef can be cooled and left in the fridge until just before you serve it, as the rest of the cooking is very quick.

4. Heat a large non-stick frying pan or wok and add the shredded coconut. Cook for 2–3 minutes or until toasted, stirring constantly. This step isn't essential but it will bring extra flavour to the curry.

5. Add the oil to the pan, then add the reserved sliced onion and stir-fry for 3–4 minutes until golden brown. Add the beef mixture and the remaining curry leaves, reduce the heat slightly and stir-fry for 5–6 minutes until the meat is hot and nicely browned and looks dry but glossy and rich. Serve with bread or rice, a selection of chutneys and lime halves.

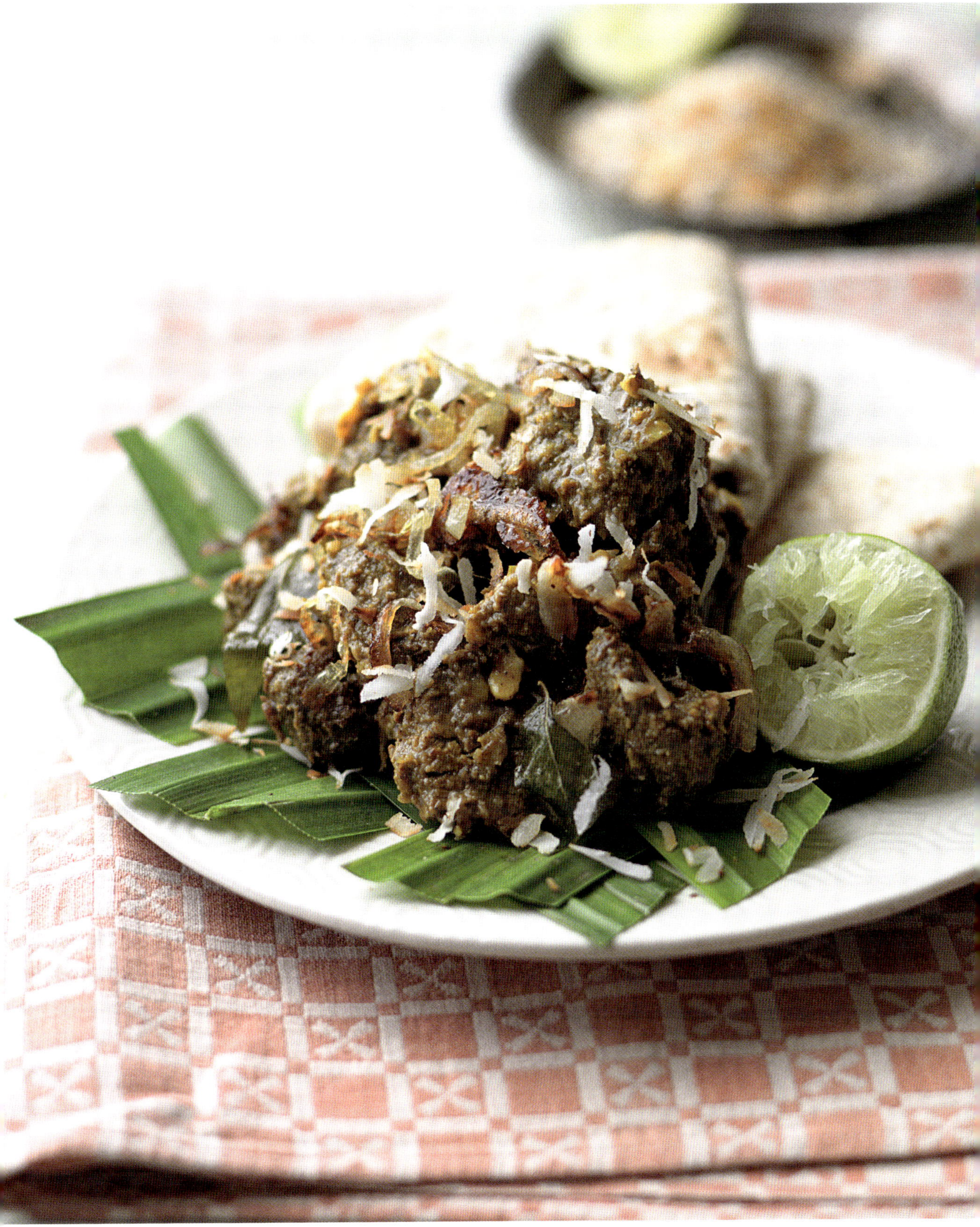

1. Indian shepherd's pie...166
2. Mushroom bourguignon cobbler...168
3. Aubergine katsu...170
4. Nut & spinach roast with wild mushroom gravy...172
5. Chilli bean burgers...174
6. Leek, asparagus & Gruyère tart...176
7. Caribbean chickpea & spinach curry...178
8. Baked bean pie...180
9. Soba noodles with miso mushrooms...182
10. Shakshuka...184

veggie

"I've never gone total vegetarian but I've always cooked and enjoyed plenty of veggie dishes for myself and my family. You won't miss meat with any of these recipes – they're just fantastic."

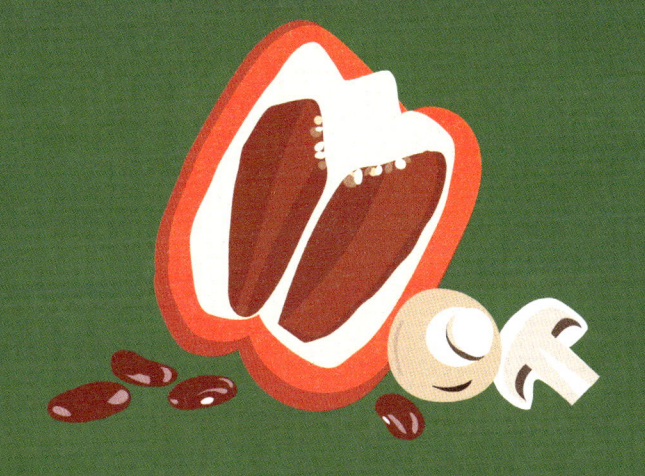

Indian shepherd's pie

SERVES 4–6

1 tbsp oil
1 large onion, very finely chopped
1 large carrot, coarsely grated
1 celery stick, very finely diced
1 green or red pepper, very finely diced
100g celeriac, turnip or swede, very finely diced
100g butternut squash, very finely diced
200g green beans, sliced into rounds
25g root ginger, finely chopped
2 garlic cloves, finely chopped
1 tbsp mild curry powder
500ml vegetable stock
100g cooked brown lentils
1 tsp tamarind paste
2 tsp Pickapeppa sauce or mushroom ketchup
1 tbsp cornflour
salt and black pepper

MASALA POTATO TOPPING
1kg floury potatoes
2 tbsp vegetable oil
1 tsp cumin seeds
1 tsp mustard seeds
1 onion, finely chopped
1 green chilli, finely chopped
100ml milk
25g butter (optional)
small bunch of coriander, chopped
100g vegetarian Cheddar, grated (optional)
olive oil or butter

One of our most popular recipes, this gives the shepherd's pie a whole new look, with a veg curry filling and a spicy mash topping. It's simple to make, but do be sure to cut the vegetables nice and small – half centimetre dice or smaller is good. To make this vegan, just use plant-based milk and leave out the butter and cheese.

1. Heat the oil in a large pan and add all the vegetables. Cook them over a medium-high heat, stirring regularly, until they start to brown and soften, then add the ginger, garlic and curry powder. Cook for another 2–3 minutes, stirring constantly, until well combined, then season.

2. Pour in the stock and add the lentils, tamarind paste and Pickapeppa sauce or mushroom ketchup. Bring to the boil, then partially cover the pan and turn down the heat. Simmer for up to 30 minutes, until the vegetables are completely tender. Mix the cornflour with cold water to make a smooth, runny paste, then stir this into the vegetables. Simmer, stirring constantly, until the sauce thickens.

3. For the topping, bring a large pan of water to the boil, add the potatoes and season with salt. Simmer for 10–15 minutes until the potatoes are knife tender, then drain well and tip them back into the pan. Leave over a low heat to steam off excess water.

4. Heat the oil in a frying pan and add the cumin and mustard seeds. When the seeds start popping, add the onion and chilli. Cook over a medium-high heat until the onion has browned.

5. Mash the potatoes with the milk and add the butter, if using. Add the onion mixture and chopped coriander and mix thoroughly. Preheat the oven to 200°C/Fan 180°C/Gas 6.

6. Put the filling in a large, 30 x 20cm, ovenproof dish. Spread the potato evenly on top, then sprinkle over the cheese, if using. Rough up the surface with a fork and drizzle over a little oil or add knobs of butter. Bake the pie for about 30 minutes until nicely browned and piping hot.

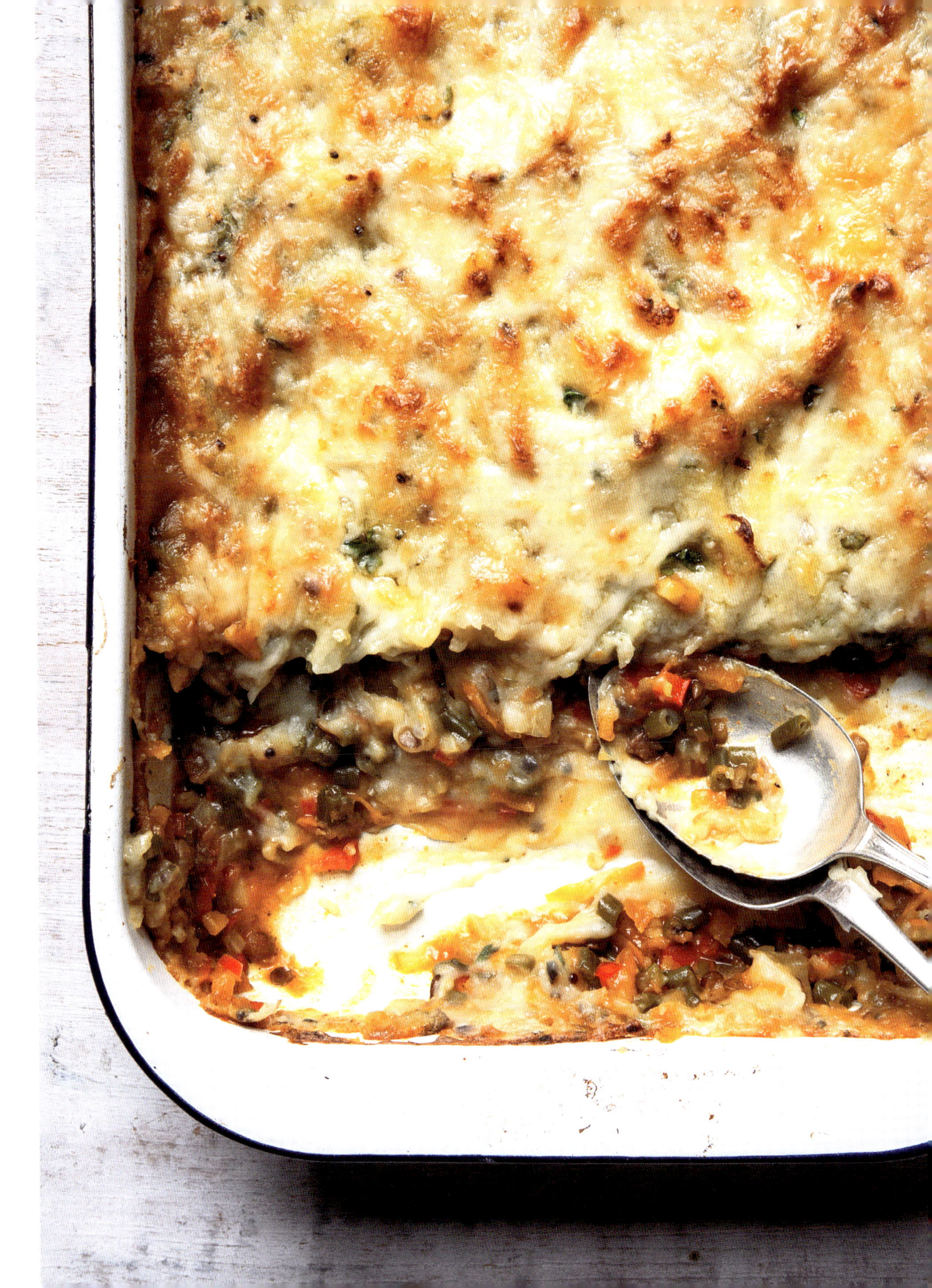

Mushroom bourguignon cobbler

SERVES 4

2 tbsp olive oil
12 button onions or shallots, peeled and left whole
300g carrots, cut into chunks
½ tsp sugar
25g butter
750g mushrooms (mix of portobello, chestnut, button, cremini), thickly sliced
1 large thyme sprig
2 bay leaves
a few sage leaves, finely chopped
200ml red wine
300ml mushroom or vegetable stock
1 tbsp mushroom ketchup
1 tsp Dijon mustard
salt and black pepper

COBBLER TOPPING
200g self-raising flour
1 tsp baking powder
½ tsp salt
1 tsp dried sage
50g vegetarian blue cheese, crumbled
1 egg, beaten
75ml buttermilk

TO SERVE
parsley, finely chopped

This has the rich gutsy flavour of a traditional bourguignon but with mushrooms instead of red meat. It's a really tasty vegetarian meal and ideal for a special occasion. It could have been a pie or a veggie crumble, but we decided to go with a cobbler topping, enriched with blue cheese. If you're not keen on blue cheese, though, Cheddar would work fine.

1. First make the bourguignon. Heat the oil in a large flameproof casserole dish and add the onions or shallots and the carrots. Fry over a high heat, stirring regularly, until they are dappled with dark brown patches. Sprinkle over the sugar and continue to cook for another couple of minutes to help them caramelise. Remove them from the dish and set aside.

2. Now add the butter to the casserole dish. When it starts to foam, add the mushrooms and cook over a high heat until they have reduced down. Put the onions or shallots and the carrots back in the dish and season them generously with salt and pepper. Add the herbs, then pour in the red wine. Bring to the boil and leave to bubble until the wine has reduced by at least a third. Add the stock, mushroom ketchup and mustard and stir until completely combined.

3. Bring back to the boil, then turn down to a simmer and cover the dish with a lid. Cook for half an hour, perhaps a little longer, until the vegetables are completely tender.

4. For the cobbler topping, put the flour and baking powder in a bowl and add half a teaspoon of salt. Add the sage and cheese, then mix in the egg and buttermilk to make a fairly sticky dough. Preheat the oven to 200°C/Fan 180°C/Gas 6.

5. Form the dough into 12 small balls and space them out over the top of the bourguignon. Cover and simmer for 10 minutes, then transfer the dish to the oven, uncovered, for a further 10–15 minutes until the cobbler topping has puffed up and is lightly browned. Serve in shallow bowls with a garnish of finely chopped parsley.

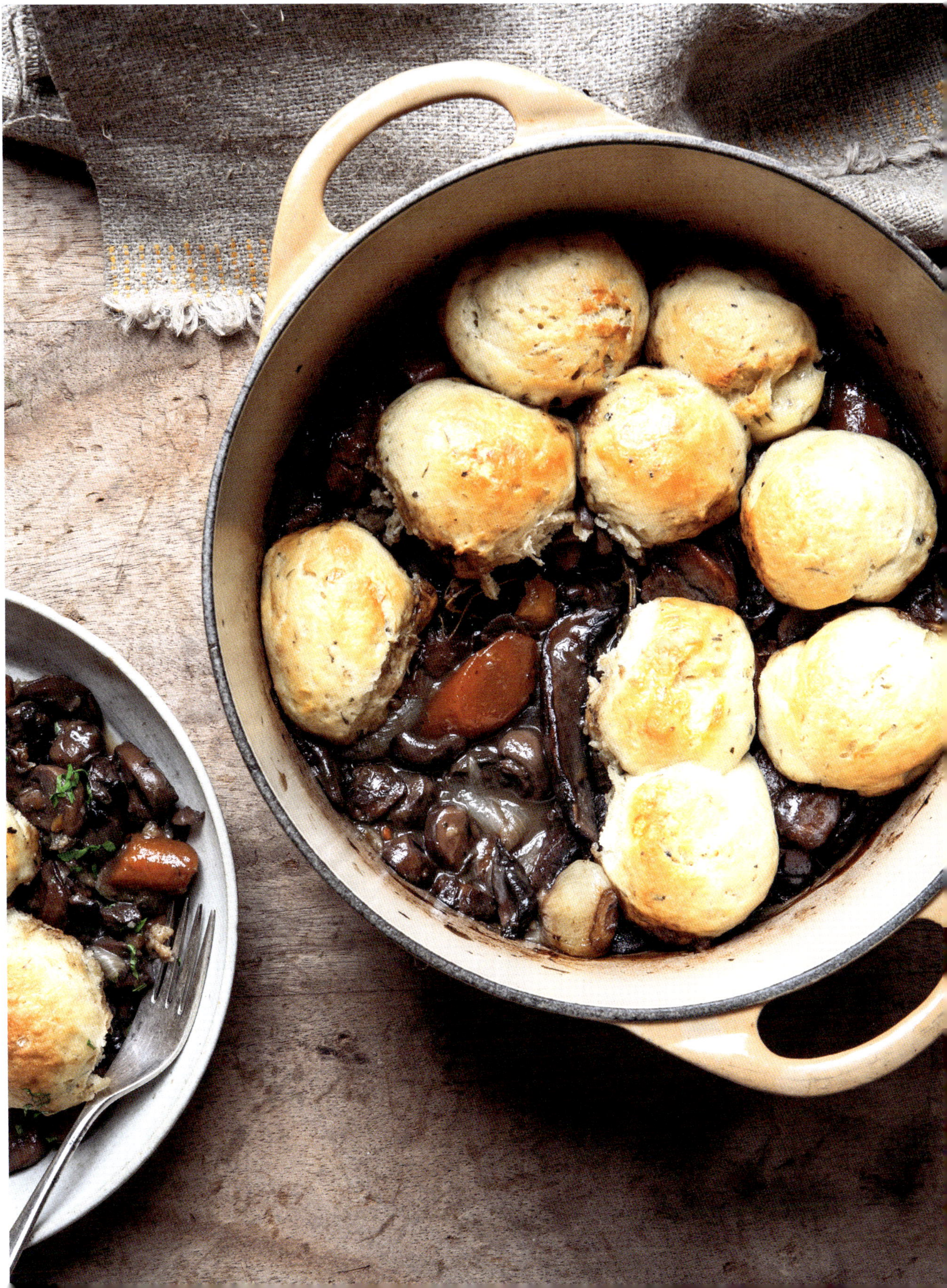

Aubergine katsu

SERVES 4

KATSU SAUCE
2 tbsp vegetable or coconut oil
1 onion, finely chopped
100g sweet potato, finely diced
3 garlic cloves, finely chopped
10g root ginger, grated
2 tbsp medium curry powder
1 tbsp plain flour
400ml vegetable stock
1 tbsp mango chutney
1 tbsp tomato ketchup
1 tbsp soy sauce
1 tbsp maple syrup
½ tsp sesame oil
salt and black pepper

PICKLES
6 radishes, thinly sliced
½ cucumber, cut into long ribbons
1 tsp salt
1 tsp caster sugar
3 tbsp rice wine vinegar

BREADED AUBERGINES
vegetable oil, for brushing
100g plain flour
panko breadcrumbs
2 large aubergines, cut into 1cm rounds

TO GARNISH
1 tsp black sesame seeds
4 spring onions, cut in half lengthways and shredded as finely as possible

Give me a katsu and I'm happy, so I was dead pleased when we came up with this fantastic veggie version, using aubergine slices. Once the sauce is made, the rest is easy, as the aubergines are baked rather than fried. They soak up far less oil that way. Served with the lightly pickled radishes and cucumber, this is a real cracker of a dish and it's vegan too.

1. First make the katsu sauce. Heat the oil in a saucepan and add the onion and sweet potato. Fry the vegetables over a medium heat until they've taken on some colour around the edges. Add the garlic, ginger, curry powder and flour and continue to cook and stir for another 2–3 minutes until everything is well combined.

2. Add the stock along with the mango chutney, ketchup, soy sauce and maple syrup. Season with salt and pepper. Bring to the boil, then turn the heat down and simmer, stirring regularly, until the vegetables are cooked through. Add the sesame oil and blitz everything in a food processor until smooth. Taste and add more seasoning, ketchup or maple syrup if you think it necessary. Set aside.

3. Next make the pickles. Put the vegetables in a bowl and sprinkle them with the salt, sugar and rice wine vinegar. Transfer to a colander and leave to drain for about half an hour.

4. For the aubergines, preheat the oven to 200°C/Fan 180°C/Gas 6. Brush a couple of baking trays generously with oil and spread the breadcrumbs on a plate. Mix the flour with about 150ml of water until you have a smooth batter the thickness of double cream – if it seems too thick, add a little more water. Season with salt. Immerse the aubergine slices in the batter, then one by one, remove, shake off any excess and dip in the breadcrumbs. Make sure all the sides are well covered.

5. Arrange the aubergine slices on the oiled baking trays, then brush the slices with more oil. Bake for 30–35 minutes, turning once, until the aubergines are cooked through and the breadcrumbs are golden.

6. Warm the sauce through and drizzle it over the aubergines. Serve with the pickles and garnish with sesame seeds and spring onions.

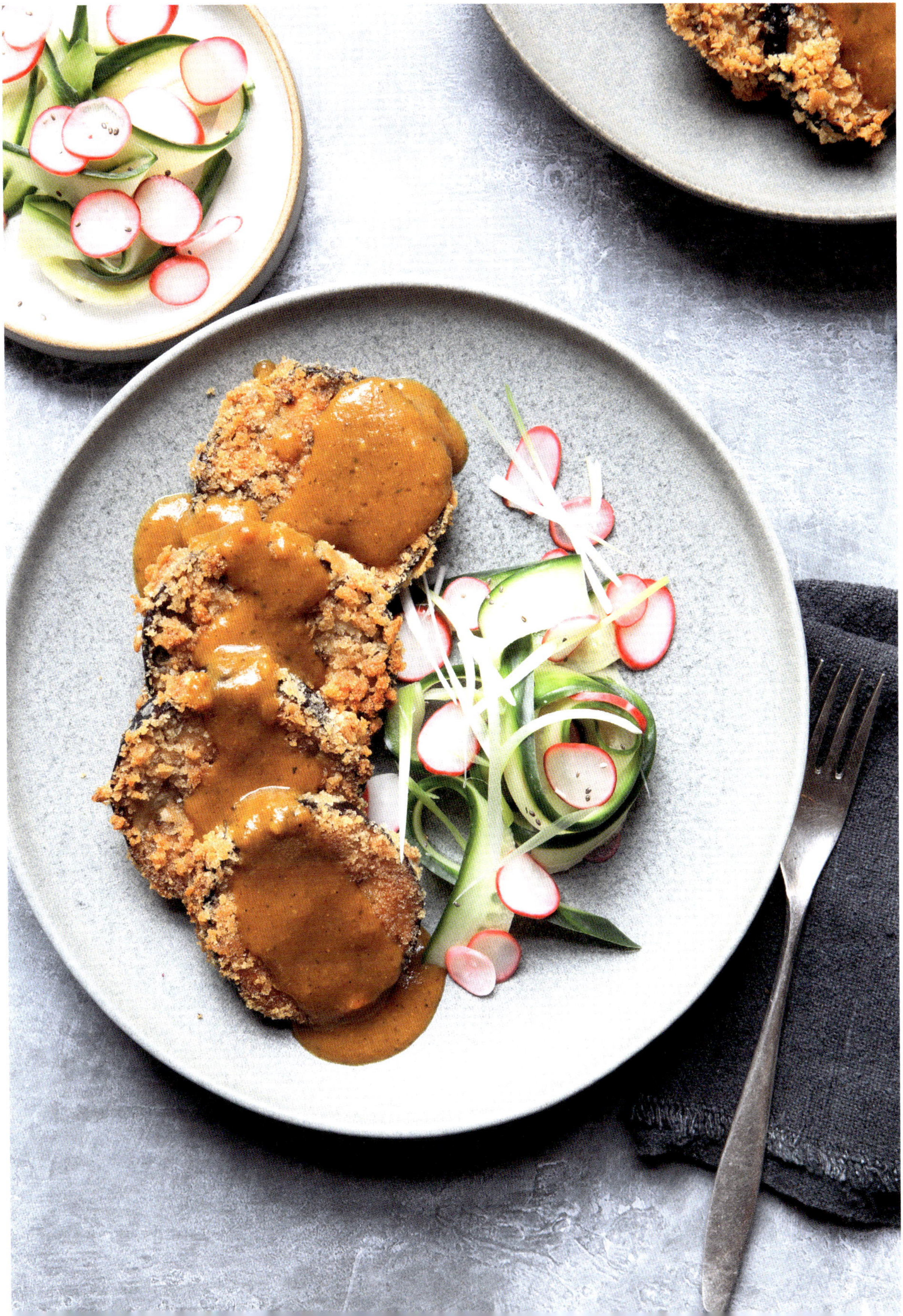

Nut & spinach roast with wild mushroom gravy

SERVES 4

200g spinach leaves
250g unsalted mixed nuts
25g unsalted cashew nuts
½ onion, finely chopped
1 carrot, grated
200g canned tomatoes, drained and chopped
50g sundried tomatoes in olive oil, roughly chopped
1 egg, beaten
100g vegetarian cheese, finely grated
½ tsp dried sage
½ tsp finely chopped fresh mint
1½ tbsp freshly chopped curly parsley
1 garlic clove, finely chopped
1 tsp vegetable stock concentrate
butter, for greasing
salt and black pepper

WILD MUSHROOM GRAVY
2 tbsp olive oil
a knob of butter
1 banana (long) shallot, finely diced
1 garlic clove, finely chopped
250g wild mushrooms
300ml vegetable stock
2 tbsp soy sauce
1 tbsp plain flour
1 tbsp softened butter

We wrote this for our Christmas cookbook many years ago and I still reckon it's one of the tastiest nut roast recipes. I have vegetarians in my family and they're more than happy to see this on the table. I've seen the non-veggies steal a slice too!

1. Preheat the oven to 180°C/Fan 160°C/Gas 4. Blanch the spinach in a pan of boiling water, then drain it well and squeeze out as much water as you can. Chop the spinach finely and set it aside. Put all the nuts in a food processor and pulse until finely chopped, but don't reduce them to a powder.

2. Tip the nuts into a large mixing bowl and add the onion, carrot, canned and sundried tomatoes, egg, cheese, sage, mint, parsley, spinach, garlic, stock and seasoning, then mix everything together well.

3. Grease a loaf tin with butter and pour in the nut mixture. Cut a piece of greaseproof paper to fit the loaf tin, grease it and lay it over the top to stop the mixture burning. Bake in the preheated oven for about an hour until cooked through. Turn it out on to a plate for slicing.

4. For the mushroom gravy, gently heat the oil and knob of butter in a pan. Add the diced shallot and cook gently for 5 minutes or until transparent, then add the garlic and cook for another 2 minutes. Add the mushrooms and cook gently for a further 5 minutes.

5. Add the stock and soy sauce, then season to taste and leave the gravy to simmer, covered, for 10 minutes. Mix the tablespoon of flour into the tablespoon of butter and stir into the gravy to thicken it. Serve the gravy piping hot with the nut roast.

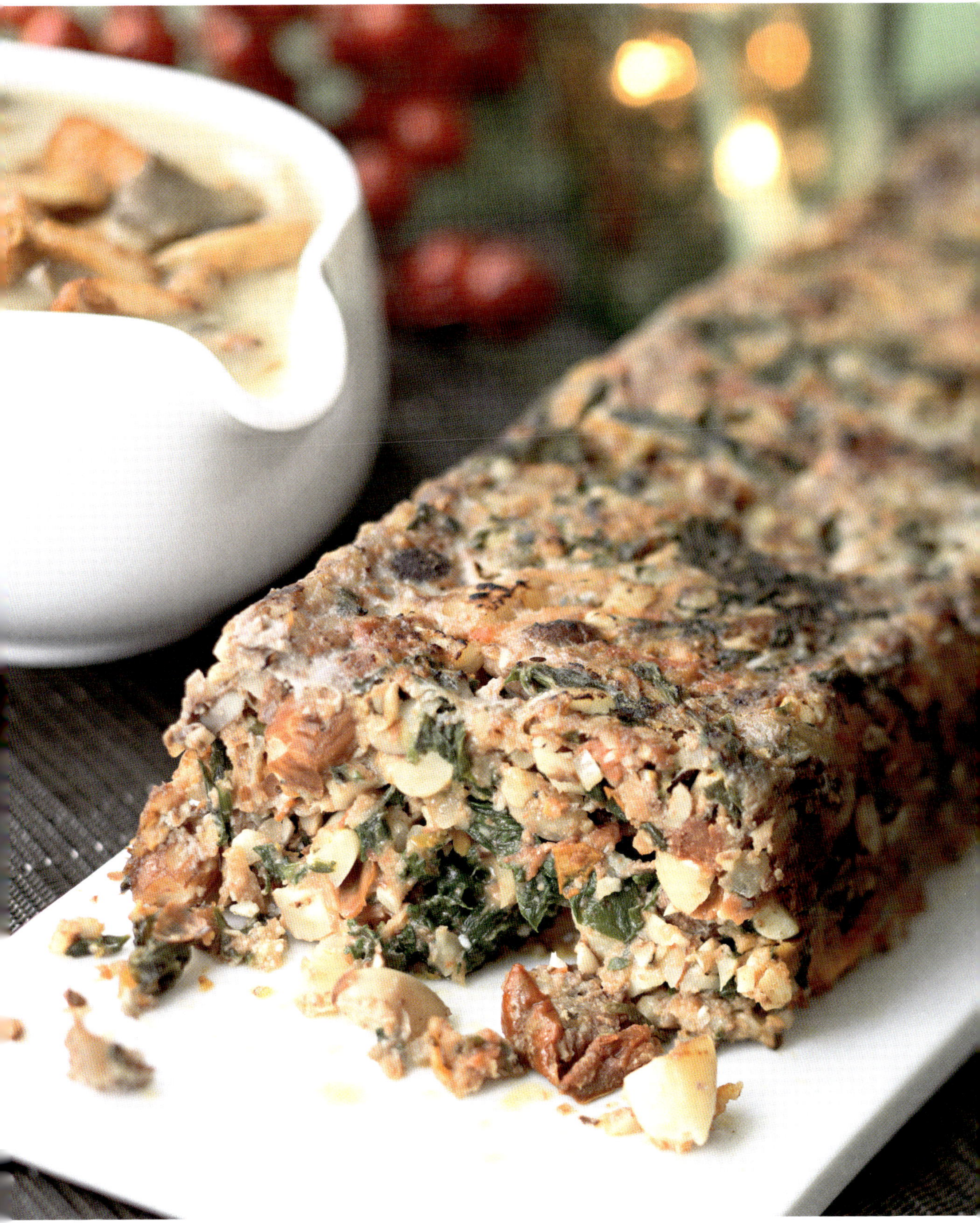

Chilli bean burgers

SERVES 4

2–3 tbsp olive oil
1 small onion, very finely chopped
½ red pepper, very finely chopped
1 small carrot, finely grated
2 jalapeños, very finely chopped (include seeds)
3 tbsp coriander stems, finely chopped
4 garlic cloves, finely chopped
1–2 tsp chilli paste or hot sauce (such as chipotle)
1 tbsp soy sauce
1 tsp ground cumin
½ tsp ground cinnamon
400g can of black, pinto or kidney beans, drained
50g cooked brown rice
75g breadcrumbs
1 egg
salt and black pepper

TO SERVE
1 avocado
juice of 1 lime
slices of vegetarian cheese (optional)
4 burger buns
4 lettuce leaves
4 slices of red onion
soured cream (optional)
coriander leaves, to garnish
hot sauce

With black beans, chilli, avocado and soured cream, this is a Mexican-style take on the veggie burger and mega tasty these are too. Do allow time to chill the burger patties in the fridge before cooking. It really does help both the flavour and the texture.

1. Heat a tablespoon of the oil in a frying pan. Add the onion, red pepper and carrot and cook until the onion is soft and translucent and the vegetables are collapsed down and glossy, but dry. Add the jalapeños, coriander stems and garlic and stir for another couple of minutes. Stir in the chilli paste or hot sauce, soy sauce, cumin and cinnamon and season with salt and pepper. Set aside to cool.

2. Put the beans into a bowl and mash them roughly – you want a mixture of textures. Add the rice, breadcrumbs, egg and the cooled vegetables. Season with more salt and pepper and mix thoroughly.

3. Heat a little more oil in the frying pan. Take a dessertspoonful of the mixture and form it into a small patty. Fry it briefly on both sides and taste for heat and seasoning. Add more salt, pepper or chilli to the main mixture if needed. When you are happy with the flavour, shape the mixture into 4 patties and chill them for at least an hour – this will help the flavour develop.

4. When you are ready to eat, remove the patties from the fridge. Peel the avocado, remove the stone and slice the flesh. Toss the slices in the lime juice and season with salt.

5. Heat more oil in a frying pan and add the patties. Cook over a medium heat until a brown crust forms underneath and the patties come away from the pan with ease. Carefully flip them to fry the other side. If serving with cheese, add it to the burgers now and put something over the pan to help the cheese melt – a lid partially covering the pan is fine.

6. Lightly toast the burger buns, then layer on the lettuce leaves, onion slices, avocado and burgers. Add soured cream, if using. Garnish with coriander leaves and serve with extra hot sauce.

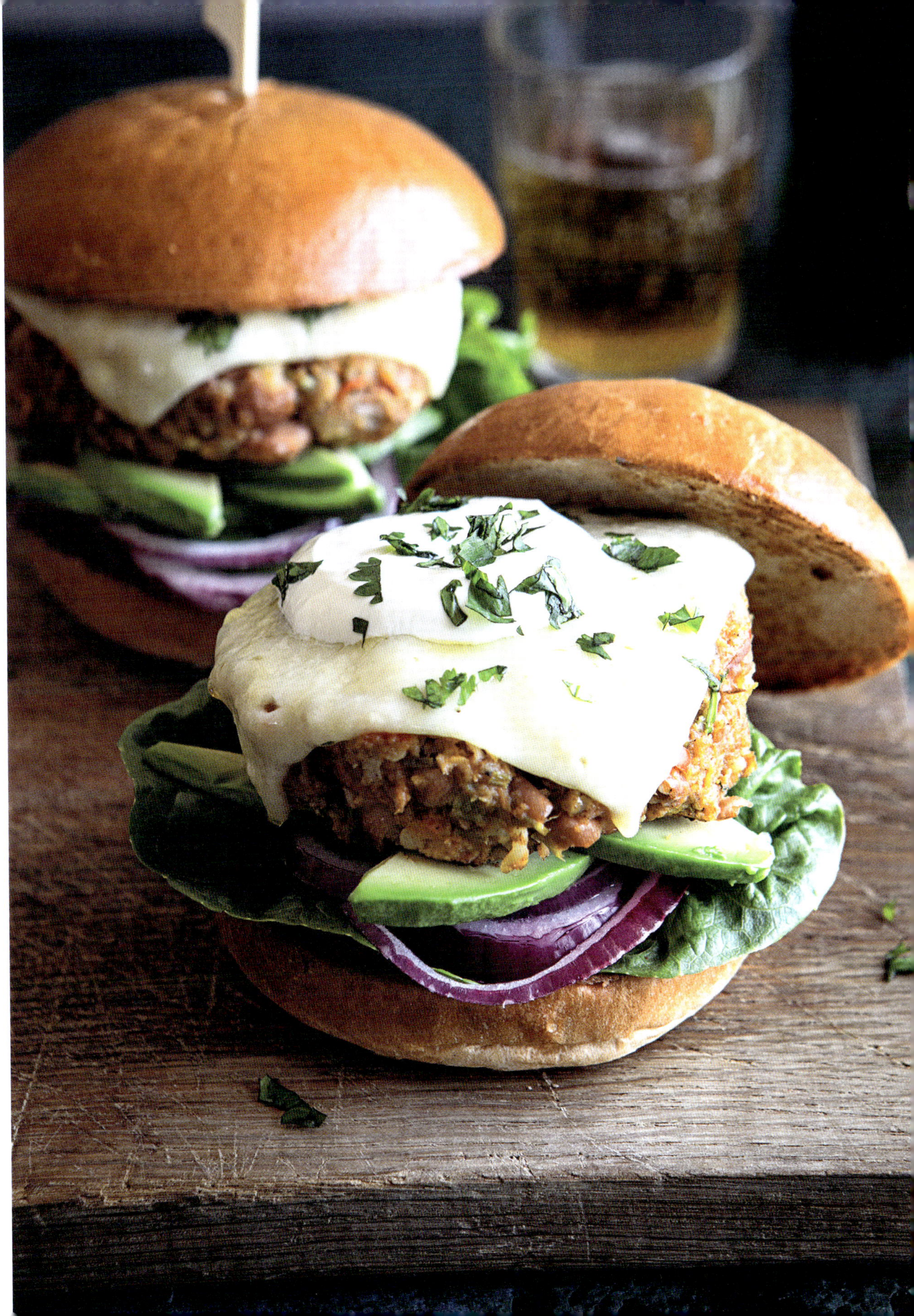

Leek, asparagus & Gruyère tart

SERVES 8

1 tbsp olive oil
10g butter
2 leeks, sliced into rounds
200g asparagus, trimmed and cut into short lengths, diagonally
4 eggs
300ml double cream
150g Gruyère cheese, grated
salt and black pepper

PASTRY
125g cold butter, diced
250g plain flour
50g Parmesan-style vegetarian cheese, grated
1 tsp finely chopped thyme leaves
1 egg yolk
1–2 tbsp ice-cold water

A properly made savoury tart is a joy to behold – and eat – and this combo of leeks, asparagus and cheese is no exception. You could, of course, buy the pastry but our cheese and thyme flavoured shortcrust is so good. By the way, Gruyère cheese is generally fine for vegetarians, as it's made with vegetarian rennet, but do check to make sure.

1. To make the pastry, rub the butter into the flour until the mixture has the texture of fine breadcrumbs. Season with salt and add the cheese and thyme. Stir in the egg yolk with a knife, then add ice-cold water a teaspoon at a time, cutting it in as you go, until the pastry starts to come together. Form the pastry into a ball and wrap it in cling film. Chill in the fridge for half an hour.

2. Roll the pastry out to line a 28cm flan tin. Make sure the pastry is pushed well into the corners, then prick the base all over with a fork. If you have time, put the pastry in the freezer for 10 minutes before baking. Preheat the oven to 200°C/Fan 180°C/Gas 6.

3. Lay a piece of baking parchment over the pastry and add baking beans. Put the tin on a baking tray and bake for 15–20 minutes. Remove the beans and parchment and bake the pastry uncovered for a further 5 minutes. Take the tin and baking tray out of the oven and turn the heat down to 180°C/Fan 160°C/Gas 4.

4. To make the filling, put the olive oil and butter in a frying pan that has a lid. When the butter has melted, add the leeks. Season them with salt and pepper, then add a splash of water. Cover the pan and cook the leeks over a low heat for 10 minutes. Add the asparagus and cook for a further 5 minutes. By now, the vegetables should be glossy and just tender. Take the pan off the heat and set aside to cool.

5. Break the eggs into a bowl, add the cream and whisk until smooth. Season with salt and pepper. Sprinkle half the cheese over the base of the pastry case, then add the leeks and asparagus. Pour half the egg and cream mixture over the vegetables, then sprinkle the remaining cheese on top. Put the flan tin and baking tray into the oven, then pull the oven shelf out a little so you can pour in the remaining filling.

6. Bake the tart for 35–40 minutes, until the filling is just set with a slight wobble in the centre. Remove the tart from the oven and allow it to cool slightly before serving.

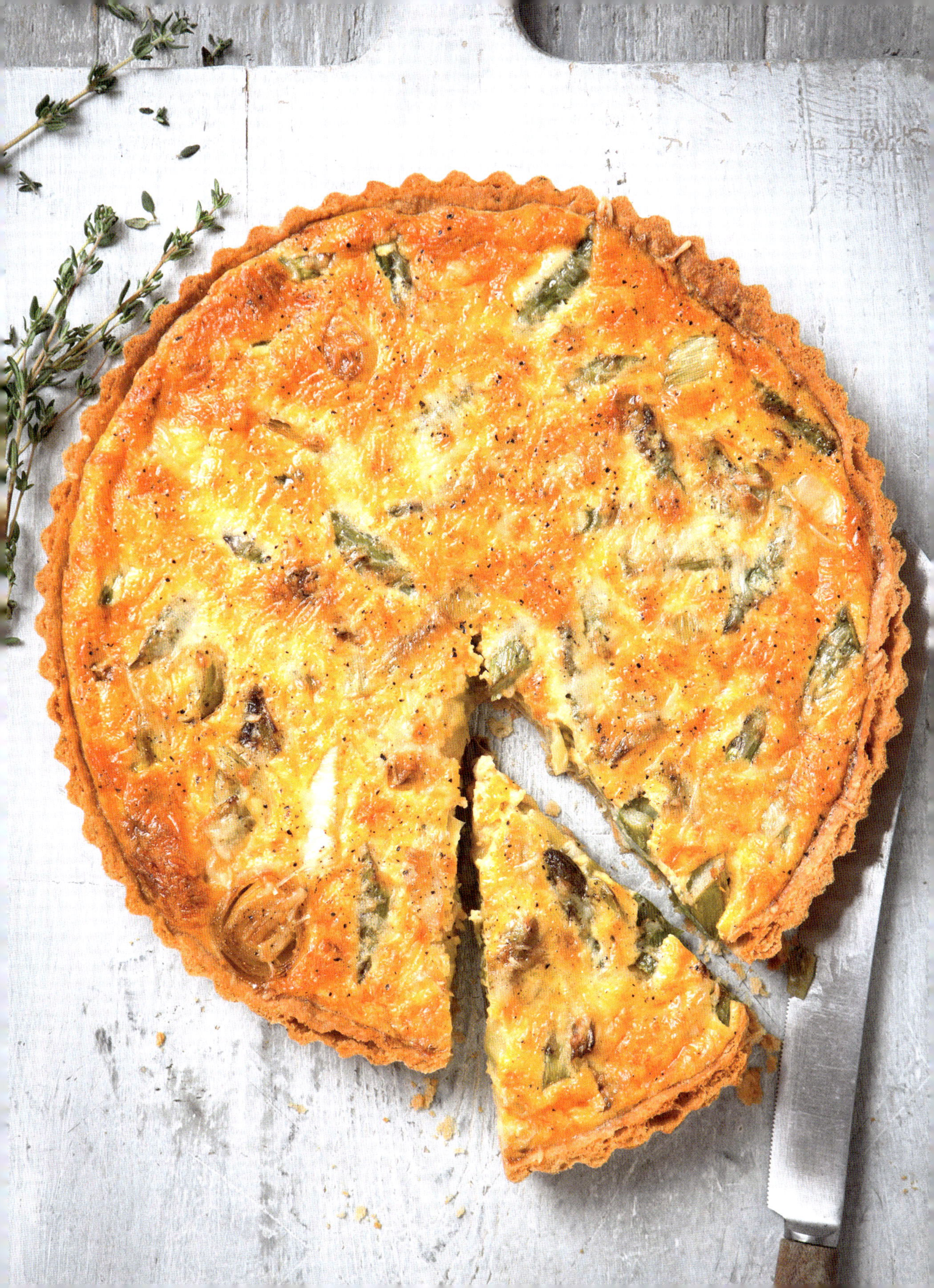

Caribbean chickpea & spinach curry

SERVES 4

1 tbsp coconut oil
1 onion, sliced into thin wedges
3 garlic cloves, finely chopped
250g pumpkin or squash, diced
1 tbsp Caribbean curry powder (shop-bought or see p.269)
1 scotch bonnet or 1–2 tsp scotch bonnet hot sauce
1 large thyme sprig
400ml can of coconut milk
2 x 400g cans of chickpeas, drained
250g frozen spinach (whole leaf, no need to defrost)
salt and black pepper

PLANTAIN
1 large, semi-ripe plantain
zest and juice of 1 lime
½ tsp Caribbean curry powder
1 tbsp coconut oil

TO GARNISH
2 spring onions, finely sliced (include the greens)
squeeze of lime juice

Curries are a big thing in the Caribbean and this is a great recipe, full of spice and flavour – really satisfying. It's vegan too, without even trying. To complete the Caribbean vibe, serve this with some fried plantain dressed with lime juice. You can buy plantains in the supermarket, just look for ones that are semi-ripe – turning yellow, but not brown spotted. Very green plantains are a bit too starchy for this recipe and ripe ones are too sweet.

1. Heat the coconut oil in a large saucepan or a flameproof casserole dish. Add the onion and sauté over a medium-high heat for a few minutes until it starts to brown. Add the garlic and pumpkin or squash and stir for another couple of minutes.

2. Add the curry powder and stir to coat the vegetables. If using the scotch bonnet, pierce it with a knife and add it, whole, to the saucepan along with the thyme. Pour over the coconut milk and stir to make sure the base of the saucepan is completely deglazed and you've scraped up all the sticky bits, then add the chickpeas and frozen spinach. Season with salt and pepper. If using hot sauce, stir it in at this point, adding a teaspoon at a time until you get the amount of heat you want.

3. Bring to the boil, then turn the heat down and partially cover the pan. Simmer for 15–20 minutes until the pumpkin or squash is tender and the sauce is slightly reduced.

4. While the curry is simmering, prepare the plantain. Peel and slice it on the diagonal, then toss it in the lime zest, juice and curry powder and season with salt. Heat the coconut oil in a frying pan and fry the plantain on both sides until well browned.

5. Fish out the scotch bonnet, if using, from the curry and serve garnished with the plantain, finely sliced spring onions and a squeeze of lime juice.

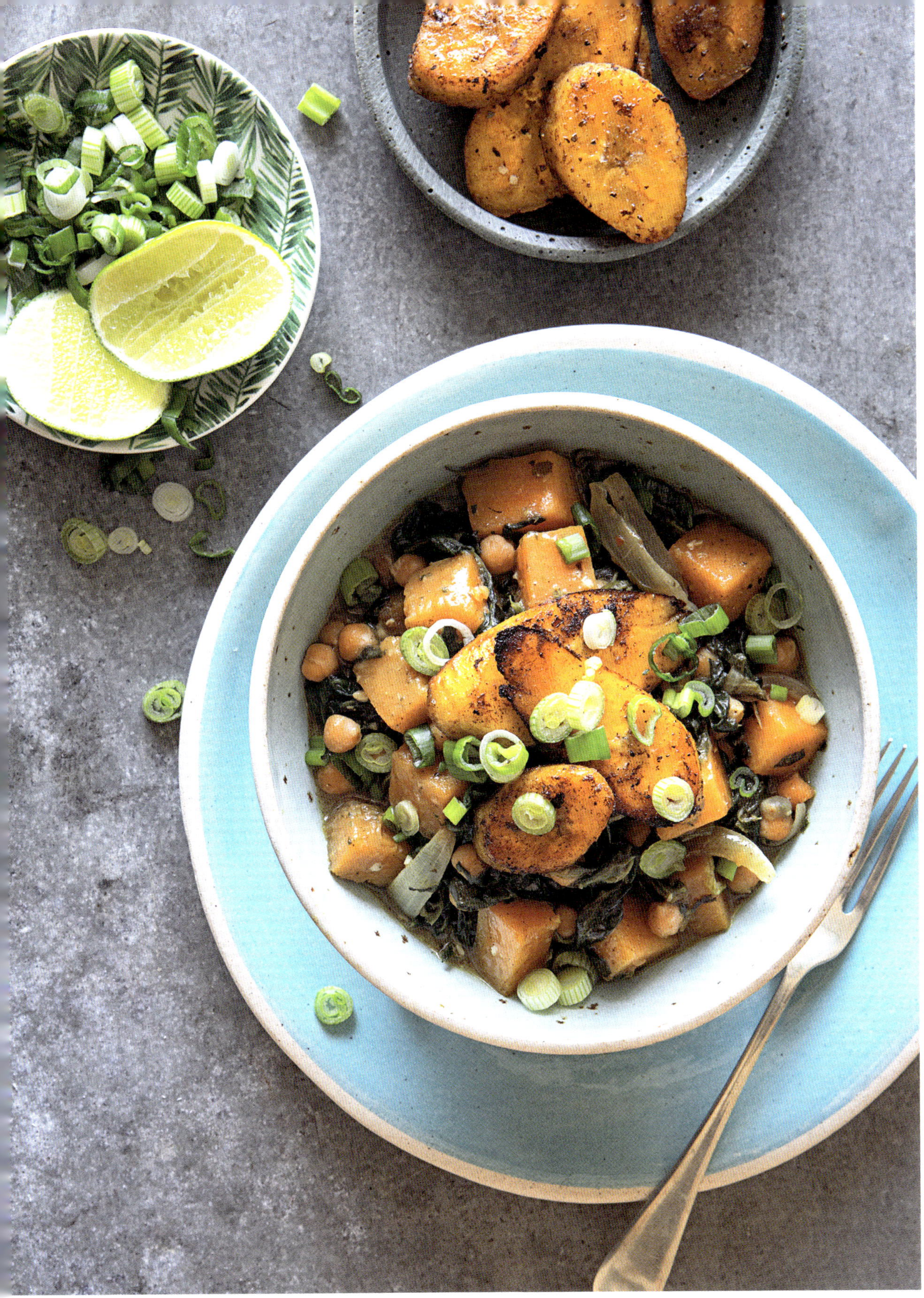

Baked bean pie

SERVES 4–6

750g potatoes, cut into 1.5–2cm cubes
25g butter, plus extra for greasing
2 medium onions, thinly sliced
small bunch of parsley, finely chopped
800g baked beans (2 cans)
1 tbsp wholegrain mustard
100g vegetarian Cheddar, grated
100g Gruyère, grated
75g vegetarian mozzarella, grated or torn
salt and black pepper

Most of us have a couple of tins of baked beans in the store cupboard and with the addition of some potato, onion and cheese you can turn them into the most warming, comforting dish you can imagine. A big hug of a meal, with a touch of mustard adding a welcome little edge of heat.

1. Put the potatoes in a steamer basket and steam them over simmering water for 8–10 minutes until tender.

2. Heat the butter in a frying pan and add the onions. Fry them over a medium heat until they are soft and translucent and starting to brown around the edges. Reserve a tablespoon of the parsley and stir the rest into the onions. Preheat the oven to 200°C/Fan 180°C/Gas 6.

3. Butter a deep ovenproof dish and add the onions and baked beans. Season with black pepper and stir to combine.

4. Put the steamed potatoes in a bowl. Stir in the mustard and season with salt and pepper. Stir in 75g each of the Cheddar and the Gruyère, then spoon the potato mixture over the baked beans. Mix the remaining cheese, including the mozzarella, with the reserved parsley and sprinkle over the top.

5. Bake in the oven for 25–30 minutes until the cheese has melted and browned and the baked beans are bubbling up under the potatoes.

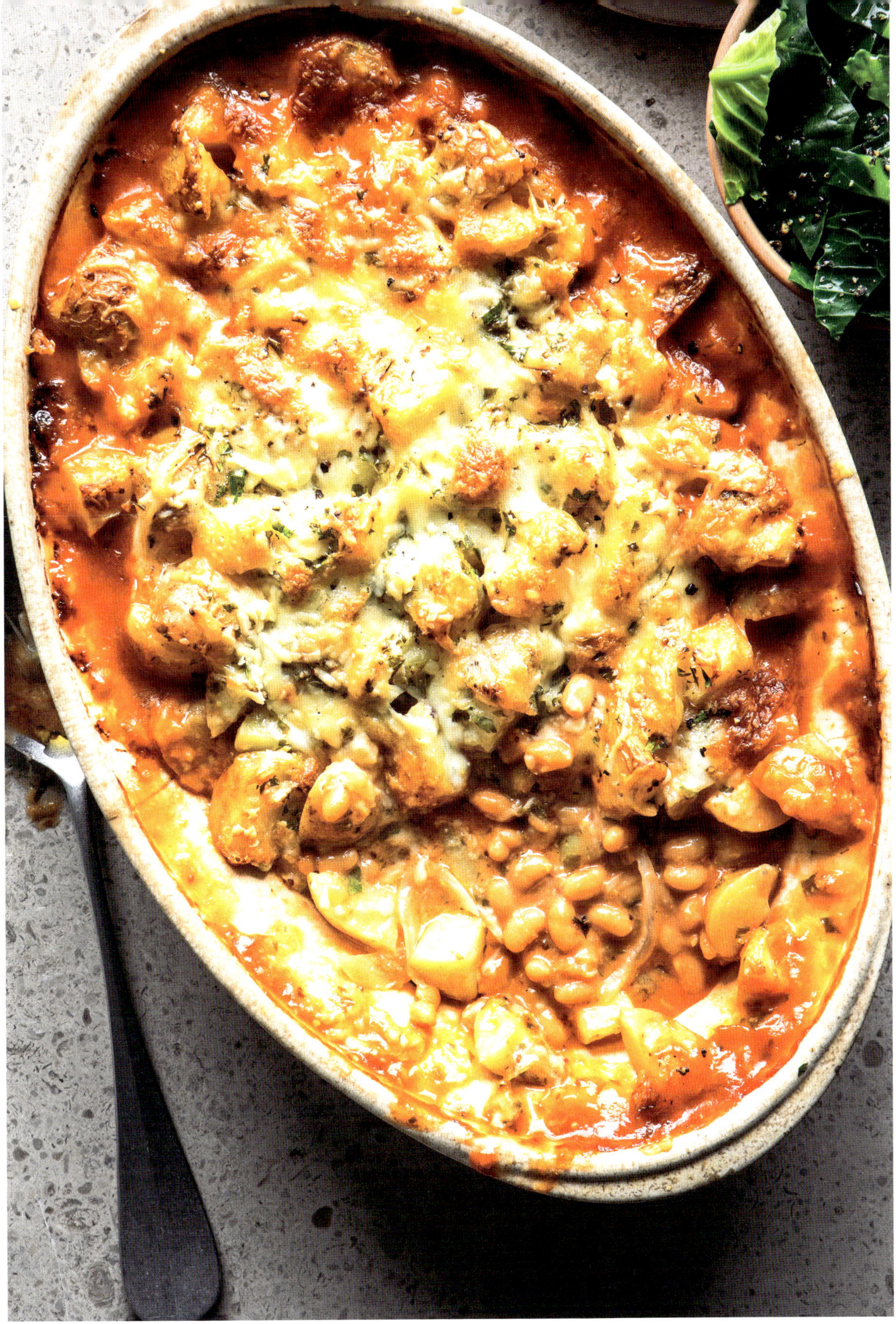

Soba noodles with miso mushrooms

SERVES 4

SAUCE
75g miso paste
2 tsp honey
3 tbsp dark soy sauce
1 tbsp rice vinegar
1 tbsp mirin
salt and black pepper

NOODLES
400g soba noodles
2 tsp sesame oil
1 tbsp soy sauce

MUSHROOMS
1 tbsp vegetable oil
500g mushrooms, sliced
25g root ginger, cut into matchsticks
3 garlic cloves, finely chopped

TO FINISH
1 tbsp sesame oil
sesame seeds
4 spring onions, sliced
a few coriander sprigs (optional)

When you're in the mood for a noodle nothing else will do. This recipe is dead tasty and mega quick to put together, so you can satisfy your craving in no time. Use any mushrooms you have available, but a mixture of shiitake and chestnut works well – and you could add a little asparagus too if you like. Fast food and fabulous.

1. First make the sauce. Whisk everything together and taste for seasoning. Add a little salt and pepper if necessary, then set aside.

2. Cook the noodles according to the packet instructions. Make sure you cook them in plenty of water and start testing for doneness after 2–3 minutes, as they can overcook very quickly. Drain the noodles thoroughly and run them under cold water to stop them cooking. Toss them in the sesame oil and soy sauce and set aside.

3. For the mushrooms, heat the vegetable oil in a wok. When the air over the oil is shimmering, add the mushrooms and stir-fry briskly for a few minutes until just cooked. Add the ginger and garlic and cook for a further couple of minutes, then pour in the sauce. Bring to the boil and simmer for 2 minutes.

4. Add the noodles to the wok and toss them gently to warm them through. Divide everything between 4 bowls and garnish with a little more sesame oil, sesame seeds, spring onions and coriander, if using.

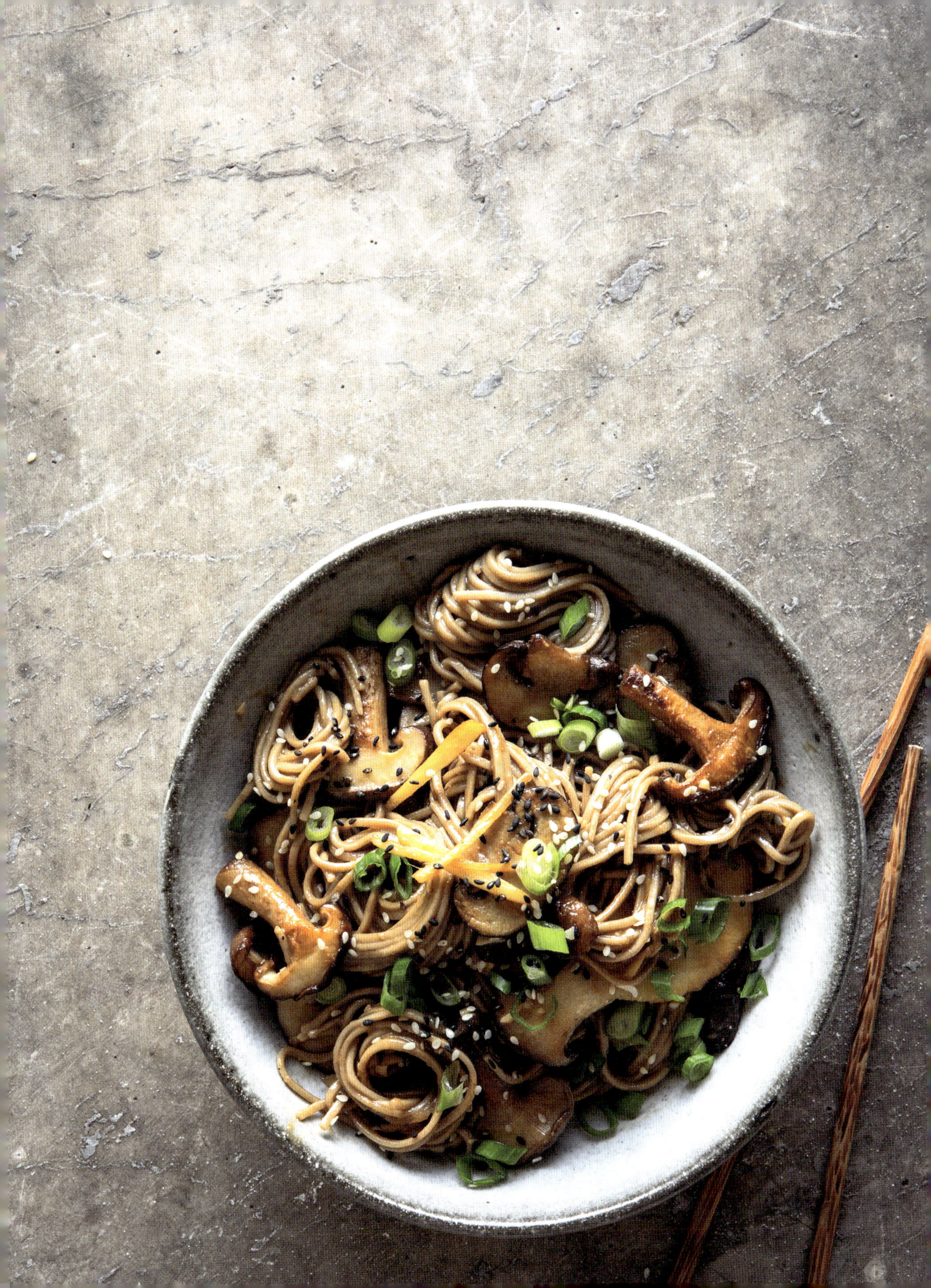

Shakshuka

SERVES 4

3 tbsp olive oil
2 large onions, sliced
2 red peppers, deseeded and cut into long slices
2 green peppers, deseeded and cut into long slices
4 garlic cloves, finely chopped
½ tsp cumin seeds
½ tsp caraway seeds
½ tsp cayenne pepper
1 tbsp tomato or red pepper purée
8 ripe tomatoes, chopped, or 2 x 400g cans of chopped tomatoes
1 tsp sugar (optional)
small bunch of coriander, roughly chopped
small bunch of parsley, roughly chopped
8 eggs
salt and black pepper

TO SERVE
cayenne pepper
Greek-style yoghurt

Enjoy this Middle Eastern dish for brunch, supper or at any time of day. It's a savoury sensation. There are loads of different variations but this is a goody I reckon. You could add a little crumbled feta on top, if you like.

1. Heat the oil in a large frying pan that has a lid. Add the onions and peppers and season them with salt and pepper. Cook over a medium heat until the veg have softened but still have a little bite – you don't want them to collapse down too much.

2. Add the garlic and cook for a further 2 minutes, then sprinkle the cumin and caraway seeds and the cayenne into the pan. Stir in the tomato or red pepper purée and cook for a couple more minutes until the paste starts to separate. Add the tomatoes with a splash of water.

3. Simmer the sauce for about 10 minutes, uncovered, until it has reduced a little. Taste after 5 minutes and add a little sugar if you think the tomatoes need it. Keep an eye on the texture – you don't want the sauce runny, but it mustn't be too dry, either. If it does look dry, add another splash of water. When the sauce has reduced, stir in the herbs.

4. Make 8 little wells in the sauce. One at a time, break the eggs into a cup and drop them carefully into the wells. Cook for a few more minutes until the whites are just set and the yolks are still runny. You might find it hard to make enough space for 8 eggs in one pan. If so, divide the sauce between 2 pans and cook 4 eggs in each. Sprinkle some cayenne over a little bowl of yoghurt and serve on the side.

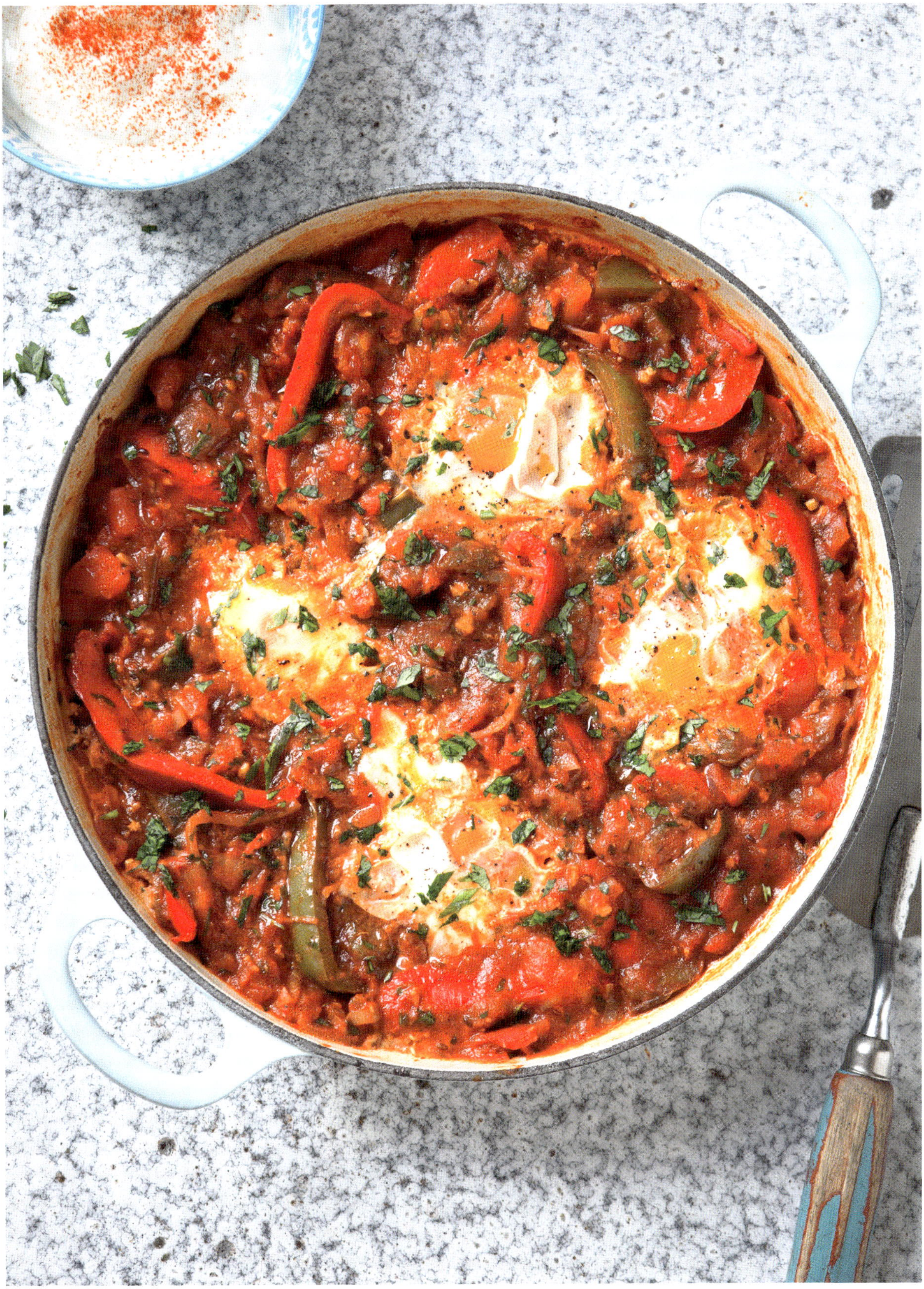

1   Tandoori chicken...188

2   Seekh kebabs...190

3   Classic burgers...192

4   Skirlie-stuffed chicken...194

5   Pot-roast chicken...196

6   Roast loin of pork with prune & apple stuffing...198

7   Traditional honey-glazed gammon...200

8   Chinese roast belly pork...202

9   Slow-roast shoulder of lamb...204

10   Roast beef topside...206

grills & roasts

> There's something so special about a big roast or the smell of something sizzling on the barbecue. It means there's a gathering around food and that's what this chapter celebrates.

Tandoori chicken

SERVES 4

1kg chicken thighs or drumsticks or a mixture, bone in, but skinned
4 garlic cloves, crushed
30g root ginger, peeled and grated
150g natural yoghurt
2 tbsp lemon juice
a few drops of red food colouring (optional)

SPICE MIX
1 tbsp ground cumin
1 tbsp ground coriander
1 tbsp Kashmiri chilli powder
1 tsp ground cardamom
1 tsp ground turmeric
1 tsp sweet smoked paprika
½ tsp ground ginger
½ tsp ground cinnamon
¼ tsp ground cloves
¼ tsp cayenne
salt and black pepper

RAITA
200g natural yoghurt
2 tsp dried mint
pinch of sugar

Tender and juicy with a sticky, spicy coating, tandoori chicken is an all-time Biker favourite. For best results and the most flavour, get started the day before so you can marinate the chicken overnight. This is great cooked on the barbecue but also good in the oven or under a grill. If you don't have Kashmiri chilli powder, you can use a mild red chilli powder instead.

1. First, make the spice mix by putting all the spices in a bowl with a teaspoon of salt and plenty of freshly ground black pepper.

2. Slash the flesh of the chicken pieces at intervals and put them in a bowl. In a separate bowl, mix the garlic and ginger with the yoghurt and lemon juice. Stir in the spice mix and the food colouring, if using.

3. Cover the chicken with the yoghurt mixture and mix well to make sure all the pieces are covered. The best thing to do is to get in there with your hands and rub the marinade into the cuts in the flesh. Cover the bowl with cling film and leave the chicken in the fridge to marinate for at least 3 hours, but preferably overnight.

4. Take the chicken out of the fridge an hour before you want to cook it so it can come up to room temperature. Prepare your barbecue. When the coals are hot, make sure they are either to one side or in the centre of the grill and place the chicken pieces so they are away from the direct heat. Cook, covered, for about half an hour, turning regularly and spraying with water on occasion until the meat is cooked through. Transfer the meat to the direct heat just to char it a little.

5. You can also bake the chicken in the oven or put it under the grill. To bake, preheat the oven to 180°C/Fan 160°C/Gas 4. Bake for 30 minutes, then turn up the heat to 220°C/Fan 200°C/Gas 7 for a further 5 minutes.

6. To grill, preheat the grill to high and cook the chicken for 10–12 minutes on each side. It should be cooked through and nicely charred in places.

7. To make the raita, mix the yoghurt with the mint, sugar and season with salt. Serve the chicken with lemon wedges and raita.

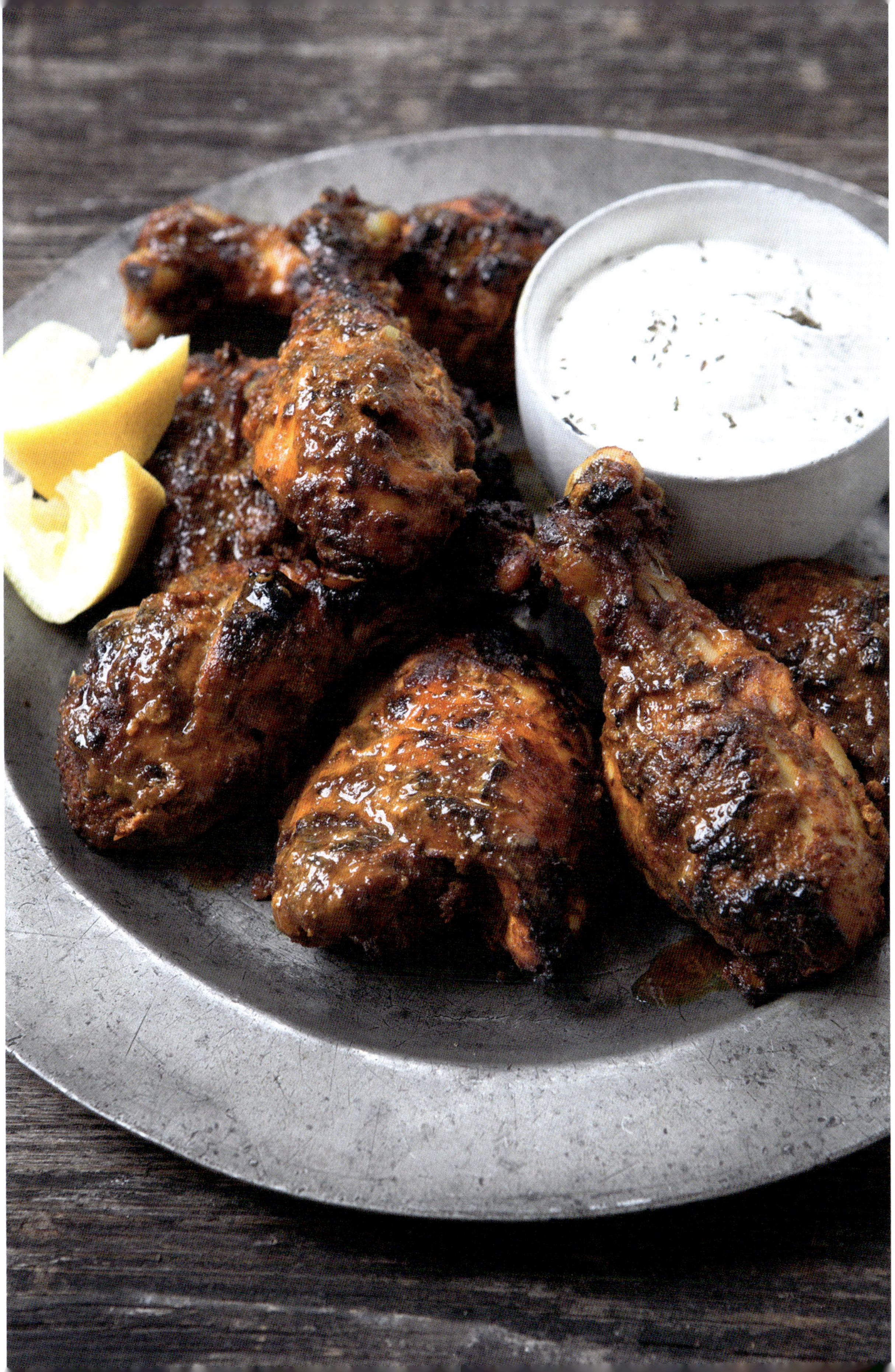

Seekh kebabs

MAKES 12

1 small onion, roughly chopped
¼ green pepper, roughly chopped
2 plump green chillies
15g root ginger, peeled and roughly chopped
3 garlic cloves, roughly chopped
2 tsp garam masala (shop-bought or see p.269)
¼ tsp hot chilli powder
1 tbsp tomato purée
400g lean minced lamb
3 tbsp finely chopped fresh coriander leaves
vegetable oil (if frying or for greasing skewers)
1–3 tbsp plain flour (optional)
salt and black pepper

TO SERVE
lemon wedges, mixed salad, dips and chutneys

Minced lamb has never tasted so good. These spicy kebabs can be shaped around skewers and grilled, or cooked like sausages in a frying pan with a little oil. Either way they hold together well and are mind-blowingly good to eat I promise you.

1. Put the onion, green pepper, chillies, ginger, garlic, garam masala, chilli powder, tomato purée and a teaspoon of salt in a food processor. Season with lots of freshly ground black pepper – add more than you think you'll need to be sure of a great flavour.

2. Blitz the ingredients into as smooth a paste as possible You'll probably need to remove the lid of the food processor and push the mixture down with a spatula a few times. Add the lamb and blitz once more. Tip the mixture into a bowl and stir in the coriander. Cover with cling film and chill for about an hour to allow the mixture to stiffen a little.

3. Divide the mince mixture into 12 portions. If using skewers, grease them with oil and shape each portion of the mixture into a long sausage shape around the skewer. Preheat the grill and grill the kebabs until cooked through.

4. Alternatively, roll each portion of the mixture into a ball, then shape it into a fairly thin sausage, about 15cm long. If your mixture becomes a little sticky, either roll with wet hands or dust your hands with plain flour as you roll. Heat 4 or 5 tablespoons of oil in a large non-stick frying pan. Gently place a few kebabs into the pan and cook for about 10 minutes over a medium heat until golden brown and cooked through, turning them often. Keep each batch warm while you fry the next. You shouldn't need to add any extra oil as some will be released through the fat in the lamb.

5. Serve the kebabs hot with lemon wedges for squeezing, salad and some dips and chutneys. This mince mixture also makes excellent kofta balls that can be eaten cold or made in advance and warmed through in a hot pan or on a baking tray in a preheated oven.

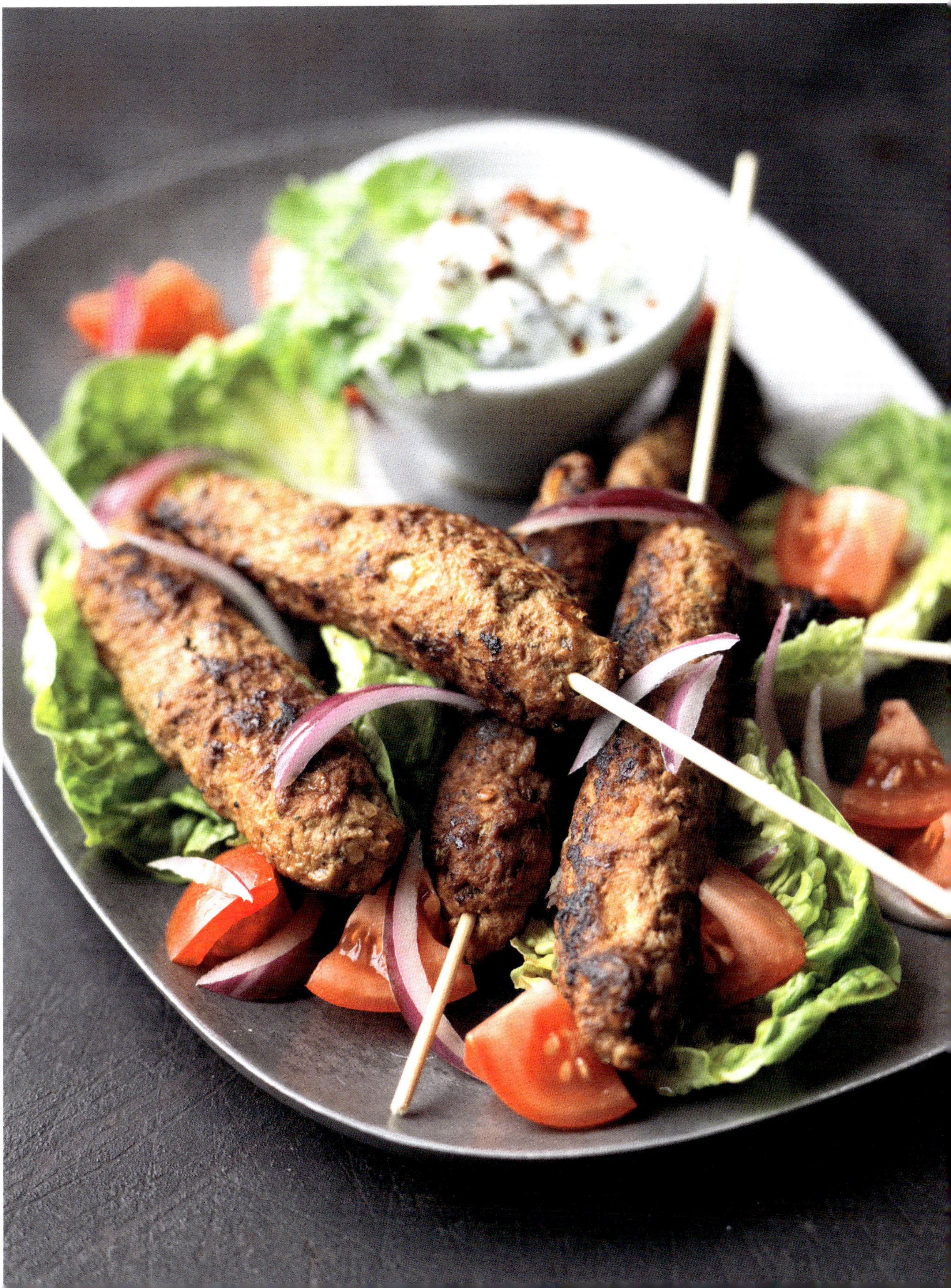

Classic burgers

SERVES 4

800g chuck steak, trimmed of any gristle or hard pieces of fat
50g bone marrow, finely diced (optional)
4 burger buns, split
salt and black pepper

BURGER SAUCE
100g mayonnaise
2 tbsp tomato ketchup
a squeeze of lemon juice
1 large gherkin, finely chopped
1 tsp garlic powder
½ tsp chipotle paste or other hot sauce

TOPPINGS
tomatoes
red onion
gherkins
lettuce

You'll find a veggie burger in the earlier 'veggie' chapter, but I just had to include a proper beef burger as well and this recipe can't be beat. These burgers are made with chuck steak, not mince, and I like to add a little bit of fat for a beautifully juicy result. The bone marrow option is delicious but if you don't fancy that, add a little bacon fat instead – see the tip below. Pile on your favourite toppings, then add the burger sauce – superb.

1. First prepare the steak. Make sure it's well chilled – in fact, you can freeze the meat, then let it thaw partially and you'll find it much easier to cut. Then put the meat through a coarse mincer, or chop it very finely by hand. It should be fine enough to stick together when you squeeze a handful. Add the bone marrow, if using.

2. Season the mixture with salt and black pepper, divide the mixture into 4 and then shape into round patties 2–2.5cm thick. The mincing and chopping will help bring the meat up to room temperature, but if not, leave the burgers to stand for a while.

3. Meanwhile, make the burger sauce. Simply mix all the ingredients together and season with salt and black pepper.

4. Heat a non-stick frying pan or a barbecue. When the pan or grill is too hot to hold your hand over, add the burgers – there's no need for oil, as some fat will render out of the meat. Leave for 4 minutes, by which time the burgers should be very well seared and have a thick crust. Flip them and cook for another 3 minutes for rare meat, 4 minutes for medium-rare, 5 for medium and up to 6 for well done.

5. Once the burgers are cooked to your liking, leave them to rest for a couple of minutes. Meanwhile, put the burger buns cut-side down on the pan or barbecue to toast very slightly and take up some of the meat flavours. Serve with the burger sauce and your choice of toppings.

BIKER TIP
If you want to add bacon instead of bone marrow, fry 4 rashers of streaky bacon slowly in a pan to render as much fat as possible. Allow the fat to cool, then add it to your burger mixture. Use the bacon rashers to garnish your burgers. If you want a cheesy topping, add some once you've flipped the burgers.

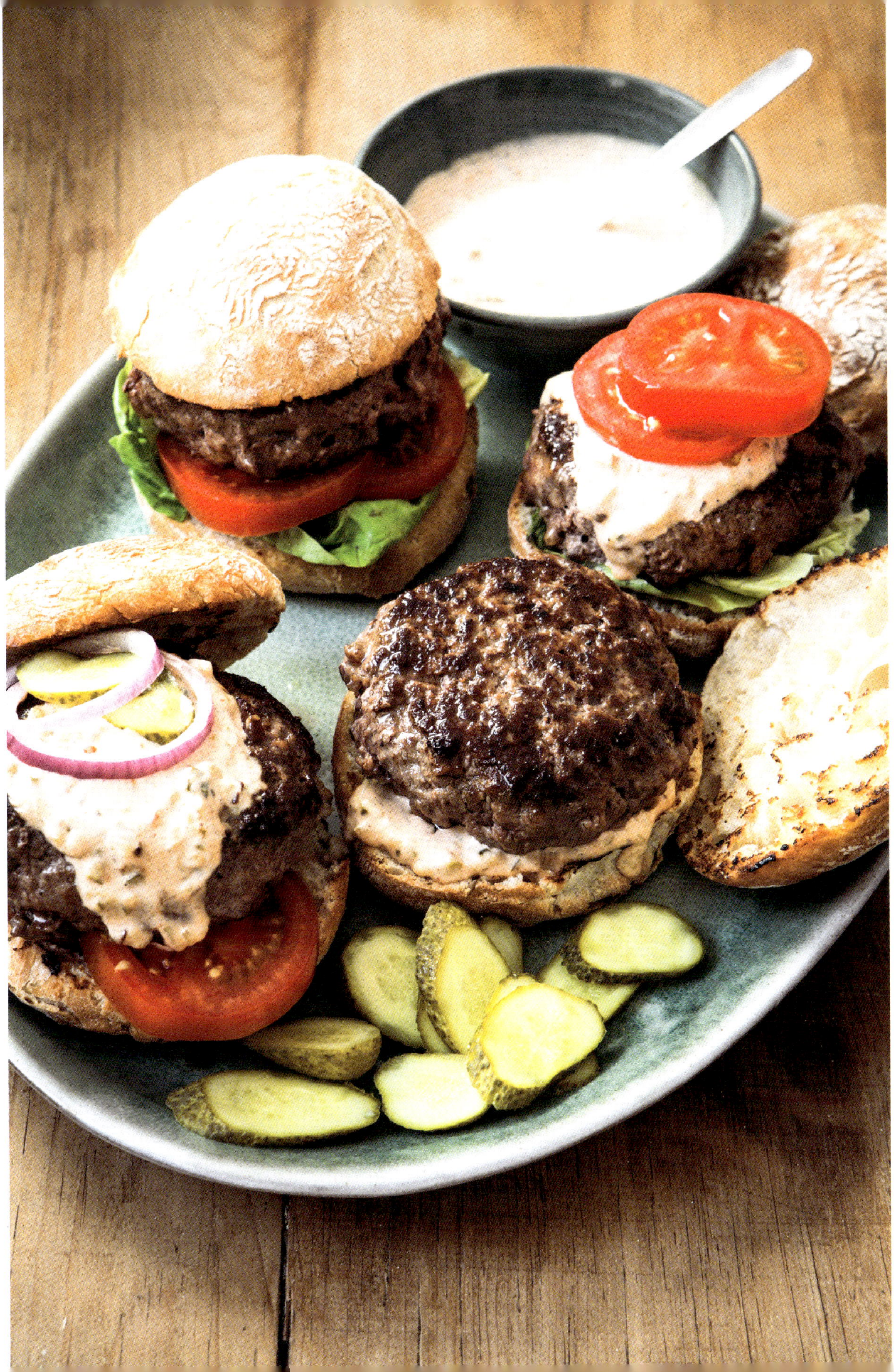

Skirlie-stuffed chicken

SERVES 4–6

1 x 1.5–1.8kg oven-ready chicken
1 large onion, sliced into thick rounds
1 thyme sprig
25g butter
squeeze of lemon juice
salt and black pepper

SKIRLIE STUFFING
50g butter or dripping
1 large onion, finely chopped
a few sage leaves, finely chopped
a few parsley sprigs, finely chopped
125g oatmeal (medium or coarse) or pinhead oats
100ml chicken stock
1 egg, beaten

GRAVY
1 tbsp flour
100ml white wine
300ml chicken stock

You can't go wrong with a roast chicken. one of the very best of Sunday dinners, and here's a version with a Scottish flavour. The chicken is stuffed with an oatmeal and herb mixture, known as skirlie, which soaks up juices and flavour from the bird. Totally delicious. A traditional Scottish recipe, skirlie can also be served as a side dish.

1. If possible, the day before you want to roast your chicken, remove it from any packaging and put it on a plate. Sprinkle with salt, then place it in the fridge, uncovered or loosely wrapped in kitchen paper. This helps to make the skin really crispy. Remove the chicken from the fridge at least an hour before you want to start roasting it.

2. To make the stuffing, melt the butter or dripping in a frying pan and add the onion. Fry it over a medium-high heat until softened and starting to brown, then stir in the herbs and the oatmeal or oats. Season with salt and plenty of black pepper – add more than you think you need! Pour over the chicken stock, then cook gently for 15–20 minutes, stirring regularly, until the oatmeal has cooked to an al dente texture. It will be quite crumbly and look quite dry. Remove from the heat and leave to cool, then stir in the egg.

3. Preheat the oven to 220°C/Fan 200°C/Gas 7.

4. Stuff the skirlie into the main cavity of the chicken, then weigh the stuffed chicken so you can work out how long to cook it for. Arrange the onion slices in the centre of a roasting tin and add the thyme, then place the chicken on top. Spread the butter over the chicken and sprinkle over the lemon juice.

5. Roast the chicken for 15 minutes, then reduce the oven temperature to 180°C/Fan 160°C/Gas 4. Cook the chicken for 20 minutes per 500g. When the cooking time is up, check for doneness. A temperature probe should read 72°C in the centre of the stuffing and in the thickest part of the leg and any juices should run clear. The legs will also feel loose.

6. Remove the chicken and onion from the roasting tin and cover loosely with foil. Pour the pan juices into a jug, then sprinkle the flour over the roasting tin. Place over a low heat and stir to scrape up any brown bits on the base of the tin – the flour will form a roux with any fat. Add the white wine and bring it to the boil, stirring to make sure the roasting tin base is completely clean. Transfer to a saucepan, add the stock and any juices from the resting chicken and simmer until you have a reduced and thickened gravy. Serve with the chicken and stuffing and some green vegetables.

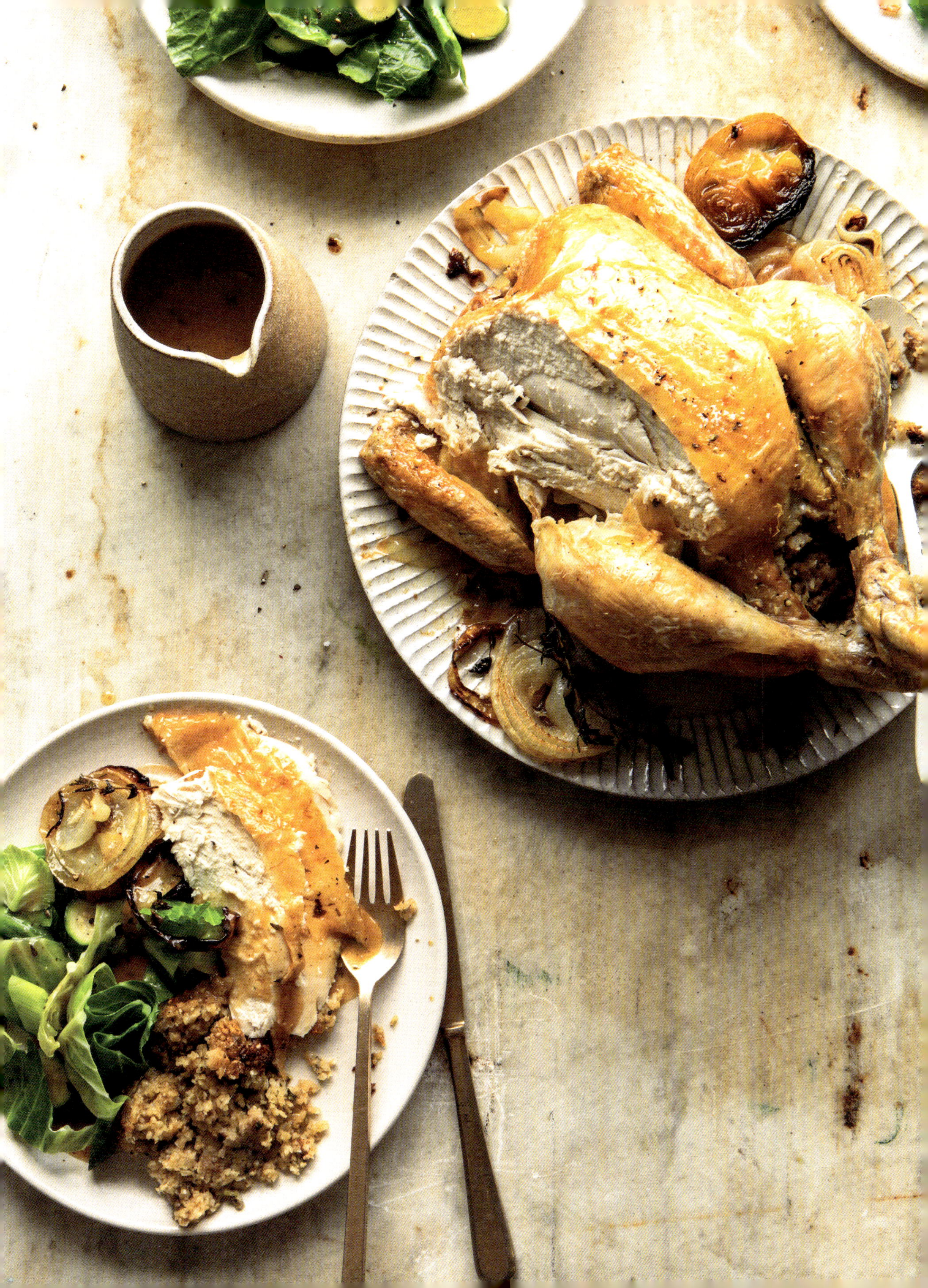

Pot-roast chicken

SERVES 4–6

1 tbsp olive oil
15g butter
100g bacon lardons
150g baby new potatoes, left whole
2 carrots, cut into chunks
2 celery sticks, cut into chunks
200g button mushrooms, left whole
1 x 1.5–1.8kg oven-ready chicken
2 bouquet garnis (tarragon, bay, thyme and parsley)
2 strips of pared lemon zest
1 garlic bulb, split into cloves but not peeled
100ml white wine
250ml chicken stock
2 or 3 leeks, cut into chunks
salt and black pepper

TO SERVE
1 tbsp finely chopped tarragon leaves
1 tbsp finely chopped parsley leaves

Here's a great chicken dinner without all the faff. The bird and all the veg are nestled into one pot and cooked to perfection. Then all you need to do is reduce the cooking juices to make a tasty gravy and dinner is ready. Tastes amazing and the bonus is that there's very little washing up to do.

1. Preheat the oven to 200°C/Fan 180°C/Gas 6. Heat the oil and butter in a large flameproof casserole dish, then add the bacon, potatoes, carrots and celery. Cook over a medium to high heat until everything is well browned, the bacon looks crisp and plenty of fat has rendered out. Add the mushrooms when everything else is nearly ready. Remove the vegetables and bacon with a slotted spoon and set them aside.

2. Take the chicken and put one bouquet garni and the lemon zest in the cavity. Place the chicken in the casserole dish, breast-side down, and brown it well on all sides, then turn it breast-side up. Sprinkle the garlic around the chicken and tuck in the other bouquet garni. Arrange all the browned vegetables and bacon around the sides, then season well.

3. Pour the wine around the chicken and bring it to the boil. Allow it to boil for a couple of minutes, then add the stock. Turn the heat down and place a lid on the dish. Transfer it to the oven and leave to cook for 30 minutes, then add the leeks. Put the lid back on and put the dish back in the oven for another 15 minutes.

4. Take the lid off and leave the dish in the oven for another 15 minutes to allow the chicken to crisp up. Check for doneness. A temperature probe should read 72°C in the centre of the stuffing and in the thickest part of the leg and any juices should run clear. The legs will also feel loose.

5. Transfer the chicken to a warm serving platter, draining off any liquid from the cavity back into the casserole dish. Using a slotted spoon, arrange the vegetables around the chicken. Cover with foil and leave the chicken to rest and keep warm.

6. Squash the garlic flesh out of the cloves back into the gravy. Put the casserole dish on the hob, bring the gravy to the boil and cook until it's reduced by about half and is nice and creamy. Strain the gravy into a jug and stir in the tarragon and parsley. Serve with the chicken and vegetables.

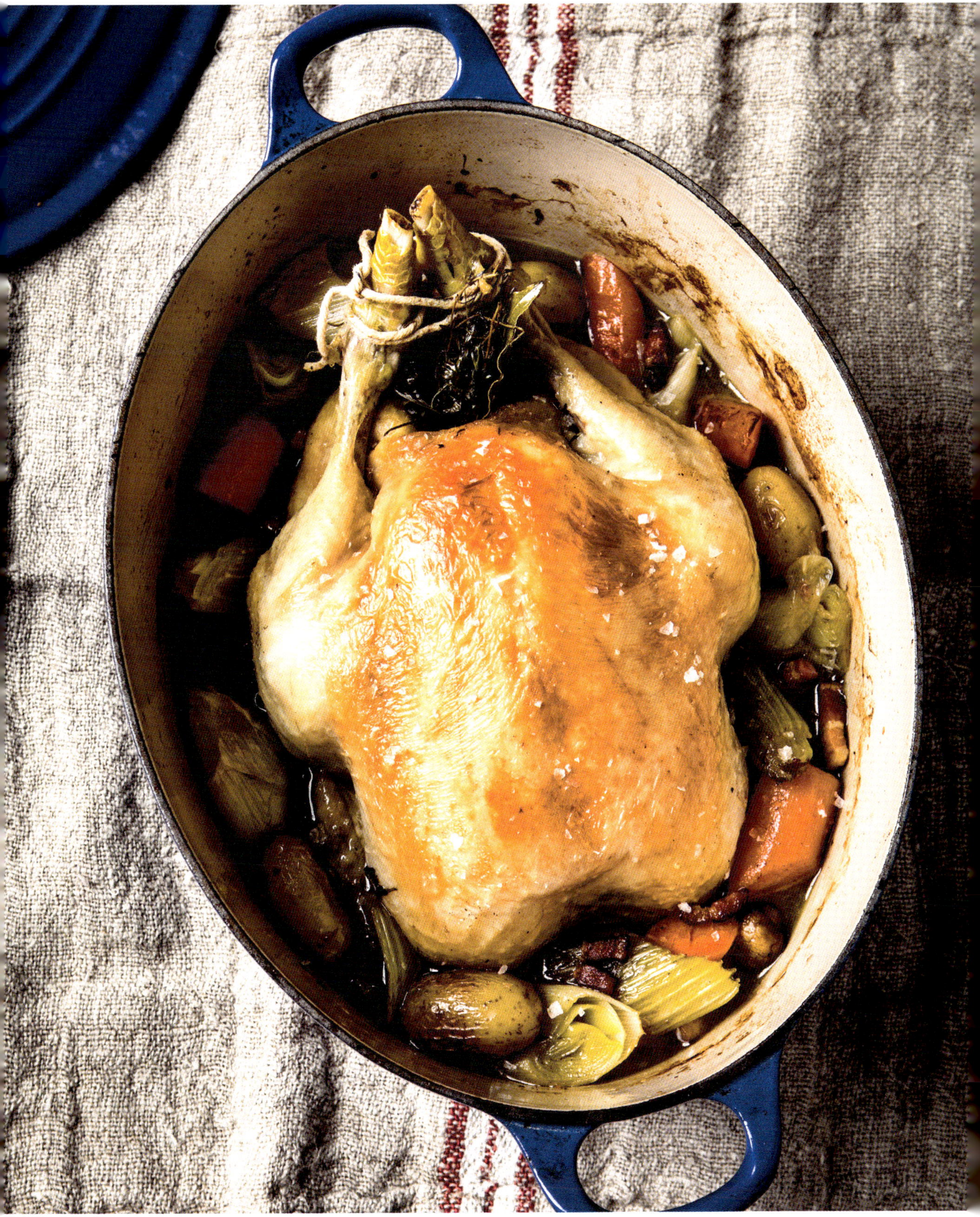

Roast loin of pork with prune & apple stuffing

SERVES 6

1 onion, thinly sliced
2kg boned loin of pork, rind scored thinly but deeply
1 tsp sea salt flakes, for the crackling

PRUNE & APPLE STUFFING
15g butter
1 tbsp olive oil
1 onion, chopped
2 garlic cloves, finely chopped
1 large Bramley apple, peeled and cut into small chunks
finely grated zest of 1 lemon
100g no-soak pitted prunes, quartered
1 tbsp clear honey
2 tsp dried sage or 2 tbsp finely shredded fresh sage leaves
50g fresh white breadcrumbs
salt and black pepper

CIDER GRAVY
2 tbsp plain flour
250ml dry cider
350ml vegetable cooking water
6–8 fresh sage leaves, finely shredded (optional)

This is a really special roast dinner, a splendid joint of pork with a fruity stuffing and crowned with everyone's favourite – crisp, crunchy crackling. The cider gravy gives the finishing touch – save the water from par-boiling your potatoes for making this. And if you're not sure about scoring the rind or making a pocket for the stuffing, ask your butcher to do it for you.

1. First make the stuffing. Melt the butter with the oil in a large non-stick frying pan. Cook the chopped onion over a low heat for about 8 minutes until softened and beginning to brown, stirring occasionally, then add the garlic and cook for another couple of minutes. Add the apple along with the lemon zest and prunes. Cook over a fairly high heat for 3–4 minutes until the apple begins to soften, stirring regularly. Stir in the honey and sage. Toss together for a couple of minutes until hot, then remove from the heat and stir in the breadcrumbs and plenty of seasoning. If you are not cooking the pork immediately, allow the stuffing to cool completely before using.

2. Preheat the oven to 230°C/Fan 210°C/Gas 8. Place the sliced onion in a pile in the centre of a large roasting tin – the pile should be about the same length as the pork. Pat the rind with kitchen paper to absorb any moisture and cut off any string that may be holding it.

3. Starting at the thin end of the joint and working towards the centre, cut between the meat and the rind – you could ask your butcher to do this for you. Open the rind out and spoon the stuffing evenly around the meat. Roll the meat up firmly, keeping the stuffing from bulging out of the pork. Cut about 5 pieces of kitchen string, 20cm long, and use them to tie the pork at even intervals – tie at each end and the middle first. Massage sea salt into the score marks made in the rind.

4. Place the pork on the onion slices and roast in the centre of the oven for 20 minutes. Turn the oven down to 190°C/Fan 170°C/Gas 5 and cook the pork for another hour. If any bits of the stuffing drop out into the tin, try to scoop them up before they burn as they might give the gravy a bitter taste. When the hour is up, take the pork out of the oven and transfer it to a baking tray. Turn the oven up to 230°C/Fan 210°C/Gas 8 and put the pork back in the oven for another 20 minutes, until the crackling is crisp.

5. To make the gravy, spoon off as much of the fat as possible from the original roasting tin, leaving all the softened onion and flavoursome, sticky sediment. Throw away any burnt onion. Place the tin on the hob, sprinkle over the flour

BIKER TIP

If you like, add small apple halves or quarters to the tin for the last 20 minutes of the cooking time and serve them with the pork instead of making apple sauce.

and stir it into the pork juices. Pour over the cider and bring to the boil, stirring constantly. Cook for 2 minutes, then add the water and return to the boil. Leave to simmer for a few minutes, stirring occasionally, until all the sticky sediment has been scraped up from the bottom of the tin. Strain through a sieve into a saucepan and season to taste with salt and pepper.

6. When the pork is ready, put it on a large, warmed serving platter, cover loosely with foil and leave it to rest for 15–20 minutes. Just before serving, warm the gravy until bubbling. Tip any pork resting juices into the gravy and heat through for a few minutes and added the fresh sage leaves, if using. Carve the pork into thick slices and serve with the cider gravy and lots of mash and greens.

Traditional honey-glazed gammon

SERVES 10–20

2–4kg boned and rolled smoked gammon
2 onions, peeled and halved
2 carrots, scrubbed and cut into short lengths
2 celery sticks, cut into short lengths
4 bay leaves
12 black peppercorns
small handful of whole cloves

GLAZE
4 tbsp runny honey
4 tbsp prepared English mustard

A beautiful, clove-studded, glazed gammon is a welcome sight on your table at Christmas or at any time of year. And it's no more trouble to cook a big piece than a smaller joint, so is ideal for a party. Enjoy hot with some braised red cabbage and Cumberland or parsley sauce, while any leftovers are delicious served cold too. Just remember to take the gammon out of the fridge half an hour beforehand. Double-smoked works a treat for this recipe if you can get your hands on some.

1. Put the gammon in a large saucepan and cover with cold water. Bring to the boil over a high heat, then remove the pan from the heat and drain all the water away. Refill the pan with fresh water, add the onions, carrots, celery, bay leaves and peppercorns. Return to the heat and bring to the boil. Reduce the heat, cover and leave the gammon to simmer gently for 20 minutes per 500g. If your pan isn't quite big enough for the water to cover the joint completely, turn it over halfway through the cooking time.

2. When the gammon is ready, remove the pan from the heat and carefully lift the meat from the water and place it on a board. Leave to cool for 15 minutes. Don't throw the stock away – use it for making a delicious pea and ham soup.

3. Preheat the oven to 200°C/Fan 180°C/Gas 6. Using a small knife, carefully cut away and peel off the rind, leaving as much of the fat as possible. Score the fat in a diamond pattern and push a clove into the centre of each diamond. Line a roasting tin with a large piece of foil and place the gammon inside. Bring the sides of the foil up to create a bowl shape that the gammon can nestle inside.

4. To make the glaze, mix the honey and mustard together until smooth and brush half evenly over the gammon, including the face. Bake in the centre of the oven for 10 minutes. Take the tin out of the oven and brush the remaining honey mixture over the gammon. Put the meat back in the oven, placing the tin so the opposite side of the gammon is facing the back. Cook for 10–15 minutes until the fat is glossy and golden brown. If the top starts to get too brown in places, cover loosely with small pieces of foil. Leave to stand for about 15 minutes before carving.

5. Put the gammon on a serving platter or board. Pour any of the marinade that's collected in the foil into a small pan and warm it through gently. Carve the gammon into thin slices and serve dribbled with a little of the hot glaze liquor to serve.

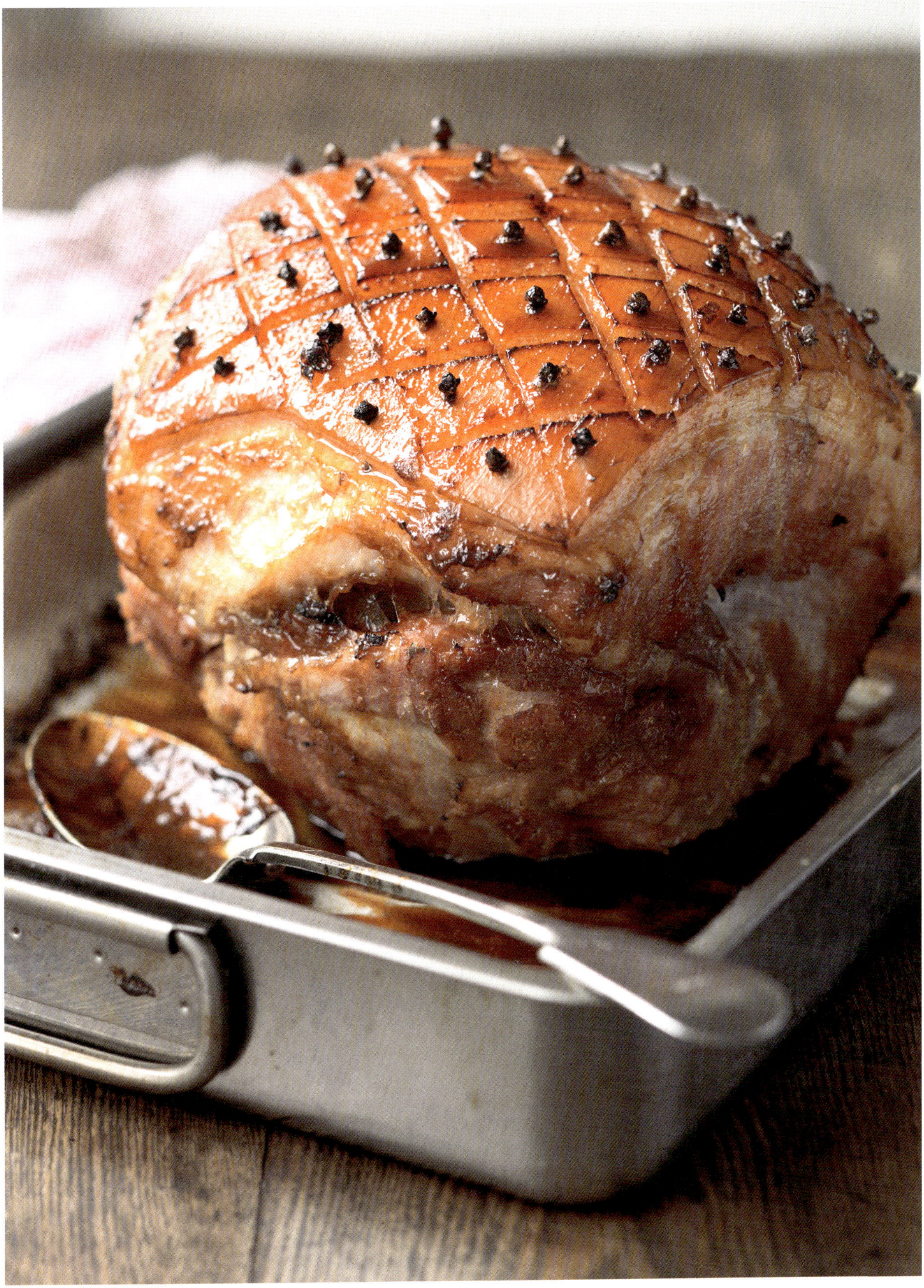

Chinese roast belly pork

SERVES 4

1 piece of boned belly pork (about 1.5kg), scored
2 tsp Chinese 5-spice powder
600g waxy potatoes, cut into chunks
1 onion, finely chopped
1 garlic bulb, broken into cloves
3 star anise
2 tbsp soy sauce
50ml mirin
salt and black pepper

A Sunday roast with a spicy Asian flavour, this recipe, with juicy belly pork and cracking crackling, is a winner. The potatoes are cooked in the same tin as the meat so they soak up all the lovely juices, then all you need to add are some greens such as pak choi or good old spinach or cabbage.

1. Pat the pork dry and rub salt on to the skin and into the score lines. Mix more salt and pepper with the Chinese 5-spice and rub this over the flesh (not the skin). Leave the meat in the fridge for at least 2 hours, preferably overnight. Take the pork out of the fridge, pat it dry again and bring up to room temperature.

2. Preheat the oven to 220°C/Fan 200°C/Gas 7. Spread the potatoes over the base of a roasting tin, then sprinkle them with the onion, garlic cloves and star anise. Season with salt. Mix the soy sauce and mirin with 100ml of water and pour the mixture over the potatoes. Place the pork on top.

3. Roast in the oven for 20 minutes, then reduce the temperature to 180°C/Fan 160°C/Gas 4 and continue to roast for a further 2 hours. By this time, the pork should be tender, with much of the fat rendered out, and the skin should be very crisp and slightly blistered. If the pork isn't quite done, leave it for another 20–30 minutes.

4. Remove the pork from the oven and leave it to rest. Strain off any liquid to serve as a thin gravy. Remove the garlic cloves and either squeeze the flesh out of the skins and whisk it into the liquid, or leave them to serve as they are. Put the roasting tin back in the oven for 20–25 minutes so that the now exposed potatoes can crisp up.

5. Serve the pork thickly sliced with the gravy, potatoes and perhaps some Chinese greens on the side.

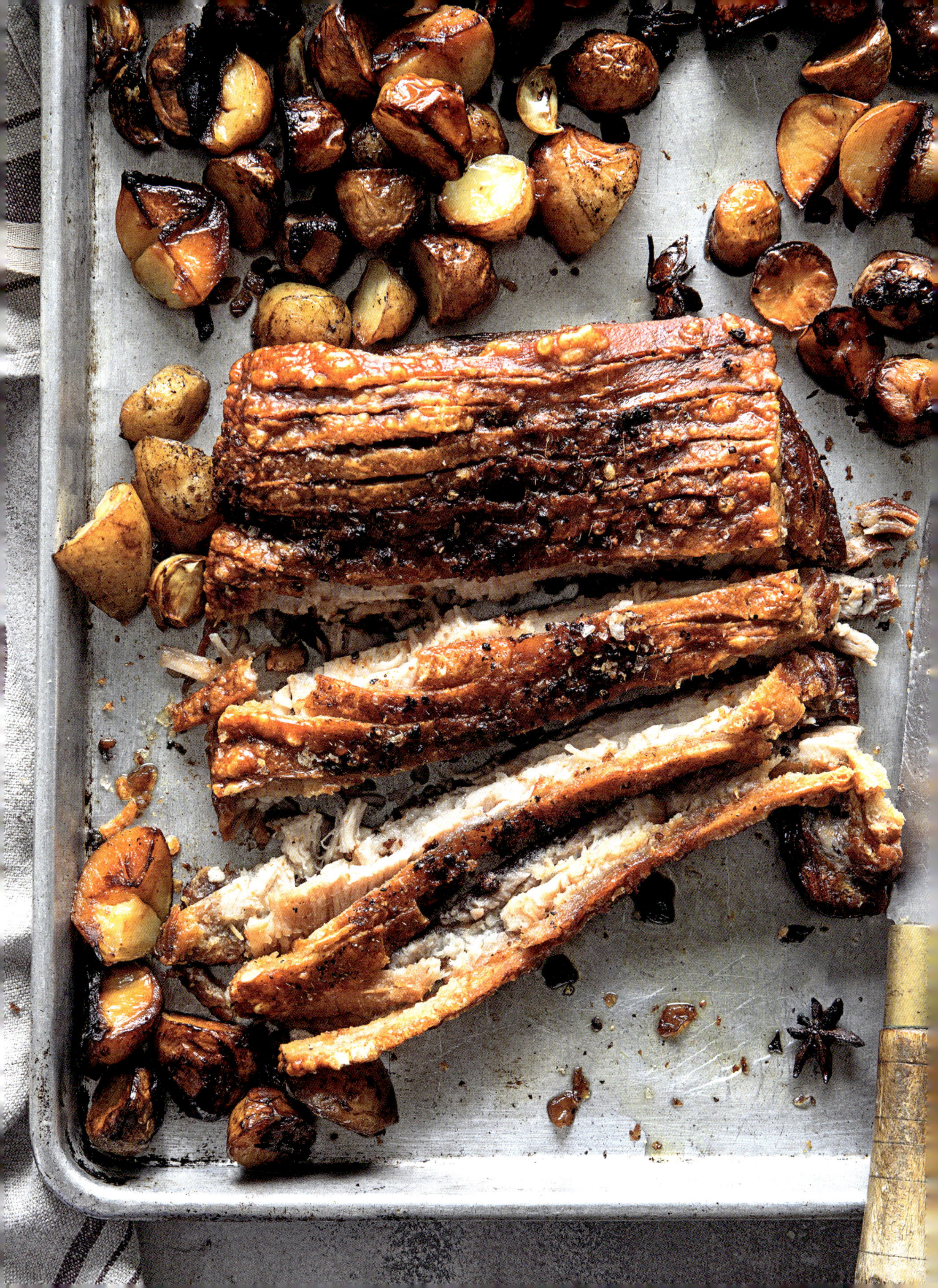

Slow-roast shoulder of lamb

SERVES 4-6

1 x 1.5–2kg lamb shoulder, on the bone
1 tbsp olive oil
1 tsp dried oregano
½ tsp ground cinnamon
2 red onions, sliced into wedges
1 lemon, sliced
3 or 4 rosemary sprigs
2 oregano sprigs
3 bay leaves
1 garlic bulb, separated into unpeeled cloves
250ml white wine
2 tbsp capers
2 tbsp chopped green olives
up to 1 tsp honey (optional)
salt and black pepper

TO SERVE (OPTIONAL)
roast new potatoes with garlic and rosemary (see p.256)

Nothing better than a slow-roast. Yes, the meat has to be cooked for ages but once it's in, you can go off, put your feet up and let the oven do its magic. You'll be rewarded with meltingly soft, tender, flavoursome meat. Shove some new potatoes into the oven to roast, make the gravy and you have the most fabulous feast with surprisingly little effort.

1. Preheat the oven to 220°C/Fan 200°C/Gas 7. Rub the skin of the shoulder of lamb with olive oil. Sprinkle over the oregano and cinnamon and season with plenty of salt and pepper.

2. Spread the onions, lemon, herbs and garlic over the base of a large roasting tin, placing the garlic cloves in the centre to make sure they are covered by the lamb. Put the lamb shoulder on top. Pour the white wine and 100ml of water around the meat.

3. Roast the lamb for 20 minutes so it develops a crust, then turn the heat down to 150°C/Fan 130°C/Gas 2. Roast for 2½–4 hours, depending on the size of your joint. Start checking after 2½ hours – when the lamb is ready the bone will feel loose and the meat will be very soft and tender.

4. Remove the tin from the oven and place the lamb on a warmed serving dish. Cover with foil. Strain the contents of the roasting tin and add the onions and lemon slices to the platter. Push everything else – including the garlic – through a sieve, then cool until the fat settles on top – this won't take long.

5. Transfer the strained juices to a saucepan and place over a medium heat to warm through. Have a taste and season to your liking. Stir in the capers and olives and add the honey if the sauce is too sharp.

6. Serve the lamb with the gravy at the table and some roast new potatoes.

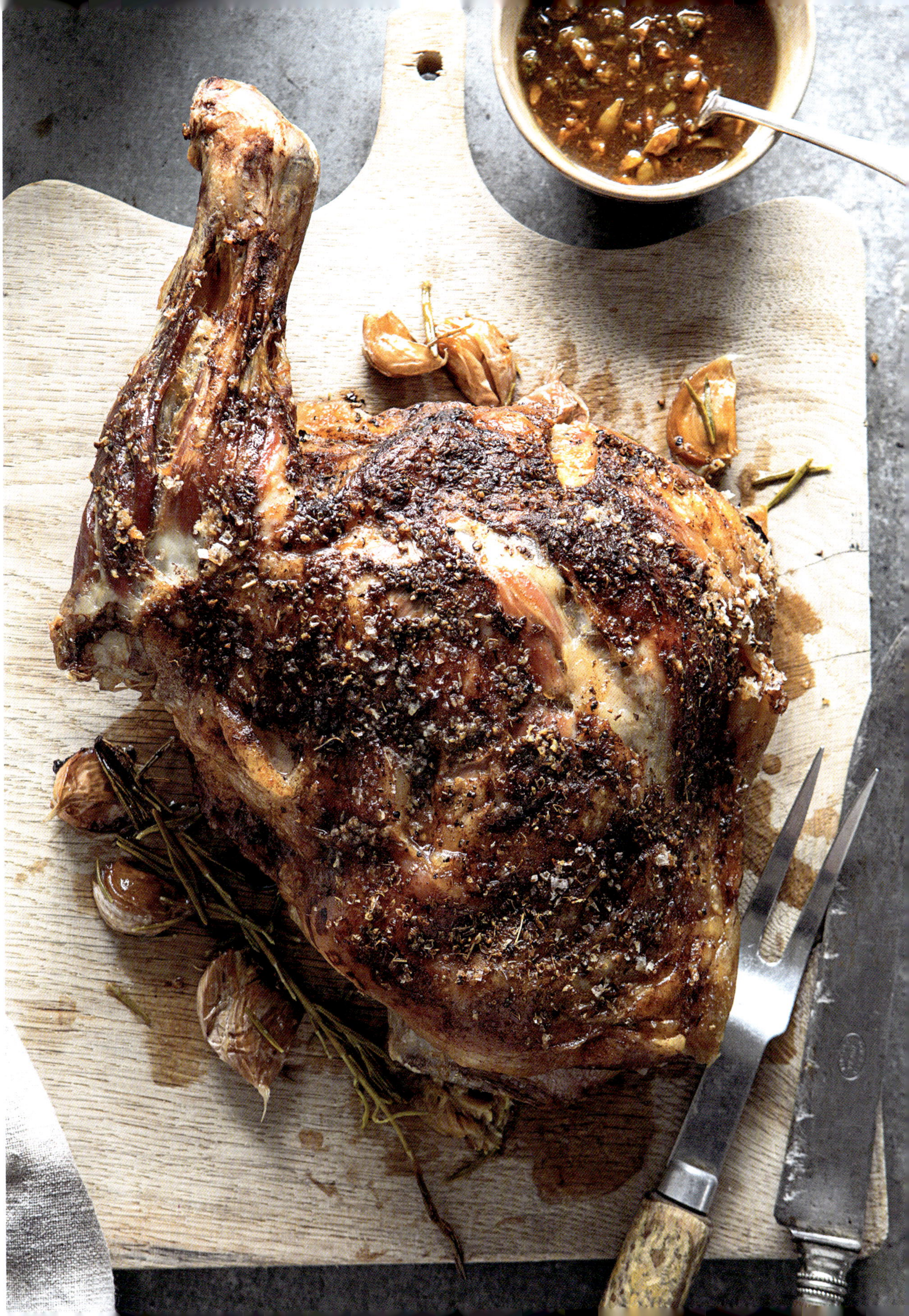

Roast beef topside

SERVES 6–8

1.5kg piece of topside, tied
2 tsp ground black peppercorns
1 tbsp English mustard powder
1 tsp onion or garlic powder (optional)
1 tsp dried thyme

GRAVY
1 tbsp flour
100ml red or white wine
400ml well-flavoured beef stock
1 tsp redcurrant jelly (optional)
salt and black pepper

TO SERVE
roast potatoes (see p.254)
Yorkshire pudding (see p.262)
green vegetables

Beef is the classic Sunday roast, but rib or sirloin are both mega expensive these days. Topside is a lot cheaper and it still makes an excellent juicy roast. Just make sure you allow the meat to come up to room temperature before putting it in the oven, then let it rest after cooking and you'll have a Sunday dinner to be proud of.

1. Be sure to take the meat out of the fridge at least 45 minutes to an hour before you want to roast it, so it can come up to room temperature. Preheat the oven to its highest setting and note the weight of the meat so you can work out the roasting time.

2. Mix the peppercorns, mustard powder, onion or garlic powder, if using, and the dried thyme in a small bowl. Sprinkle this mixture over the joint, pressing it in as you go, until the meat is completely covered. Put the beef in a roasting tin, place it in the preheated oven and roast for 15 minutes.

3. Reduce the oven temperature to 200°C/Fan 180°C/Gas 6. Roast the beef for a further 12 minutes per 500g if you want to serve it rare, 15 minutes per 500g for medium rare, 17 minutes per 500g for medium, and 20 minutes per 500g for well-done meat.

4. When the beef is cooked to your liking, remove it from the oven. Put the meat on a platter or carving board, cover it with foil and leave it to rest for 20 minutes.

5. Meanwhile, make the gravy. Strain the contents of the roasting tin into a jug and set it aside for a few minutes – the fat will rise to the top. Put the roasting tin over a low heat. Take a tablespoon of fat from the jug and add it to the roasting tin, then sprinkle in the flour. Stir thoroughly, making sure you scrape up all the sticky bits from the bottom of the tin, as they add flavour.

6. Pour the wine into the pan and stir continuously. Gradually add the beef stock and the separated pan juices, stirring until you have a nice gravy. Pour the gravy into a small saucepan; the bottom of the roasting tin should look clean. Leave the gravy on a fairly low heat and add any juices from the resting meat. Season with salt and pepper and, if you would like a little sweetness, add a teaspoon of redcurrant jelly.

7. Carve the beef and serve with, roast potatoes, Yorkshire pudding, green veg and the piping hot gravy.

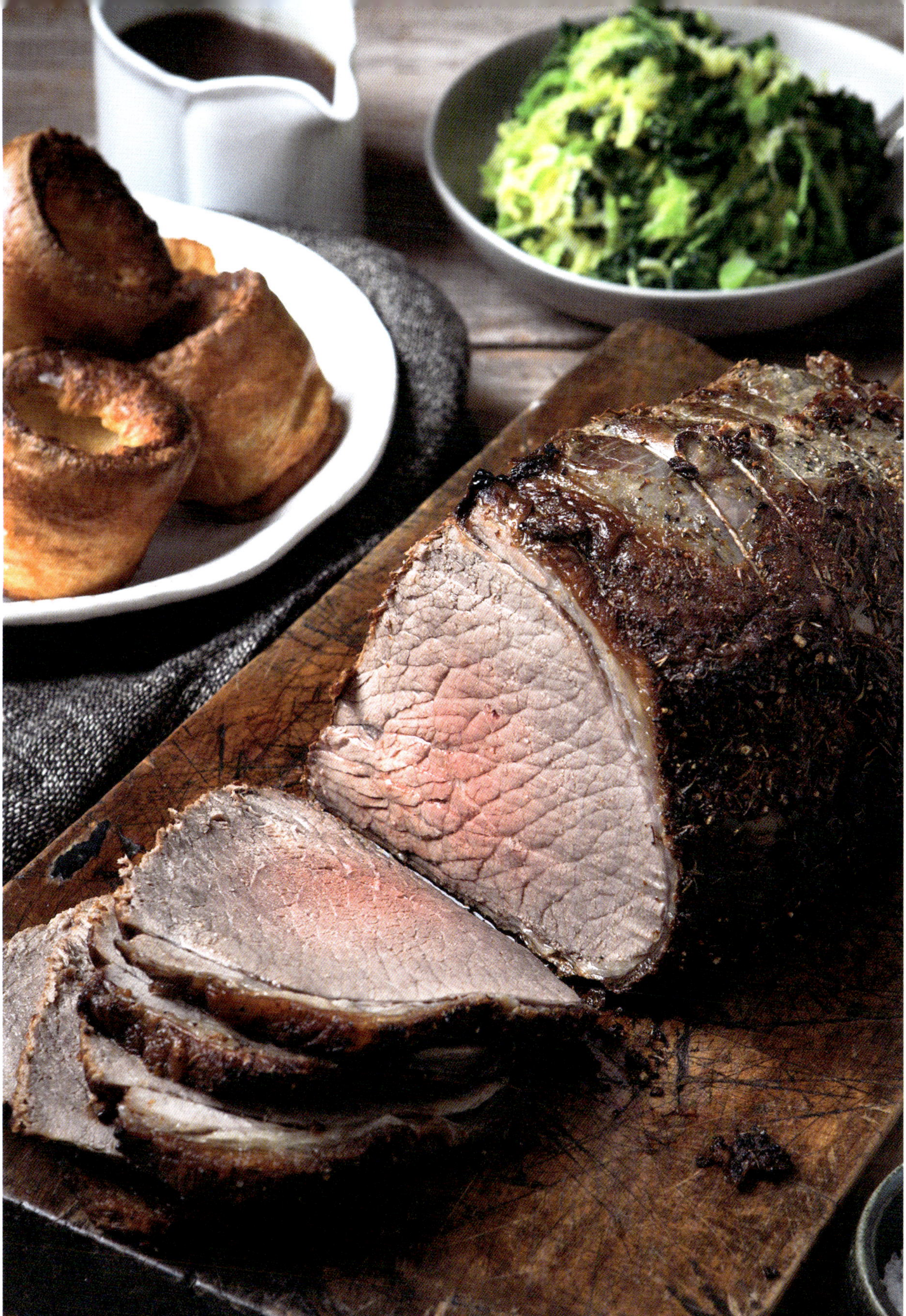

1. Cinnamon swirls...210
2. Stem ginger & lemon drizzle cake...212
3. Chocolate cake...214
4. Cherry & chocolate cheesecake...216
5. Spicy fruit loaf...218
6. Biker brownies...220
7. Caramelised almond & raisin cookies...222
8. Gingerbread cake...224
9. Dundee cake...226
10. Brown butter cupcakes...228

bakes

❝ Nothing beats the smell of a bake in the oven – it says you're home. There's a joy and a magic about baking and it's a great way to treat those you love. ❞

Cinnamon swirls

MAKES 16

375ml whole milk
100g butter, diced
75g light brown soft sugar
650g strong plain flour, plus extra for dusting
7g fast-action dried yeast
a good pinch of salt
1 egg, beaten

FILLING
100g butter
100g light brown soft sugar
25g ground almonds
2 tbsp ground cinnamon

TOPPING
25g butter
½ tsp ground cinnamon
2 tsp caster sugar

The aroma of cinnamon and sugar as these are baking is so tempting you'll hardly be able to bear the wait until they are cooked and cool enough to eat. Just be patient – it will be worth it. This is one of my favourite bakes.

1. Line 2 baking trays with baking parchment. Pour the milk into a pan and add the butter and sugar. Place the pan over a medium heat until the butter has melted and the mixture is warm, but don't let it get too hot. Remove from the heat and set aside.

2. Put the flour in a bowl, add the yeast and mix well, then stir in the salt. Stir the beaten egg into the warm milk and pour it all on to the flour mixture. Mix with a wooden spoon, then with your clean hands until the mixture forms a soft, spongy dough.

3. Lightly dust a work surface with flour, turn out the dough and knead for about 10 minutes. The dough will be fairly wet to begin with, but within a few minutes it should feel less sticky – sprinkle a little extra flour over the surface while kneading if necessary. Set aside while you make the filling.

4. For the filling, cream the butter in a bowl with the brown sugar, ground almonds and cinnamon. Roll out the dough on a floured work surface to form a rectangle of about 35 x 50cm. Use a rubber spatula or a palette knife, to spread the filling over the dough, taking it all the way to the edges.

5. Roll the dough up from one of the longest sides, keeping it fairly tight. Trim the ends and cut the dough into 2cm rounds – brush them with a little water if they begin to undo. Place the rounds on the baking trays, leaving plenty of room between them, and leave to rise in a warm place for 45–60 minutes or until doubled in size.

6. Preheat the oven to 220°C/Fan 200°C/Gas 7. For the topping, melt the butter in a small pan and brush it over the cinnamon swirls. Mix the ground cinnamon and caster sugar and sprinkle this over the buns. Bake the swirls for 10–12 minutes or until well risen and pale golden brown. Leave to cool on the tins for a few minutes before serving.

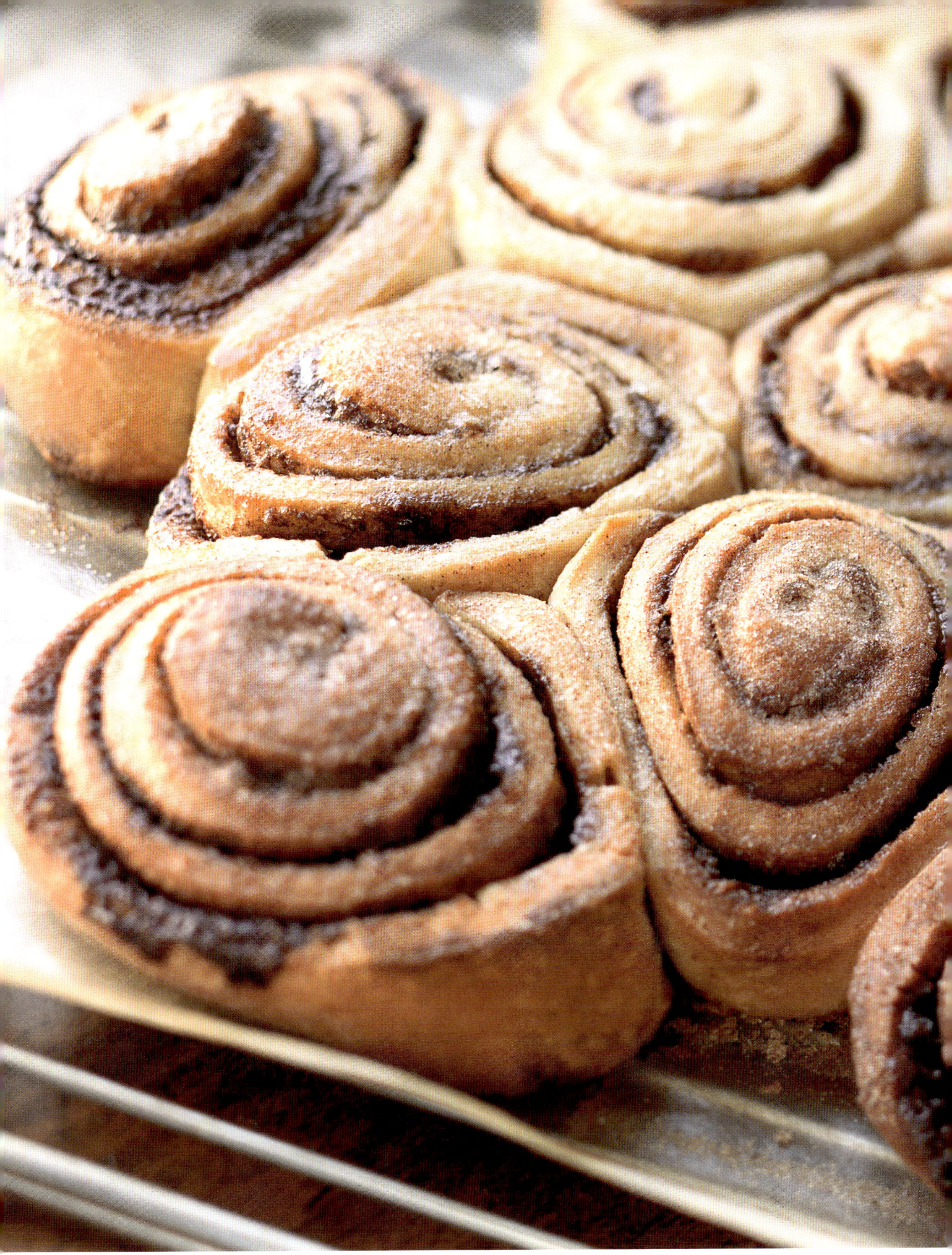

Stem ginger & lemon drizzle cake

MAKES ABOUT 12 SLICES

175g butter, softened, plus extra for greasing
175g golden caster sugar
2 balls of stem ginger, rinsed, dried and very finely chopped
zest of 1 lemon
pinch of salt
3 eggs
225g self-raising flour
3–4 tbsp milk

TOPPING
juice of 1 lemon
2–3 tbsp ginger syrup
1 ball of stem ginger, rinsed, dried and finely chopped
2 tbsp granulated sugar

A lemon drizzle cake is always a good teatime treat and adding some chopped stem ginger and ginger syrup makes it even better. It's easy to make too and a top version of a classic.

1. Preheat the oven to 180°C/Fan 160°C/Gas 4. Grease a large loaf tin with butter and line it with baking parchment.

2. Beat the butter and sugar together with the finely chopped stem ginger, the lemon zest and a generous pinch of salt, until soft and fluffy. Add the eggs, one at a time, plus a couple of tablespoons of the flour with each addition. Fold in the rest of the flour and just enough of the milk to give the batter a reluctant dropping consistency.

3. Scrape the mixture into the prepared tin and put it in the oven. Bake for about 45 minutes until the cake is well risen, springy to the touch and has shrunk away slightly from the sides of the tin. The top may crack a little, but that's normal for this type of cake. Leave the cake in the tin.

4. Mix the lemon juice, ginger syrup and stem ginger together. Pierce the cake all over with a skewer. Add the granulated sugar to the syrup and pour it all over the cake while it is still warm from the oven. Try to make sure most of the syrup goes on top, rather than down the sides. Rearrange some of the stem ginger as necessary, so it is evenly spread over the cake. Leave the cake in the tin to cool completely, then store it in an airtight container.

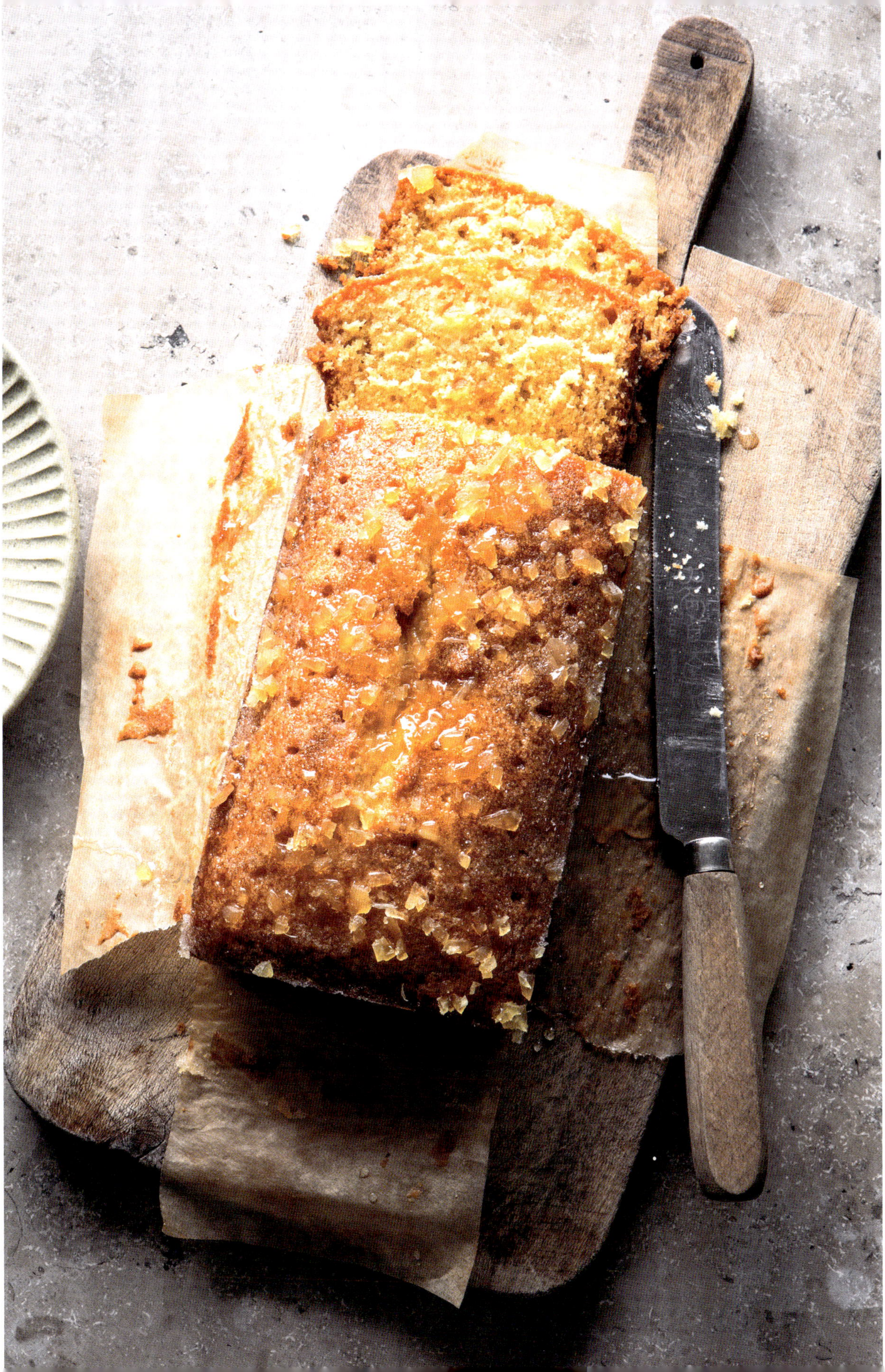

Chocolate cake

SERVES 8–10

100g dark chocolate (70% cocoa solids), broken up
25g cocoa powder
250ml just-boiled water
200g plain flour
2 tsp baking powder
½ tsp bicarbonate of soda
¼ tsp salt
200g butter, softened
250g light brown soft sugar
3 eggs
1 tsp vanilla extract
125ml soured cream

BUTTERCREAM ICING

75g dark chocolate (70% cocoa solids), broken up
25g cocoa powder
2 tbsp just-boiled water
1 tsp vanilla extract
150g butter, softened
300g icing sugar
pinch of salt
1–2 tbsp milk

DECORATION (OPTIONAL)
chocolate curls

Everyone needs a good chocolate cake in their baking repertoire and this one is a keeper. It's easy to make and can be dressed up as much as you like for a celebration. One thing to mention – be sure to use proper cocoa powder, not drinking chocolate. It has a much better flavour.

1. Preheat the oven to 180°C/Fan 160°C/Gas 4. Line 2 x 20cm sandwich tins with baking parchment.

2. Put the chocolate and cocoa powder in a bowl and pour over the hot water. Whisk until the chocolate has completely melted and you have a smooth liquid. Set aside.

3. Whisk the flour, baking powder, bicarbonate of soda and salt together.

4. Beat the butter and sugar together until very soft and aerated. Beat in the eggs, one at a time, then add all the remaining ingredients, including the chocolate liquid and the flour mixture. Combine, keeping mixing to a minimum. You should end up with a rich, pourable batter.

5. Divide the batter between the lined tins. Bake the cakes in the oven for 25–30 minutes until well risen and springy to the touch. Remove from the oven and leave the cakes in their tins for 10 minutes, before turning them out on to a wire rack to cool.

6. To make the icing, put the chocolate, cocoa and water in a bowl and set over a pan of simmering water. Stir until the chocolate has completely melted, then add the vanilla extract. Remove the bowl from the heat and leave to cool slightly. Beat the butter until soft and aerated, then add the icing sugar and a pinch of salt. Continue to beat until smooth, then add the chocolate mixture. Continue to beat to combine, adding up to 2 tablespoons of milk if the mixture is very stiff.

7. Spread a third of the icing over one of the cakes and place the other cake on top. Spread the rest of the icing over the top and sides of the cakes. Leave to set before serving. Add some lovely curls of chocolate, if you like.

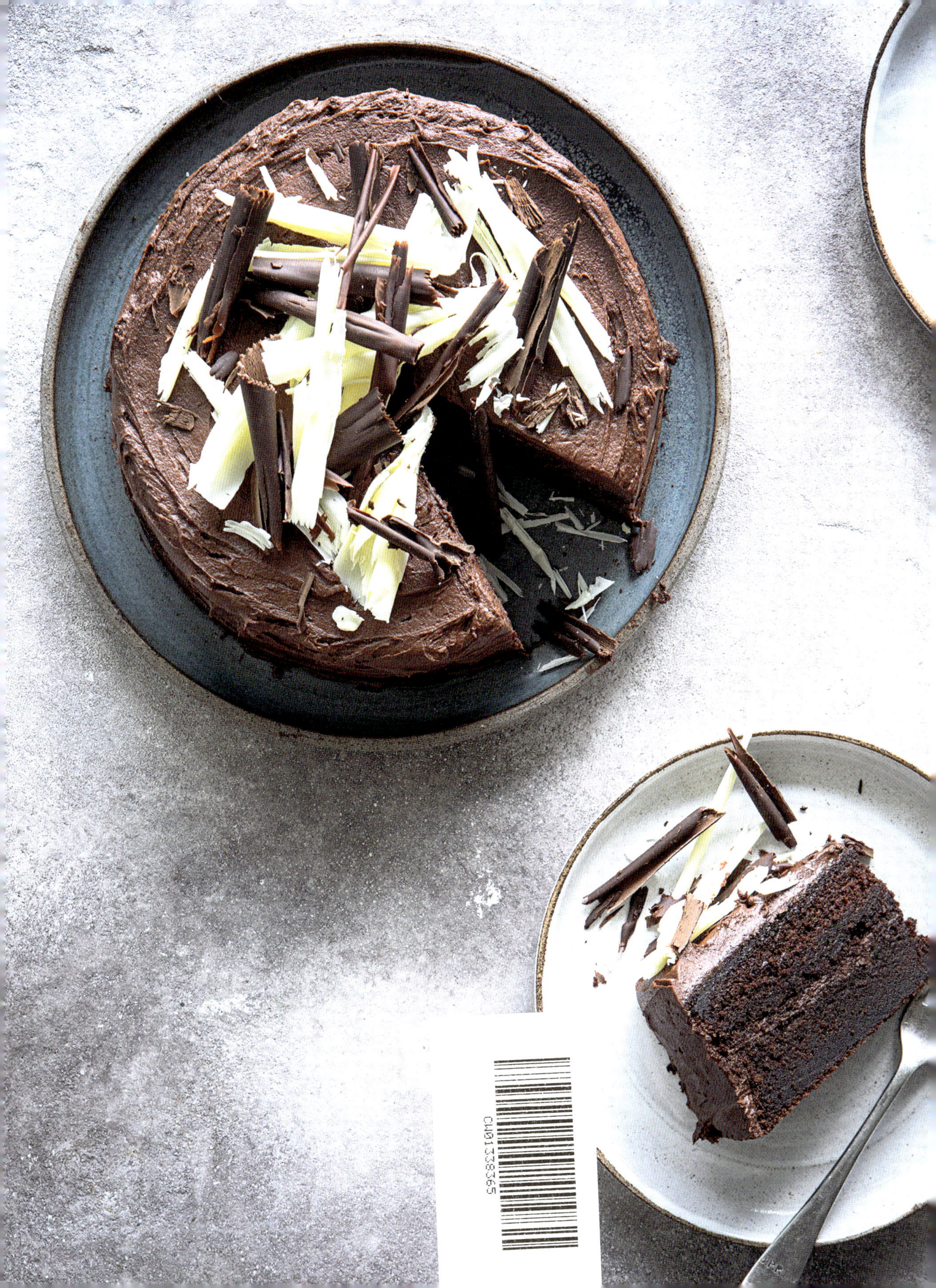

Cherry & chocolate cheesecake

SERVES 8

CHOCOLATE BASE
200g biscuits, such as digestive or similar
75g dark or milk chocolate
75g butter

CHERRY FILLING
300g frozen cherries, defrosted
2 tbsp icing sugar
2 tsp cornflour
1 tsp lemon juice
1 tsp Kirsch (optional)

CREAM CHEESE FILLING
250g mascarpone cheese
350g cream cheese
100g icing sugar
1 tsp vanilla extract
pinch of salt
300ml double cream

TOPPING
fresh cherries, if in season, or chocolate curls

A while back, Dave and I did a survey, asking people to tell us about their favourite dishes, whether mains, bakes, puddings and so on. Cheesecake came up again and again, so we developed what I think is a particularly delicious version, with a chocolate base and cherries in the filling. Top tip: use frozen cherries, as you can get them at any time of year, they keep their colour well and they're already pitted, so easier to deal with.

1. First make the base. Blitz the biscuits in a food processor or put them in a bag and give them a good bash with a rolling pin. Put the chocolate and butter in a heatproof bowl and place the bowl over a saucepan of simmering water. When they have both melted, remove the bowl from the heat and add the biscuit crumbs. Stir well until everything is combined.

2. Line a 23cm-diameter cake tin with a circle of baking parchment. Press the crumb mixture into the base, making sure it comes up the sides a little, then put it in the fridge to chill until firm.

3. Put the cherries in a saucepan with their juices, add the sugar, then stir until it has dissolved. Mix the cornflour with a little water and add this mixture to the cherries, along with the lemon juice and Kirsch, if using. Stir until the sauce thickens a little. Leave to cool.

4. To make the cream cheese filling, beat the mascarpone, cream cheese, icing sugar and vanilla extract together with a pinch of salt until thick and smooth. Whisk the double cream in a separate bowl until thickened to the soft peak stage. Beat the cream into the cream cheese mixture until it has a stiff consistency that won't drop off a spoon.

5. Spoon the cherries into the centre of the cheesecake base, aiming to leave a border all the way round. Pile on the cream cheese filling, working from the edges inwards to make sure the cherries are sealed in. Smooth the filling down as well as you can, then put the cake in the fridge to chill for several hours until completely set, preferably overnight.

6. If fresh cherries are in season, pile some on top or add some chocolate curls. You could even have some extra cream or ice cream on the side.

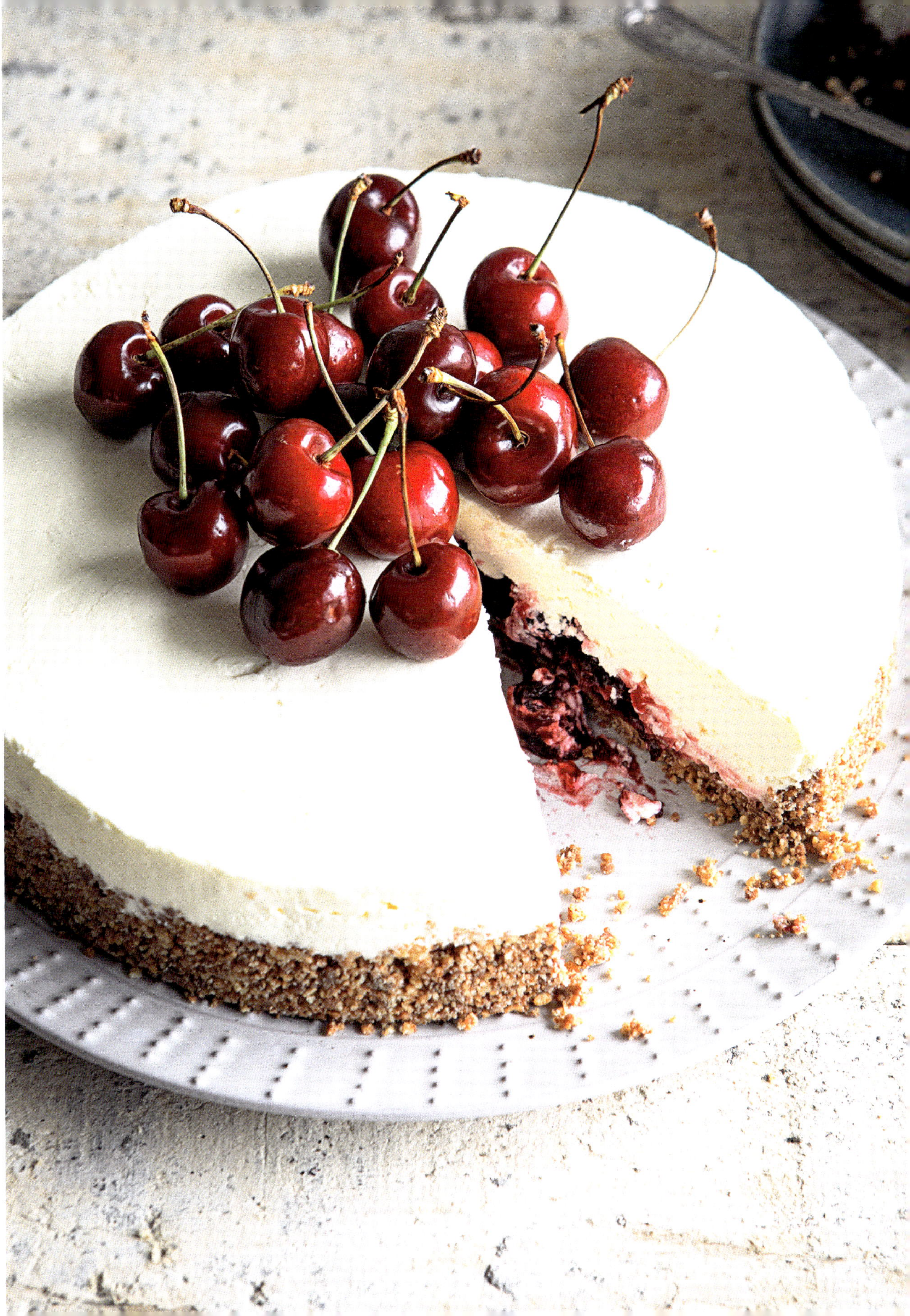

Spicy fruit loaf

MAKES 1 LOAF

150g sultanas or raisins
100g currants
100g glacé cherries, halved
50g prunes, roughly chopped
350ml hot strong tea
2 balls of stem ginger, finely chopped (optional)
100g light brown soft sugar
2 eggs, beaten
300g wholemeal or white self-raising flour
2 tsp mixed spice
pinch of salt

A slice of this goes down very well with a cup of tea when you feel that little slump in the afternoon. It's really easy to make and you can use whatever combination of dried fruit you want – I do like to whack some cherries in there. This loaf smells amazing as it comes out of the oven, but hold off if you possibly can as it's even better if it's kept for a couple of days to mature. Just saying.

1. Put all the dried fruit into a large bowl and pour over the tea – there should be enough to completely submerge the fruit. Cover and leave to soak for several hours, or preferably overnight. The fruit will swell up and the liquid will have thickened to a syrup.

2. When you are ready to bake the loaf, preheat the oven to 160°C/Fan 140°C/Gas 3 and line a large (900g) loaf tin with baking paper.

3. Stir the stem ginger, if using, into the fruit, followed by the sugar and the eggs. Sprinkle over the flour with the spice and a good pinch of salt, then stir everything together – the mixture should have a slow dropping consistency.

4. Pour the mixture into the prepared tin and bake for 60–75 minutes. Start checking after an hour – the loaf should have shrunk away from the sides and be firm but springy when you press it. Leave it to cool in the tin.

5. Remove the loaf from the tin once cool, wrap it in foil and leave it for a day or so before eating it, if possible. The top will become slightly glossy and sticky in that time. This keeps well in an airtight container for up to 2 weeks.

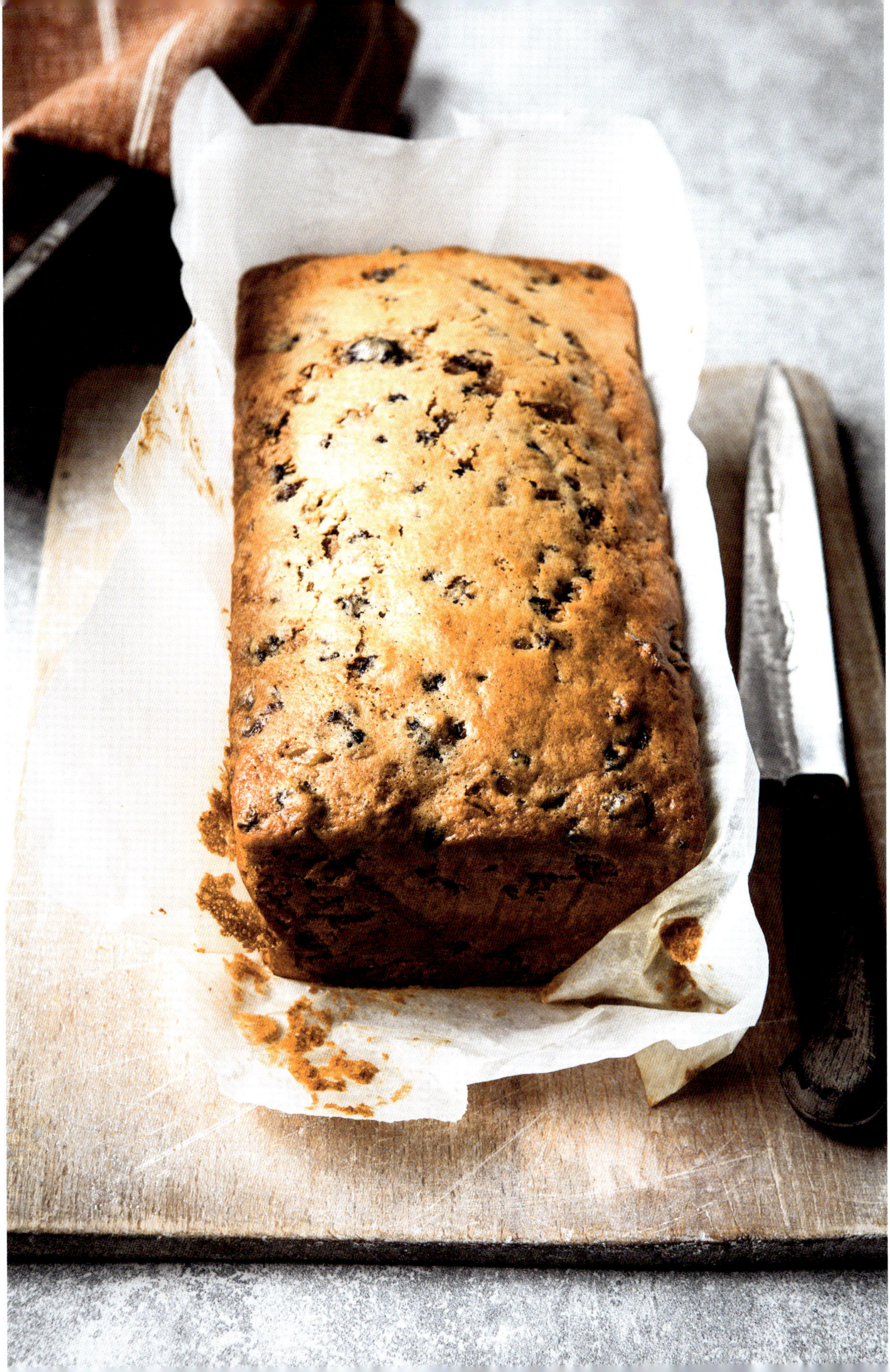

Biker brownies

MAKES 12

100g plain flour
50g cocoa powder
¾ tsp baking powder
pinch of salt
300g dark chocolate (minimum 70% cocoa solids)
250g butter
250g granulated sugar
4 eggs
100g hazelnuts, roughly chopped
100g chocolate hazelnut spread (optional)
50ml hazelnut liqueur (optional)

You won't be able to resist these brownies. When we first wrote the recipe we made the chocolate hazelnut spread and the liqueur optional but I have to say – it really is worthwhile adding them. Makes these extra specially fudgy and amazing. Nice with a cup of tea or try them warm for pudding with a good dollop of vanilla ice cream.

1. Preheat the oven to 170°C/Fan 150°C/Gas 3½. Line a 30 x 20cm straight-sided brownie tin with foil or non-stick baking paper.

2. Sift the flour, cocoa and baking powder together in a bowl and add a generous pinch of salt. Break 250g of the chocolate into a heatproof bowl and place the bowl over a pan of barely simmering water. Make sure the bottom of the bowl does not touch the water. Leave the chocolate to melt, stirring regularly.

3. When the chocolate has melted, remove the bowl and leave the chocolate to cool slightly. Roughly chop the remaining chocolate and set it aside.

4. Beat the butter and sugar together in a bowl until very light and fluffy. Add the eggs, one at a time, then pour in the melted chocolate. Mix thoroughly, then add a third of the flour mixture. Stir to combine, then repeat with the other two-thirds of flour. Add half the hazelnuts and all the reserved chopped chocolate and stir to combine. Scrape the mixture into the tin.

5. If using the chocolate spread and hazelnut liqueur, mix them together to make a smooth paste. Make little wells in the brownie batter and add spoonfuls of the mixture.

6. Sprinkle the remaining hazelnuts on top and press them down lightly into the mixture. Bake in the preheated oven for about 30 minutes, testing the brownies after 25 minutes. When they are ready, a wooden skewer should come out with a few crumbs attached – it shouldn't be wet, but it shouldn't be completely clean either.

7. Leave the brownies to cool in the tin. If you can bear to wait, put the tin in the fridge overnight to rest the brownies before cutting them – it will help them settle into a consistency that isn't too cake-like. Cut into triangles or squares and store them in an airtight tin.

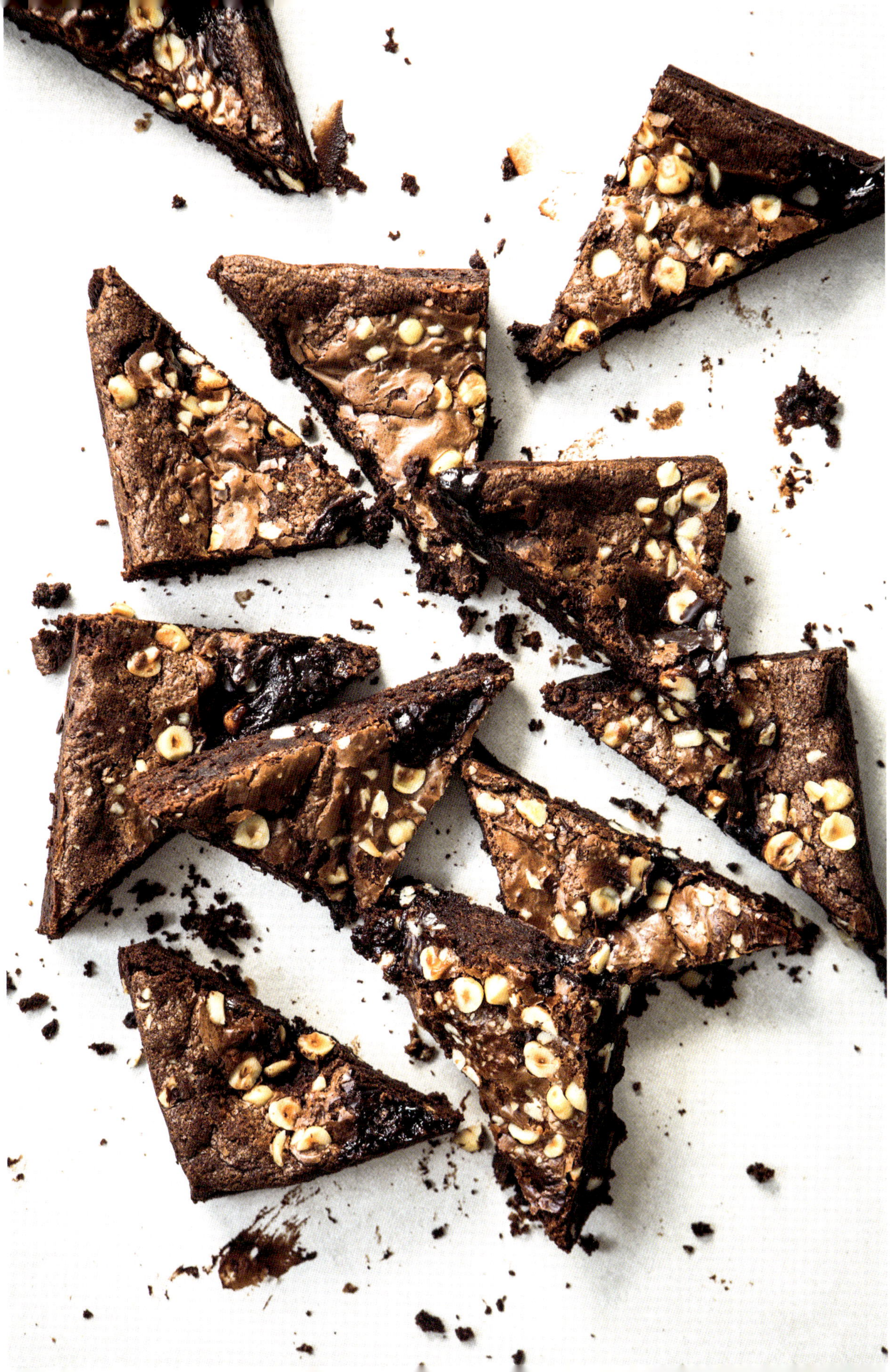

Caramelised almond & raisin cookies

MAKES ABOUT 24

175g plain flour
¼ tsp bicarbonate of soda
¼ tsp baking powder
pinch of salt
125g butter
100g light brown soft sugar
100g granulated sugar
125g almond butter
1 egg
½ tsp vanilla extract or a few drops of almond extract
100g raisins

CARAMELISED ALMONDS
50g granulated sugar
100g almonds
(skin on is fine)

I like a nice bit of crunch in a cookie and the caramelised almonds in this recipe add lots of lovely texture. Nice to know you have a batch of these stashed away for a teatime treat or to pop in a lunchbox.

1. First caramelise the almonds. Put the sugar in a frying pan with 75ml of water. Slowly bring to the boil, stirring until the sugar has dissolved, then keep stirring as the liquid thickens to a syrup.

2. Add the almonds and continue to cook, while stirring constantly, until the syrup darkens, becomes sticky and eventually turns to a powder around the almonds. Remove the pan from the heat, then tip the almonds on to a plate and leave to cool. Roughly chop half the almonds, then finely chop the rest to the consistency of coarse breadcrumbs.

3. Preheat the oven to 170°C/Fan 150°C/Gas 3½. Line 2 or 3 baking trays with baking parchment.

4. Put the flour, bicarb and baking powder in a bowl with a pinch of salt and mix thoroughly. Put the butter and both sugars in a separate bowl and beat until well combined and aerated. Beat in the almond butter, followed by the egg and the vanilla extract. Add all the dry ingredients and the raisins to the butter mixture and mix to form a soft, thick dough.

5. Scoop spoonfuls of the mixture – each cookie should be roughly a heaped tablespoon – and space them out over the baking trays. Flatten them down lightly. If you want to be sure all your cookies are about the same size, weigh the dough first and divide it by 24 to get an idea of how large each cookie should be.

6. Bake the cookies for 12–14 minutes until well spread out and golden brown around the edges – this will give you a chewy-centred cookie. For a crunchier cookie, leave for a couple of minutes longer.

7. Remove the cookies from the oven and leave them to cool on the baking trays. Store in an airtight container.

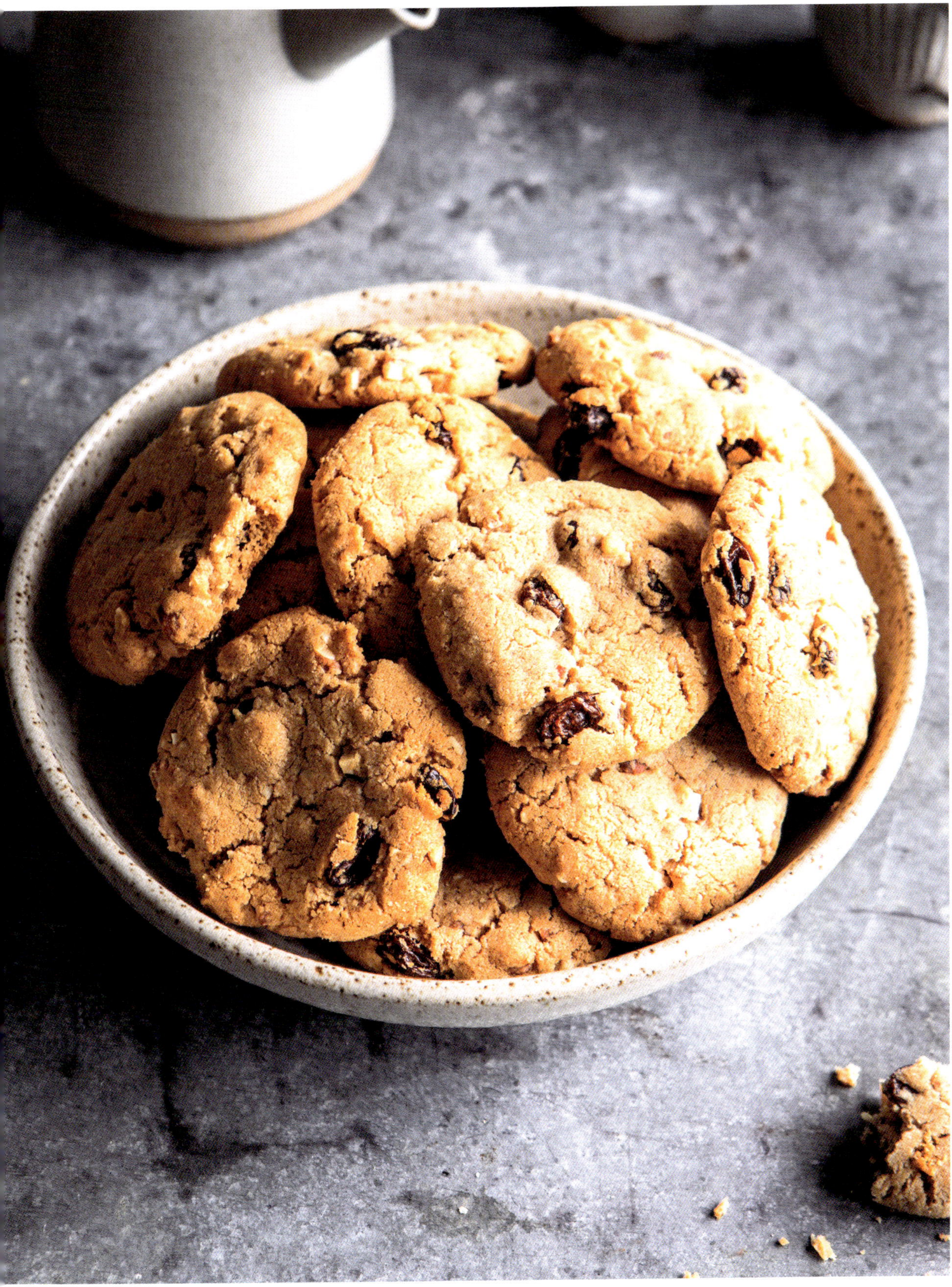

Gingerbread cake

MAKES 12

300g plain flour
2 tbsp ground ginger (or to taste – this makes for quite a hot cake)
½ tsp cayenne pepper
½ tsp ground cinnamon
½ tsp ground allspice
¼ tsp ground mace
generous pinch of ground cloves
150g butter
125g dark brown muscovado sugar
150g golden syrup
200g black treacle
1 jar of stem ginger
250ml milk
1 heaped tsp bicarbonate of soda
2 eggs, lightly beaten

This spicy cake has always been a favourite in Dave's neck of the woods and he had fond memories of the gingerbread his Auntie Mary used to make when he was a child. It's one of those bakes that really benefits from being wrapped up once cool and kept for a few days before slicing and eating. It gets beautifully sticky as it matures, so is worth the wait. I love the stem ginger in this but if you don't have any, make it without and use an extra 50g of golden syrup instead of the stem ginger syrup. The cake will be almost as good.

1. Preheat the oven to 170°C/Fan 150°C/Gas 3½. Line a 30 x 20cm tin with baking paper – a straight-sided brownie tin is just right.

2. Sift the flour into a large bowl, add the spices and mix lightly to combine.

3. Put the butter, sugar, golden syrup, treacle and 50g of the syrup from the jar of stem ginger into a pan. Place over a gentle heat and allow everything to melt together.

4. Remove the pan from the heat and whisk in the milk, bicarbonate of soda and eggs. Gradually add the contents of the pan to the flour, making sure everything is well combined, and you have a very wet, pourable batter. Drain the balls of stem ginger and rinse them, then chop them finely. Stir the chopped stem ginger into the batter.

5. Pour the batter into the prepared tin and bake the cake in the oven for 45–60 minutes. When the edges of the gingerbread have pulled back slightly from the sides of the tin and the top is springy to the touch, it will be done.

6. Leave the gingerbread to cool in the tin for 30 minutes and then turn it out on to a wire rack. Ideally, wrap the gingerbread and keep it for a few days before eating – the gingerbread's stickiness will develop as it matures.

BIKER TIP

To make it easier to spoon out syrup and treacle, oil the spoon first and the syrup or treacle will just slide off.

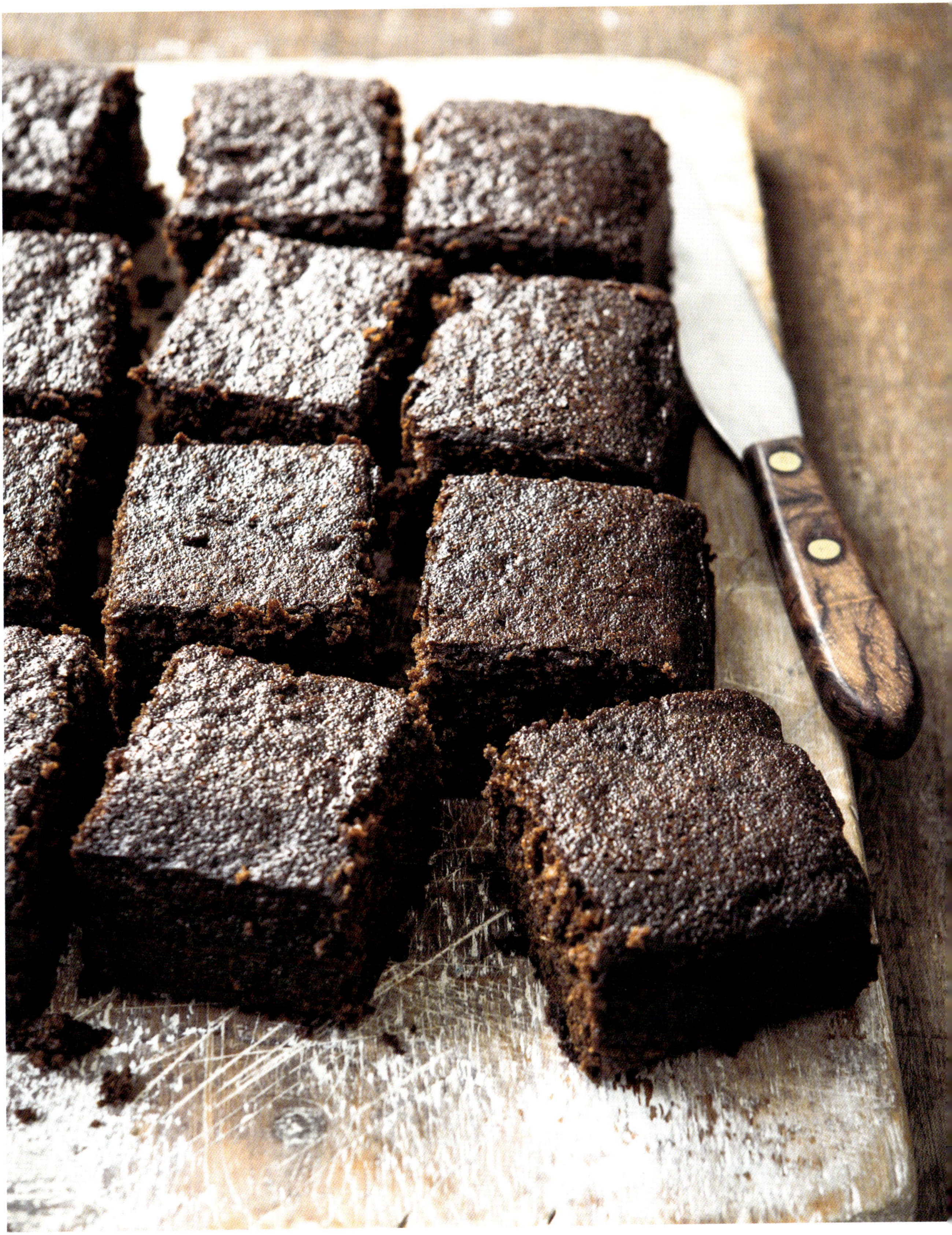

Dundee cake

SERVES 10

175g softened butter, plus extra for greasing
175g light brown soft sugar
3 tbsp orange marmalade
3 eggs, beaten
225g self-raising flour
25g ground almonds
1 heaped tsp ground mixed spice
400g mixed dried fruit
75g glacé cherries, halved
2 tbsp whisky or milk
60g blanched almonds, to decorate
1 tsp granulated or caster sugar, to decorate

Legend has it that this traditional Scottish cake was first made for Mary, Queen of Scots way back in the 16th century. If so, she certainly had good taste. One of the characteristics of this rich fruit cake is that it always contains some marmalade and is decorated simply with blanched almonds, rather than marzipan and icing. It's simple to make and great served with a hunk of good mature cheese.

1. Preheat the oven to 150°C/Fan 130°C/Gas 2. Grease a 20cm loose-bottomed cake tin and line it with a double layer of baking paper.

2. Beat the butter and sugar in a food processor or with a hand-held electric beater for 3–4 minutes, or until very light and fluffy.

3. Add the marmalade and mix for a few seconds more. Slowly add the eggs, one at a time, beating well after each addition.

4. Add the flour, almonds and mixed spice to the batter. Mix slowly until well combined, then stir in the dried fruit and cherries with a large metal spoon. Add the whisky or milk and mix until well combined.

5. Spoon the mixture into the cake tin, smooth the surface and carefully arrange the blanched almonds in circles on top.

6. Bake the cake for 1½–2 hours, or until it's well risen, firm and golden-brown. Test the cake by inserting a skewer into the centre. If the skewer comes out clean, the cake is done. Leave the cake to cool for 10 minutes, then remove it from the tin, peel off the paper and set aside to cool on a wire rack.

7. Sprinkle the top of the cake with granulated sugar and store it in a cake tin.

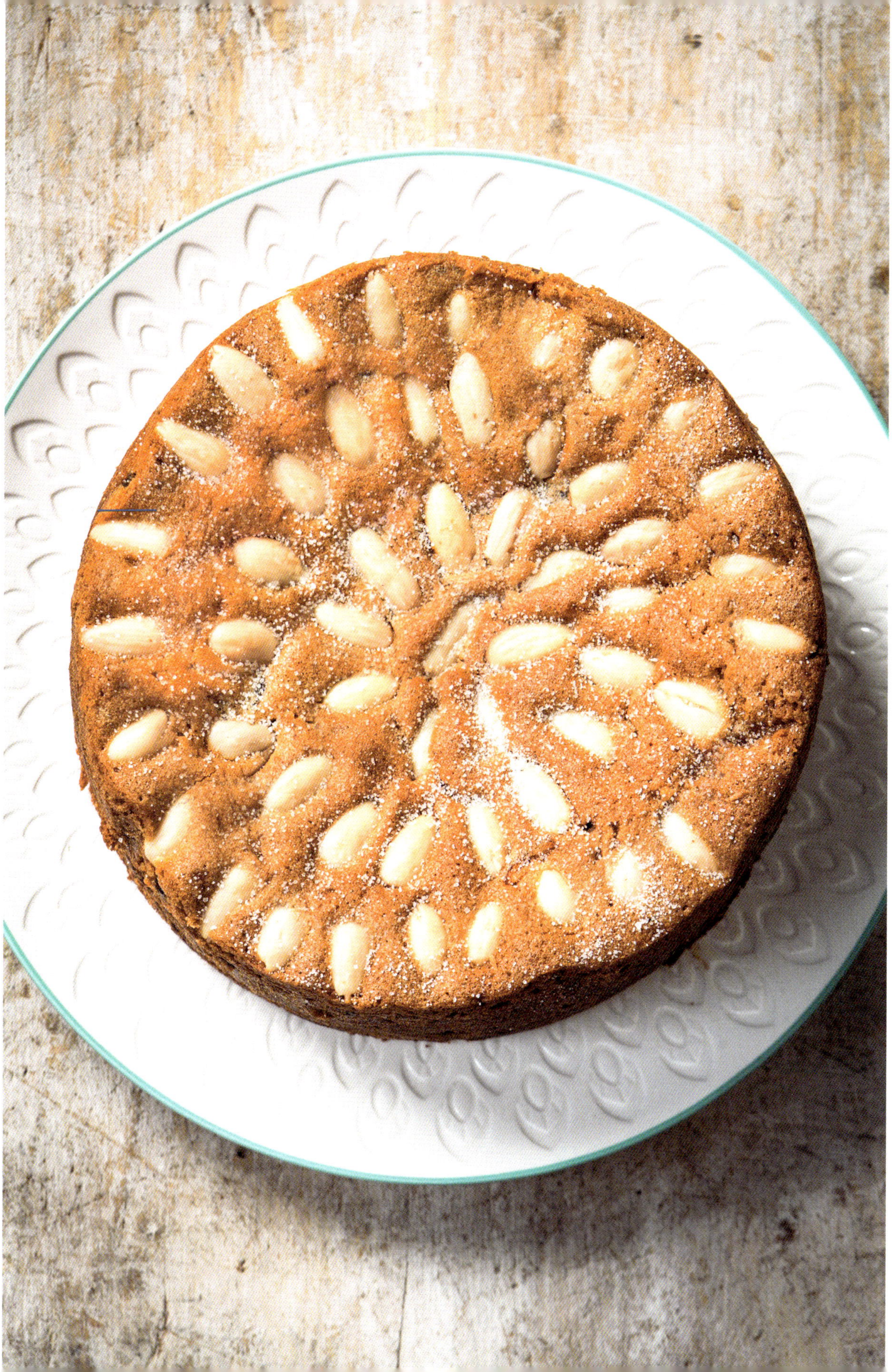

Brown butter cupcakes

MAKES 12

175g plain flour
1 tsp baking powder
¼ tsp bicarbonate of soda
pinch of salt
125g brown butter, softened (see p.275)
50g light brown soft sugar
25g dark brown soft sugar (or another 25g light brown soft sugar)
50ml maple syrup
2 eggs
75ml buttermilk
a few drops of vanilla extract
1 tbsp demerara sugar (optional)

STRAWBERRY SAUCE
300g strawberries
squeeze of lemon juice
25g icing sugar
pinch of salt

ERMINE ICING
40g flour
225ml whole milk
125g caster sugar
pinch of salt
225g butter, softened
½ tsp vanilla extract

TO SERVE
hundreds and thousands or similar
4 chocolate flakes, cut into thirds

Dave and I got a bit carried away when we first wrote this recipe. We could, of course, have made regular cupcakes with the tasty addition of brown sugar and brown butter giving them extra flavour. But no, we decided to get creative and make them look like little soft-scoop ice creams, using this special ermine icing which is easy to make into swirls. We had fun and I hope you do too. And don't forget the chocolate flakes!

1. Preheat the oven to 180°C/Fan 160°C/Gas 4 and line a cupcake tin with 12 paper cases.

2. Put the flour in a bowl with the baking powder, bicarbonate of soda and a generous pinch of salt. Whisk to remove any lumps.

3. Put the brown butter in a bowl with the brown sugars and maple syrup. Beat with electric beaters until very soft and well aerated. Add an egg and 2 tablespoons of the flour mixture, then beat until well combined. Add another egg and 2 tablespoons of the flour and mix again. Add the remaining flour, then fold in the buttermilk and vanilla extract.

4. Spoon the mixture into the cupcake cases – each one should take a heaped tablespoon. Sprinkle over a little demerara sugar, if using, for extra crunch. Bake the cakes in the preheated oven for 20–25 minutes until well risen and golden brown. Leave to cool.

5. To make the strawberry sauce, purée the strawberries with the lemon juice, sugar and a pinch of salt. Push everything through a sieve if you want to remove the tiny seeds, then chill until needed – the mixture will thicken.

6. To make the icing, put the flour in a saucepan. Place over a medium heat and gradually whisk in the milk. When it's all incorporated, stir or whisk until the mixture thickens to a paste the texture of a thick béchamel. It will do so quite suddenly, so make sure you stir constantly. Remove from the heat and transfer the mixture to a bowl. Beat in the sugar with a generous pinch of salt until the sugar dissolves and the sauce thins out a little. It may have an unappetising grey tinge to it at this point, but don't worry, it will not affect the finished icing. Cover and leave to cool to room temperature. You can also chill the paste at this point until you are ready to use it.

7. Put the butter in a bowl and beat with electric beaters until it's very soft and aerated. Give the flour and milk paste a good whisk, just to make sure it is lump-free, then gradually add it to the butter, a tablespoon at a time until it is all incorporated. Add the vanilla extract and beat again for 2 or 3 minutes, then taste. Add a little more vanilla extract if necessary and beat again.

8. To assemble, pipe the icing over the cupcakes in nice swirls to resemble soft-scoop ice cream, then sprinkle over some hundreds and thousands or similar. Add a piece of flake to each one and serve with the strawberry sauce.

1. Apple & cherry crumble...232
2. Lemon meringue pie...234
3. Lemon & blueberry pavlova...236
4. Pear & almond tart...238
5. Bakewell trifle...240
6. Chocolate fondants...242
7. Pistachio & rose kulfi...244
8. Baked rice pudding & blackberry compote...246
9. Pineapple & rum sticky toffee pudding...248
10. Banana crème brûlée...250

puddings

> **"** I don't know about you, but however stuffed I am, I always seem to be able to find room for pudding! Some of these recipes are childhood favourites while others are more recent discoveries, but all are lip-smackingly good. **"**

Apple & cherry crumble

SERVES 4

FILLING
400g cherries, pitted
3 eating apples, peeled, cored and chopped
1 tbsp cornflour
1 tbsp caster sugar
1 tbsp cherry liqueur or Kirsch (optional)

TOPPING
100g plain flour
50g ground almonds
pinch of salt
125g butter, softened
50g flaked almonds (optional)
35g demerara sugar

TO SERVE
custard (shop-bought or see p.273)

You can't beat a good crumble. They're so quick and easy to make and you can use almost any fruit you fancy. Apple is, of course, the classic but adding cherries turned out to be a great success – their flavour goes so well with the almonds in this topping. Frozen cherries are fine and I generally use eating apples in puds so I don't need to add much sugar to the filling. For extra crunch, add a couple of tablespoons of oats to the topping mix.

1. Preheat the oven to 200°C/Fan 180°C/Gas 6.

2. Put the cherries and apples in an ovenproof dish and sprinkle over the cornflour. Mix thoroughly, making sure no lumps or flecks of cornflour remain, then stir in the sugar and the cherry liqueur or Kirsch, if using.

3. To make the topping, put the flour and ground almonds in a bowl with a generous pinch of salt. Add the butter and rub it in until the mixture is clumpy. Stir in the flaked almonds, if using, and the sugar. Sprinkle the topping over the fruit.

4. Bake in the preheated oven for 35–40 minutes until the top is golden and some of the juice from the fruit is starting to break through. Serve with custard or cream.

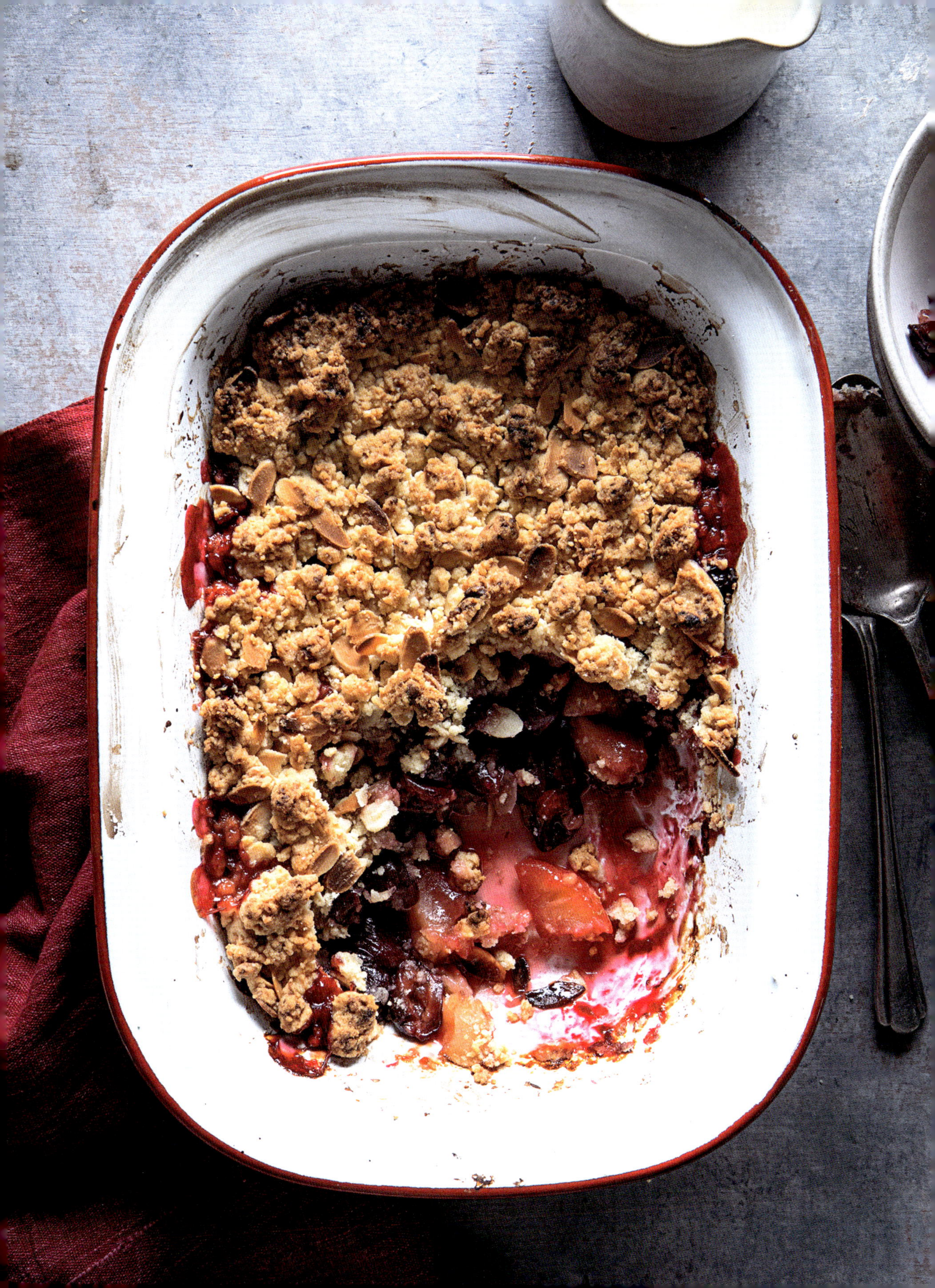

Lemon meringue pie

SERVES 6

butter, for greasing
50g cornflour
350ml cold water
200g caster sugar
zest and juice of 4 lemons
3 egg yolks
1 whole egg

MERINGUE TOPPING
3 eggs whites
175g caster sugar
½ tsp vanilla extract

PASTRY
200g plain flour,
    plus extra for dusting
1 tsp caster sugar
125g cold butter,
    cut into cubes
1 egg, beaten

My mam was such a great cook and made a wicked lemon meringue pie. I hope our recipe matches up to hers – tastes like perfection to me.

1. Preheat the oven to 200°C/Fan 180°C/Gas 6. Grease a 20cm flan tin.

2. To make the pastry, place the flour and sugar in bowl, then rub in the butter until the mixture resembles fine breadcrumbs. Add the egg and cut it in with a knife until the pastry comes together. Don't overwork the pastry or it will be tough. You can make the pastry in a food processor if you prefer.

3. Tip the pastry on to a floured board, knead briefly, then roll it out to the thickness of a pound coin, turning the pastry and flouring the surface regularly. Use the pastry to line the prepared tin. Trim the edges neatly, prick the base lightly with a fork and chill the pastry in the fridge for 30 minutes.

4. To make the filling, put the cornflour in a small bowl and mix with enough of the 350ml of cold water to make a thin paste, then set aside. Pour the remaining water into a pan and add the sugar, lemon zest and juice – you should have about 225ml of lemon juice. Heat gently until the sugar dissolves then bring to the boil. Reduce the heat slightly and quickly stir in the cornflour paste – the mixture should thicken immediately.

5. Cook over a low heat for 3 minutes, stirring until thickened and glossy. Remove from the heat and cool for 5 minutes. Whisk the egg yolks with the whole egg until smooth, then whisk vigorously into the filling mixture. Set aside to cool for 25 minutes.

6. Put the pastry case on a baking tray, line it with crumpled baking paper and fill with baking beans. Bake the pastry for 15 minutes then take it out of the oven and remove the paper and beans. Put the pastry back in the oven for a further 3–4 minutes until the surface is dry. Remove from the oven and reduce the temperature to 150°C/Fan 130°C/Gas 2.

7. For the meringue topping, whisk the egg whites in a large bowl until stiff, then gradually whisk in half the sugar. Add the vanilla extract and whisk in the remaining sugar.

8. Stir the cooled lemon filling and pour it into the pastry case. Cover very gently with large spoonfuls of the meringue topping, starting at the sides then working your way into the middle, then gently swirl the top. Bake for 25 minutes or until the meringue is set and very lightly browned. Leave to cool before removing from the tin.

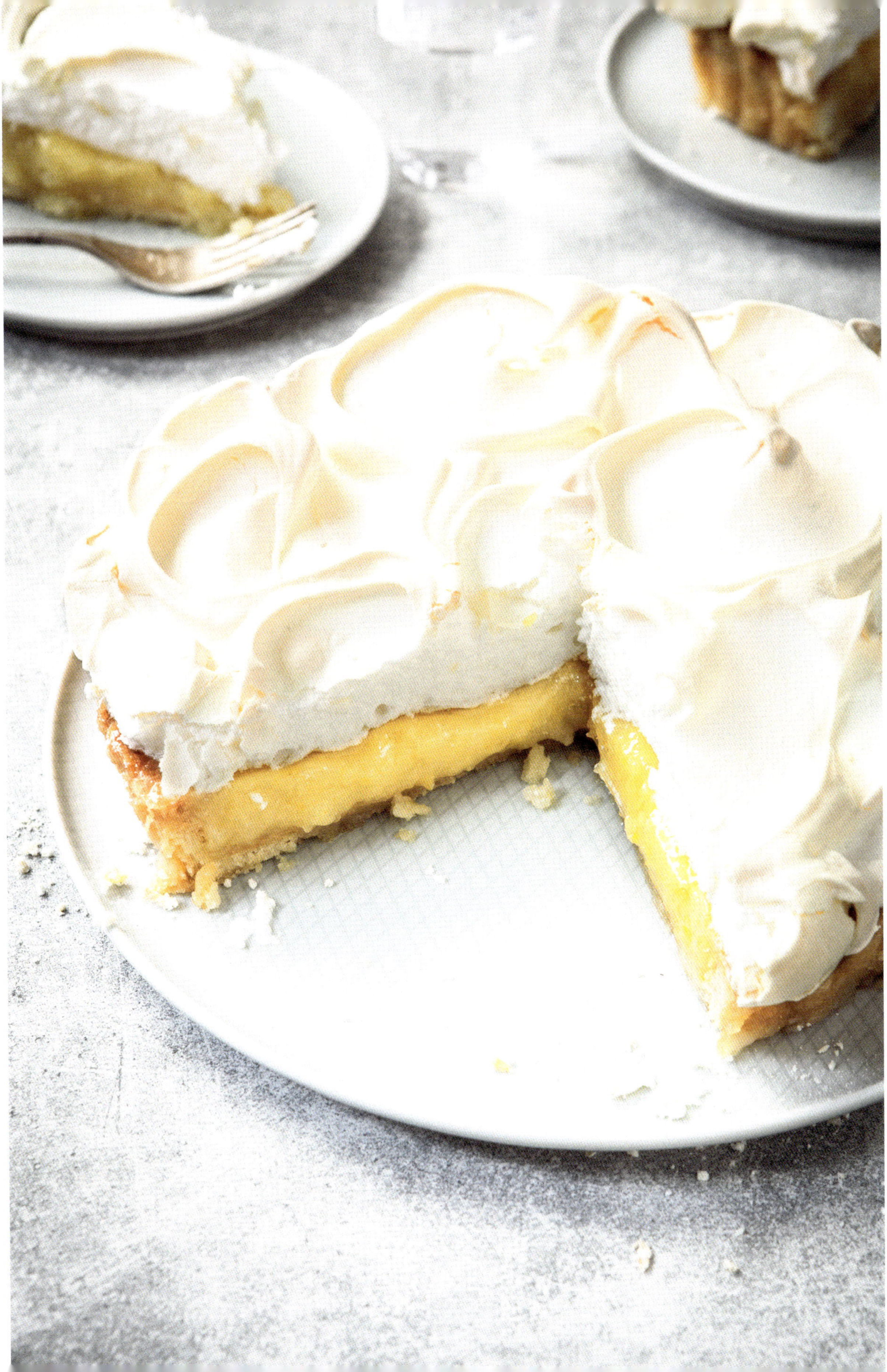

Lemon & blueberry pavlova

SERVES 6

MERINGUE BASE
6 large egg whites
300g caster sugar
1 tsp cornflour
1 tsp white wine vinegar

SYRUP
100g granulated sugar
juice and pared zest of 2 lemons
2 tbsp yuzu, grapefruit or mandarin juice (optional, add more lemon juice if you prefer)
1 tbsp tequila (optional)

TO ASSEMBLE
300ml double or whipping cream
1 tbsp icing sugar
300g blueberries

Fruity and fabulous, this tangy pavlova is just begging for a party to go to. Everyone's favourite celebration dessert.

1. Preheat the oven to 160°C/Fan 140°C/Gas 3. Line a baking sheet with baking parchment and draw a 23cm circle on the baking parchment as guidance for the meringue base.

2. Whisk the egg whites until they form soft peaks, then gradually add the sugar, a tablespoon at a time to start with. Whisk vigorously between each addition, until the meringue is stiff and glossy. Mix the cornflour and vinegar together and whisk into the meringue.

3. Pile the meringue on to the circle drawn on your baking parchment, making sure you leave a dip in the middle, and build the sides up a bit. Place the meringue in the oven, then right away turn the temperature down to 150°C/Fan 130°C/Gas 2. Bake for an hour, then turn off the heat, leave the oven door ajar and allow the pavlova to cool in the oven.

4. To make the syrup, put the sugar and the lemon juice and zest into a small saucepan. Slowly heat, stirring constantly, until the sugar has dissolved, then bring to the boil. Turn down to a simmer and cook until the syrup reaches the thread stage – this will take about 10 minutes and the mixture should reach a temperature of 112°C. To check, drizzle a small amount of the syrup into a glass of cold water – it it's ready, it will form fine threads, not dissolve.

5. Add the yuzu or other citrus juice and bring the syrup back to the same temperature, then remove the pan from the heat. Add the tequila, if using, and leave to cool down – the syrup should thicken as it cools – then strain.

6. Whip the cream with the icing sugar until thick but not too stiff. Put the cream into the dip you made in the middle of the meringue and drizzle over half the syrup. Give the cream a couple of quick stirs, then add a little more syrup. Pile on the blueberries and drizzle over the remaining syrup.

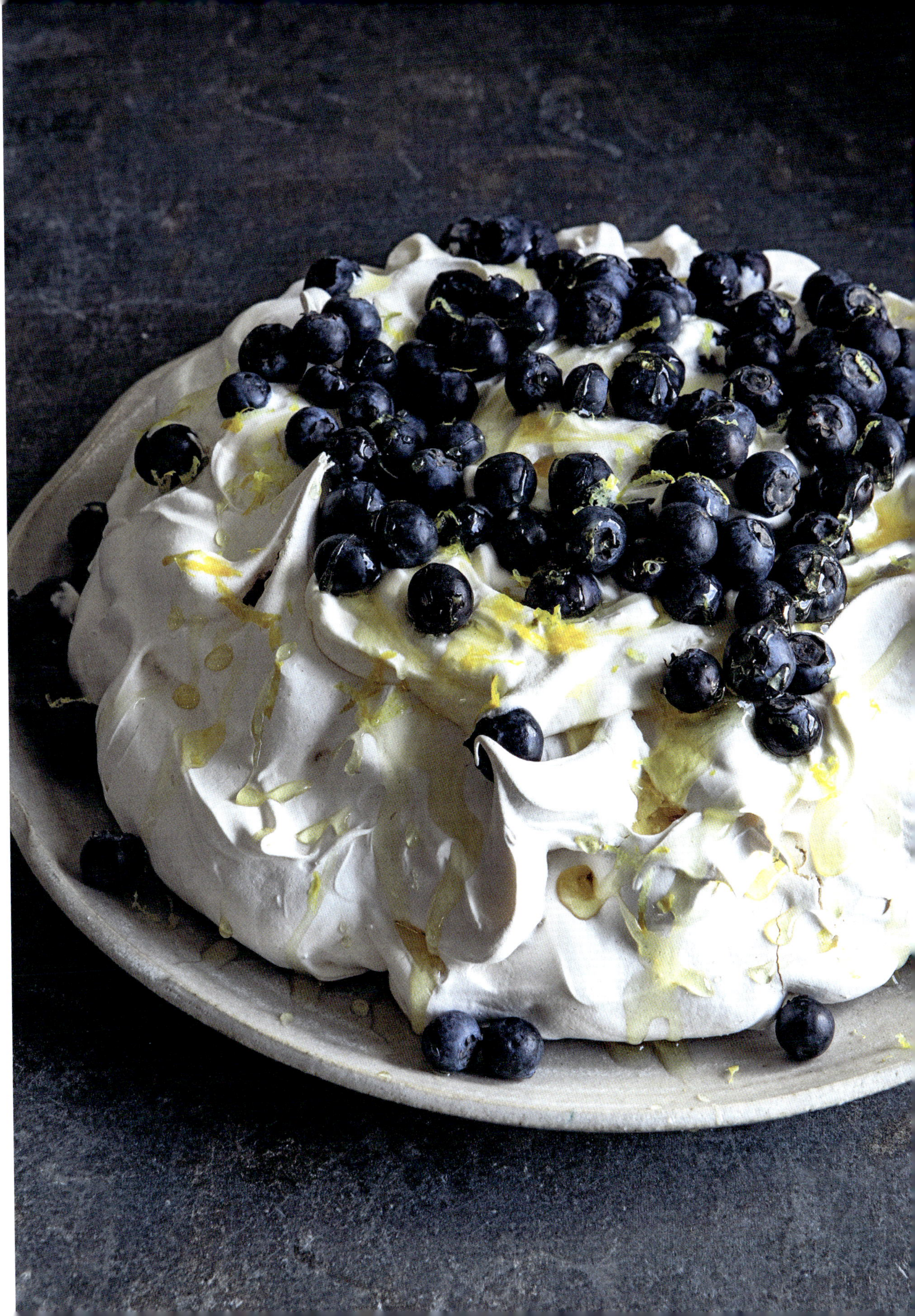

Pear & almond tart

SERVES 4–6

1 x 320g sheet of ready-rolled puff pastry
1 egg, beaten
a few drops of almond extract (optional)
1 tsp ground cardamom
50g icing sugar
125g ground almonds
420g can of pears in syrup
icing sugar, for dusting

TO SERVE
2 tbsp chocolate sauce (shop-bought or see p.274)

This fruit tart looks really classy and fancy, but it's a doddle to make and can be whipped up in no time, using ready-rolled puff pastry and a can of pears. You can even use shop-bought chocolate sauce if you like or make your own using the recipe on page 274. Simply scrumptious.

1. Preheat the oven to 200°C/Fan 180°C/Gas 6. Unroll the puff pastry sheet on to a baking tray and score a 2cm border all the way around. Brush the pastry with a little of the beaten egg.

2. Add the almond extract, if using, to the rest of the egg, then mix with the ground cardamom, icing sugar and ground almonds. The mixture should clump together and look a bit like crumble topping. Sprinkle it over the puff pastry, making sure it stays within the scored border.

3. Drain the pears, reserving the syrup, and slice them thinly. Arrange the slices over the ground almond mixture and dust with icing sugar.

4. Bake the tart in the oven for about 25 minutes until the pastry has puffed up and turned a rich golden brown and the pears have taken on some colour. Brush the pears and the pastry with some of the pear syrup, then drizzle with the chocolate sauce.

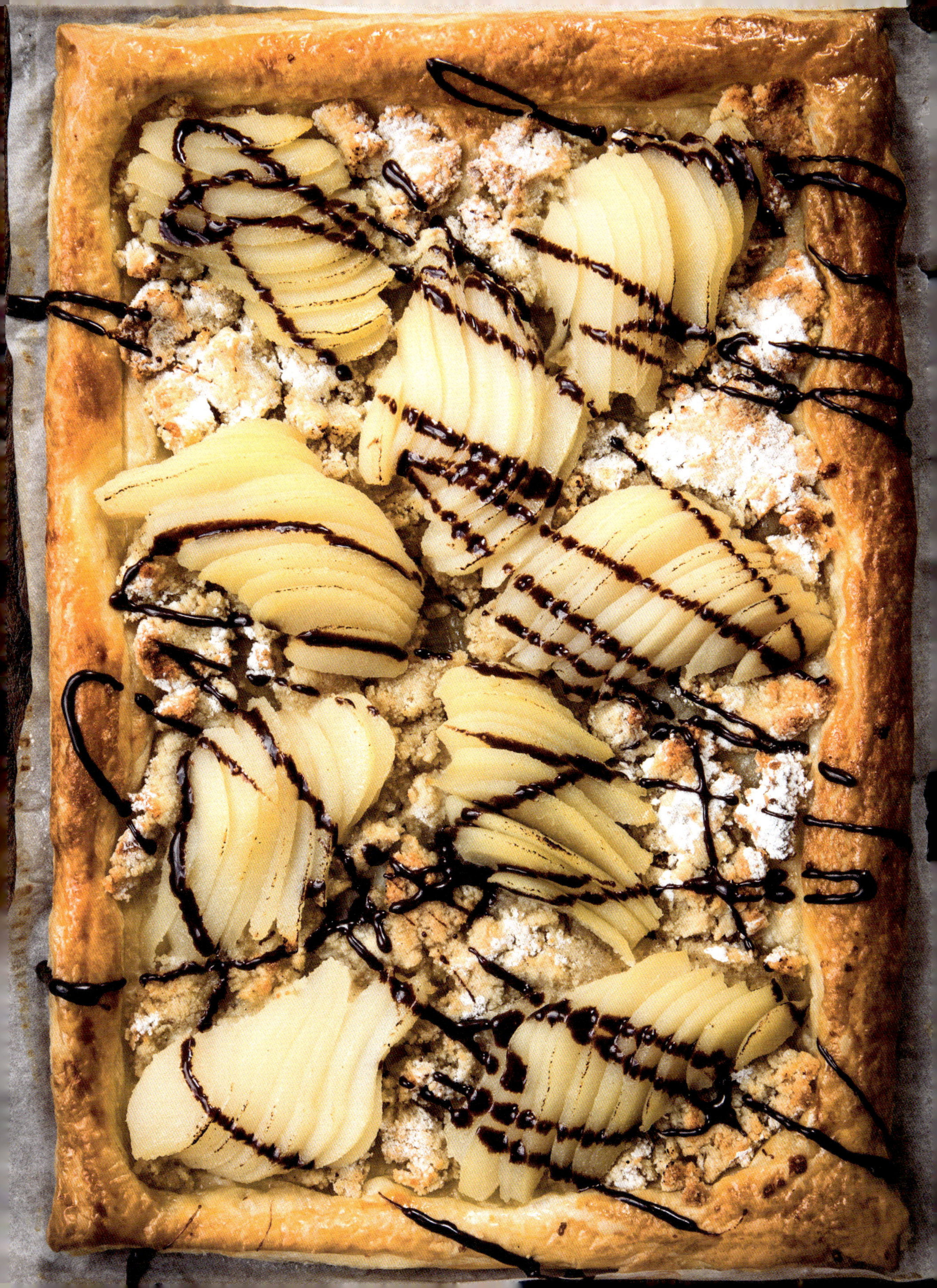

Bakewell trifle

SERVES AT LEAST 6

SPONGE
25g self-raising flour
1 tsp baking powder
85g ground almonds
pinch of salt
110g butter, softened
110g caster sugar
a few drops of almond extract (optional)
2 eggs, beaten
1–2 tbsp milk

TRIFLE CUSTARD
250ml whole milk
250ml double cream
50g ground almonds (optional)
1 vanilla pod, split
a few drops of almond extract
5 egg yolks
75g caster sugar
2 tsp cornflour

TO ASSEMBLE
2 tbsp raspberry jam
100g amaretti biscuits
100ml Oloroso sherry or almond liqueur
200g raspberries
500g double cream
30g flaked almonds, toasted

Welcome to the highly successful marriage of a trifle with a Bakewell tart. They are very happy together and I know you will be too.

1. Preheat the oven to 200°C/Fan 180°C/Gas 6 and line a 20cm round cake tin with baking parchment.

2. Mix the flour and baking powder with the ground almonds and a pinch of salt. In a separate bowl, cream the butter and sugar with the almond extract, if using, until pale and fluffy, then incorporate the beaten eggs and the flour mixture, adding just enough milk to make a batter with a dropping consistency. Scrape the batter into the lined cake tin.

3. Bake the cake in the oven for 25–30 minutes until it's golden brown and springy but firm to the touch. Remove from the oven and leave to stand for a few minutes before transferring to a rack to finish cooling.

4. To make the custard, put the milk, cream and ground almonds, if using, into a saucepan with the vanilla pod and a few drops of almond extract. Bring to just below boiling point, then remove the pan from the heat and set aside.

5. Put the egg yolks, caster sugar and cornflour into a bowl. Whisk until the mixture is very pale and the consistency of fairly stiff foam.

6. Remove the vanilla pod from the milk, then pour the milk on to the egg mixture, whisking constantly until combined. Pour back into the saucepan. Cook, stirring constantly, until the custard thickens – this will happen very quickly so don't leave it unattended. Whisk until smooth, then transfer to a jug and cover with oiled cling film to stop a skin forming – make sure the cling film is in contact with the surface of the custard. When the custard is cool, put it in the fridge to chill.

7. To assemble, cut the cake in half horizontally and sandwich the halves with the jam. Cut into chunks and arrange them over the base of your trifle bowl. Top with the amaretti biscuits, then pour over the sherry.

8. Add the raspberries in a single layer on top, then pour over the custard. Whip the cream until it forms soft peaks, then smooth it over the custard. Sprinkle with toasted almonds and chill for at least an hour before serving.

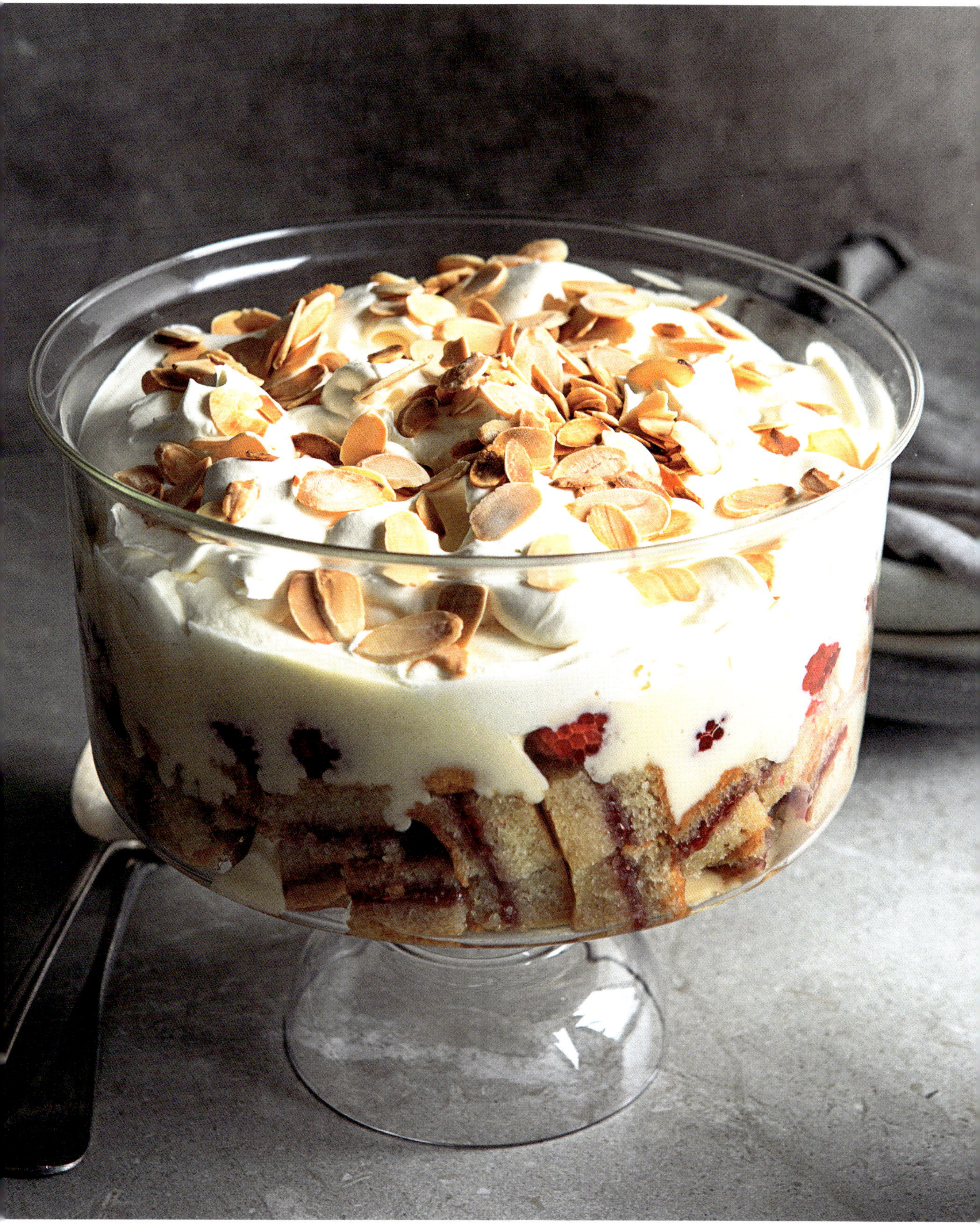

Chocolate fondants

SERVES 6

150g butter, plus extra for greasing
1 tsp cocoa powder
1 tsp plain flour
150g dark chocolate (70% cocoa solids), broken into pieces
3 large eggs
3 large egg yolks
50g caster sugar
finely grated zest of 2 limes
25g self-raising flour

TO SERVE

crème fraiche, clotted cream or ice cream

A favourite with **MasterChef** *contestants, these little beauties are not difficult to make but the timing is crucial. Too long in the oven and they turn out dry instead of oozing gloriously gooey chocolate. Follow our instructions to the letter and you should be fine. The other great thing about these is you can prepare them in advance, ready to go in the oven at the last minute, so they're ideal for a special meal.*

1. Generously grease 6 x 175ml dariole moulds with butter, then line the base of each with a small circle of baking paper.

2. Mix the cocoa powder and plain flour in a bowl and sift a little into each dariole mould, rolling them around to coat the base and sides. Shake out any excess.

3. Bring some water to a simmer in a saucepan. Place a heatproof bowl over the water, making sure the bottom of the bowl doesn't touch the water. Add the chocolate and butter to the bowl and stir until melted and smooth. Remove the bowl from the pan and set aside to cool for 10 minutes.

4. Meanwhile, whisk the eggs, egg yolks, caster sugar and half the lime zest together in a bowl, using electric beaters. When the mixture is pale and thick, and the whisk leaves a trail across the mixture when lifted out, the mixture is ready.

5. Gently fold in the cooled, melted chocolate mixture using a large, metal spoon, until just combined. Sift in the flour and fold in until just combined.

6. Pour the fondant mixture into the prepared moulds, cover them with cling film and chill in the fridge for at least 30 minutes and up to 8 hours.

7. To cook the fondants, preheat the oven to 200°C/Fan 180°C/Gas 6. Remove the fondants from the fridge and allow them to come up to room temperature. Take off the cling film and place the moulds on a baking tray.

8. Bake for 11 minutes, or until the sponge has risen but the puddings still have a slight wobble. Remove them from the oven.

9. Using a folded, dry tea towel or oven glove to protect your hand, loosen the chocolate fondant from the sides of each dariole mould using a blunt, round-edged knife and turn them out on to plates. Remove the circles of baking paper and top the fondants with spoonfuls of crème fraiche, clotted cream or ice cream. Sprinkle with the rest of the lime zest and serve immediately.

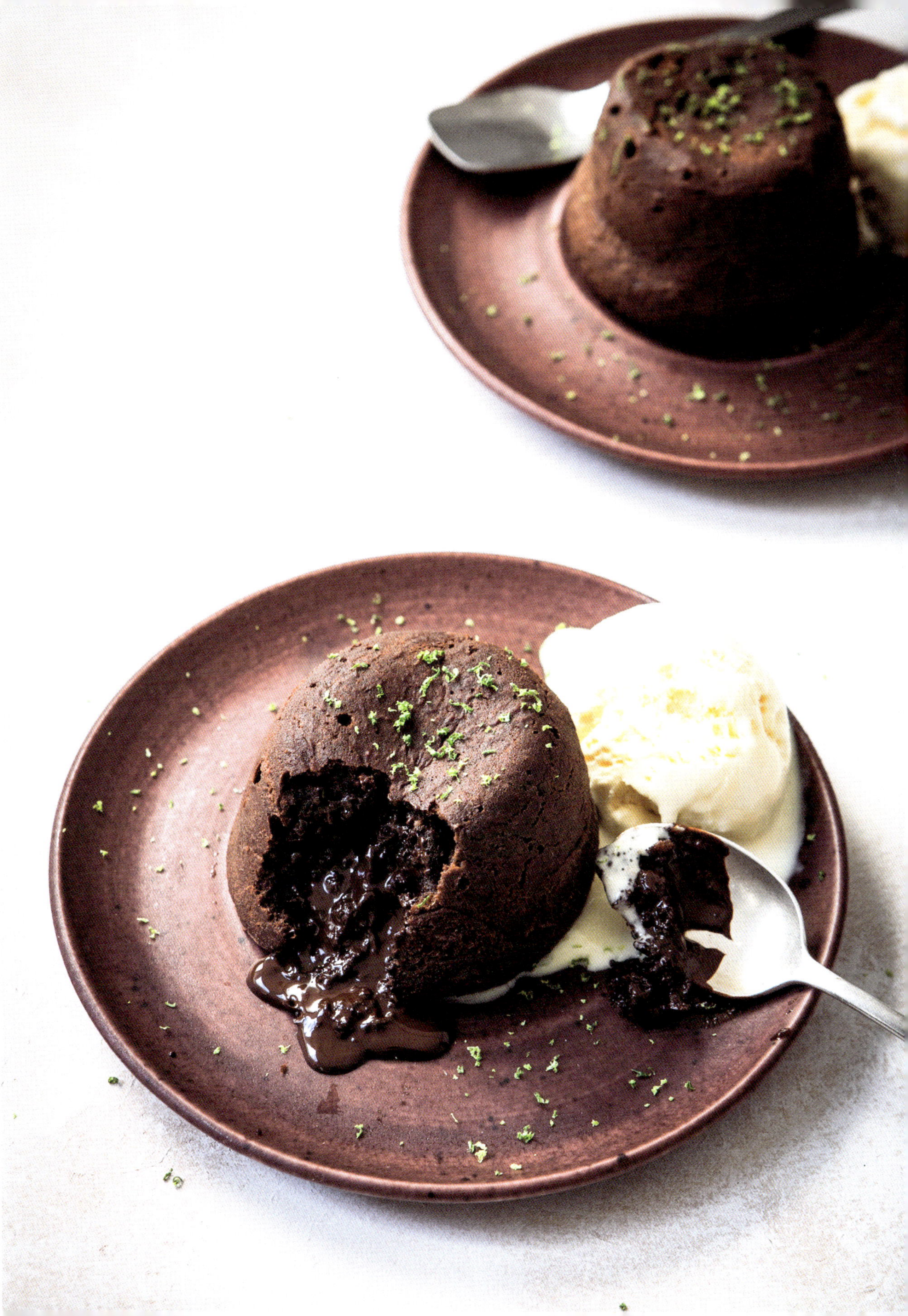

Pistachio & rose kulfi

SERVES 6

50g shelled, unsalted pistachio nuts
25g flaked almonds
150ml whole milk
50g caster sugar
1 x 410g can and 1 x 170g can of evaporated milk
200ml double cream
1 tsp rose water
few drops of green food colouring (optional)
fresh rose petals, to decorate (optional)

Kulfi is the Indian answer to ice cream and very good it is too – perfect for cooling you down after enjoying a hot, spicy curry. The traditional way of preparing it is to cook milk very, very slowly until it is thick and reduced, but this does take a while and the milk can easily burn. When Dave and I were working on our **Great Curries** *book, we fell in love with kulfi and came up with this way of making it with evaporated milk. It makes the process way quicker and the result still tastes totally amazing.*

1. Put 25g of the pistachio nuts and the flaked almonds in a spice grinder and blitz them to a powder. Roughly chop the remaining nuts and set them aside for decorating the kulfi.

2. Pour the milk into a saucepan and stir in the ground nuts and sugar. Heat through gently until the sugar dissolves, stirring constantly, but don't let the milk boil. Remove the pan from the heat and stir in the evaporated milk, double cream and rose water. Add a little green food colouring if you like, just enough to give the mixture a pretty pastel green colour. Leave to cool.

3. When the mixture is cool, taste to check the level of rose water and add a little more if necessary. Pour the mixture into 6 paper cups and put them on a small baking tray. Cover with cling film and pop them in the freezer.

4. As the kulfi begins to freeze, give it a stir with a fork every hour after the first 2 hours in the freezer to break up the ice crystals. After about 5 hours, the kulfi will be very stiff and almost too thick to stir. At this point, cover the cups tightly with foil and freeze them until solid. You can freeze them for up to 2 weeks.

5. When ready to serve, take the kulfi out of the freezer and leave to stand for 10 minutes, then turn them out on to small plates. Sprinkle the kulfi with the reserved chopped pistachios and rose petals, if using, and serve.

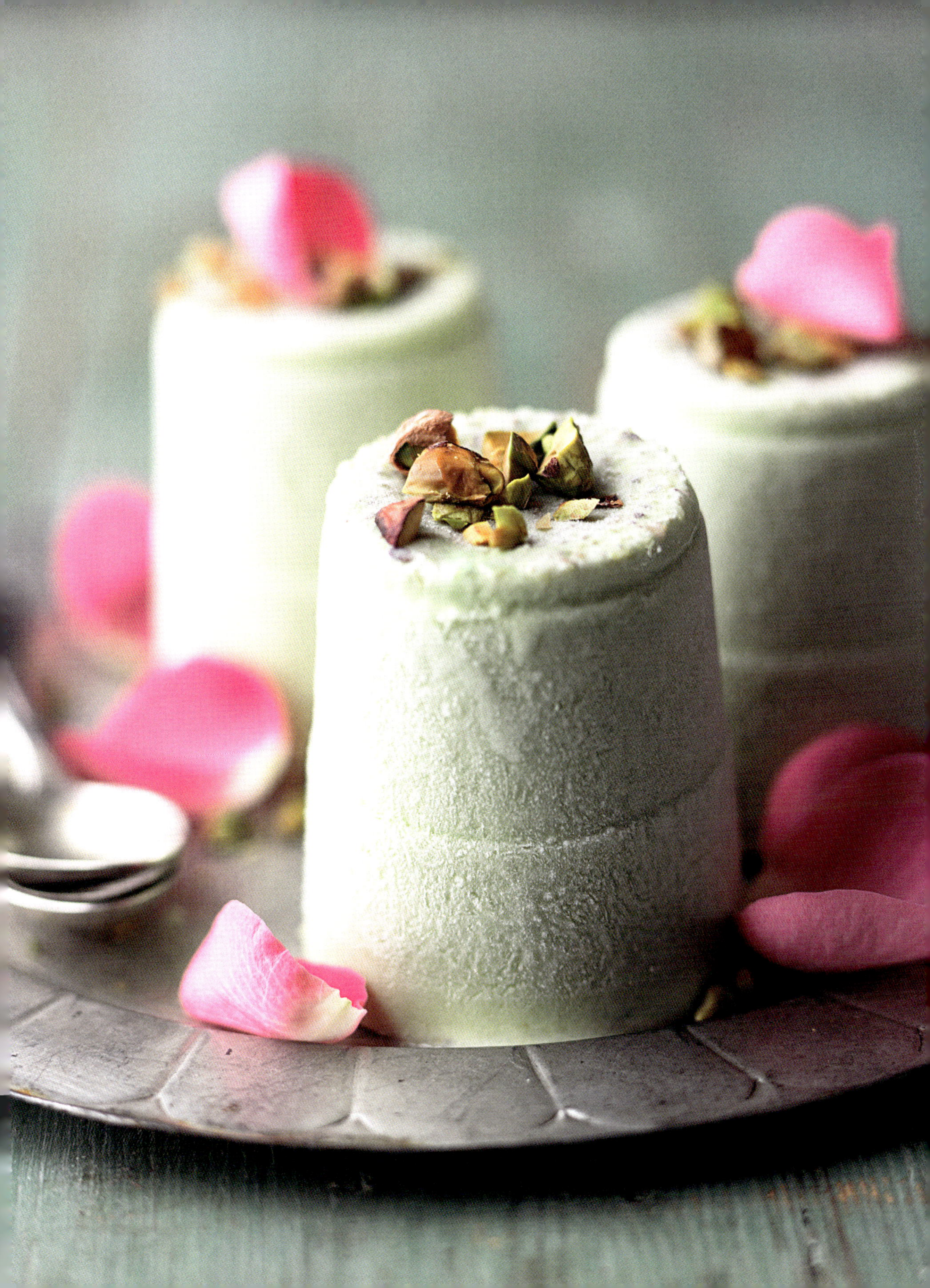

Baked rice pudding & blackberry compote

SERVES 4–6

750ml whole milk
2 bay leaves
1 mace blade
25g butter, diced, plus extra for greasing
125g pudding rice
50g light brown soft sugar
1 x 410ml can of evaporated milk
rasp of nutmeg

BLACKBERRY COMPOTE (OPTIONAL)
300g blackberries
50g caster sugar
pinch of salt
2 bay leaves
squeeze of lemon juice
1 tbsp crème de mûre or cassis (optional)

I do love a rice pudding and this is my mam's recipe which includes some evaporated milk as well as ordinary milk. I know you can make the pudding faster on top of the stove, but to my mind this version is better, and once it's in the oven you don't have to watch over it or do anything, just wait for the magic to happen. It's nice with just a blob of jam on top – that's how we used to have our pud – but if you want to go a bit more special, make this blackberry compote. It's fab.

1. Put the milk in a saucepan with the bay leaves and mace blade. Heat slowly and remove the pan from the heat just before the milk reaches boiling point. Leave to cool down to room temperature.

2. Preheat the oven to 150°C/Fan 130°C/Gas 2. Generously grease a 1.5-litre ovenproof dish with butter.

3. Strain the infused milk and pour it into the dish with the rice, brown sugar and evaporated milk. Stir to combine, then drop in the cubes of butter and grate some nutmeg over the top.

4. Bake the pudding for about 2½ hours until the rice has swelled and softened and a rich brown skin has developed on top.

5. For the compote, put the blackberries and sugar in a pan with a pinch of salt. Scrunch up the bay leaves slightly – they won't break, just bruise – and add them to the pan. Squeeze over the lemon juice and stir, then leave everything to macerate for a few minutes. The sugar will start to dissolve.

6. Place the pan over a gentle heat and slowly bring the compote to the boil, stirring regularly, until the blackberries have started to break down and the sauce has started to thicken. Add the crème de mûre or cassis, if using. Leave to cool and remove the bay leaves just before serving with the rice pudding.

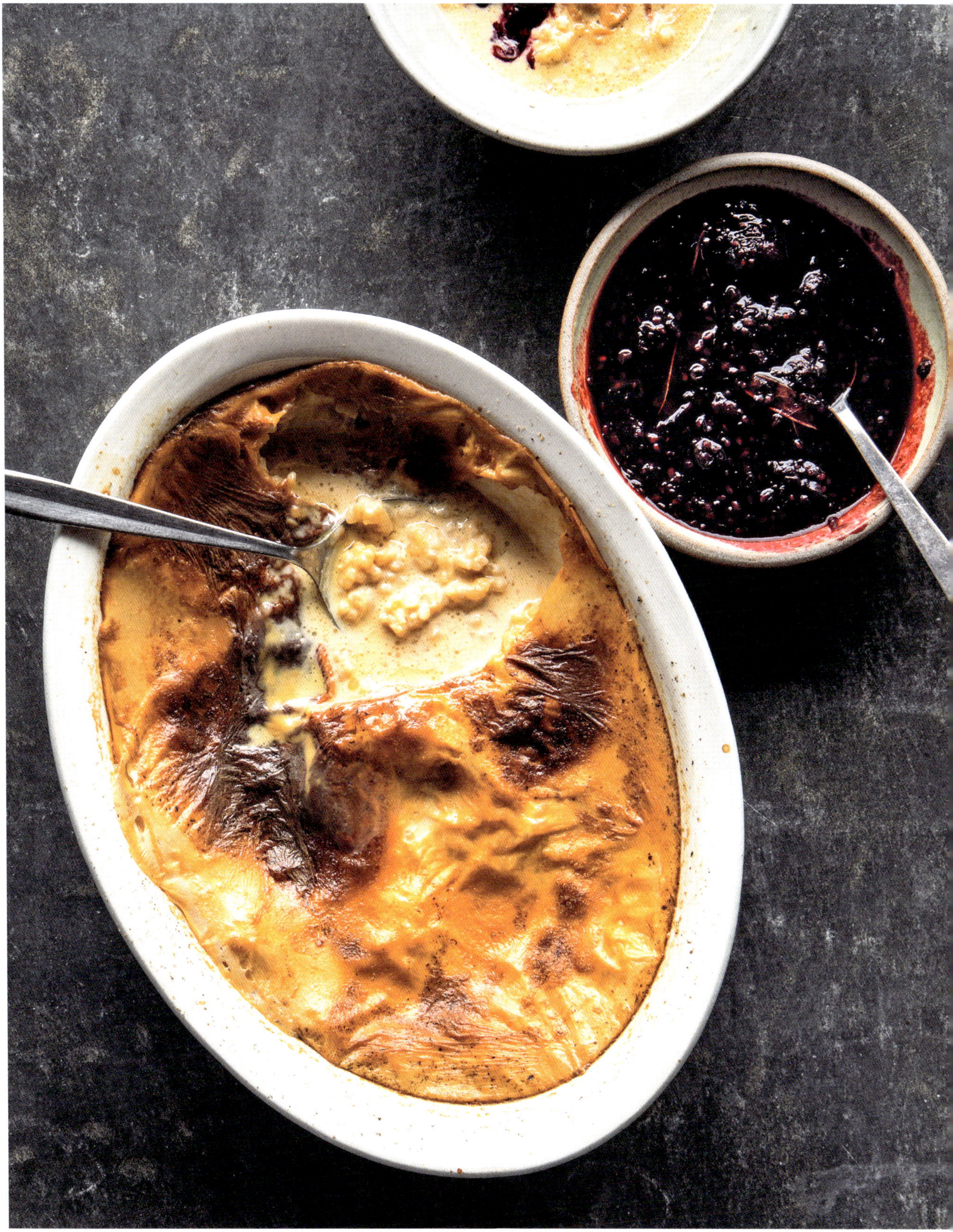

Pineapple & rum sticky toffee pudding

SERVES 4–6

PINEAPPLE
50g butter, softened
25g light brown soft sugar
25g dark brown soft sugar
large (425g) can of pineapple rings in juice

SPONGE
200g medjool dates
175ml just-boiled water
25ml rum
1 tsp bicarbonate of soda
175g self-raising flour
½ tsp salt
85g butter, softened
75g light brown soft sugar
75g dark brown soft sugar
1 tbsp treacle
2 eggs, beaten
100ml milk (or use pineapple juice from the can)
50g crystallised pineapple, chopped (optional)

RUM BUTTERSCOTCH SAUCE
175g dark brown soft sugar
50g butter
200ml double cream
1–2 tbsp rum, to taste

TO SERVE (OPTIONAL)
cream or ice cream

This is a sticky toffee pud all dressed up with rum and pineapple for an evening out. Turbo-charged or what? Just one word of warning – don't use a loose-bottomed tin and make sure the baking parchment liner is completely sealed, otherwise the butter/sugar mix will leak through.

1. First prepare the pineapple. Preheat the oven to 180°C/Fan 160°C/Gas 4. Line a square brownie tin with some baking parchment or a liner. Rub the lined base of the tin with butter. Mix the sugars together and sprinkle them over the butter. Drain the pineapple rings – reserve the juice to use in the sponge if you like. Arrange the rings over the top and set the tin aside.

2. For the sponge, finely chop the dates and cover them with the boiled water and the rum. Add the bicarbonate of soda and leave to stand until the dates have swollen and softened and the liquid is thick.

3. Mix the flour and salt in a bowl. Beat the butter, sugars and treacle together in a separate bowl until very soft and aerated, then add the flour and eggs. Pour in the milk or pineapple juice and mix briefly, then stir in the dates including their soaking liquid. Stir in the crystallised pineapple, if using.

4. Pour the sponge mixture over the pineapple rings, then bake in the oven for 30–35 minutes until well risen and springy to the touch. Turn out on to a large serving plate and remove the baking paper – you should have something that looks a bit like a dark pineapple upside-down pudding.

5. While the pudding is baking, make the rum butterscotch sauce. Melt the sugar, butter and half the cream in a small pan, stirring until the sugar has completely dissolved. Slowly bring to the boil and let it bubble for a couple of minutes, then remove the pan from the heat. Add the remaining cream and the rum and stir to combine. Transfer to a jug.

6. Serve the pudding with the sauce poured over and some extra cream or ice cream, if you like.

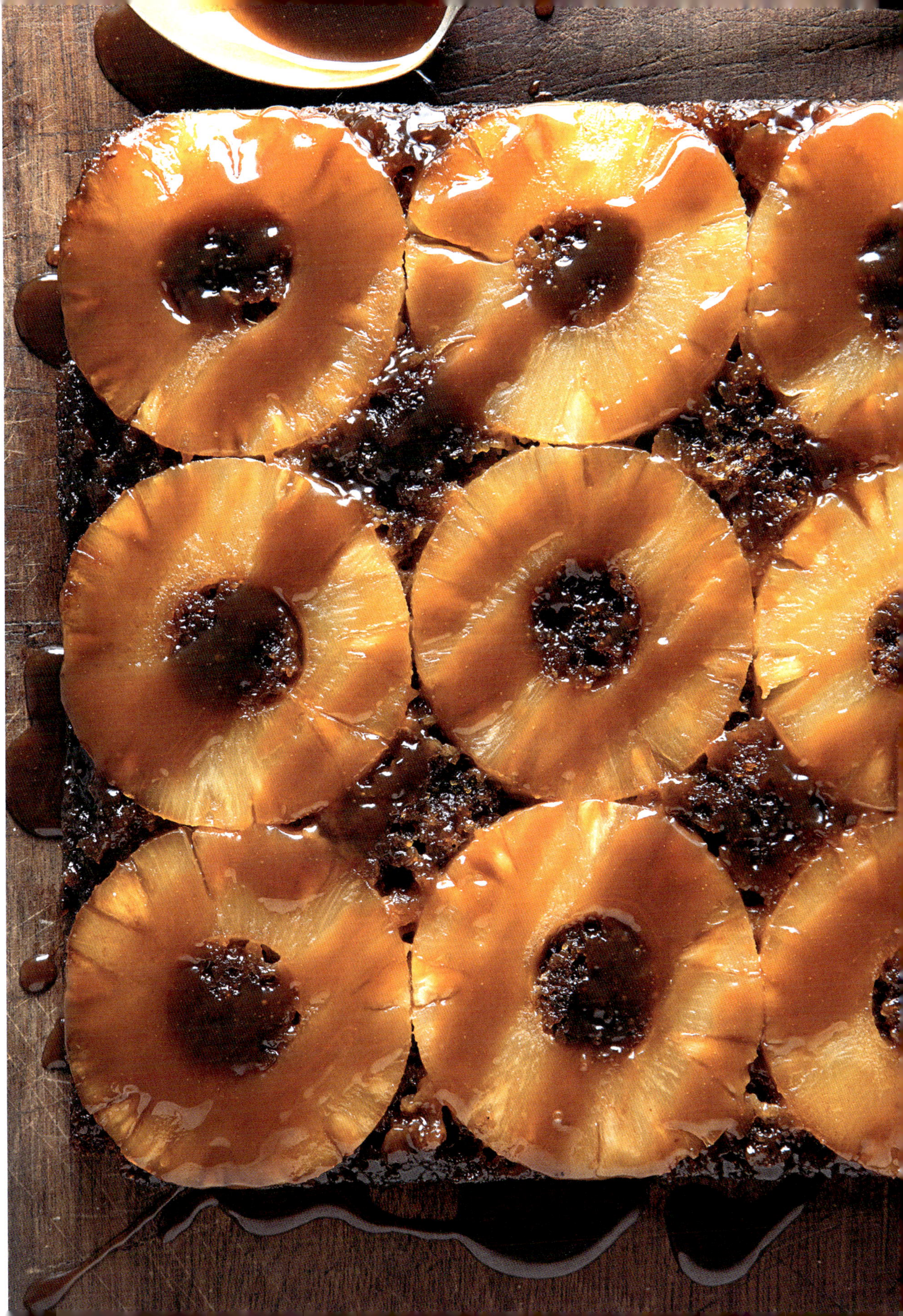

Banana crème brûlée

SERVES 4

25g butter, plus extra for greasing
25g dark brown soft sugar
pinch of salt
pinch of ground cinnamon
4 bananas, peeled and sliced diagonally
25ml rum

CUSTARD
600ml double cream
1 vanilla pod, split
6 egg yolks
15g light brown soft sugar
15g dark brown soft sugar

TOPPING
2 tbsp demerara sugar

Dave and I both loved a nice bowlful of banana and custard when we were kids, so we decided we needed to make a grown-up version. Here's our childhood favourite re-imagined as an extra special crème brûlée. You'll love it and it's another of those useful puds that you can prepare mostly in advance, then finish at the last minute with the browning of the top.

1. Grease 4 shallow ramekins with butter and set them aside. Melt the butter in a frying pan and when it starts to foam, add the sugar, salt and cinnamon. Stir until the sugar has melted.

2. Add the slices of banana and cook them for a couple of minutes on each side until lightly browned. Heat the rum in a small saucepan or a ladle and set it alight, then carefully pour it over the bananas. When the flames subside, divide the bananas between the ramekins.

3. To make the custard, put the double cream in a saucepan with the vanilla pod. Heat until the cream is almost boiling, then remove the pan from the heat and leave the cream to infuse for 10 minutes.

4. Lightly whisk the egg yolks with the sugar in a bowl, just to combine, then pour the cream over the eggs in a continuous thin stream until all is combined. Rinse out the saucepan and pour everything back into it, including the vanilla pod.

5. Stir the mixture continuously over a low to medium heat until you have a thick, just pourable custard. Do not leave the custard unattended as it may split. To guard against this, have a bowl of iced water at the ready. If your custard does split, plunge the saucepan into the water, then beat the custard like crazy with a whisk. When the custard is well thickened – this will take at least 10 minutes – pour it over the bananas. When cool, put the ramekins in the fridge to chill, preferably for at least 6 hours.

6. For the burnt sugar topping, first make sure the surface of the custard is completely dry – blot it with kitchen paper if necessary. Sprinkle the sugar over the top, then put the ramekins under a very hot grill or blast them with a blowtorch until the sugar is browned and bubbling. Serve at once.

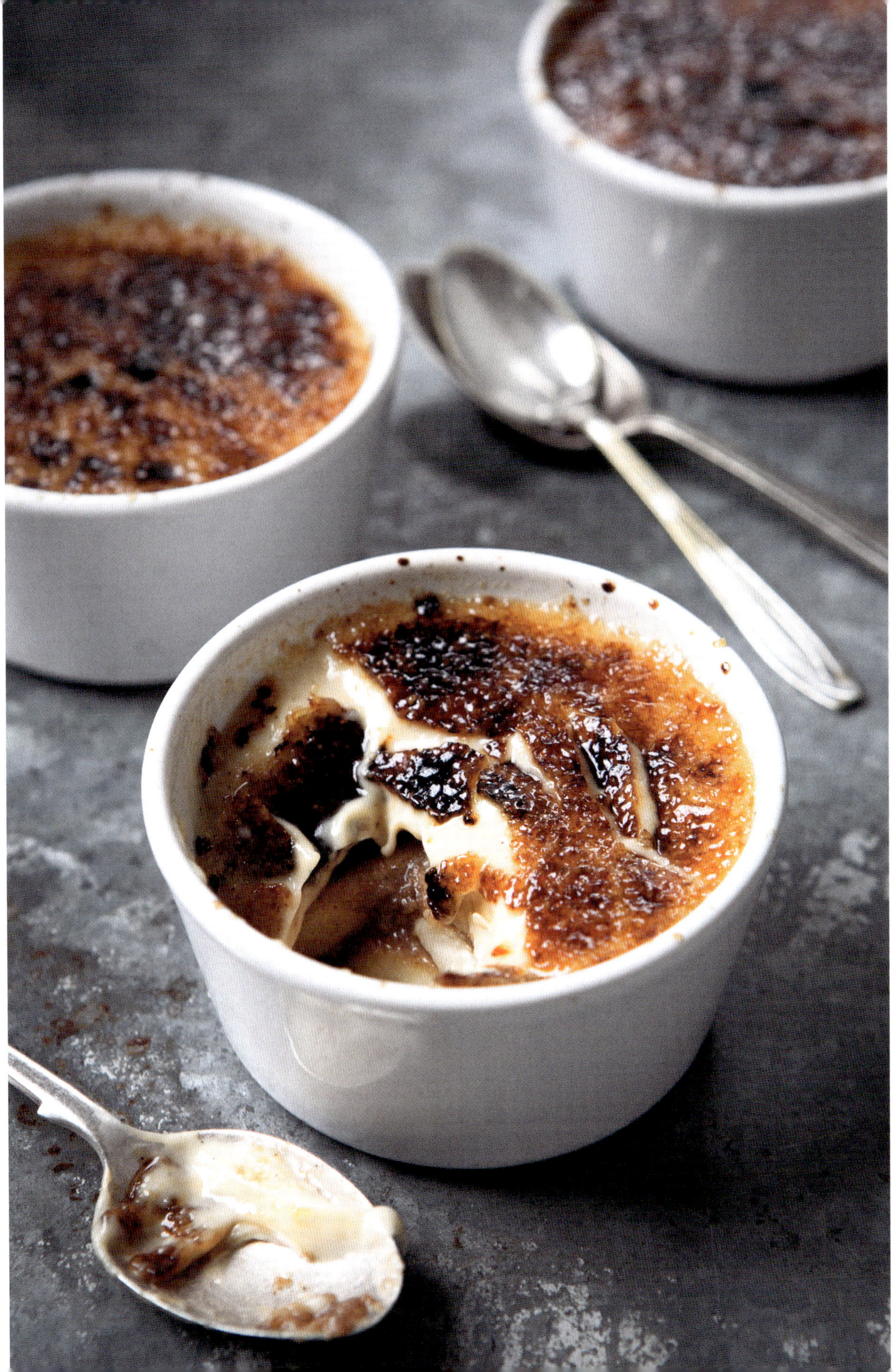

Triple-cooked chips...254
Roast potatoes...254
Colcannon...255
Dauphinoise potatoes...255
Boulangère potatoes...256
Roast new potatoes with garlic & rosemary...256
Potato salad...257
Mulled cider red cabbage...257
Three-root mash...258
Root vegetable purées...258
A quick dal...259
Cauliflower cheese...259
Pickled eggs...260
Marinated eggs (tamago)...260
Bacon jam...261
Basil pesto...261
Twice-cooked pork (char siu)...262
Yorkshire pudding...262
Puffy puris...263
Fresh pasta...264

Shortcrust pastry...265
Cranberry relish...265
Hollandaise sauce...266
Mayonnaise...266
Tartare sauce...267
Tomato sauce...267
Medium curry powder...268
Vindaloo spice paste...268
Our garam masala...269
Caribbean curry powder...269
Vegetable stock...270
Fish stock...270
Chicken stock...271
Beef stock...271
Onion gravy...272
Chicken gravy...272
Pancake batter...273
Proper custard...273
Vanilla ice cream...274
Chocolate sauce...274
Buttercream icing...275
Brown butter...275

sides & basics

"Here are some of the best side dishes, sauces and other cooking essentials that have featured in the Hairy Biker cookbooks. These can make a great meal fabulous."

Triple-cooked chips

SERVES 4

1kg floury potatoes, preferably Maris Pipers
groundnut or sunflower oil, for deep-frying
sea salt

1. Peel the potatoes and cut them into thick batons, about 1.5 x 1.5 x 6cm. Run them under cold water to remove as much starch as possible, then put them in a large pan.

2. Cover the chips with cold water and slowly bring it to the boil. Simmer gently for 20–25 minutes, until the potatoes are tender when tested with the point of a knife and you can see lines and cracks start to develop. Using a slotted spoon, remove the chips very carefully from the pan and drain them on some kitchen paper. Pat them dry.

3. Half fill a deep-fat fryer or large saucepan with oil and heat to 130°C. Never leave a pan of hot oil unattended. Fry the chips in a couple of batches, until they have developed a crust but not taken on any colour – this will take about 5 minutes. Remove each batch when it's ready and set aside.

4. Heat the oil to 180°C. Return the chips to the pan, again in a couple of batches, and fry them for 1–2 minutes until they're very crisp and a deep golden-brown.

5. Drain the chips on kitchen paper, then sprinkle them with salt and serve at once. If you prefer, you could cook the chips in beef dripping. You'll need about 1.5kg.

Roast potatoes

SERVES 4–6

1.5kg floury potatoes, such as Maris Pipers or King Edwards
100g goose or duck fat
2 tbsp semolina
salt and black pepper

1. Peel the potatoes and cut them into large chunks. Put the potatoes in a pan of cold, salted water, bring to the boil and boil for about 5 minutes. Drain well in a colander, then tip the potatoes back into the saucepan and shake them to scuff up the surfaces. This helps to make lovely crispy roasties.

2. Meanwhile, preheat the oven to 200–220°C/Fan 180–200°C/Gas 6–7 and melt the fat in a roasting tin. It must be good and hot. Sprinkle the semolina over the potatoes and carefully tip them into the sizzling fat. Season liberally and roast the potatoes until golden. This will take 45–50 minutes, depending on the size of the potatoes. Serve at once.

Colcannon

SERVES 4

750g potatoes, such as
   Maris Pipers or
   King Edwards
50g butter
1 onion, finely chopped
100g curly kale,
   roughly shredded
200ml double cream
salt and black pepper

1. Peel the potatoes and cut them into chunks. Try to make sure the pieces are roughly the same size, so they cook evenly.
2. Put the potatoes in a pan of salted water and bring to the boil. Once the water is boiling, turn down the heat and simmer the potatoes for about 20 minutes or until soft.
3. Meanwhile, heat 25g of the butter in a large heavy-based frying pan and gently fry the onion for 5 minutes, or until softened, stirring regularly. Add the kale and cook for 2–3 minutes, then set aside.
4. Drain the potatoes in a large colander, tip them back into the pan and leave them to stand for a couple of minutes. Warm the cream and the rest of the butter in a small pan, then add the mixture to the potatoes and mash them until smooth. Season to taste. Add the softened kale and stir together until lightly combined, then serve immediately.
5. If you're not quite ready to serve, preheat the oven to 140°C/Fan 120°C/Gas 1 and put a heatproof dish in the oven to heat up. Transfer the colcannon to the warmed dish, cover it with foil and leave in the oven until needed.

Dauphinoise potatoes

SERVES 4–6

1 garlic clove, cut in half
25g butter
1kg salad/waxy potatoes,
   such as Charlottes, thinly
   sliced
300ml double cream
400ml whole milk
1 tsp plain flour
grating of nutmeg
   (optional)
salt and black pepper

1. Preheat the oven to 180°C/Fan 160°C/Gas 4.
2. Rub a shallow gratin dish with the cut sides of the garlic, then take a small knob of the butter and rub this around the dish as well.
3. Rinse the potatoes to get rid of excess starch, then dry them as thoroughly as you can. Layer them in the gratin dish, seasoning them with salt and black pepper as you go.
4. Put the double cream and milk in a jug and whisk in the flour – this helps to stop the cream curdling. Pour the mixture over the potatoes, then dot the remaining butter on top. Grate over some nutmeg, if using.
5. Bake in the preheated oven for an hour, then turn the heat up to 220°C/Fan 200°C/Gas 7 and bake for another 10 minutes or until the top layer of potatoes has turned a crisp golden-brown.

Boulangère potatoes

SERVES 6

2 tbsp olive oil, plus extra for greasing
1 large onion, thinly sliced
3–4 thyme sprigs, plus extra to garnish
3 garlic cloves, thinly sliced
1.2 kg floury potatoes, such as Maris Pipers, thinly sliced to the thickness of a £1 coin
400ml chicken or vegetable stock
salt and black pepper

1. Heat the oil in a large frying pan. Add the onion and thyme and fry gently, stirring occasionally, for 8–10 minutes, until the onion has softened and browned slightly. Add the garlic and continue to fry for 2–3 minutes, then season to taste with salt and black pepper.

2. Preheat the oven to 200°C/Fan 180°C/Gas 6. Grease a 20 x 30cm roasting tin or ovenproof dish with a little oil. Arrange a layer of potato slices to cover the base of the dish. Sprinkle over a third of the fried onions. Continue layering the potato slices and onion mixture, ending with a layer of potatoes.

3. Pour over the stock until it just reaches the top layer of potatoes. Season again with black pepper and garnish with a few thyme sprigs. Cook for about 1¼ hours or until the potatoes are tender and lovely and brown on top.

Roast new potatoes with garlic & rosemary

SERVES 4

1kg new potatoes, unpeeled
50ml olive oil
1 garlic bulb
a few rosemary sprigs
salt and black pepper

1. Preheat the oven to 200°C/Fan 180°C/Gas 6.

2. Cut any larger potatoes into chunks, then put them in a saucepan and cover them with water. Add salt, then bring to the boil and simmer for 5 minutes. Drain well.

3. Pour the olive oil into a roasting tin and heat for a couple of minutes in the oven. Remove and add the potatoes, carefully shaking them around to coat them in the hot oil.

4. Separate the garlic bulb into cloves but leave them unpeeled. Add these to the tin, together with all but one of the rosemary sprigs. Season with plenty of salt and black pepper.

5. Put the roasting tin in the oven and roast the potatoes for about 45 minutes, turning them over every so often. Chop the spikes from the reserved sprig of rosemary and toss them over the potatoes before serving.

Potato salad

SERVES 4

400g new potatoes, unpeeled
3 tbsp mayonnaise
1 tbsp crème fraiche
2 tbsp baby capers, drained
50g baby gherkins, drained and sliced
2 tsp lemon juice
grated zest of 1 lemon
1 tbsp chopped parsley
salt and black pepper

1. Scrub the potatoes well. Bring a pan of salted water to the boil. Add the potatoes, bring the water back to the boil and cook them for 15–18 minutes, or until just tender. Drain the potatoes in a colander, then rinse them under running water until they're cold.

2. Mix the mayonnaise, crème fraiche, capers, gherkins and lemon juice in a large bowl until well combined.

3. Cut the potatoes into quarters, add them to the mayonnaise dressing with the lemon zest and stir well. Season to taste with salt and black pepper and sprinkle with parsley before serving.

Mulled cider red cabbage

SERVES 6–8

1 small red cabbage
25g butter
1 large onion, finely sliced
2 star anise
1 cinnamon stick
¼ tsp freshly grated nutmeg
1 bay leaf
8 tbsp cider
2 tbsp light muscovado sugar
2 tbsp redcurrant jelly
salt and black pepper

1. Finely slice the cabbage, chucking out the core and any tough pieces. Use a pan that has a tight-fitting lid and is large enough to hold all the cabbage. Melt the butter in the pan and cook the onion, uncovered, for 5 minutes until it's soft but not browned.

2. Add the star anise, cinnamon stick, nutmeg and bay leaf, then the cabbage, cider and sugar. Stir until everything is thoroughly mixed and the sugar has dissolved. Season generously. Bring to the boil, then cover the pan tightly and simmer for about 1 hour, stirring occasionally, until the cabbage is very tender and the liquid has evaporated.

3. Stir in the redcurrant jelly and allow it to melt. Remove the star anise and cinnamon stick before serving.

Three-root mash

SERVES 4

400g carrots
250g parsnips
500g celeriac
50g butter
a few gratings of nutmeg
salt and black pepper

1. Cut the vegetables into 2.5cm chunks. Put them in a large saucepan, cover with cold water and bring to the boil. Turn down the heat slightly and simmer for 25–30 minutes, or until the vegetables are very tender.

2. Drain the vegetables in a colander and then tip them back into the pan. Add the butter, grated nutmeg and lots of salt and pepper to taste, then mash thoroughly until smooth.

Root vegetable purées

SERVES 4

500g celeriac, parsnips, sweet potatoes or Jerusalem artichokes, diced
250g floury potatoes, diced
50ml whole milk, warmed through
25g butter
2 tsp wholegrain mustard (optional)
herbs (optional – see tip)
salt and black pepper

1. Bring a large saucepan of water to the boil and add a generous amount of salt. Add whichever root vegetables you want and the potatoes, then simmer until they are all very tender.

2. Drain thoroughly and tip the veg back into the pan. Cover with a tea towel and leave the pan over a very low heat for 5 minutes, shaking the pan every so often, to dry the vegetables out.

3. Put the veg through a potato ricer or use a regular masher – don't be tempted to use a stick blender, as it will make the potatoes go gluey. Season again with salt and pepper, then add the milk and butter. Add mustard, if using – it does go very well with celeriac and Jerusalem artichokes. Mix thoroughly and keep the purée warm until served.

BIKER TIP

If you want to add herbs to the mash, take small bunches and separate leaves from stems. Use any herbs you like, but sage works particularly well with parsnips and Jerusalem artichokes; thyme with celeriac and sweet potato; and parsley with sweet potato. Add the stems to the cooking water and discard them when you drain the vegetables. Finely chop the leaves. Melt the butter and add the leaves. Swirl the herbs around in the butter or oil before stirring them through the mashed vegetables.

A quick dal

SERVES 4

1 tbsp vegetable oil
3 garlic cloves, crushed
15g root ginger, grated
½ tsp ground turmeric
½ tsp ground cinnamon
½ tsp ground cumin
½ tsp ground coriander
½ tsp ground cardamom
a pinch of asafoetida
200g lentils (any split sort or mung beans), well rinsed
salt and black pepper

GARNISH (OPTIONAL)
1 tbsp vegetable oil
1 tsp mustard seeds
12 curry leaves
a few coriander leaves
a few green chillies, chopped

1. Heat the oil in a large pan and add the garlic, ginger and spices – you don't have to add all the spices, but it's good to use at least a pinch of turmeric and a pinch of asafoetida. Stir to combine and cook for a couple of minutes.

2. Stir in the lentils and add a litre of water. Season with plenty of salt and pepper, then bring to the boil and turn the heat down to a simmer. Cook until the dal is tender – this will take anything from 20 minutes for red lentils to up to 40 minutes for firmer varieties.

3. For the garnish, if using, heat the vegetable oil in a small frying pan and add the mustard seeds and curry leaves. When the mustard seeds start popping and the curry leaves look dry and start to crackle, remove the pan from the heat and pour the mixture over the dal.

4. Serve the dal sprinkled with coriander leaves and green chillies.

Cauliflower cheese

SERVES 4–6

1 large cauliflower
25g butter
2 tbsp plain flour
250ml whole milk
½ tsp English mustard powder
200g Gruyère cheese, grated
pinch of grated nutmeg
50g Parmesan cheese, grated
salt and black pepper

1. Trim the cauliflower and break it into florets. Bring a big pan of water to the boil, add the florets and boil them for about 10 minutes until just soft. Drain and set aside. Preheat the oven to 180°C/Fan 160°C/Gas 4.

2. Melt the butter in a small saucepan and beat in the flour. Add the milk, stirring all the time, to make a thick white sauce. Add the mustard powder and grated Gruyère while stirring, then season with salt and black pepper.

3. Put the cauliflower florets in an ovenproof dish, pour in the cheesy sauce and sprinkle with the pinch of nutmeg. Sprinkle the grated Parmesan on top. Place in the preheated oven and bake for about 15 minutes or until the sauce is bubbling and the top is golden.

Pickled eggs

MAKES 6

6 eggs
350ml cider vinegar
1 tbsp salt
1 tbsp sugar
1 tsp chilli flakes or a few dried chillies (optional)

1. First find a jar that's large enough to hold all 6 eggs – a Kilner jar is ideal. To sterilise it, run it through the hottest setting in your dishwasher, or wash it in plenty of hot, soapy water, then rinse thoroughly. Put it in a low oven (140°C/Fan 120°C/Gas 1) to dry completely.

2. Bring a saucepan of water to the boil, then gently lower in the eggs. Boil them for 7 minutes exactly, then take the pan off the heat, remove the eggs and run them under cold water to stop them cooking. When they are cool enough to handle, peel them carefully.

3. Put the cider vinegar in a saucepan with 150ml of water and the salt and sugar. Slowly bring the mixture to the boil, stirring to dissolve the sugar, then simmer for 5 minutes. If using chilli, add it for the last minute.

4. Pack the eggs into the jar, then pour over the pickling mixture. Seal the jar and leave to cool completely. Leave the eggs for at least 2 weeks before eating, preferably a month, then store the jar in the fridge once opened.

Marinated eggs (tamago)

MAKES 6

6 eggs
200ml dark soy sauce
100ml mirin
100ml sake
50g light brown soft sugar
2 star anise

1. Bring a saucepan of water to the boil, then turn the heat down to a simmer. Add the eggs and simmer them gently for exactly 6 minutes. Remove the eggs from the pan and immediately plunge them into cold water to stop them cooking.

2. Mix the soy sauce, mirin, sake and sugar together, stirring until the sugar has dissolved. Add the star anise.

3. Peel the eggs and put them in a container just big enough to hold them snugly, then pour the marinade over them. If any of the eggs break the surface of the marinade, weigh them down by putting some scrunched-up greaseproof paper on top.

4. Leave the eggs in the marinade for at least 3 hours, but preferably overnight. To serve, cut the eggs in half and add to Asian dishes – they are particularly good in ramen (see p.50)

Bacon jam

MAKES 1 LARGE JAR

500g smoked streaky bacon, finely diced
2 medium onions, very finely chopped
2 garlic cloves, finely chopped
1 thyme sprig, left whole
75ml cider vinegar
75g light brown soft sugar
50ml maple syrup
100ml strong espresso coffee
100ml bourbon, whisky or brandy
1 tbsp chipotle paste or 1 tsp chilli powder

1. Put the bacon in a large saucepan and fry it over a medium heat until it's starting to crisp up and brown. Add the onions and continue to cook until softened and they have slightly caramelised. Add the garlic and thyme and cook for another minute or so.

2. Add the vinegar, sugar, maple syrup, coffee and alcohol to the saucepan. Cook over a low heat, stirring constantly to dissolve the sugar. Stir in the chipotle paste or chilli powder, then leave to simmer gently for about an hour, until the mixture is thick and syrupy.

3. Using a stick blender, if you have one, or an ordinary jug blender, blend the mixture quite roughly – you want to keep plenty of texture in there, so a couple of blasts should be enough. Stir again to mix.

4. Transfer the jam to a clean, sterilised jar and store it in the fridge. It will keep for up to a month.

Basil pesto

MAKES ABOUT 250ML

50g pine nuts or blanched almonds
generous pinch of salt
1 garlic clove
leaves from 2 large bunches of basil
zest of ½ lemon
25g Parmesan cheese, grated
up to 150ml extra virgin olive oil, plus extra for storing

1. Put the pine nuts or almonds in a dry frying pan and toast them, shaking the pan regularly, until they start to turn light brown. Transfer them to a food processor and leave to cool.

2. Add the salt and garlic to the processor, then pulse a few times to break up the nuts and garlic. Add the basil and lemon zest, then pulse a few more times, pushing the basil down as necessary to make a coarse paste.

3. Add the Parmesan, then start drizzling in the oil while continuing to pulse. The pesto should be lightly emulsified but not smooth. Add just enough oil to create quite a thick paste. The pesto shouldn't be runny.

4. Use right away or transfer the pesto to a jar and top with extra olive oil to keep the surface fresh. Store in the fridge.

Twice-cooked pork (char siu)

SERVES 4–6

750g piece of pork loin, skinned, trimmed of fat, and rolled and tied
250ml soy sauce
100ml sake
100ml mirin
50ml hoisin sauce
3 garlic cloves, sliced
30g root ginger, sliced
2 star anise
vegetable oil, for frying
black pepper

1. Prick the pork loin all over with a sharp skewer or needle, then put it in a saucepan. The pork should fit quite snugly, so don't use a pan that's bigger than necessary. Add all the ingredients, except the vegetable oil, and season with black pepper. Pour in water until the pork is just covered – ideally no more than about 500ml. Bring the water to the boil, then turn down the heat and cover the pan. Leave to simmer very gently for a couple of hours, until the pork is tender.

2. If possible, leave the pork to cool in the liquid, preferably overnight, then remove it, reserving the cooking liquid. Pat the meat dry and wrap it tightly in cling film and chill – the wrapping and chilling will help to firm up the meat and make it easier to slice thinly.

3. To serve, cut the meat into very thin slices. Heat some vegetable oil in a frying pan and fry the slices of pork, ladling in small amounts of the cooking liquid, so it reduces and clings to the slices in a sticky sauce. Serve with greens and steamed rice or noodles. Alternatively, drop the slices – fried or not as you prefer – into ramen broth (see p.50).

Yorkshire pudding

MAKES 1 LARGE OR 12 SMALL

150g plain flour
½ tsp salt
2 eggs, beaten
275ml whole milk
2 tbsp vegetable oil or goose fat

1. Put the flour in a bowl and whisk it lightly to get rid of any lumps, then add the salt. Make a well in the middle and add the eggs. Work the eggs into the flour, then gradually add the milk. Alternatively, put everything in a food processor and blitz until smooth. Leave to stand for an hour.

2. Preheat the oven to 200°C/Fan 180°C/Gas 6. Put the oil or goose fat in a Yorkshire pudding tin and place it in the oven until smoking hot. Give the batter a stir, then quickly pour it into the tin and pop it back into the oven.

3. Bake for about 30 minutes until the pudding has risen and is a beautiful golden-brown. If you're making individual puds, use a muffin pan and bake them for about 15 minutes.

Puffy puris

MAKES 12

200g wholewheat atta flour, plus extra for rolling
½ tsp fine sea salt
4 tsp sunflower oil, plus ¼ tsp
150ml water (75ml just-boiled and 75ml cold)
about 1 litre sunflower oil, for frying

1. Atta flour is used to make Indian breads and is available in supermarkets. Put the flour and salt in a large bowl and make a well in the centre. Pour the 4 teaspoons of oil into the flour and rub together with your fingertips until the flour comes together in a loose clump. It should look like slightly damp sand. Add the water to the flour, a couple of tablespoons at a time, mixing well between each addition. Bring the mixture together to form a dough that's wet and sticky but still quite firm.

2. Knead the dough in the bowl until it's smooth and no longer sticky, then add the remaining ¼ teaspoon of oil and knead again for 30 seconds. Take a pea-sized piece of the dough and set it aside.

3. Divide the dough into 12 portions and roll them into small balls. Take a ball and flatten it into a disc. Sprinkle a little flour on to the work surface and, using a rolling pin, roll the disc into a 12cm circle about the thickness of a 2 pence coin. It is important that it has an even thickness, so take it slowly, lifting and turning the pastry frequently. Put the disc on a very lightly floured tray and repeat to make 11 more.

4. Pour about a litre of oil in a large saucepan or sauté pan, about 4cm deep. Heat the oil to 190°C, using a cooking thermometer to check the temperature. You can also take half the reserved tiny ball of dough and drop it into the oil. If it rises to the surface immediately, the oil is hot enough to fry the puris. It is important that the oil is the right temperature or the puris won't puff up as they fry. Never leave a pan of hot oil unattended.

5. Brush any excess flour off a puri and using a heatproof slotted spoon, lower it into the hot oil. Push it under, paddling it gently with the bowl of the spoon so it remains submerged. As the puri begins to puff up, work the spoon around it to encourage the hot oil to create enough steam inside the disc to puff. Cook for 8–10 seconds once completely puffed, then carefully turn it over and fry on the other side for a further 8–10 seconds.

6. Lift the puri out of the hot oil and drain well on kitchen paper. Continue frying the rest of the puris in the same way, but make sure the oil remains at 190°C, so the puris puff up properly and don't become greasy. Be ready to increase or reduce the heat accordingly. Serve warm with prawns, as on page 24, or with any curry.

Fresh pasta

MAKES ABOUT 600G

500g Italian '00' flour
5 eggs
pinch of salt

1. If making your pasta by hand, sift the flour into a bowl, then turn it out on to a clean work surface. Make a large well in the middle, break the eggs into it and add a generous pinch of salt.

2. Break up all the yolks, then, using a circular motion with your fingers, start working in the flour from the sides. When you have worked most of it in, start shaping the dough into a ball. If it is still on the dry side, wet your hands which should give enough extra liquid to work the dough together. When the dough has formed a ball, knead it for about 10 minutes until smooth. It will still feel quite firm at this stage.

3. If you want to make the pasta in a stand mixer, sift the flour and salt into the bowl and fit the dough hook. With the motor running on a slow setting, gradually add the eggs, one at a time, until the mixture comes together. Knead the dough in the mixer for about 5 minutes.

4. Divide the dough into 2 balls, wrap them in cling film and leave them to rest for an hour before rolling. You can freeze the dough at this stage if you like.

5. To roll the pasta, flatten each piece of dough down slightly and start on the widest setting of your pasta machine. Roll the pasta through, then move down a setting. Repeat twice more, reducing the setting each time, then fold the pasta in half and start again. Repeat the procedure. By this point the pasta will be very long so cut it in half. Put one of the pieces under a damp cloth, then fold the other piece into 3 – it should be the same width as the machine if you give it one turn. Roll through again, starting at the widest setting then reducing until it is about 1.5mm thick.

6. Cut the pasta as required for your recipe – for lasagne sheets, cut to fit your lasagne dish. Otherwise cut it into thick ribbons (pappardelle) about 2cm wide, or into thinner tagliatelle.

7. You can use this pasta fresh or dry. To dry the lengths, lay them out over a pasta drier (a clothes horse also works well), or roll the ribbons into loose nests. Leave them to dry out completely, then store them in a cool dark place until needed.

Shortcrust pastry

MAKES ABOUT 500G

300g plain flour, plus extra for dusting
75g butter, chilled and diced
75g lard, chilled and diced (or another 75g butter)
pinch of salt
1 egg, beaten (optional)
iced water

1. Put the flour, butter and lard, if using, in a bowl and add a generous pinch of salt. Rub the fat into the flour, using just your fingertips to keep it as cool as possible, until the mixture resembles fine breadcrumbs. Give the bowl a gentle shake – this will help any larger lumps move to the top which you can then rub until finer, as necessary.

2. If using the egg, whisk it with a tablespoon of iced water before adding it to the bowl – mixing with the water helps the egg yolk disperse more evenly. Add just enough iced water to the bowl to form a dough.

3. Knead the dough very gently until smooth, then turn it out on to a floured work surface. If the dough is too soft to manage or if you're making things like pasties, you'll need to chill the pastry before rolling so wrap it in cling film and leave it in the fridge for half an hour. If you are using the pastry to line a tart tin, you might like to roll it and line the tin, then chill.

4. If you need to roll out pastry that has been chilled for too long and is hard, remove it from the fridge at least half an hour before you want to use it and cover it with a damp tea towel. This will help soften it up a bit and stop it from feeling too dry or crumbly around the edges. Use the pastry as needed.

Variations

SWEET PASTRY: Add 1 tablespoon of icing sugar. You can also flavour a sweetened dough with some citrus zest – add the zest of 1 lemon or orange or 2 limes with the flour.
A MORE ROBUST PASTRY: Use suet in place of the 75g of lard or extra butter.
NUTTY PASTRY: Substitute ground almonds or hazelnuts for up to half the flour.

Cranberry relish

SERVES 4

250g cranberries (fresh or frozen)
100g caster sugar
juice of 1 orange
1 tsp orange zest
50ml port (optional)
pinch of salt

1. Put all the ingredients in a saucepan, including the port, if using, and stir over a low heat until all the sugar has dissolved. Turn up the heat until the mixture is just boiling and continue to cook until at least half the cranberries have burst.

2. Remove the pan from the heat and leave the relish to cool – the consistency will thicken and become jammy.

Hollandaise sauce

MAKES 250ML

50ml white wine vinegar
a few peppercorns
1 bay leaf
1 shallot, finely diced
1 blade of mace
250g unsalted butter, diced
3 egg yolks
pinch of salt
squeeze of lemon
    juice (optional)
pinch of sugar (optional)
finely chopped tarragon
    (optional)

1. Put the white wine vinegar in a small saucepan with 50ml of water, the peppercorns, bay leaf, shallot and mace. Bring to the boil and simmer until the liquid has reduced down to 2 tablespoons.

2. Place the butter in a medium saucepan over a low heat and allow it to melt, but make sure it doesn't burn. When the butter has melted, take the pan off the heat.

3. Put the egg yolks in a heatproof bowl with a pinch of salt. Whisk in the white wine vinegar reduction, then place the bowl over a pan of simmering water. Gradually add the melted butter, just a few drops at a time to start with, and keep whisking until it starts to thicken. Then keep pouring the butter in a slightly faster, steady stream until it is all incorporated and you have a thick, glossy sauce.

4. Taste for seasoning and add a squeeze of lemon juice or a pinch of sugar to balance the flavours. Add the chopped tarragon, if using. Serve warm or if making the sauce for use in the salmon pie with spinach on page 124, cool it by putting the bowl into a larger bowl filled with iced water.

Mayonnaise

MAKES A GOOD BOWLFUL

2 egg yolks
1 tsp mustard
250ml sunflower or
    groundnut oil
squeeze of lemon juice or
    a few drops of vinegar
salt and black pepper

1. Put the egg yolks in a bowl with the mustard and a little salt. Mix them together until well combined.

2. Start drizzling in the oil, a few drops at a time, whisking constantly, until the mixture has thickened. Keep adding the oil, very gradually, until you have incorporated it all. If it the mayonnaise seems to be becoming greasy or too thick to work with, add a few drops of warm water and whisk thoroughly before adding any more oil.

3. Taste the mayonnaise, then add more seasoning and a squeeze of lemon or a few drops of vinegar if you think it needs acidity.

Tartare sauce

SERVES 4

1 egg yolk
pinch of salt
1 tsp Dijon mustard
250ml neutral-tasting oil (sunflower or groundnut)
zest of 1 lime
4 tbsp cornichons, finely chopped
3 tbsp capers, finely chopped
a few chives, snipped
a few tarragon leaves
a few basil leaves
a squeeze of lime juice
1 tsp sriracha sauce (optional)

1. Put the egg yolk in a bowl or food processor with a generous pinch of salt and the mustard. Whisk or pulse briefly, then very gradually start adding the oil.

2. When the mixture has emulsified, start adding the oil in a steady, slightly faster stream until it is all incorporated and you have a thick mayonnaise. Stir through the remaining ingredients and taste for seasoning.

Tomato sauce

SERVES 6-8

6 tbsp olive oil
2 onions, very finely sliced
6 garlic cloves, finely chopped
250ml red wine
4 x 400g cans of tomatoes or 1.5kg plum tomatoes, peeled and chopped
2 tsp dried oregano
1 tsp fresh thyme leaves
2 bay leaves
pinch of sugar (optional)
salt and black pepper

1. Heat the olive oil in a large saucepan and add the onions. Sauté them very gently until very soft – this will take at least 15 minutes.

2. Add the garlic and cook for another 3–4 minutes over a very gentle heat, then pour in the red wine. Boil until the wine is reduced by at least half, then add the tomatoes and herbs. Season with salt and pepper.

3. Bring the sauce to the boil, then turn down the heat, cover the pan and simmer for an hour. At this point taste the sauce and if it seems acidic, add a generous pinch of sugar. Continue to simmer, uncovered, for about half an hour until well reduced. Great with pasta.

Medium curry powder

MAKES 1 SMALL JAR

1 tbsp cumin seeds
1 tbsp coriander seeds
1 tsp mustard seeds
1 tsp nigella seeds
½ tsp fenugreek seeds
3cm piece of cinnamon stick, broken up
6 dried curry leaves (optional)
1 tsp ground turmeric
1 tsp chilli powder
1 tsp sweet paprika
1 tsp garlic granules
¼ tsp asafoetida

1. Put all the whole spices and the curry leaves, if using, into a dry frying pan – preferably not a non-stick one. Toast over a medium heat until the aroma is strong and the mustard seeds are popping.

2. Transfer the toasted spices and curry leaves to a bowl to cool, then grind them to a fine powder in a spice grinder or with a pestle and mortar.

3. Mix with the turmeric, chilli powder, sweet paprika, garlic granules and asafoetida and store in an airtight jar.

Vindaloo spice paste

MAKES 1 SMALL JAR

8 green cardamom pods
1 tsp black peppercorns
8 cloves
5cm piece of cinnamon stick
1 tsp cumin seeds
½ tsp coriander seeds
2 tbsp Kashmiri chilli powder
1 tsp ground turmeric
1 tbsp tamarind purée
1 tbsp vinegar (cider or red wine)
25g root ginger, roughly grated
4 garlic cloves, roughly chopped

1. Crush the cardamom pods lightly until they crack. Tip them on to a board and open all the pods. Using the tip of a knife, scrape the seeds into a dry frying pan – preferably not a non-stick one – and chuck out the shells.

2. Add the other whole spices to the pan and toast until they have a strong aroma. Remove and cool, then blitz in a spice grinder.

3. Transfer them to a food processor with the remaining ingredients and blitz to a paste, adding water to help it combine if necessary. Spoon the paste into a jar or bowl and keep it in the fridge.

Our garam masala

MAKES 1 SMALL JAR

12 cardamom pods
3cm piece of cinnamon stick
2 tbsp coriander seeds
1 tbsp cumin seeds
1 tsp whole cloves
3 dried bay leaves
scant 2 tsp black peppercorns
½ whole nutmeg
½ tsp ground turmeric
½ tsp ground ginger

1. Crush the cardamom pods lightly until they crack. Tip them on to a board and open all the pods. Using the tip of a knife, scrape the seeds into a dry frying pan – preferably not a non-stick one – and chuck out the shells.

2. Add the cinnamon, coriander and cumin seeds, cloves, bay leaves and peppercorns to the pan and toast over a medium heat for 1–2 minutes, stirring until you can smell the spices strongly. Watch them carefully so they don't burn.

3. Allow the spices to cool a little. Tip them into an electric spice grinder or use a pestle and mortar, then grind or pound to a fine powder.

4. Finely grate the nutmeg and stir into the other spices. Add the turmeric and ginger and mix well. Use what you need and put the rest into a small airtight jar. Keep in a dark place and try to use within a month.

Caribbean curry powder

MAKES 1 SMALL JAR

4cm piece of cinnamon stick, broken up
2 tbsp coriander seeds
2 tsp cumin seeds
1 tsp mustard seeds
1 tsp white peppercorns
½ tsp allspice berries
½ tsp fenugreek
seeds from 6 cardamom pods
4 cloves
2 mace blades
2 dried bay leaves
1 tbsp ground turmeric
½ tsp onion salt

1. Put all the whole spices and the bay leaves in a dry frying pan – preferably not a non-stick one. Toast the spices over a medium heat, shaking regularly, until the aroma intensifies and the mustard seeds are popping. Transfer to a bowl to cool.

2. Grind the spices in a spice grinder or with a pestle and mortar to form a fine powder, then mix with the turmeric and onion salt. Store in an airtight jar.

Vegetable stock

MAKES ABOUT 1.5 LITRES

1 tsp olive oil
2 large onions, roughly chopped
3 large carrots, chopped
200g squash or pumpkin, unpeeled, diced
4 celery sticks, sliced
2 leeks, sliced
100ml white wine or vermouth
large thyme sprig
large parsley sprig
1 bay leaf
a few peppercorns

1. Heat the olive oil in a large saucepan. Add all the vegetables and fry them over a high heat, stirring regularly, until they start to brown and caramelise around the edges. This will take at least 10 minutes. Add the white wine or vermouth and boil until it has evaporated away.

2. Cover the vegetables with 2 litres of water, add the herbs and peppercorns. Bring to the boil, then turn the heat down to a gentle simmer. Cook the stock, uncovered, for about an hour, stirring every so often.

3. Check the stock – the colour should have some depth to it. Strain it through a colander or a sieve lined with muslin or kitchen paper into a bowl. Store it in the fridge for up to a week or freeze it.

Fish stock

MAKES ABOUT 1.5 LITRES

1.5kg fish heads and bones from white fish (ask your fishmonger)
1 tbsp salt
2 tbsp olive oil
1 onion, finely chopped
2 leeks, finely sliced
½ fennel bulb, finely chopped
1 celery stick, sliced
2 garlic cloves, sliced
200ml white wine
bouquet garni (2 sprigs each of parsley, tarragon and thyme)
2 bay leaves
a few peppercorns
1 piece of thinly pared lemon zest

1. Put the fish heads and bones in a bowl, cover them with cold water and add the salt. Leave to stand for an hour, then drain and wash thoroughly under running water. This process helps to draw out any blood from the fish and gives you a much clearer, fresher-tasting stock.

2. Heat the olive oil in a large saucepan. Add the onion, leeks, fennel, celery and garlic. Cook the vegetables over a medium heat for several minutes until they start to soften without taking on any colour.

3. Add the fish heads and bones and pour over the wine. Bring to the boil, then add 2 litres of water. Bring back to the boil, skim off any mushroom-coloured foam that appears on the surface, then turn the heat down to a very slow simmer. Add the herbs, peppercorns and lemon zest and leave to simmer for 30 minutes, skimming off any foam every so often.

4. Strain the stock through a colander or sieve into a bowl, then line the sieve with muslin or kitchen paper and strain the stock again. Don't push it through as that will result in a cloudier stock. Leave to cool, then keep in the fridge for 3–4 days or freeze it.

Chicken stock

MAKES ABOUT 1 LITRE

at least 1 chicken carcass, pulled apart
4 chicken wings (optional)
1 onion, unpeeled, cut into quarters
1 large carrot, cut into large chunks
2 celery sticks, roughly chopped
1 leek, roughly chopped
1 tsp black peppercorns
3 bay leaves
large parsley sprig
small thyme sprig
a few garlic cloves, unpeeled (optional)

1. Put the chicken bones and the wings, if using, into a saucepan, just large enough for all the chicken to fit quite snugly. Cover with cold water, bring to the boil, then skim off any foam that collects. Add the remaining ingredients and then turn the heat down to a very low simmer. Partially cover the pan with a lid.

2. Leave the stock to simmer for about 3 hours, then remove the pan from the heat. Strain the stock through a colander or a sieve lined with muslin or kitchen paper into a bowl.

3. The stock can be used right away, although it is best to skim off most of the fat that will collect on the top. If you don't need the stock immediately, leave it to cool. The fat will set on top and will be much easier to remove.

4. You can keep the stock in the fridge for up to 5 days, or freeze it. If you want to make a larger amount of stock, save up your chicken carcasses in the freezer or add more chicken wings.

Beef stock

MAKES ABOUT 2 LITRES

1.5kg beef bones, including marrow bones if possible, cut into small lengths
500g piece of beef shin or any cheap, fairly lean cut
2 onions, unpeeled, roughly chopped
1 leek, roughly chopped
2 celery sticks, roughly chopped
2 carrots, roughly chopped
2 tomatoes
½ tsp peppercorns
bouquet garni made up of large thyme sprigs, parsley and 2 bay leaves

1. Put the beef bones and meat into a large saucepan and cover them with cold water – at least 3–3.5 litres. Bring the water to the boil and when a starchy, mushroom-grey foam appears, start skimming. Keep on skimming as the foam turns white and continue until it has almost stopped developing.

2. Add the vegetables, peppercorns and bouquet garni, turn down the heat until the stock is simmering very gently, then partially cover the pan with a lid. Leave to simmer for 3–4 hours.

3. Line a sieve or colander with 2 layers of muslin or a tea towel and place it over a large bowl. Ladle the stock into the sieve or colander to strain it. Remove the meat and set it aside, then discard everything else. Pour the strained stock into a large container and leave it to cool. The fat should solidify on top of the stock and will be very easy to remove. You can keep the stock in the fridge for 2 or 3 days or freeze it.

4. Don't chuck out the piece of meat – it's good in sandwiches or can be sliced, fried and added to salads.

Sides & basics

Onion gravy

SERVES 4

50g butter
3 onions, finely sliced
1 tsp sugar
100ml red wine
large thyme sprig
1 bay leaf
600ml well-flavoured beef stock or consommé
dash of Worcestershire sauce (optional)
salt and black pepper

TO THICKEN (OPTIONAL)
1 tbsp flour
15g butter, softened

1. Melt the butter in a wide saucepan or a lidded sauté pan and add the onions. Sauté gently until they are soft and translucent, then stir in the sugar and turn up the heat. Continue to cook, stirring regularly, until the onions are a rich brown and are caramelised.

2. Pour in the red wine, add the herbs and bring to the boil. Allow the wine to reduce down by at least two-thirds, then pour in the stock or consommé. Add the Worcestershire sauce, if using, and season with salt and pepper. Bring to the boil, then turn down the heat, cover and leave to simmer for 10 minutes.

3. The gravy can be served like this, or you can thicken it, if you prefer. To do this, mash the flour and butter together, then whisk a teaspoon at a time into the simmering gravy. Keep whisking until the mixture is dissolved and the gravy is the consistency you like.

Chicken gravy

SERVES 4

25g butter
1 shallot, very finely chopped
1 bay leaf
thyme or tarragon sprig
25g plain flour
100ml white wine
600ml well-flavoured chicken stock
100ml double cream (optional)
salt and black pepper

1. Melt the butter in a saucepan and add the shallot, bay leaf and the thyme or tarragon. Sauté until the shallot is very soft and translucent, then stir in the flour. Stir until you have a lightly toasted paste or roux – cook it for long enough for the flour to lose its raw aroma.

2. Turn up the heat and pour in the wine. It should bubble up immediately. Stir vigorously – the roux should thicken and pull away from the base of the pan. Make sure it's smooth, then start adding the chicken stock, gradually to start with. Allow each addition to bubble up, then stir until smooth. Continue until you have added all the stock. The sauce should have the consistency of thin custard.

3. Season with salt and black pepper and simmer gently for 5 minutes. For a richer sauce, add the cream and simmer gently for another couple of minutes. Remove the herbs just before serving and strain the gravy if you don't want the texture of the shallots.

Pancake batter

MAKES 10–12 PANCAKES

125g plain flour
pinch of salt
1 egg
300ml milk
25g butter

1. Put the flour in a bowl with a pinch of salt. Whisk it lightly to get rid of any lumps, then make a well in the centre. Break the egg into a ramekin and pour it into the well. Using a small whisk, gradually start combining the egg with the flour, working in from the sides until you have a very thick paste. Trickle in the milk a little at a time, whisking constantly until the batter is lump free, then add the rest of the milk. Set the batter aside to rest for about an hour.

2. When you're ready to use the batter, melt the butter in a frying pan and pour most of it into the batter. Give it a quick whisk and use as required.

Proper custard

SERVES 4–6

250ml whole milk
250ml double cream
1 vanilla pod, split,
    or 1 tsp vanilla extract
1 coffee bean (optional)
6 egg yolks
50g caster sugar

1. Put the milk and cream in a pan with the vanilla pod or extract and the coffee bean, if using (it adds depth of flavour but doesn't make the custard taste of coffee). Bring the milk and cream almost to the boil, then remove the pan from the heat and set it aside for the flavours to infuse while the mixture cools down.

2. Whisk the egg yolks and sugar together in a bowl until pale and foamy. Reheat the milk and cream, again to just below boiling point. Strain the milk mixture through a sieve into a jug and rinse out the saucepan.

3. Slowly pour the milk mixture over the eggs, whisking constantly as you do so, then pour it all back into the saucepan. Set the pan over a very low heat and stir constantly until the custard has thickened slightly and you can draw a line through it when it coats the back of a spoon.

4. Strain the custard again and if you aren't serving it immediately, put the vanilla pod, if using, back into it. Cover the custard with cling film, making sure it comes into contact with the surface to prevent a skin from forming. Leave to cool.

Vanilla ice cream

SERVES 4–6

300ml whole milk
300ml double cream
2 vanilla pods, split,
    or 2 tsp vanilla extract
4 egg yolks
100g caster sugar

1. Put the milk and the cream in a pan with the vanilla. Bring it almost to the boil, then remove it from the heat and set it aside for the flavours to infuse while the mixture cools.

2. Have a bowl of ice-cold water ready to chill the custard down once you are happy with the thickness. Whisk the egg yolks and sugar together in a bowl until pale and foamy. Reheat the milk and cream, again until just below boiling point. Strain the milk mixture through a sieve into a jug and rinse out the saucepan. Slowly pour the milk mixture over the eggs, whisking constantly as you do so, then pour it all back into the saucepan. Set the pan over a very low heat and stir constantly until the custard has thickened slightly and you can draw a line through it when it coats the back of a spoon.

3. Plunge the pan into the bowl of ice-cold water to stop the custard cooking. Cover the custard with cling film to stop a skin forming, making sure the cling film touches the surface of the custard, then chill.

4. If you have an ice-cream machine, churn the ice cream, then scoop it into a container. If you don't have a machine, pile the custard mixture into a plastic container and freeze it immediately. Remove and whisk it well every half an hour until it has completely set. Fifteen minutes before you want to serve the ice cream, take it out of the freezer and transfer it to the fridge.

Chocolate sauce

SERVES 4

200ml double or whipping
    cream
25g butter, diced
125g dark chocolate (at
    least 70% cocoa solids),
    broken up
generous pinch of sea salt
1 tbsp brandy or liqueur
    (optional)

1. Put the cream, butter and chocolate in a pan. Add the salt and heat gently until everything has melted. Remove the pan from the heat and whisk until you have a smooth sauce. Add the alcohol, if using, then pour into a jug.

2. Use the sauce immediately – for instance, to pour over the pear tart on page 238 – or allow it to cool, then transfer to the fridge. The sauce will set to a spreadable consistency and can be used as a spread. To reheat, warm it very gently in a saucepan until it melts, making sure it doesn't boil and separate.

Buttercream icing

MAKE ENOUGH TO ICE A REGULAR SANDWICH CAKE

200g butter, softened
400g icing sugar
a few drops of vanilla extract
up to 2 tbsp milk
a few drops of food colouring (optional)

1. Make sure the butter is very soft before you start. Put the butter in a bowl with all the icing sugar and very gently stir them together with a wooden spoon. This should stop you getting icing sugar clouds in your kitchen. When the mixture is looking lumpy and is no longer powdery, switch to electric beaters or beat more vigorously. Continue beating until the mixture is very soft, light and airy.

2. Add the vanilla extract and beat in a little milk to loosen the mixture – you want a reluctant dropping consistency. Add food colouring, if using – just a drop or two at a time – right at the end, making sure you beat well between each addition. Keep adding until you are happy with the colour.

3. Chill the icing until you need it and beat again to loosen a little before using.

Variations

COFFEE: Replace the milk with 2 tablespoons of strong coffee.

CHOCOLATE: Add 25g of cocoa powder with the icing sugar. Replace the milk with 100g of dark chocolate, melted and cooled a little.

CITRUS ZEST: Add the zest of 1 lemon or orange or the zest of 2 limes at the start of the recipe.

JAM: Purée 50g of jam, then beat this into the buttercream.

Brown butter

160g unsalted butter

1. Put the diced butter in a frying pan – if possible, use a light-coloured, enamel-based pan, as it makes it easier to see what's happening.

2. Heat the butter over a medium heat until it has melted. Bring it to the boil, stirring constantly, until the white milk solids that initially foam at the top of the butter, sink and turn brown. They will turn brown very quickly, so don't take your eye off the pan for a moment.

3. As soon as you see the solids turning brown, remove the pan from the heat and pour the butter into a bowl. Up to you whether you keep the brown bits or not – there is a lot of flavour in them so they are great for baking. Leave to cool until the butter is solid but still very soft – you can speed this up in the fridge if you like. Once cool, it can be used as needed.

Index

A

almonds
　Apple & cherry crumble 232
　Bakewell trifle 240
　Basil pesto 261
　Caramelised almond & raisin cookies 222
　Dundee cake 226
　Lamb pasanda 158
　Nutty pastry 265
　Pear & almond tart 238
apples
　Apple & cherry crumble 232
　Prune & apple stuffing 198
　Rainbow coleslaw 58
　Roast beetroot, goat's cheese & apple salad 60
　Waldorf salad 64
Arroz al horno 114
asparagus
　Leek, asparagus & Gruyère tart 176
　Spring vegetable pilaf 118
　Steak & asparagus salad 74
aubergines
　Aubergine katsu 170
　Roasted aubergine pasta 96
　Auntie Daeng's green curry 148
avocados
　Chilli bean burgers 174

B

bacon
　Bacon jam 261
　Classic burgers 192
　Pigs in blankets 140
　Seafood chowder 44
　Special fried rice 104
Baked bean pie 180
Baked rice pudding & blackberry compote 246
bakes
　Biker brownies 220
　Caramelised almond & raisin cookies 222
　Cherry & chocolate cheesecake 216
　Cinnamon swirls 210
　Spicy fruit loaf 218
　see also cakes
Bakewell trifle 240
Banana crème brûlée 250
banana shallots
　Wild mushroom gravy 172
　see also Thai shallots
barley, pearl
　Scotch broth 52
Basil pesto 2610
batter
　Gram (chickpea) flour batter 20, 26
　Muffin batter 30
　Pancake batter 273

bean sprouts
　Crispy noodles with prawns & crab 70
beans *see* baked, broad, butter, cannellini, green, kidney, pinto *and* runner beans
beef
　Auntie Daeng's green curry 148
　Beef stock 271
　Celebratory lasagne 88–9
　Classic burgers 192
　Cottage pie 134
　Dry Keralan beef curry 162
　Our 'proper' Bolognese 80
　Roast beef topside 206
　Steak & asparagus salad 74
　Steak & mushroom pie 130
beetroot
　Roast beetroot, goat's cheese & apple salad 60
　Bhajis, Pickled onion 20
　Biker brownies 220
biryani
　Extra special lamb biryani 156–7
　Vegetable biryani 100–1
black pudding
　Arroz al horno 114
blackberries
　Baked rice pudding & blackberry compote 246
blueberries
　Lemon & blueberry pavlova 236
Boulangère potatoes 256
bouquet garni 196, 270, 271

bread
  Bruschetta 14
  Croutons 40, 66
  Garlic bread pizzas 22
broad beans
  Ricotta and broad bean bruschetta 14
  Spaghetti alla greens 94
  Spring vegetable pilaf 118
  Summery minestrone 38
Brown butter 275
  Brown butter cupcakes 228–9
  Brownies, Biker 220
  Bruschetta 14
  Burrata, Parma ham & grilled peach salad 56
butter
  Brown butter 275
  Buttercream icing 214, 275
butter beans
  Fish & chorizo traybake 136
Buttercream icing 275
  Chocolate buttercream icing 214
butternut squash
  Caribbean chickpea & spinach curry 178
  Chicken & sausage traybake 138
  Curried chicken pie 128
  Indian shepherd's pie 166
  Moroccan tomato soup 34
  Vegetable stock 270

C

cabbage, red
  Mulled cider red cabbage 257
  Rainbow coleslaw 58
cabbage, Savoy
  Scotch broth 52
Caesar salad 66

cakes
  Chocolate cake 214
  Dundee cake 226
  Gingerbread cake 224
  Stem ginger & lemon drizzle cake 212
cannellini beans
  Summery minestrone 38
Caramelised almond & raisin cookies 222
Caribbean chickpea & spinach curry 178
Caribbean curry powder 269
carrots
  Beef stock 271
  Chicken soup 46
  Chicken stock 271
  Cottage pie 134
  Cumberland sausage pie 132
  Mushroom bourguignon cobbler 168
  Oxtail soup with parsley dumplings 48
  Pork ramen 50
  Pot-roast chicken 196
  Rainbow coleslaw 58
  Scotch broth 52
  Shepherd's pie 134
  Three-root mash 258
  Traditional honey-glazed gammon 200
  Traybake Christmas dinner 140
  Vegetable biryani 100–1
  Vegetable stock 270
cauliflower
  Cauliflower cheese 259
  Cauliflower tikka masala 146
  Vegetable biryani 100–1
  Celebratory lasagne 88–9
celeriac
  Indian shepherd's pie 166

  Root vegetable purées 258
  Three-root mash 258
celery
  Beef stock 271
  Chicken soup 46
  Chicken stock 271
  Cumberland sausage pie 132
  Fish stock 270
  Oxtail soup with parsley dumplings 48
  Pot-roast chicken 196
  Scotch broth 52
  Seafood chowder 44
  Traditional honey-glazed gammon 200
  Vegetable stock 270
  Waldorf salad 64
celery, Chinese
  Thai prawn noodle salad 72
Char siu 262
chard
  Spring vegetable pilaf 118
cheese
  Baked bean pie 180
  Cauliflower cheese 259
  Celebratory lasagne 88–9
  Cheese & Marmite scones 18
  Classic cheese & onion pie 122
  Leek, asparagus & Gruyère tart 176
  Lobster mac 'n' cheese 84
  Roast beetroot, goat's cheese & apple salad 60
  Spaghetti carbonara 90
  see also mascarpone; mozzarella; paneer; ricotta
cheesecake
  Cherry & chocolate cheesecake 216

cherries
　Apple & cherry crumble 232
　Cherry & chocolate cheesecake 216
cherries, glacé
　Dundee cake 226
　Spicy fruit loaf 218
chicken
　Auntie Daeng's green curry 148
　Caesar salad 66
　Chicken & sausage traybake 138
　Chicken, ham & leek pie 126
　Chicken Kiev pasta bake 82
　Chicken soup 46
　Chicken stock 271
　Chicken tikka masala 152
　Curried chicken pie 128
　Egg fried rice 102
　Hairy Biker paella 108
　Pork ramen 50
　Pot-roast chicken 196
　Skirlie-stuffed chicken 194
　Special fried rice 104
　Tandoori chicken 188
　Teriyaki chicken salad 68
　Traybake Christmas dinner 140
　see also Prawns on puri
chickpeas
　Arroz al horno 114
　Caribbean chickpea & spinach curry 178
　Cauliflower tikka masala 146
　see also gram flour
chillies
　Auntie Daeng's green curry 148
　Chilli bean burgers 174
　Dry Keralan beef curry 162
　Extra special lamb biryani 156–7
　Pickled onion bhajis 20
　Seekh kebabs 190
　Thai prawn noodle salad 72

　Tom yum soup 42
　Traditional lamb saag 160
　Vindaloo sausage rolls 12
　Chinese roast belly pork 202
　Chips, Triple-cooked 254
chocolate
　Biker brownies 220
　Cherry & chocolate cheesecake 216
　Chocolate cake 214
　Chocolate fondants 242
　Chocolate sauce 274
chorizo
　Arroz al horno 114
　Fish & chorizo traybake 136
　Hairy Biker paella 108
　Chowder, Seafood 44
　Christmas dinner, Traybake 140
cider
　Cider gravy 198–9
　Mulled cider red cabbage 257
　Cinnamon swirls 210
clams
　Seafood with saffron fregola 86
　Classic burgers 182
　Classic cheese & onion pie 122
cobbler
　Mushroom bourguignon cobbler 168
coconut milk
　Auntie Daeng's green curry 148
　Caribbean chickpea & spinach curry 178
　Curried chicken pie 128
　Keralan king prawn curry 150
　Tom yum soup 42
cod
　Fish & chorizo traybake 136
　Colcannon 255
　Coleslaw, Rainbow 58
　Compote, Blackberry 246

cookies
　Caramelised almond & raisin cookies 222
　Cornbread muffins with bacon jam 30
　Cottage pie 134
courgettes
　Fish & chorizo traybake 136
　Grilled vegetable & freekeh salad 62
　'Nduja stromboli 16
　Spaghetti alla greens 94
　Spring vegetable pilaf 118
　Summery minestrone 38
crabmeat
　Crispy noodles with prawns & crab 70
　Cranberry relish 265
　Cream cheese cake filling 216
　Crispy noodles with prawns & crab 70
　Croutons 40, 66
crumble
　Apple & cherry crumble 232
　Crunchy palak paneer 144
cucumber
　Grilled vegetable & freekeh salad 62
　Pickled cucumber 170
　Yoghurt dip 112, 113
　Cumberland sausage pie 132
cupcakes
　Brown butter cupcakes 228–9
currants
　Dundee cake 226
　Spicy fruit loaf 218
curries
　Auntie Daeng's green curry 148
　Caribbean chickpea & spinach curry 178
　Cauliflower tikka masala 146

Chicken tikka masala 152
Crunchy palak paneer 144
Curried chicken pie 128
Dry Keralan beef curry 162
Keralan king prawn curry 150
Lamb kofte vindaloo 154
Lamb pasanda 158
Prawns on puri 24
Traditional lamb saag 160
see also biryani; kedgeree

curry powder
Caribbean curry powder 269
Medium curry powder 268

Custard 250
Proper custard 273
Trifle custard 240

D

dal, Quick 259
dates
Pineapple & rum sticky toffee pudding 248
Dauphinoise potatoes 255
desserts *see* puddings
dressings
Ranch dressing 68
Salad dressings 58, 60, 62, 66, 74
Dumplings, Parsley 48
Dundee cake 226

E

eggs
Chocolate fondants 242
Egg fried rice 102
Extra special lamb biryani 156–7
Lemon meringue pie 234
Marinated egg garnish 50
Marinated eggs (tamago) 260
Pancake batter 273

Pickled eggs 260
Really good kedgeree 110
Scotch pickled eggs 28
Shakshuka 184
Special fried rice 104
Vanilla ice cream 274
see also Custard
Ermine icing 228

F

fennel bulb
Vegetable stock 270
fish
Auntie Daeng's green curry 148
Fish stock 270
Really good kedgeree 110
Salmon pie with spinach 124
freekeh
Grilled vegetable & freekeh salad 62
fregola
Seafood with saffron fregola 86
French onion soup 40

G

galangal
Crispy noodles with prawns & crab 70
Tom yum soup 42
gammon
Traditional honey-glazed gammon 200
Garam masala 269
Garlic bread pizzas 22
Gingerbread cake 224
gram (chickpea) flour
Batter 20, 26
Pickled onion bhajis 20

grapes
Waldorf salad 64
gravy
Beef gravy 206
Chicken gravy 194, 272
Cider gravy 198–9
Onion gravy 272
Wild mushroom gravy 172
green beans
Hairy Biker paella 108
grills
Classic burgers 192
Seekh kebabs 190
Tandoori chicken 188

H

haddock
Fish & chorizo traybake 136
haddock, smoked
Really good kedgeree 110
hake
Fish & chorizo traybake 136
ham
Burrata, Parma ham & grilled peach salad 56
Chicken, ham & leek pie 126
see also gammon
harissa paste
Moroccan tomato soup 34
hazelnuts
Biker brownies 220
Nutty pastry 265
Honey-glazed gammon, Traditional 200

I

Ice cream, Vanilla 274
icing
  Buttercream icing 275
  Buttercream chocolate icing 214
  Ermine icing 228

J

Jerusalem artichokes
  Root vegetable purées 258

K

kaffir lime leaves
  Crispy noodles with prawns & crab 70
Kebabs, Seekh 190
Kedgeree, Really good 110
Keralan king prawn curry 150
kidney beans
  Chilli bean burgers 174
kulfi
  Pistachio & rose kulfi 244

L

lamb
  Extra special lamb biryani 156–7
  Lamb chop pakoras 26
  Lamb kofte vindaloo 154
  Lamb pasanda 158
  Scotch broth 52
  Seekh kebabs 190
  Shepherd's pie 134
  Slow-roast shoulder of lamb 204
  Traditional lamb saag 160
  Turkish lamb pilaf 112–13
Lasagne, Celebratory 88–9

leeks
  Beef stock 271
  Chicken, ham & leek pie 126
  Chicken soup 46
  Chicken stock 271
  Fish stock 270
  Leek, asparagus & Gruyère tart 176
  Pea & watercress soup 36
  Pot-roast chicken 196
  Seafood chowder 44
  Summery minestrone 38
  Vegetable stock 270
lemongrass stalks
  Tom yum soup 42
lemons
  Lemon & blueberry pavlova 236
  Lemon meringue pie 234
  Stem ginger & lemon drizzle cake 212
lentils
  Indian shepherd's pie 166
  Moroccan tomato soup 34
  A quick dal 259
lettuce
  Caesar salad 66
  Summery minestrone 38
  Teriyaki chicken salad 68
Lobster mac 'n' cheese 84

M

macaroni
  Lobster mac 'n' cheese 84
mangos
  Salsa 128
Marmite
  Cheese & Marmite scones 18
Masala potato topping 166
Masala sauce 152

mascarpone cheese
  Cream cheese cake filling
Mayonnaise 64, 266
meatballs
  Lamb kofte vindaloo 154
  Spaghetti & meatballs 78
Meringue 234
  Lemon & blueberry pavlova 236
  Lemon meringue pie 234
Minestrone, summery 38
Moroccan tomato soup 34
mozzarella
  Baked bean pie 180
  Celebratory lasagne 88–9
  Garlic bread pizzas 22
  'Nduja stromboli 16
  see also Burrata, Parma ham & grilled peach salad 56
muffins
  Cornbread muffins with bacon jam 30
Mulled cider red cabbage 257
mushrooms
  Chicken & sausage traybake 138
  Egg fried rice 102
  Mushroom bourguignon cobbler 168
  Mushroom risotto 106
  Nut & spinach roast with wild mushroom gravy 172
  Pot-roast chicken 196
  Soba noodles with miso mushrooms 182
  Steak & mushroom pie 130
mussels
  Hairy Biker paella 108
  Seafood with saffron fregola 86

N

'nduja
  'Nduja linguine 92
  'Nduja stromboli 16
noodles
  Crispy noodles with prawns & crab 70
  Soba noodles with miso mushrooms 182
  Thai prawn noodle salad 72
nuts
  Basil pesto 261
  Biker brownies 220
  Caramelised almond & raisin cookies 222
  Hollandaise sauce 266
  Nutty pastry 265
  Pistachio & rose kulfi 244
  Roast beetroot, goat's cheese & apple salad 60
  Waldorf salad 64

O

onions
  Arroz al horno 114
  Bacon jam 261
  Baked bean pie 180
  Beef stock 271
  Chicken & sausage traybake 138
  Chicken Kiev pasta bake 82
  Chicken stock 271
  Crunchy palak paneer 144
  Fish & chorizo traybake 136
  French onion soup 40
  Mushroom bourguignon cobbler 168
  Onion gravy 272
  Oxtail soup with parsley dumplings 48
  Pickled onion bhajis 20
  Scotch broth 52
  Shakshuka 184
  Traditional lamb saag 160
  Vegetable biryani 100–1
  Vegetable stock 270
Oxtail soup with parsley dumplings 48

P

paella
  Hairy Biker paella 108
pak choi
  Chinese roast belly pork 202
  Tom yum soup 42
pakoras
  Lamb chop pakoras 26
Pancake batter 273
pancetta
  Risotto carbonara 116
  Spaghetti carbonara 90
paneer
  Crunchy palak paneer 144
parsley
  Grilled vegetable & freekeh salad 62
  Parsley dumplings 48
parsnips
  Root vegetable purées 258
  Three-root mash 258
  Traybake Christmas dinner 140
pasta
  Celebratory lasagne 88
  Chicken Kiev pasta bake 82
  Fresh pasta 264
  Lobster mac 'n' cheese 84
  'Nduja linguine 92
  Our 'proper' Bolognese 80
  Roasted aubergine pasta 96
  Seafood with saffron fregola 86
  Spaghetti alla greens 94
  Spaghetti & meatballs 78
  Spaghetti carbonara 90
Pastry 122, 128, 176, 234
  Shortcrust pastry 265
pavlova
  Lemon & blueberry pavlova 236
Pea & watercress soup 36
peaches
  Burrata, Parma ham & grilled peach salad 56
peanuts
  Thai prawn noodle salad 72
Pear & almond tart 238
peas
  Egg fried rice 102
  Pea & watercress soup 36
  Special fried rice 104
  Spring vegetable pilaf 118
peppers
  Arroz al horno 114
  Fish & chorizo traybake 136
  Indian shepherd's pie 166
  Shakshuka 184
Pesto, Basil 261
Pickled eggs 260
Pickled onion bhajis 20
pies
  Baked bean pie 180
  Chicken, ham & leek pie 126
  Classic cheese & onion pie 122
  Cottage pie 134
  Cumberland sausage pie 132
  Curried chicken pie 128
  Lemon meringue pie 234
  Salmon pie with spinach 124
  Shepherd's pie 134
  Steak & mushroom pie 130
Pigs in blankets 140

pilafs
 Spring vegetable pilaf 118
 Turkish lamb pilaf 112–13
pine nuts
 Basil pesto 261
 Turkish lamb pilaf 112
Pineapple & rum sticky toffee
  pudding 248
pinto beans
 Chilli bean burgers 174
Pistachio & rose kulfi 244
pizzas
 Garlic bread pizzas 22
 see also 'Nduja stromboli
Plantain 178
pork
 Auntie Daeng's green curry 148
 Celebratory lasagne 88–9
 Chinese roast belly pork 202
 Our 'proper' Bolognese 80
 Pork ramen 50
 Roast loin of pork with prune &
  apple stuffing 198–9
 Spaghetti & meatballs 78
 Twice-cooked pork (char siu)
  262
potatoes
 Baked bean pie 180
 Boulangère potatoes 256
 Chicken soup 46
 Chinese roast belly pork 202
 Classic cheese & onion pie 122
 Colcannon 255
 Cottage pie 134
 Cumberland sausage pie 132
 Dauphinoise potatoes 255
 Indian shepherd's pie 166
 Pot-roast chicken 196
 Potato salad 257
 Roast new potatoes with garlic &
  rosemary 256

 Roast potatoes 254
 Root vegetable purées 258
 Scotch broth 52
 Seafood chowder 44
 Shepherd's pie 134
 Slow-roast shoulder of lamb 204
 Steak & asparagus salad 74
 Traybake Christmas dinner 140
 Triple-cooked chips 254
Pot-roast chicken 196
prawns
 Auntie Daeng's green curry 148
 Crispy noodles with prawns &
  crab 70
 Hairy Biker paella 108
 Keralan king prawn curry 150
 Prawns on puri 24
 Seafood with saffron fregola 86
 Special fried rice 104
 Thai prawn noodle salad 72
prunes
 Prune & apple stuffing 198
 Spicy fruit loaf 218
puddings
 Apple & cherry crumble 232
 Baked rice pudding & blackberry
  compote 246
 Bakewell trifle 240
 Banana crème brûlée 250
 Chocolate fondants 242
 Lemon & blueberry pavlova 236
 Lemon meringue pie 234
 Pear & almond tart 238
 Pineapple & rum sticky toffee
  pudding 248
 Pistachio & rose kulfi 244
Puffy puris 263
pumpkin
 Caribbean chickpea & spinach
  curry 178
 Chicken & sausage traybake 138

 Curried chicken pie 128
 Vegetable stock 270
puris
 Prawns on puri 24
 Puffy puris 263

R

radishes
 Pickles 170
 Teriyaki chicken salad 68
Rainbow coleslaw 58
raisins
 Caramelised almond & raisin
  cookies 222
 Dundee cake 226
 Spicy fruit loaf 218
Raita 188
Ramen, Pork 50
Ranch dressing 68
raspberries
 Bakewell trifle 240
 Really good kedgeree 110
rice
 Arroz al horno 114
 Baked rice pudding & blackberry
  compote 246
 Egg fried rice 102
 Extra-special lamb biryani 156
 Hairy Biker paella 108
 Mushroom risotto 106
 Really good kedgeree 110
 Risotto carbonara 116
 Special fried rice 104
 Spring vegetable pilaf 118
 Turkish lamb pilaf 112
 Vegetable biryani 100–1
ricotta cheese
 Celebratory lasagne 88–9
 Ricotta and broad bean
  bruschetta 14

risotto
  Mushroom risotto 106
  Risotto carbonara 116
roasts
  Chinese roast belly pork 202
  Pot-roast chicken 196
  Roast beef topside 206
  Roast loin of pork with prune & apple stuffing 198–9
  Skirlie-stuffed chicken 194
  Slow-roast shoulder of lamb 204
  Traditional honey-glazed gammon 200
  Root vegetable purées 258
runner beans
  Summery minestrone 38
  Vegetable biryani 100–1

S

saffron
  Extra special lamb biryani 156–7
  Hairy Biker paella 108
salads
  Burrata, Parma ham & grilled peach salad 56
  Caesar salad 66
  Crispy noodles with prawns & crab 70
  Grilled vegetable & freekeh salad 62
  Potato salad 257
  Rainbow coleslaw 58
  Roast beetroot, goat's cheese & apple salad 60
  Steak & asparagus salad 74
  Teriyaki chicken salad 68
  Thai prawn noodle salad 72
  Waldorf salad 64
Salmon pie with spinach 124
Salsa 128

sauces
  Burger sauce 192
  Chocolate 274
  Hollandaise 266
  Katsu sauce 170
  Masala sauce 152
  Rum butterscotch sauce 248
  Strawberry sauce 228
  Tartare sauce
  Tomato sauce 267
sausagemeat/sausages
  Celebratory lasagne 88–9
  Chicken & sausage traybake 138
  Cumberland sausage pie 132
  Pigs in blankets 140
  Scotch pickled eggs 28
  Vindaloo sausage rolls 12
scallops
  Seafood with saffron fregola 86
scones
  Cheese & Marmite scones 18
scotch bonnet
  Caribbean chickpea & spinach curry 178
  Curried chicken pie 128
Scotch broth 52
Scotch pickled eggs 28s
Seafood chowder 44
seafood see crabmeat; fish; prawns
  Seafood with saffron fregola 86
Seekh kebabs 190
Shakshuka 184
shallots
  Chicken gravy 272
  Hollandaise sauce 266
  Mushroom bourguignon cobbler 168
  Salad dressing 60
  Tom yum soup 42
  see also banana shallots; Thai shallots
Shepherd's pie 134
  Indian shepherd's pie 166
Shortcrust pastry 265
Skirlie-stuffed chicken 194
snacks
  Bruschetta 14
  Cheese & Marmite scones 18
  Cornbread muffins with bacon jam 30
  Garlic bread pizzas 22
  Lamb chop pakoras 26
  'Nduja stromboli 16
  Pickled onion bhajis 20
  Prawns on puri 24
  Scotch pickled eggs 28
  Vindaloo sausage rolls 12
  Soba noodles with miso mushrooms 182
soups
  Chicken soup 46
  French onion soup 40
  Moroccan tomato soup 34
  Oxtail soup with parsley dumplings 48
  Pea & watercress soup 36
  Pork ramen 50
  Scotch broth 52
  Seafood chowder 44
  Summery minestrone 38
  Tom yum soup 42
spaghetti
  Spaghetti alla greens 94
  Spaghetti & meatballs 78
  Spaghetti carbonara 90
Special fried rice 104

spinach
  Caribbean chickpea & spinach curry 178
  Crunchy palak paneer 144
  Nut & spinach roast with wild mushroom gravy 172
  Salmon pie with spinach 124
  Spaghetti alla greens 94
  Traditional lamb saag 160
spring onions
  Crispy noodles with prawns & crab 70
  Cumberland sausage pie 132
  Egg fried rice 102
  Grilled vegetable & freekeh salad 62
  Pork ramen 50
  Rainbow coleslaw 58
  Special fried rice 104
  Teriyaki chicken salad 68
Spring vegetable pilaf 118
squash *see* butternut squash
steak *see* beef
Stem ginger & lemon drizzle cake 212
Sticky toffee pudding *see* Pineapple & rum sticky toffee pudding 248
stocks
  Beef stock 271
  Chicken stock 271
  Fish stock 270
  Vegetable stock 270
Strawberry sauce 228
Stromboli, 'Nduja 16
Stuffing balls 140
sultanas
  Dundee cake 226
  Spicy fruit loaf 218
Summery minestrone 38

swedes
  Indian shepherd's pie 166
sweet potatoes 72, 134
  Aubergine katsu 170
  Root vegetable purées 258

T

tagliatelle
  Our 'proper' Bolognese 80
Tamago 260
Tandoori chicken 188
Tartare sauce 267
tarts 265
  Leek, asparagus & Gruyère tart 176
  Pear & almond tart 238
  Teriyaki chicken salad 68
  Thai prawn noodle salad 72
  Three-root mash 258
Thai shallots
  Auntie Daeng's green curry 148
  Crispy noodles with prawns & crab 70
  Thai prawn noodle salad 72
  Wild mushroom gravy 172
tikka masalas
  Cauliflower tikka masala 146
  Chicken tikka masala 152
tofu
  Tom yum soup 42
  Tom yum soup 42
tomatoes
  Arroz al horno 114
  Beef stock 271
  Cauliflower tikka masala 146
  Crunchy palak paneer 144
  Fish & chorizo traybake 136
  Grilled vegetable & freekeh salad 62
  Hairy Biker paella 108

Moroccan tomato soup 34
'Nduja linguine 92
Nut & spinach roast with wild mushroom gravy 172
Our 'proper' Bolognese 80
Roasted aubergine pasta 96
Teriyaki chicken salad 68
Thai prawn noodle salad 72
Tom yum soup 42
Tomato bruschetta 14
Tomato sauce 78, 267
traybakes
  Chicken & sausage traybake 138
  Christmas dinner 140
  Fish & chorizo traybake 136
trifle
  Bakewell trifle 240
Triple-cooked chips 254
Turkish lamb pilaf 112–13
turnips
  Indian shepherd's pie 166
  Scotch broth 52
Twice-cooked pork (char siu) 262

V

Vanilla ice cream 274
vegetarian dishes
  Aubergine katsu 170
  Baked bean pie 180
  Caribbean chickpea & spinach curry 178
  Cauliflower tikka masala 146
  Chilli bean burgers 174
  Crunchy palak paneer 144
  Indian shepherd's pie 166
  Leek, asparagus & Gruyère tart 176
  Mushroom bourguignon cobbler 168

Nut & spinach roast with wild mushroom gravy 172
Pickled onion bhajis 20
Shakshuka 184
Soba noodles with miso mushrooms 182
Spaghetti alla greens 94
Spring vegetable pilaf 118
Vegetable biryani 100–1
Vindaloo sausage rolls 12
Vindaloo spice paste 268

W

Waldorf salad 64
walnuts
 Roast beetroot, goat's cheese & apple salad 60
 Waldorf salad 64
watercress
 Pea & watercress soup 36
 Roast beetroot, goat's cheese & apple salad 60

Y

yoghurt
 Marinades 146, 158
 Raita 188
 Salad dressing 58
 Tandoori chicken 188
 Yoghurt dip 112, 113
Yorkshire pudding 262

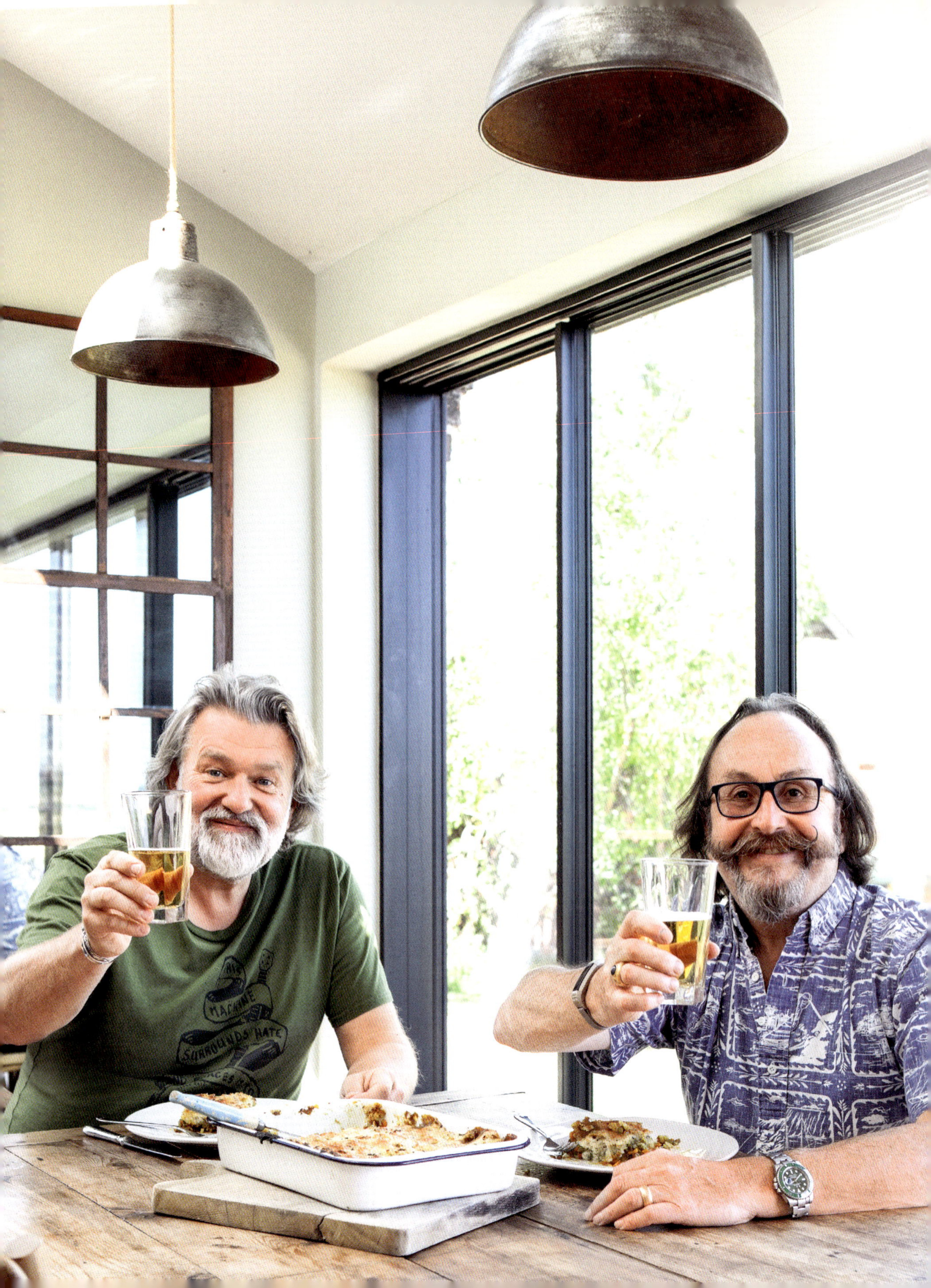
MACHINE
SURROUNDS HATE

The biggest thank you!

So many wonderful people have been involved in the creation of the Hairy Biker books.

You've all been amazing and I can't thank you enough. I hope I've included everyone here, but apologies if I've missed anyone.

Photographers: Cristian Barnett and Andrew Hayes-Watkins; recipe consultants: Justine Pattison and Catherine Phipps; editor: Jinny Johnson; designers: Kate Barr, Loulou Clark, Abi Hartshorne (Hart Studio), Claire Sivell and Lucie Stericker (Studio 7:15); food stylists: Hattie Baker, Lorna Brash, Anna Burges-Lumsden, Lisa Harrison, Suki Hayes-Watkins, Lou Kenney, Lola Milne, Nikki Morgan, Mima Sinclair and Sammy-Jo Squire; prop stylists: Sarah Birks, Giuliana Casarotti, Tamzin Ferdinando, Rebecca Newport and Rachel Vere; proofreader: Elise See Tai; indexers: Vicki Robinson and Elizabeth Wiggans.

Huge thanks, too, to all the Orion people, past and present, for all their help and support. Publishers: Vicky Eribo, Anna Valentine, Katie Espiner, Amanda Harris and Lisa Milton; editorial assistants: Zoe Yang, Tierney Witty and Kayleigh McKnight; publicity: Francesca Pearce, Sarah Lundy, Virginia Woolstencroft, Becca Bryant, Alainna Hadjigeorgiou and Angela McMahon; marketing: Louis Patel, Helena Fouracre, Lynsey Sutherland and Tom Noble; sales: Dave Murphy, Catherine Worsley, Jennifer Wilson, Victoria Laws, Barbara Ronan, Dominic Smith, Esther Waters and Jo Jacobs; cover designers: Jess Hart and Nick Shah; design coordinators: Natalie Dawkins and Helen Ewing; production managers: Claire Keep, Lucy Horrocks, Davina Cheung, Katie Horrocks, Simon Walsh and Nicole Abel.

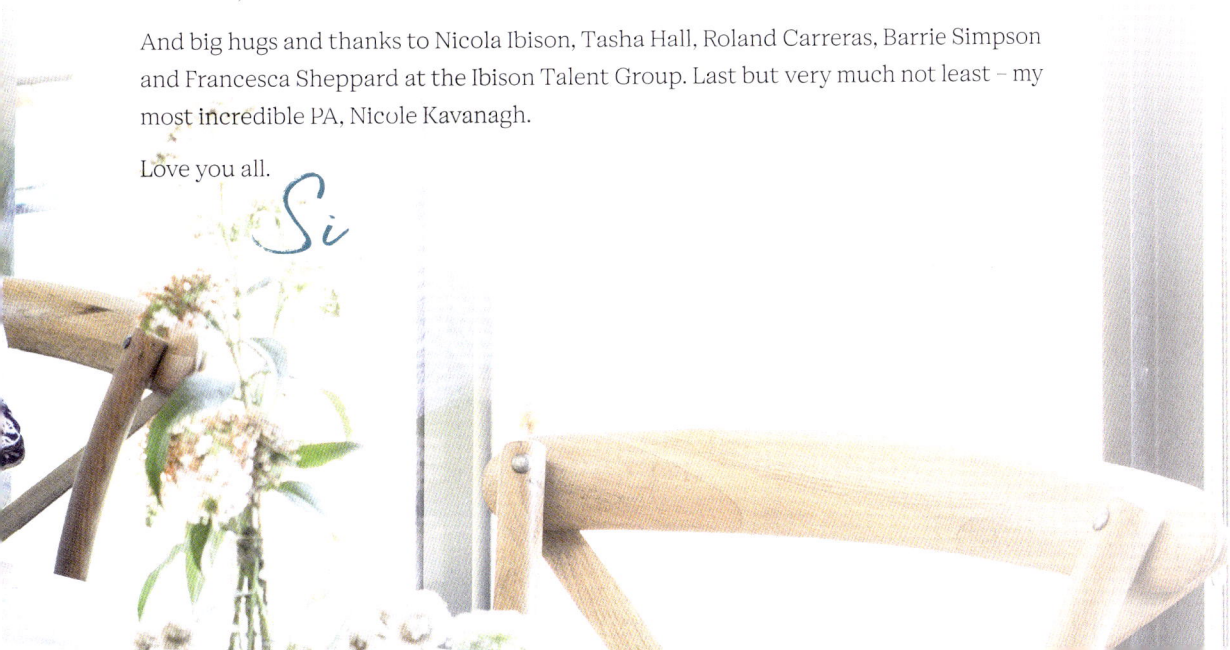

And big hugs and thanks to Nicola Ibison, Tasha Hall, Roland Carreras, Barrie Simpson and Francesca Sheppard at the Ibison Talent Group. Last but very much not least – my most incredible PA, Nicole Kavanagh.

Love you all.

Si

To all of you who've followed us over the years, bought our books and watched us on television – I know Dave would want to say a massive thank you. The legacy lives on and rightly so.

First published in Great Britain in 2025 by Seven Dials,
an imprint of The Orion Publishing Group Ltd
Carmelite House, 50 Victoria Embankment
London EC4Y 0DZ

An Hachette UK Company

10 9 8 7 6 5 4 3 2 1

Text copyright © Bytebrook Limited and Sharpletter Limited 2025

Design and layout copyright © Seven Dials 2025

The moral right of Dave Myers and Si King to be identified as the authors of this work has been asserted in accordance with the Copyright, Designs and Patents Act of 1988.

All rights reserved. No part of this publication may be reproduced, stored in a retrieval system, or transmitted in any form or by any means, electronic, mechanical, photocopying, recording, or otherwise, without the prior permission of both the copyright owner and the above publisher of this book.

A CIP catalogue record for this book is available from the British Library.

ISBN (Hardback) 978 1 3996 0734 6

ISBN (eBook) 978 1 3996 0735 3

Origination by Altaimage, London

Printed in Germany

www.orionbooks.co.uk

Publisher: Vicky Eribo
Recipe consultants: Catherine Phipps
    & Justine Pattison
Photography: Andrew Hayes-Watkins
    & Cristian Barnett
Design and art direction:
    Lucie Stericker, Studio 7:15
Editor: Jinny Johnson
Proofreader: Elise See Tai
Indexer: Vicki Robinson
Production manager: Claire Keep
Cover design: Jessica Hart